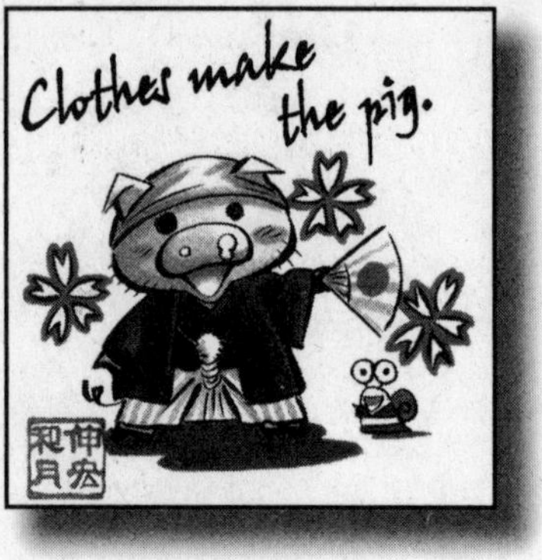
Clothes make the pig.
伸宏
和月

Wearing a kimono is part of being Japanese.
On pretty much a daily basis I wear *samue* (Buddhist monk's work clothes). In the future I want to become a man who looks good in a boater's hat and kimono. Thinking that, I went and got myself a *hakama* (kimono trousers) with a family crest on the coat.
I have to say that they are very comfortable! However...they are a real chore to maintain! And since I don't know how to put everything on properly, I can't do it alone! Including eating and going to the bathroom! And they are really expensive to boot!
I think for the time being, I will stick with my *samue*. I have been made painfully aware of my limitations.

—Nobuhiro Watsuki

Nobuhiro Watsuki earned international accolades for his first major manga series, **Rurouni Kenshin**, about a wandering swordsman in Meiji Era Japan. Serialized in Japan's *Weekly Shonen Jump* from 1994 to 1999, **Rurouni Kenshin**, available in North America from VIZ Media, quickly became a worldwide sensation, inspiring a spin-off short story ("Yahiko no Sakabatô"), an animated TV show and a series of novels. Watsuki's latest hit, **Buso Renkin**, began publication in *Weekly Shonen Jump* in June 2003.

BUSO RENKIN
VOL. 6
The SHONEN JUMP ADVANCED
Manga Edition

STORY AND ART BY
NOBUHIRO WATSUKI

English Adaptation/Lance Caselman
Translation/Toshifumi Yoshida
Touch-up Art & Lettering/James Gaubatz
Design/Yukiko Whitley
Editor/Urian Brown

Editor in Chief, Books/Alvin Lu
Editor in Chief, Magazines/Marc Weidenbaum
VP of Publishing Licensing/Rika Inouye
VP of Sales/Gonzalo Ferreyra
Sr. VP of Marketing/Liza Coppola
Publisher/Hyoe Narita

Printed in the U.S.A.

Published by VIZ Media, LLC
P.O. Box 77010
San Francisco, CA 94107

SHONEN JUMP ADVANCED Manga Edition
10 9 8 7 6 5 4 3 2 1
First printing, June 2007

THE WORLD'S MOST
CUTTING-EDGE MANGA

SHONEN
JUMP
ADVANCED
www.shonenjump.com

VIZ
MEDIA
www.viz.com

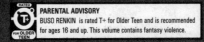

SHONEN JUMP ADVANCED MANGA EDITION

STORY & ART BY
NOBUHIRO WATSUKI

Vol. 6
A New Mission

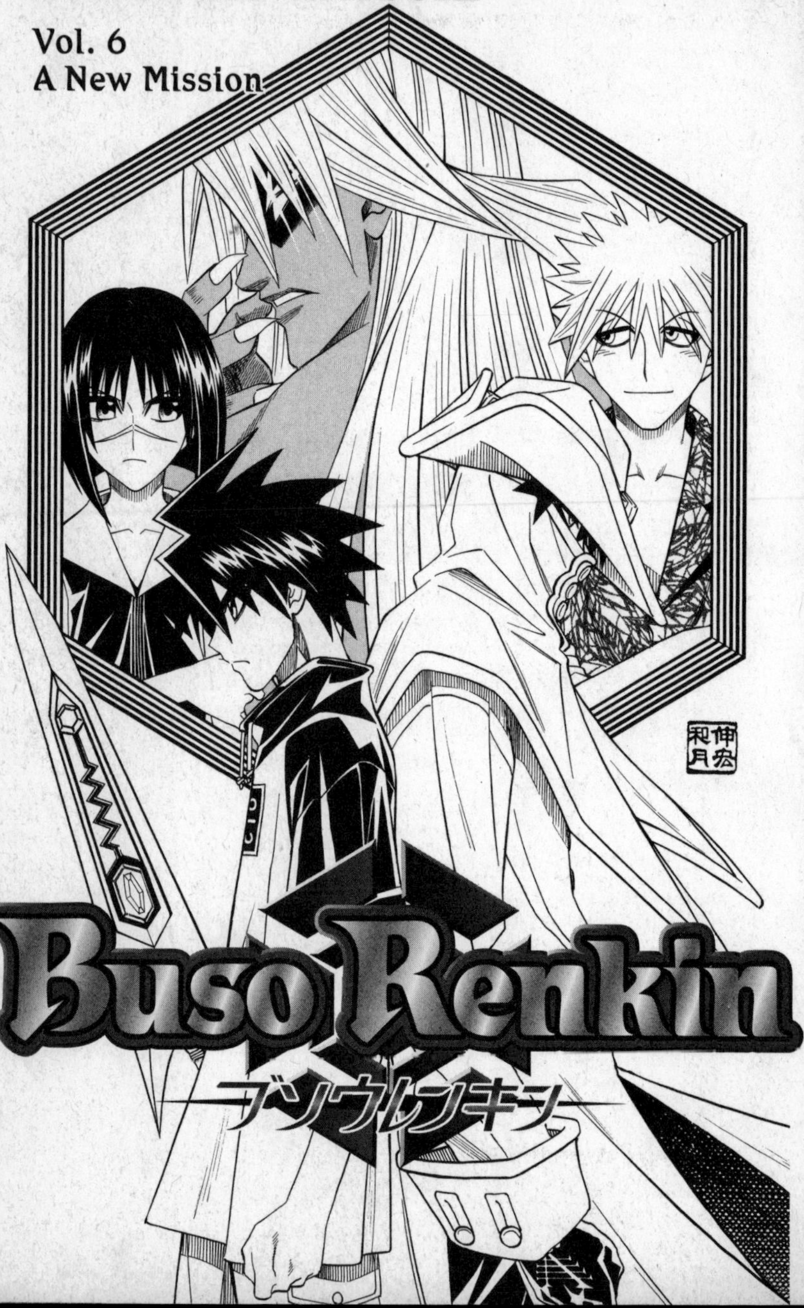
Buso Renkin
ブソウレンキン

Alchemy

Alchemy is an early proto-science combining elements of various disciplines that swept through Europe over the millennia. Its goals were the transmutation of base metals into gold and the creation of an Elixir of Immortality, neither of which succeeded. But unknown to the world at large, alchemy achieved two earthshaking supernatural successes--the homunculi and the kakugane.

Kazuki Muto

Kazuki was once killed by a homunculus but was restored to life by Tokiko, who replaced his heart with a magical talisman called a kakugane. Kazuki is 16 years old, a year older than his sister Mahiro. His Buso Renkin is a lance called "Sunlight Heart."

CHARACTERS

Homunculus

An artificial being created by alchemy. The form and powers of the homunculus differ depending on the organism it was based on. Homunculi feed on human flesh, and can only be destroyed by the power of alchemy.

Kakugane

The kakugane are forged from a magical alchemic alloy. They are activated by the deepest parts of the human psyche, the basic instincts. Each kakugane can materialize a unique weapon called a Buso Renkin.

Tokiko Tsumura

A girl chosen to be an Alchemist Warrior, an expert of Buso Renkin. Her Buso Renkin is a Death Scythe called the "Valkyrie Skirt."

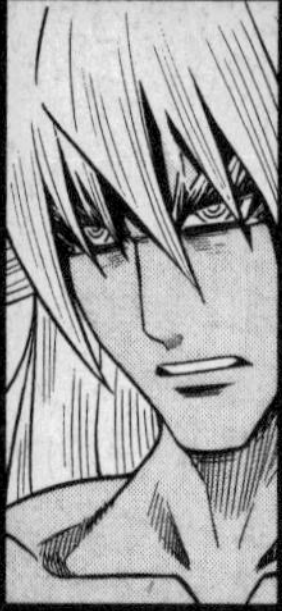
Victor

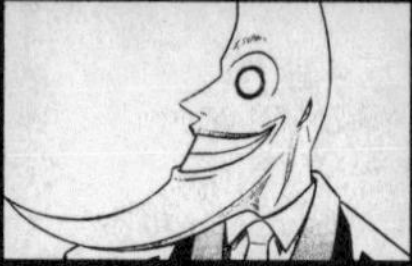
Moonface

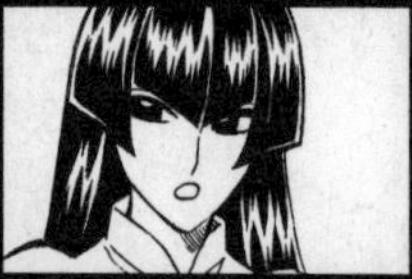
Ouka Hayasaka

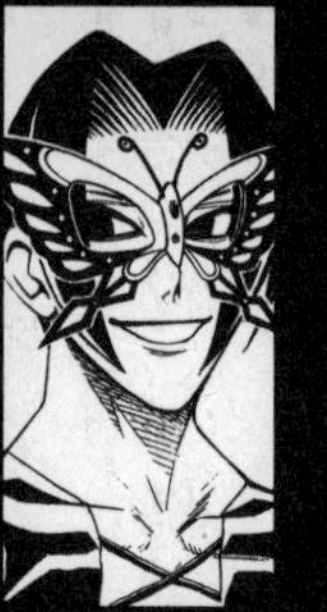
Papillon (Koushaku Chouno)

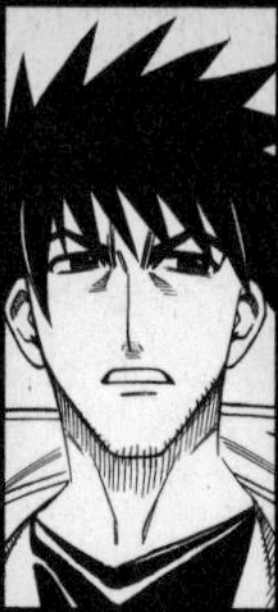
Captain Bravo (Warrior Chief)

S T O R Y

Alchemist Warrior Tokiko comes to Ginsei City and uses herself as bait for the homunculi, artificial life forms that lurk in the darkness to devour unsuspecting humans. But Kazuki Muto, a high school student, unaware of Tokiko's intentions, tries to save her and is killed. Tokiko restores Kazuki's life with an alchemic talisman called a kakugane, and he fights at Tokiko's side to save his friends.

Tokiko and Kazuki manage to defeat the homunculi created by Koushaku, which were created using his great-grandfather's research notes. However, Tokiko receives new orders from her commanding officer, the Warrior Chief: find and destroy the traitorous Alchemist Warrior who chose to become a homunculus, along with Doctor Butterfly and his organization of evil, the L.X.E. (League of eXtraordinary Elects).

Working from the information provided to them by Ouka, the location of the secret L.X.E. hideout is revealed. Kazuki, Tokiko and Captain Bravo attack the hideout only to find out it's been abandoned, leaving only Moonface to slow them down. Doctor Butterfly had already left with the "Traitorous Warrior" to feed on the students at the school and complete his recovery. Arriving at the school, Kazuki and Tokiko engage the army of homunculi in the schoolyard. In the midst of battle, Papillon, tired of his treatment by the L.X.E., appears to fight against Doctor Butterfly. Kazuki and Tokiko hurry to the roof of the school to stop the rejuvenation chamber containing the traitorous warrior before he can be released. But just as Papillon defeats Doctor Butterfly, the chamber releases the traitorous warrior named Victor, who is a completely different kind of being, neither human nor homunculus, and with a kakugane for his heart, like Kazuki. But his kakugane is unlike the others and is black in color. As Victor and Kazuki clash, Victor obliterates the Sunlight Heart, and in doing so kills Kazuki. As Victor moves to attack the grieving Tokiko, the twice-dead Kazuki rises to his feet. Kazuki's kakugane turns black and like Victor, Kazuki begins to transform, his skin becoming copper colored and his hair like the color of the light of a firefly...!

Koji Rokumasu

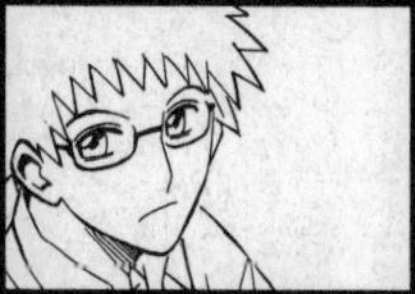

Mahiro Muto

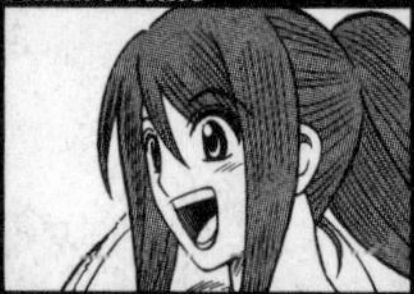

Hideyuki Okakura

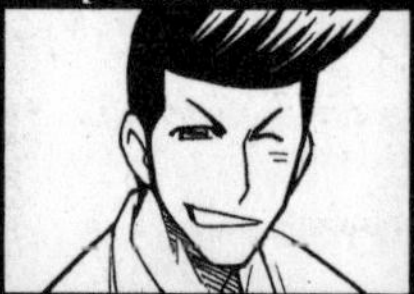

Chisato Wakamiya

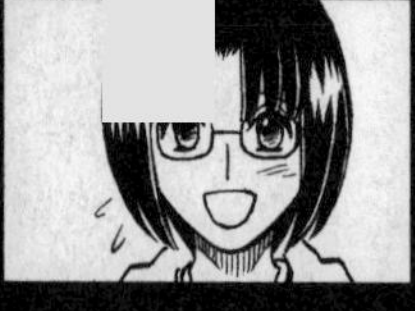

Saori Kawai

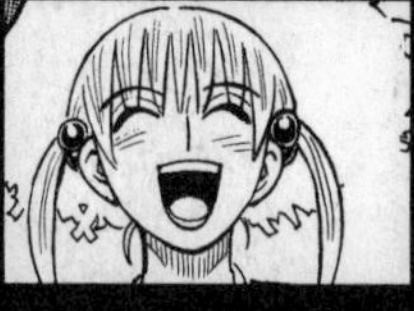

Masashi Daihama

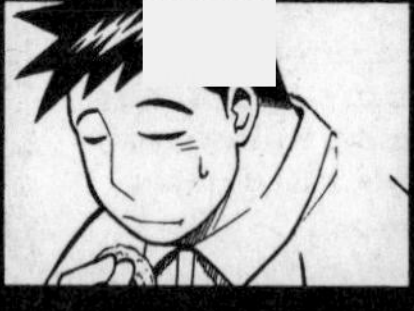

BUSO RENKIN
Volume 6: A New Mission

CONTENTS

Chapter 46: Heart Shift — 7

Chapter 47: End of the Battle — 25

Chapter 48: A Warrior's Respite — 43

Chapter 49: A New Mission — 61

Chapter 50: Say It's Not So, Bravo. — 81

Chapter 51: Crimson Ocean — 101

Chapter 52: Re-Extermination Complete — 123

Chapter 53: When the Night Ends — 143

Chapter 54: One Heart and One Mind — 163

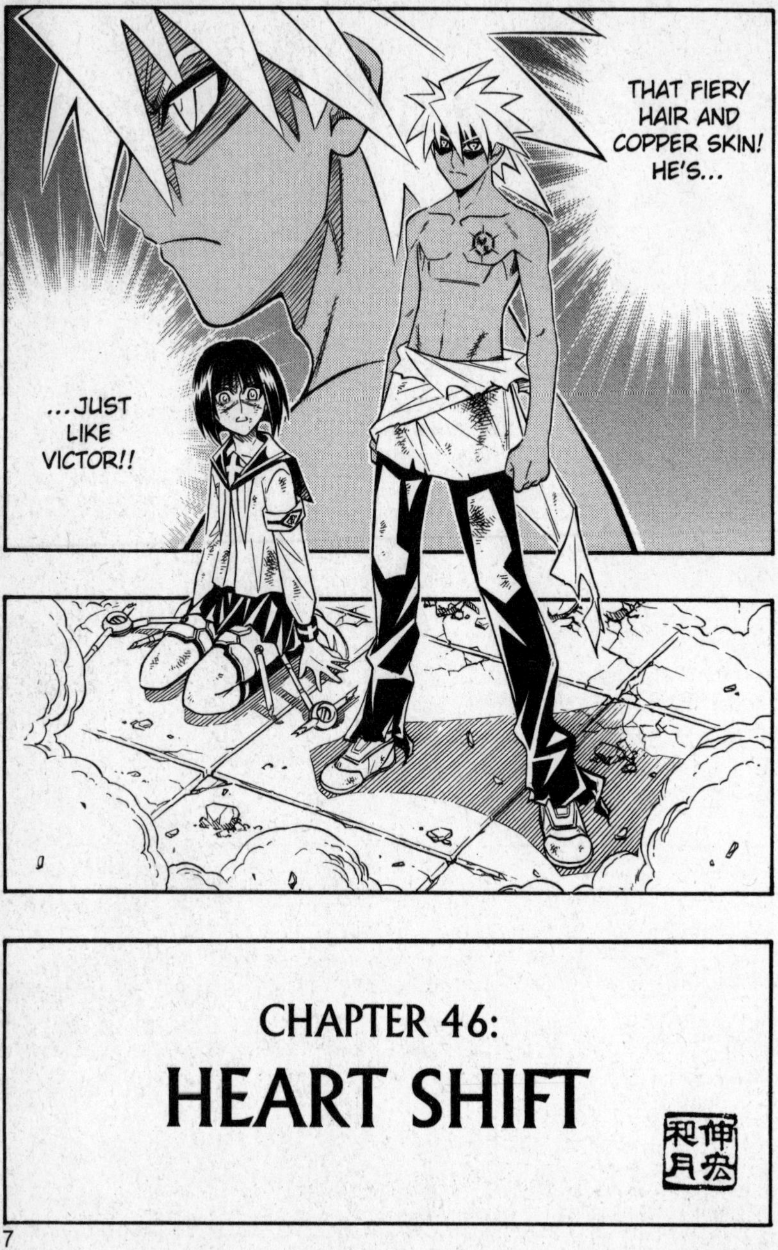
THAT FIERY HAIR AND COPPER SKIN! HE'S...
...JUST LIKE VICTOR!!

CHAPTER 46:
HEART SHIFT

伸宏和月

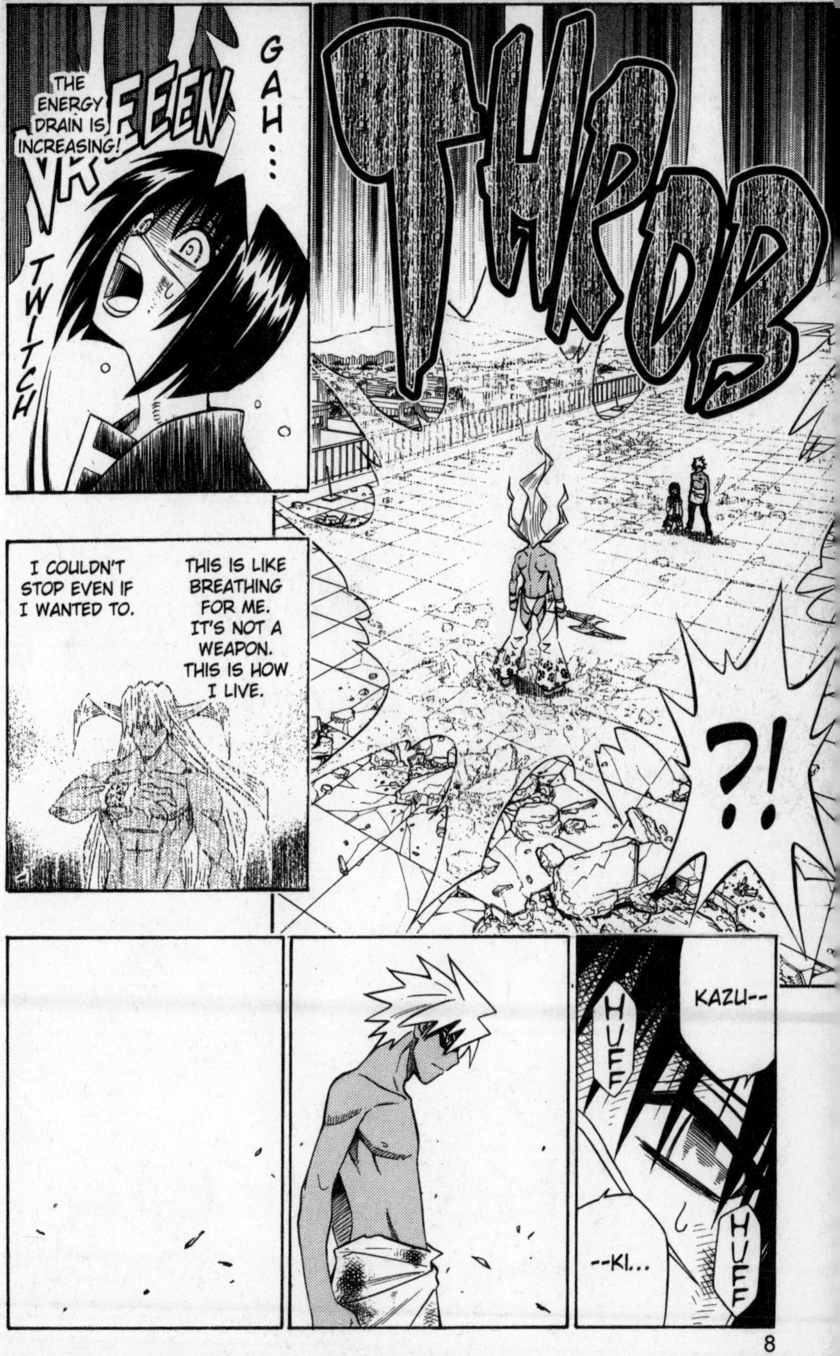
THROB
?!
GAH...
THE ENERGY DRAIN IS INCREASING!
TWITCH
THIS IS LIKE BREATHING FOR ME. IT'S NOT A WEAPON. THIS IS HOW I LIVE.
I COULDN'T STOP EVEN IF I WANTED TO.
KAZU--
HUFF
HUFF
--KI...

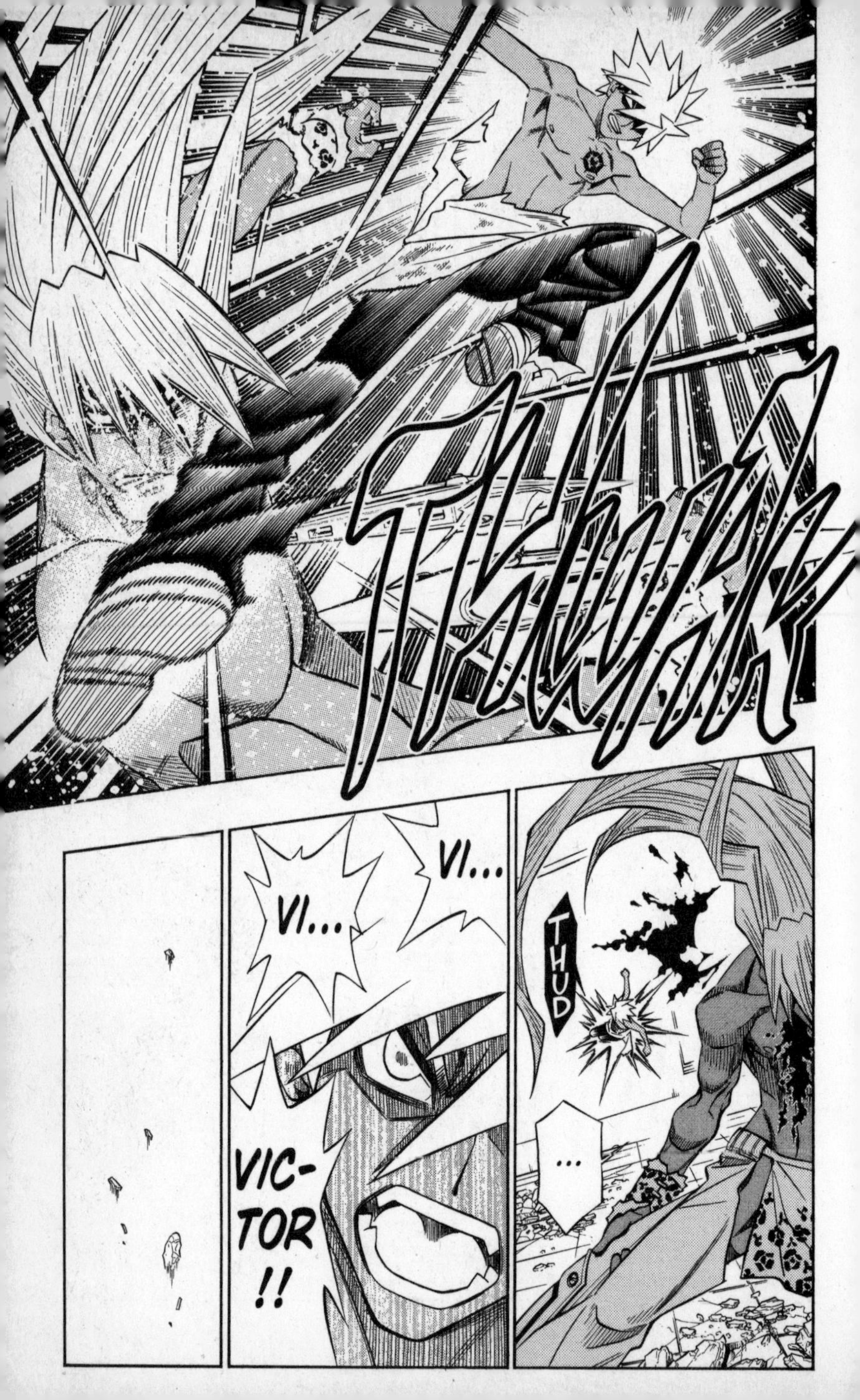
Thwak
THUD
...
VI...
VI...
VIC-
TOR
!!

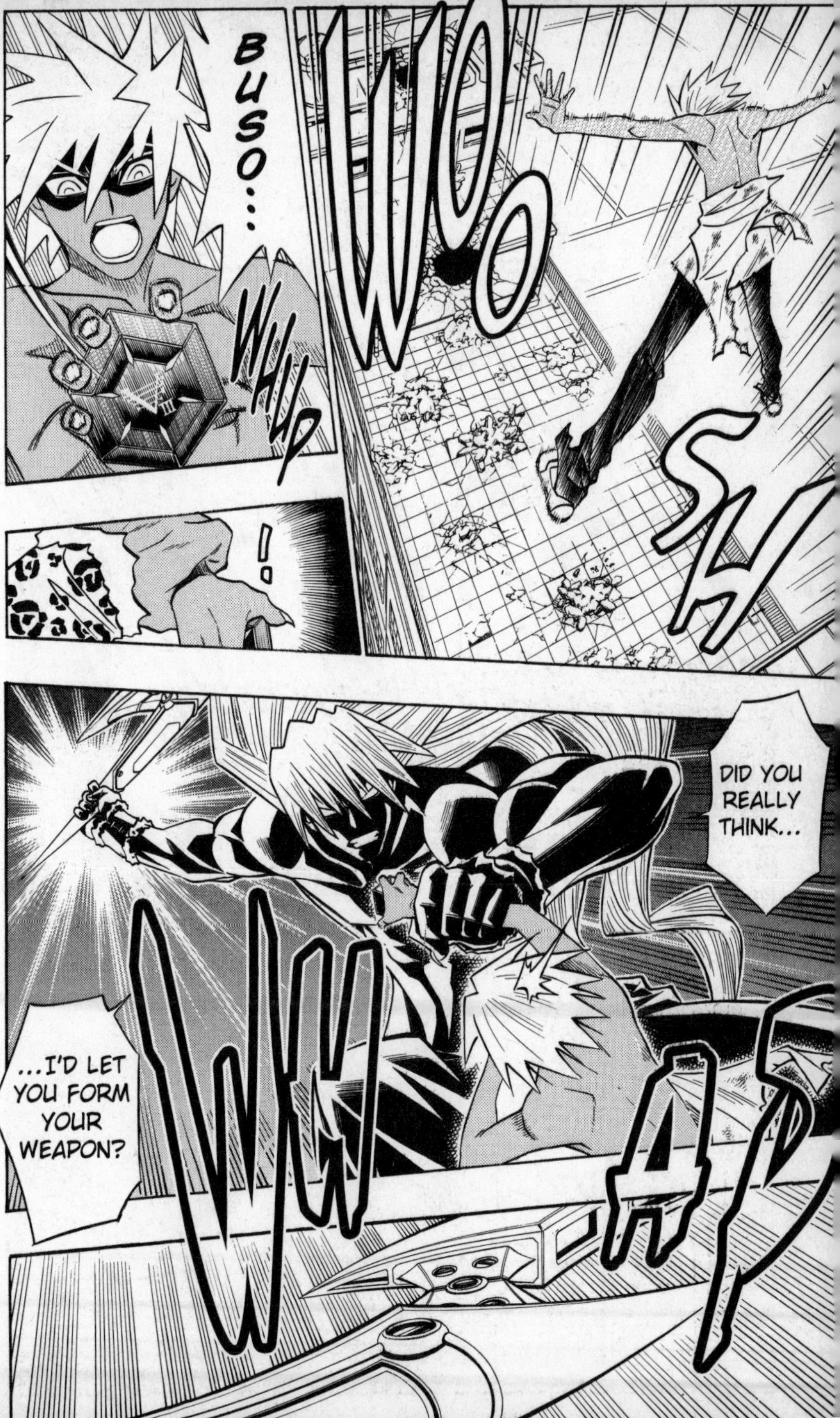
WOO
SH
BUSO...
WHUP
!
DID YOU REALLY THINK...
...I'D LET YOU FORM YOUR WEAPON?
WHAP

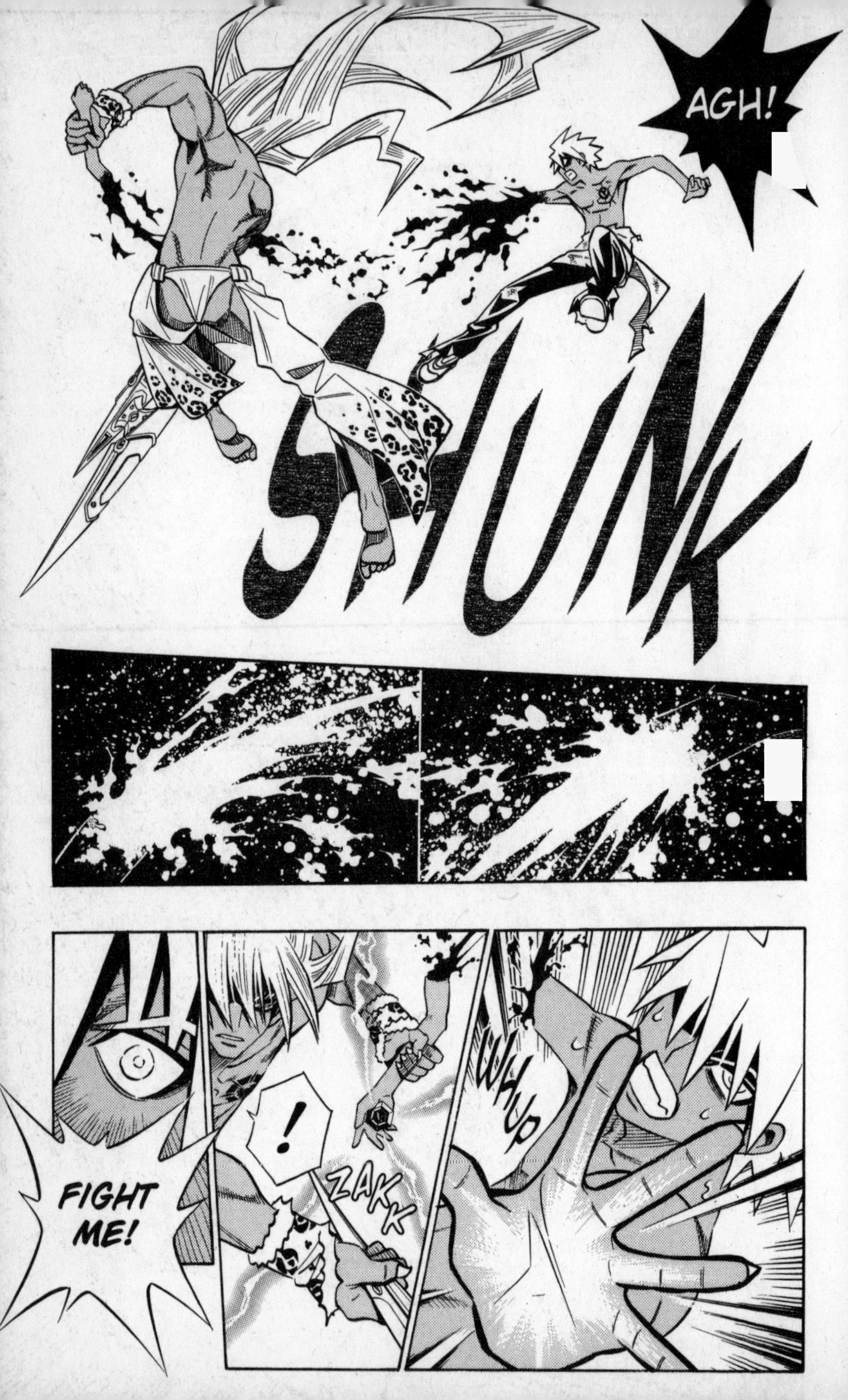
AGH!
SHUNK
WHUP
!
ZAKK
FIGHT ME!

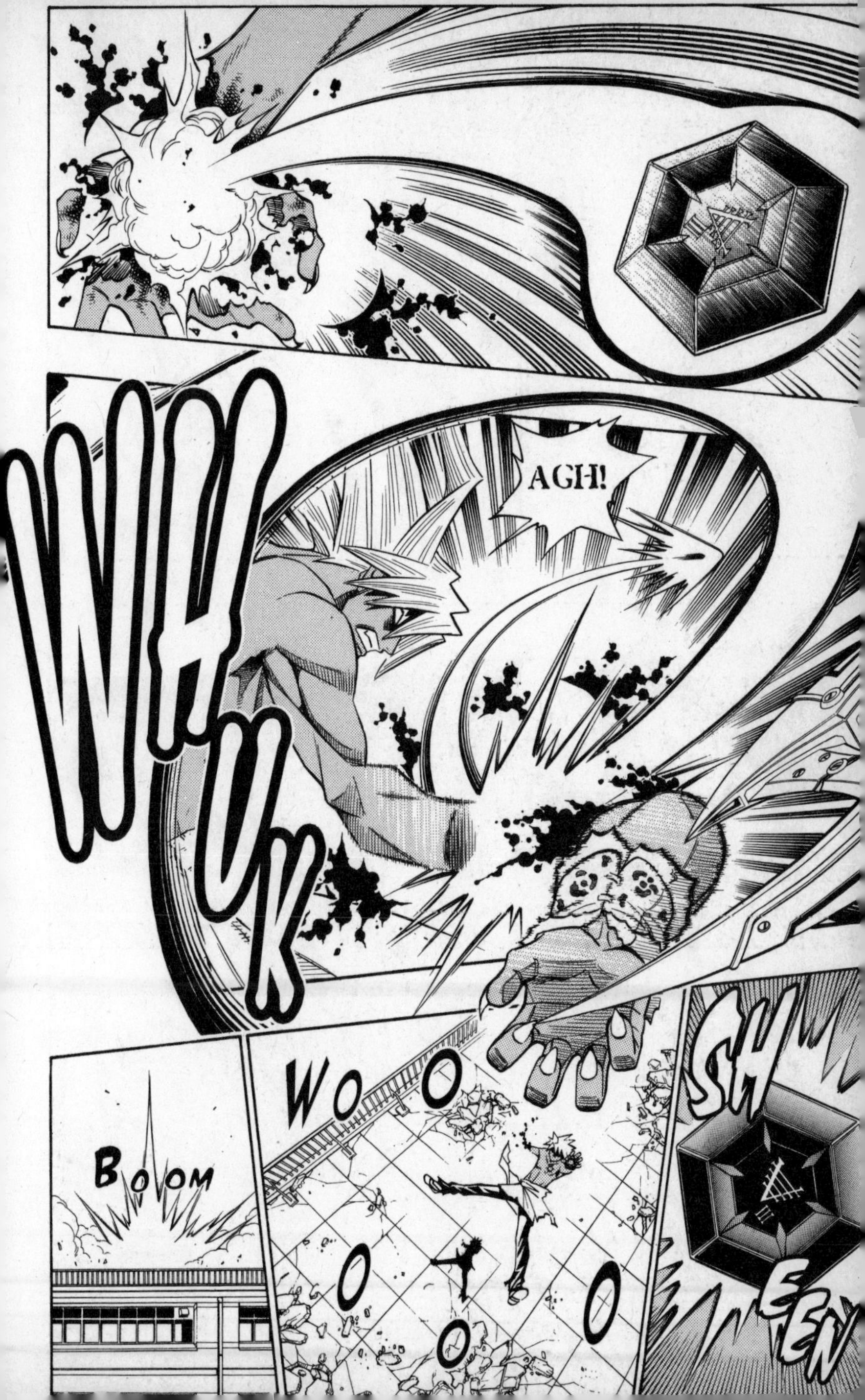
AGH!
WHACK
SHEEEN
WOOOOOO
BOOM

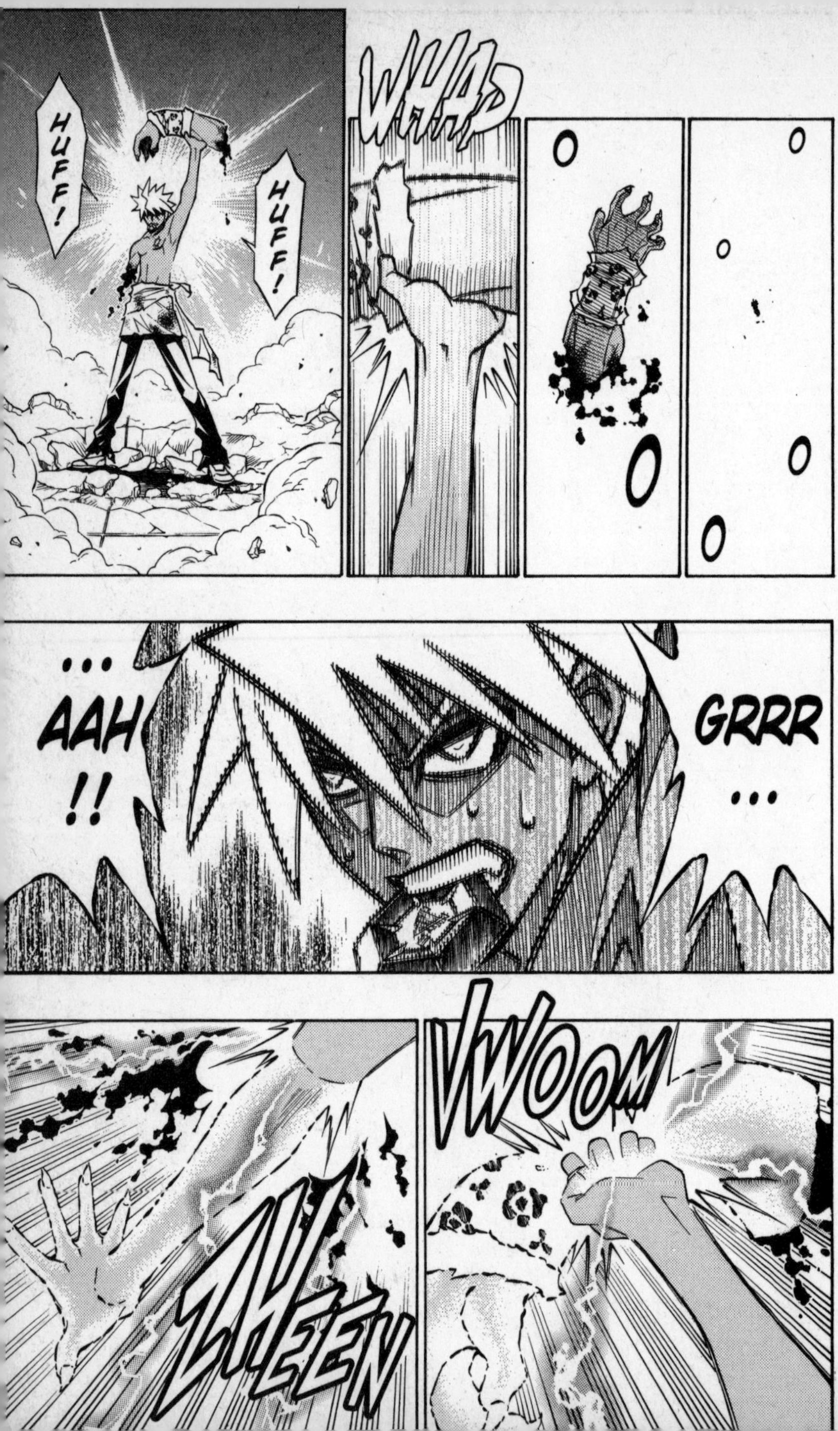
WHAP
HUFF!
HUFF!
GRRR...
...AAH!!
VWOOM
WHEEN

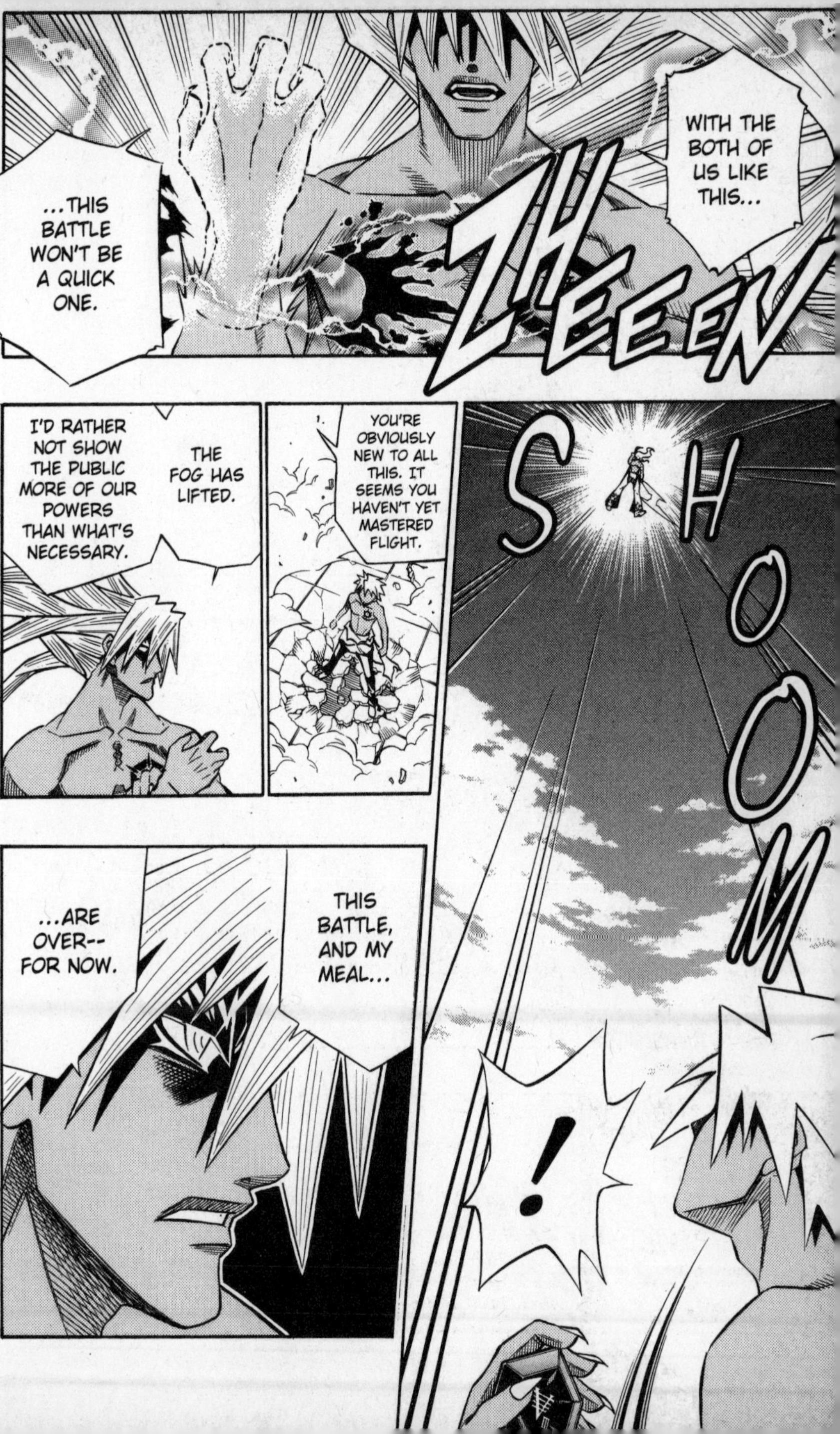
WITH THE BOTH OF US LIKE THIS...
...THIS BATTLE WON'T BE A QUICK ONE.
ZHEEEN
SHOOM
!
YOU'RE OBVIOUSLY NEW TO ALL THIS. IT SEEMS YOU HAVEN'T YET MASTERED FLIGHT.
THE FOG HAS LIFTED.
I'D RATHER NOT SHOW THE PUBLIC MORE OF OUR POWERS THAN WHAT'S NECESSARY.
THIS BATTLE, AND MY MEAL...
...ARE OVER-- FOR NOW.

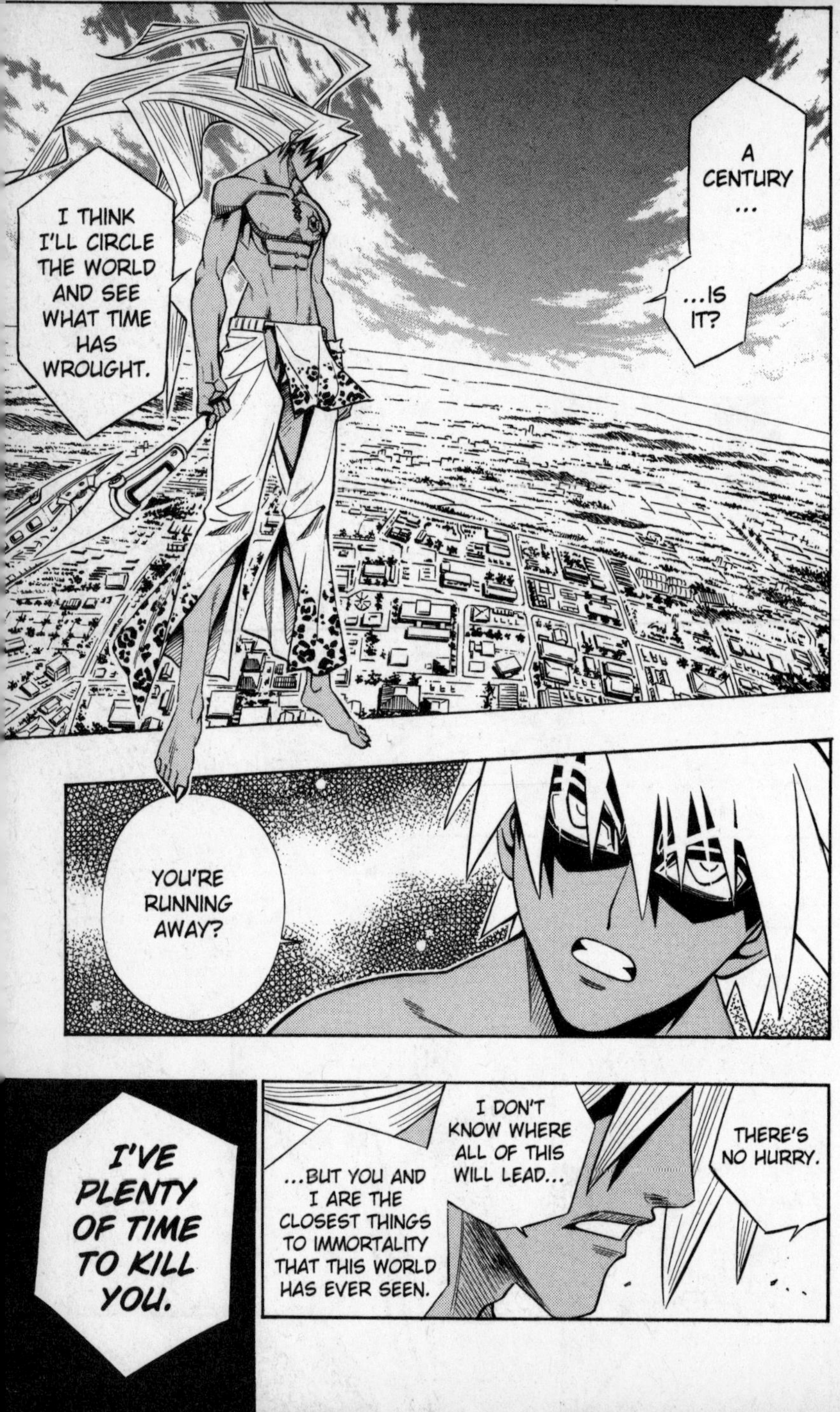
A CENTURY ...
...IS IT?
I THINK I'LL CIRCLE THE WORLD AND SEE WHAT TIME HAS WROUGHT.
YOU'RE RUNNING AWAY?
THERE'S NO HURRY.
I DON'T KNOW WHERE ALL OF THIS WILL LEAD...
...BUT YOU AND I ARE THE CLOSEST THINGS TO IMMORTALITY THAT THIS WORLD HAS EVER SEEN.
I'VE PLENTY OF TIME TO KILL YOU.

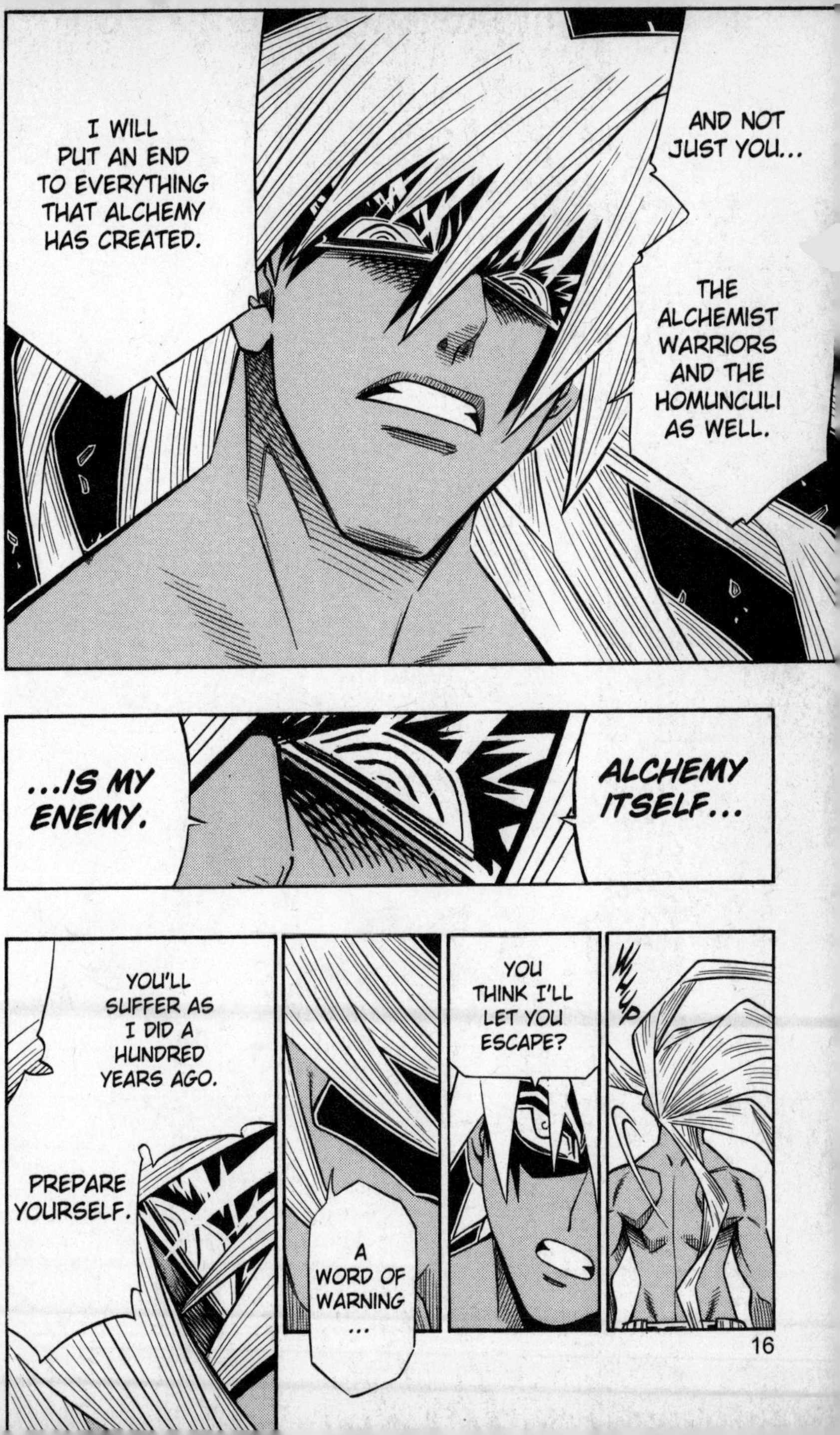
AND NOT JUST YOU...
THE ALCHEMIST WARRIORS AND THE HOMUNCULI AS WELL.
I WILL PUT AN END TO EVERYTHING THAT ALCHEMY HAS CREATED.
ALCHEMY ITSELF...
...IS MY ENEMY.
WHUP
YOU THINK I'LL LET YOU ESCAPE?
A WORD OF WARNING ...
YOU'LL SUFFER AS I DID A HUNDRED YEARS AGO.
PREPARE YOURSELF.

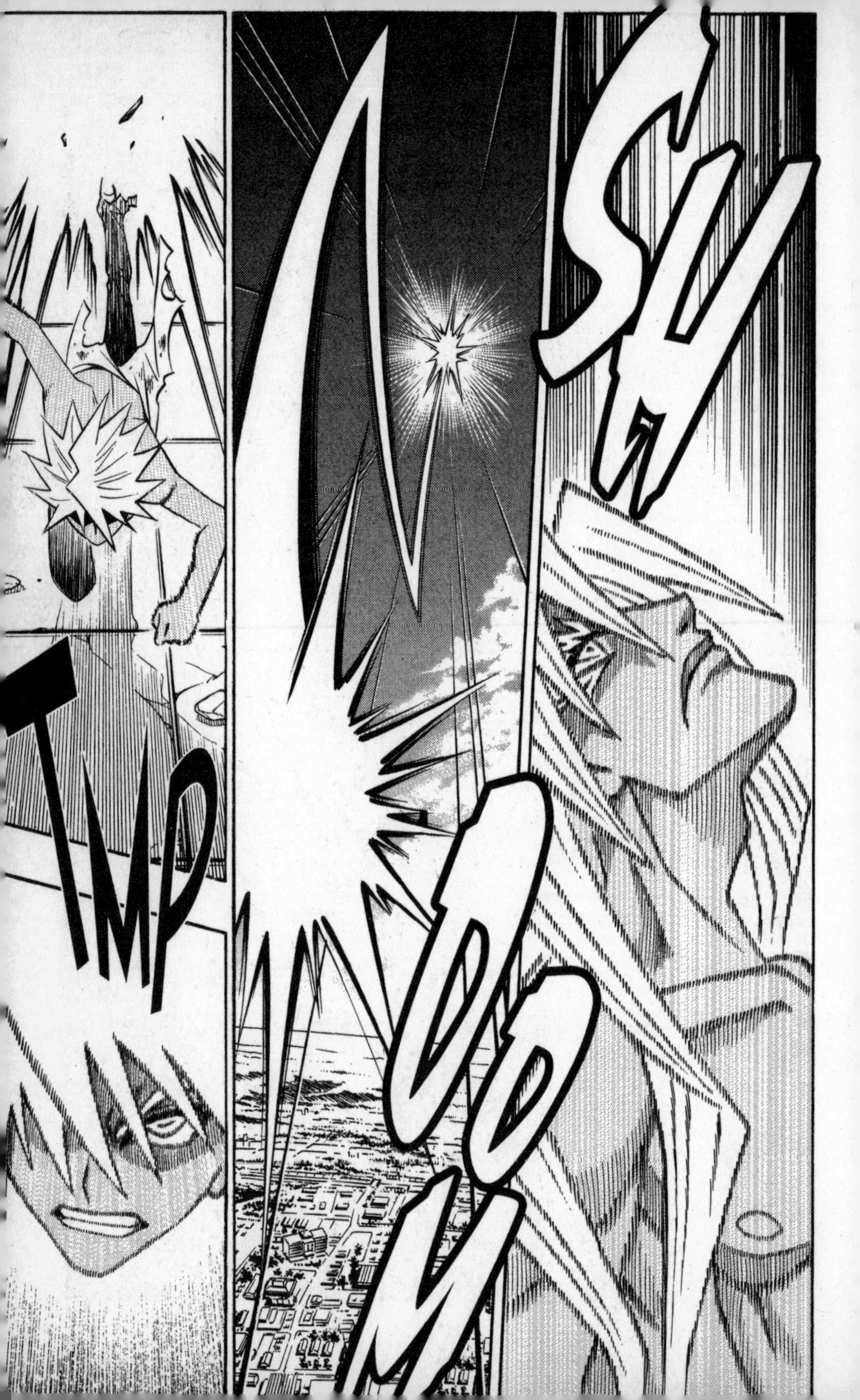
SHOOM
TMP

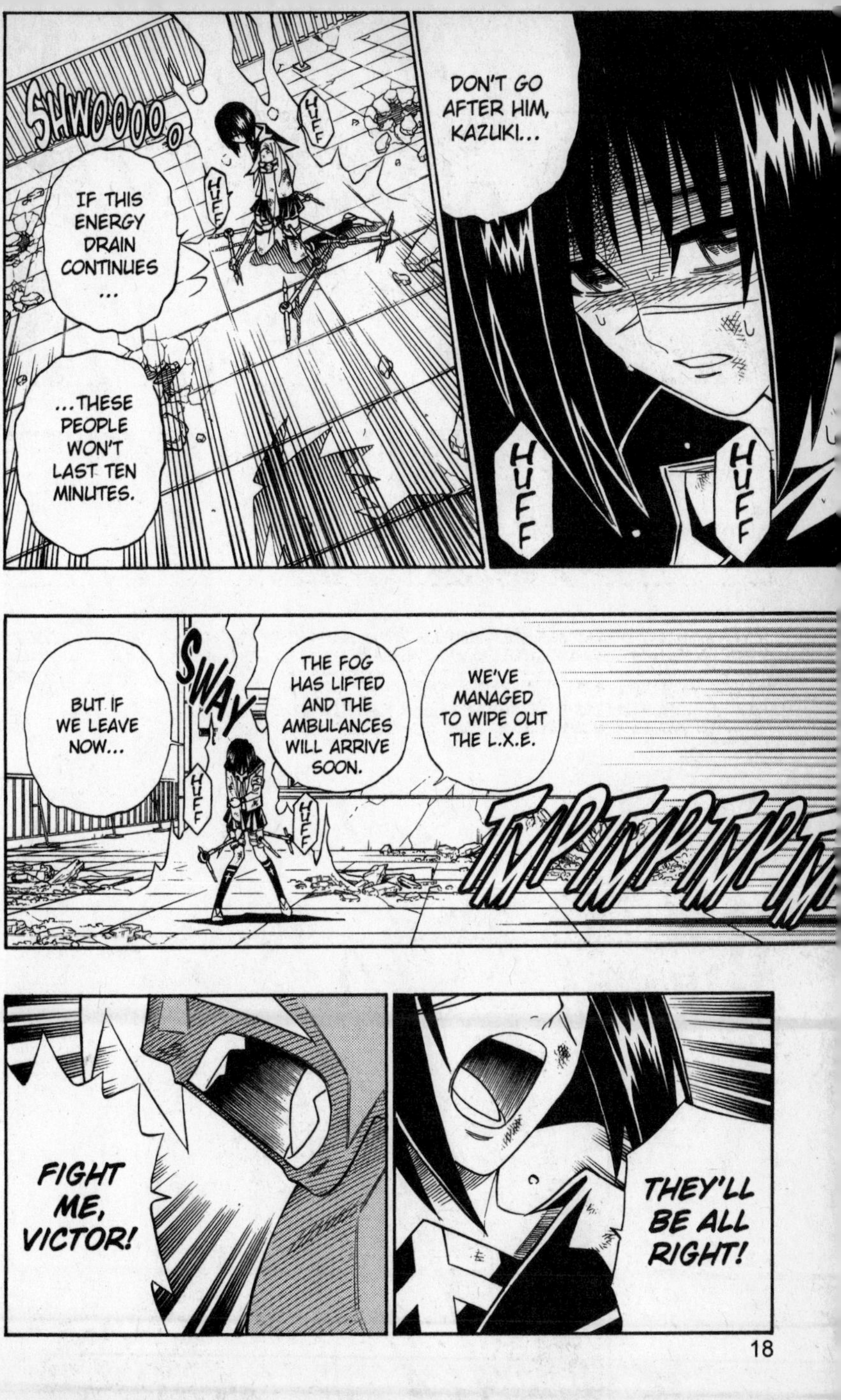
DON'T GO AFTER HIM, KAZUKI...
HUFF
HUFF
SHWOOOO
HUFF
HUFF
IF THIS ENERGY DRAIN CONTINUES ...
...THESE PEOPLE WON'T LAST TEN MINUTES.
WE'VE MANAGED TO WIPE OUT THE L.X.E.
THE FOG HAS LIFTED AND THE AMBULANCES WILL ARRIVE SOON.
SWAY
BUT IF WE LEAVE NOW...
HUFF
HUFF
THEY'LL BE ALL RIGHT!
FIGHT ME, VICTOR!

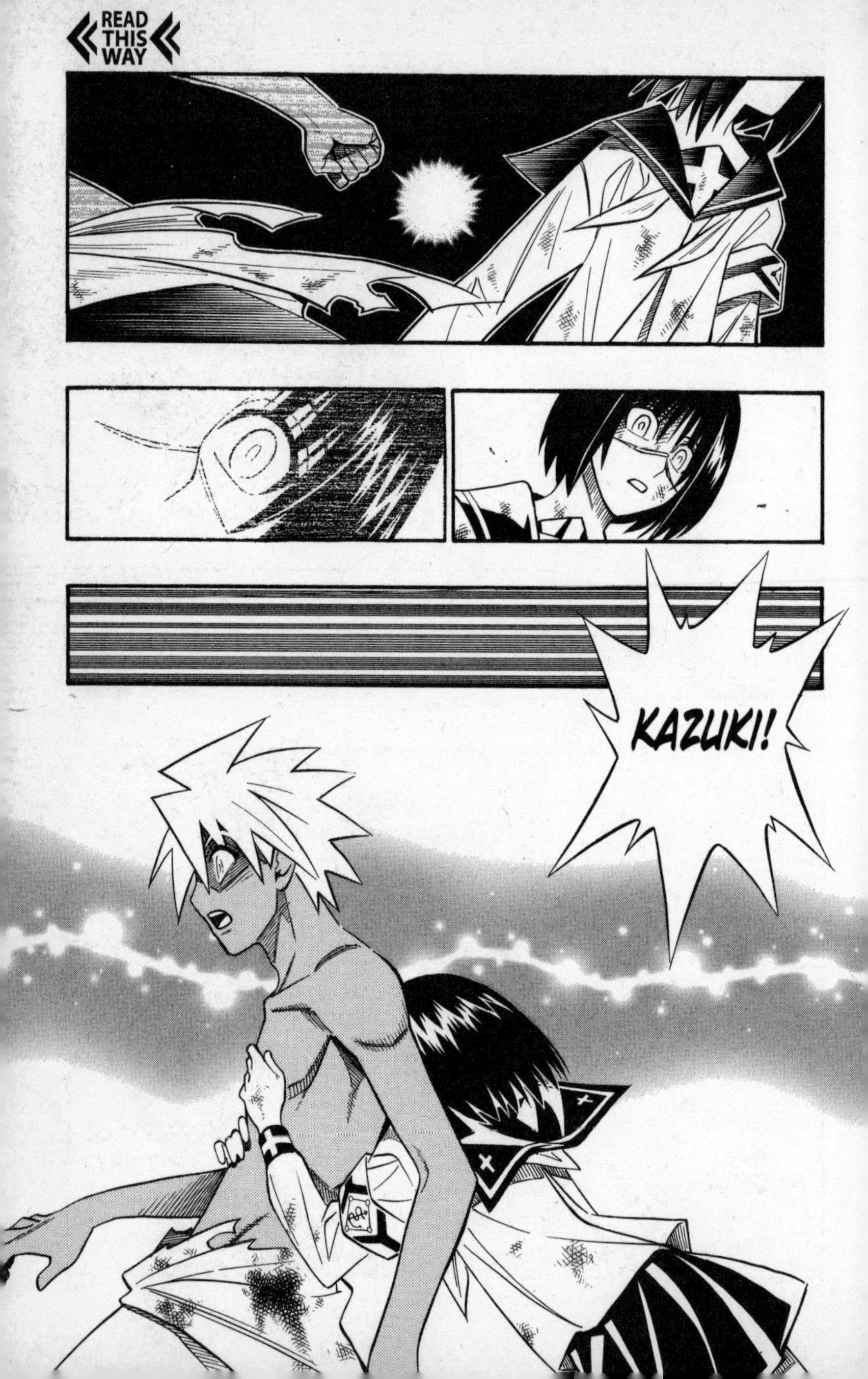
READ THIS WAY
KAZUKI!

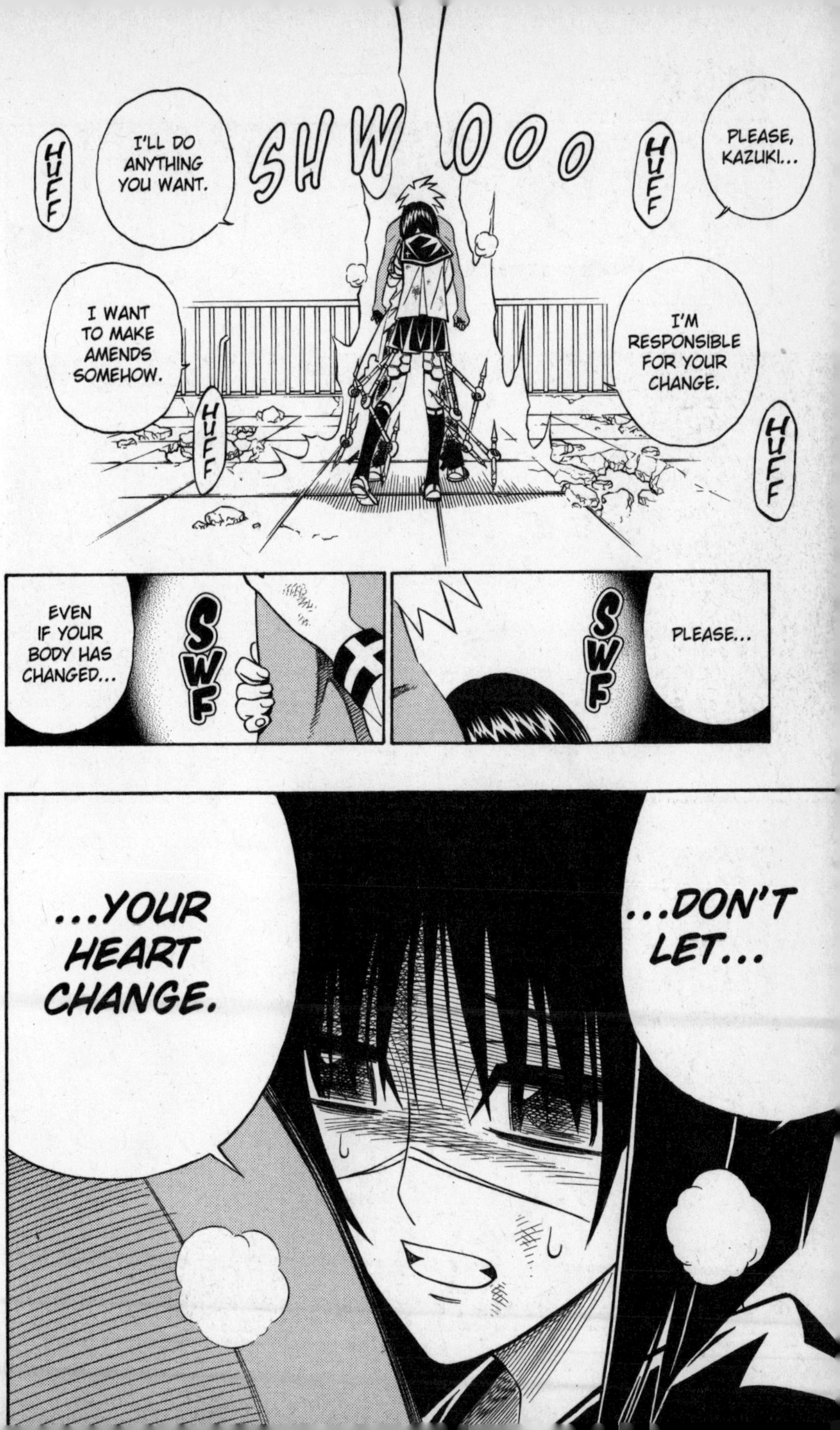
PLEASE, KAZUKI...
HUFF
I'M RESPONSIBLE FOR YOUR CHANGE.
HUFF
SHWOOO
I'LL DO ANYTHING YOU WANT.
HUFF
I WANT TO MAKE AMENDS SOMEHOW.
HUFF
PLEASE...
SWF
SWF
EVEN IF YOUR BODY HAS CHANGED...
...DON'T LET...
...YOUR HEART CHANGE.

READ THIS WAY

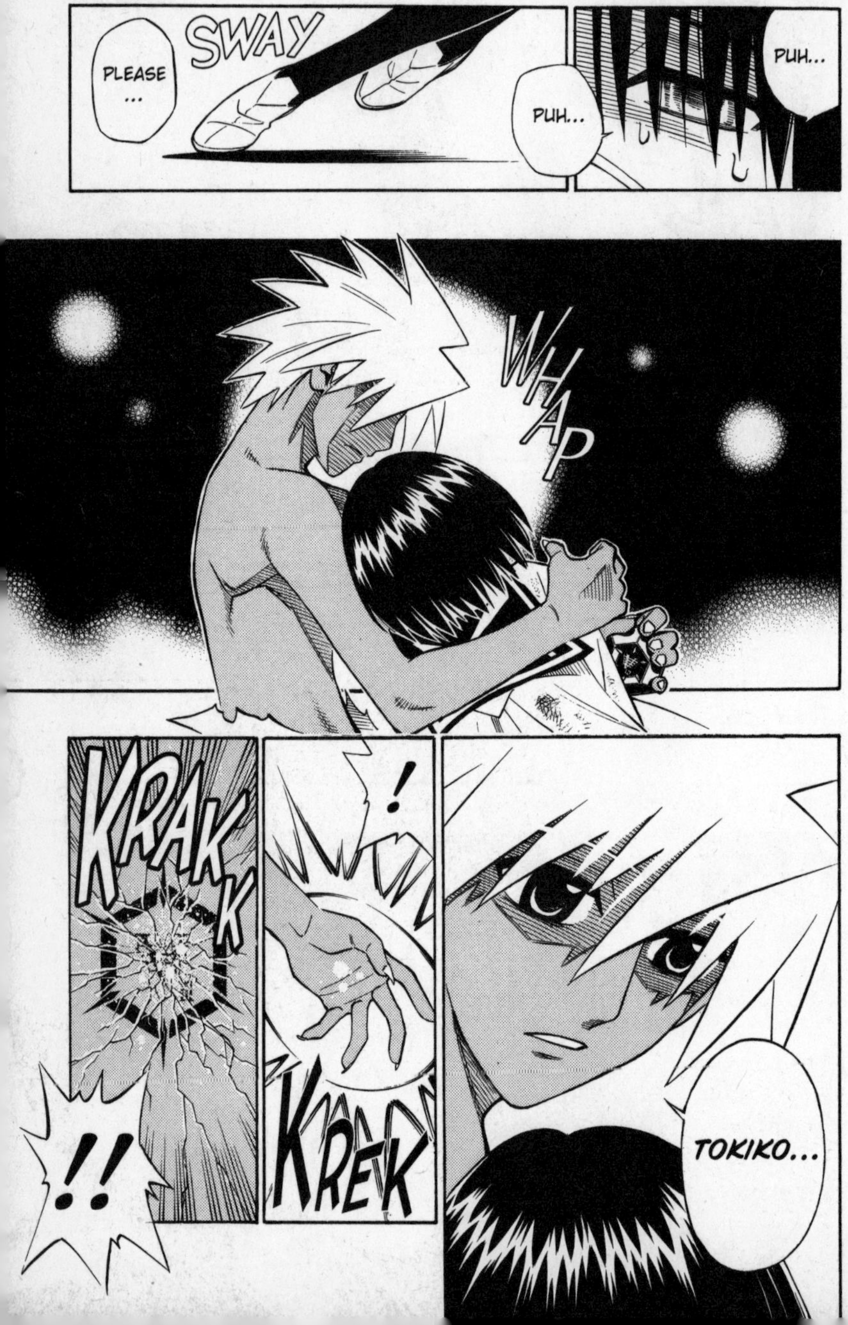
PUH...
PUH...
SWAY
PLEASE ...
WHAP
TOKIKO...
!
KREK
KRAK
K
!!

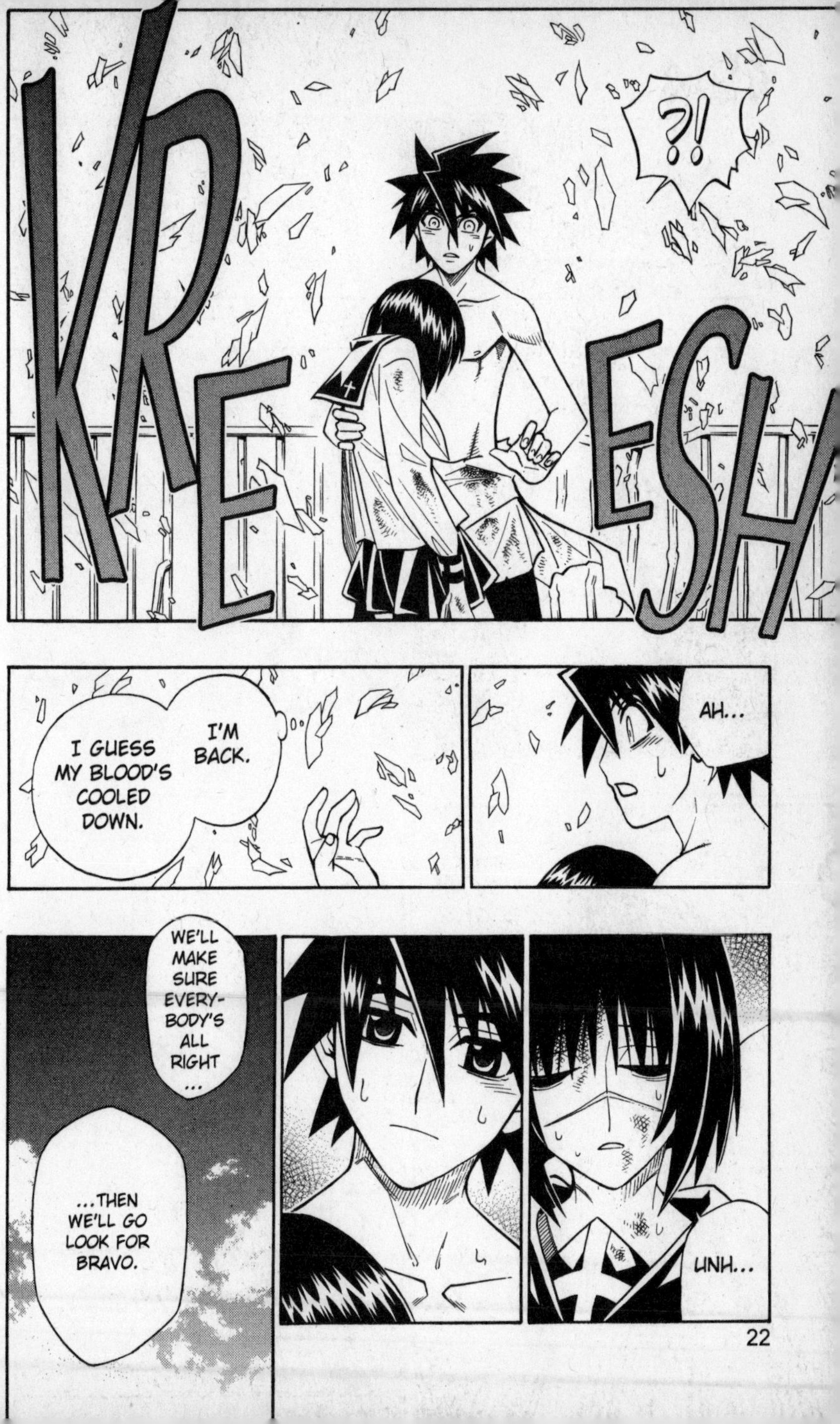
?!
KREESH
AH...
I'M BACK.
I GUESS MY BLOOD'S COOLED DOWN.
UNH...
WE'LL MAKE SURE EVERYBODY'S ALL RIGHT...
...THEN WE'LL GO LOOK FOR BRAVO.

READ THIS WAY

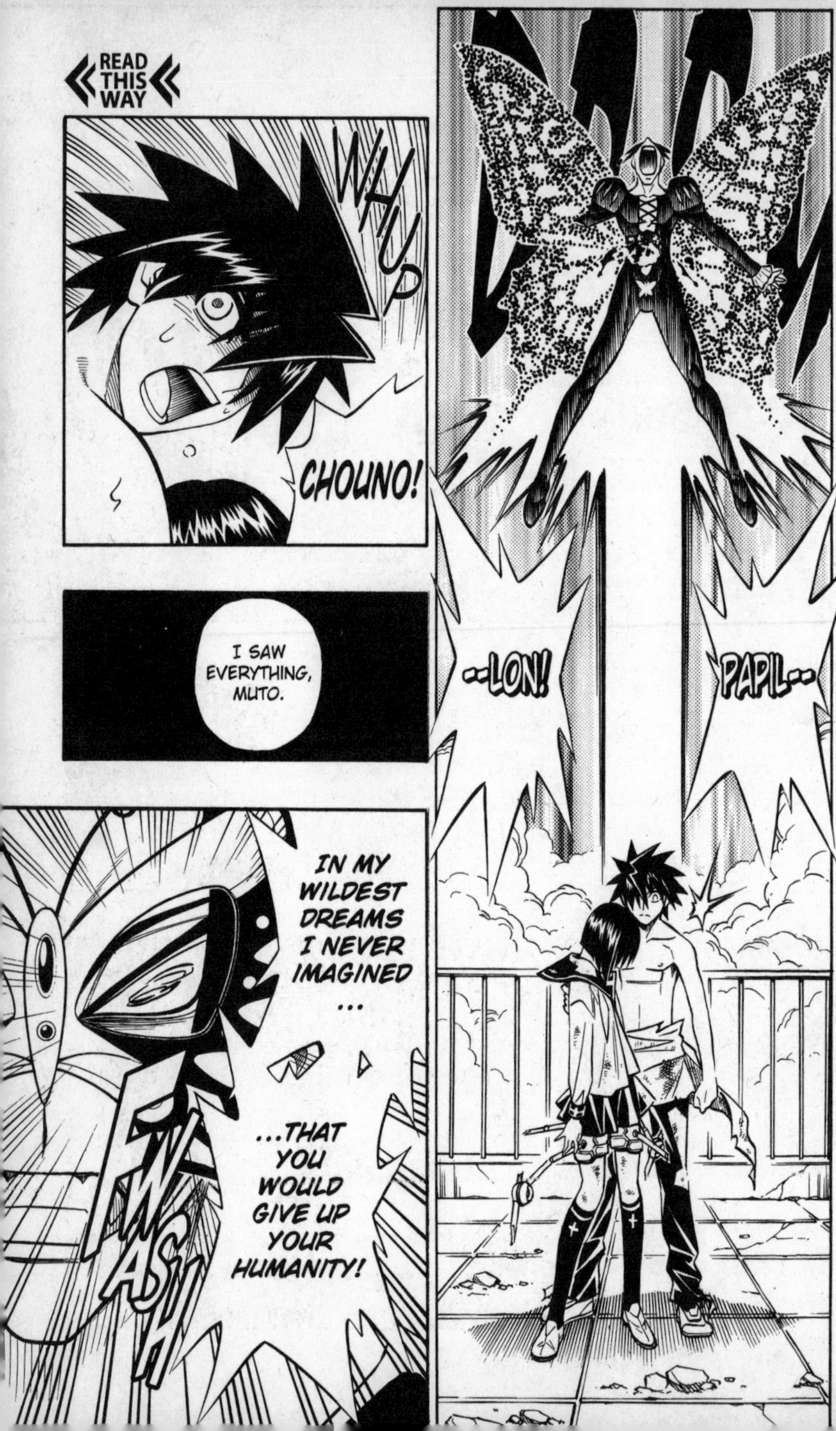
PAPIL--
--LON!
WHUP
CHOUNO!
I SAW EVERYTHING, MUTO.
IN MY WILDEST DREAMS I NEVER IMAGINED ...
...THAT YOU WOULD GIVE UP YOUR HUMANITY!
WASH

- Height: 250cm; Weight: 200kg
- Born: September 30; Libra; Blood Type: A; Age: 28
- Likes: Wife, daughter, comrades in arms
- Dislikes: Everything to do with alchemy
- Hobby: None
- Special Ability: None (He can do almost everything better than the average person.)
- Affiliations: The organization that unites the Alchemist Warriors (currently unnamed) Warrior Chief.

Character File No. 25

VICTOR

Author's Notes

- In designing Victor, I was thinking about forms that Kazuki might take in the future. Something that Kazuki has that Victor does not will probably figure in the turning point between these two characters.
- Then again, I haven't revealed much about Victor's past so the above comment may not be clear. I'll clarify in more detail at a later date.
- His design is based on the Native American warrior from the movie *Brotherhood of the Wolf*. He looks so cool in that fundoshi.
- I gave Victor white hair and red skin because I wanted to make him look like he came from some never-before-seen tribe of warriors, but it didn't turn out as well as I'd hoped.
- I wasn't feeling well at the time and things didn't look quite finished. He may look a little different when he shows up again

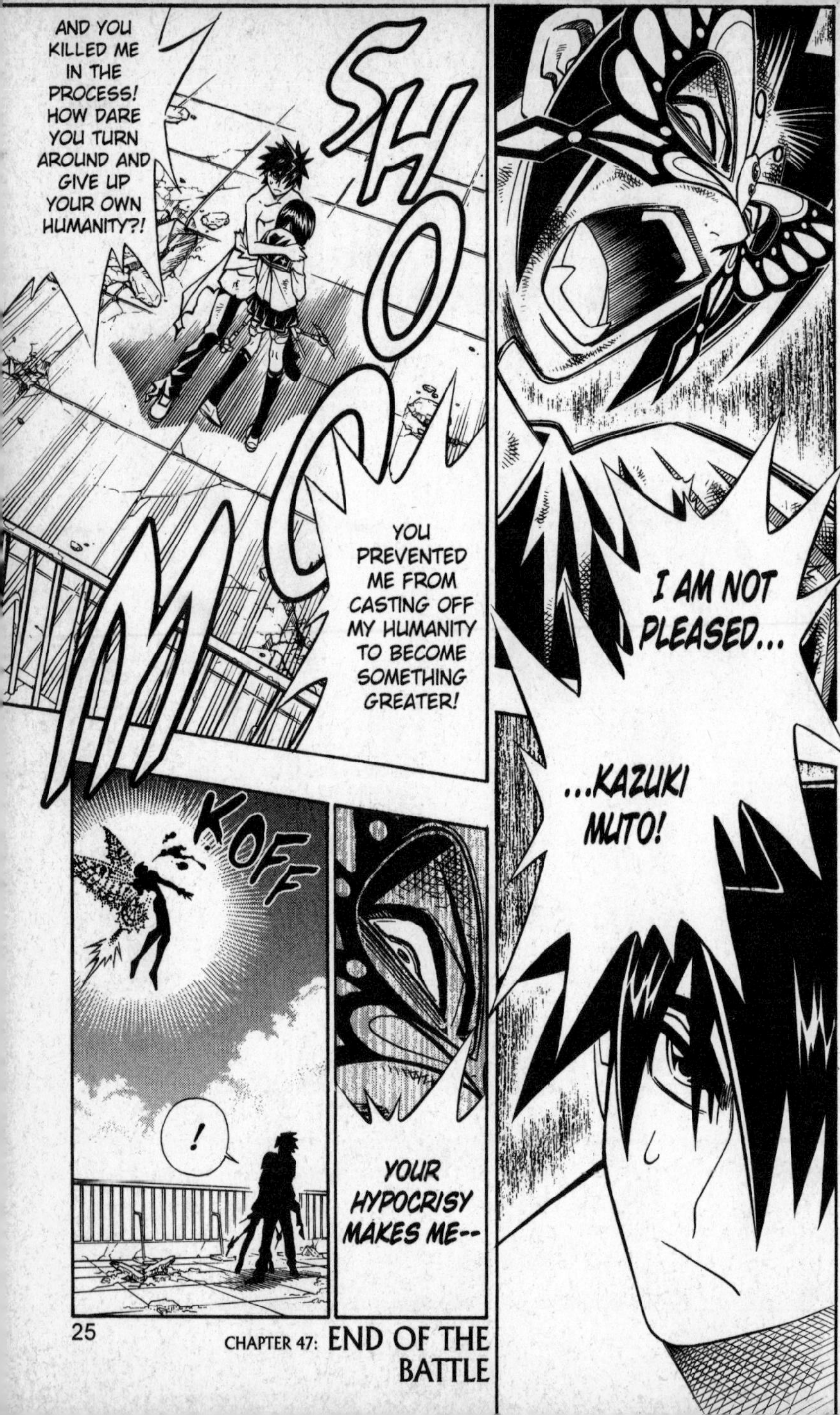
YOU PREVENTED ME FROM CASTING OFF MY HUMANITY TO BECOME SOMETHING GREATER!
AND YOU KILLED ME IN THE PROCESS! HOW DARE YOU TURN AROUND AND GIVE UP YOUR OWN HUMANITY?!
KOFF
!
YOUR HYPOCRISY MAKES ME--
I AM NOT PLEASED...
...KAZUKI MUTO!

CHAPTER 47: END OF THE BATTLE

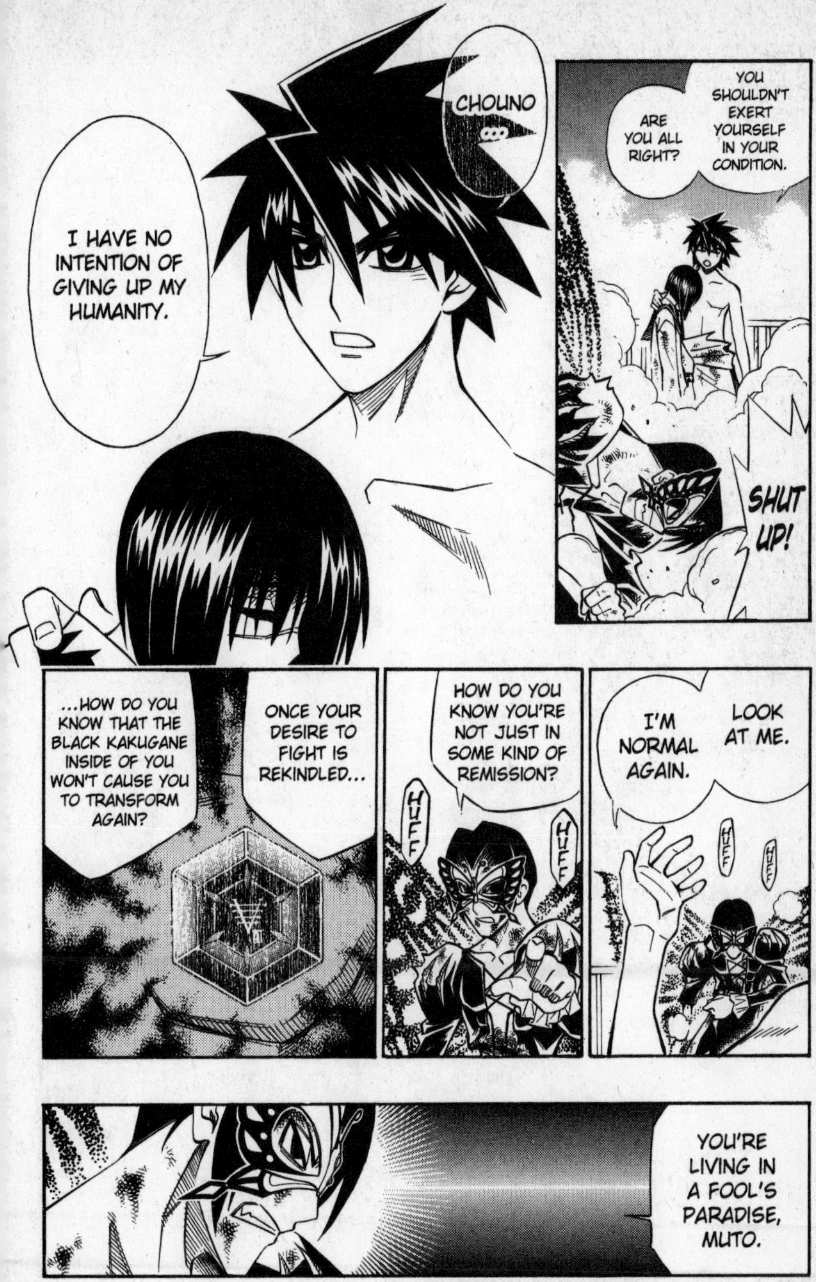
YOU SHOULDN'T EXERT YOURSELF IN YOUR CONDITION.
ARE YOU ALL RIGHT?
SHUT UP!
CHOUNO...
I HAVE NO INTENTION OF GIVING UP MY HUMANITY.
LOOK AT ME.
I'M NORMAL AGAIN.
HUFF
HUFF
HOW DO YOU KNOW YOU'RE NOT JUST IN SOME KIND OF REMISSION?
HUFF
HUFF
ONCE YOUR DESIRE TO FIGHT IS REKINDLED...
...HOW DO YOU KNOW THAT THE BLACK KAKUGANE INSIDE OF YOU WON'T CAUSE YOU TO TRANSFORM AGAIN?
YOU'RE LIVING IN A FOOL'S PARADISE, MUTO.

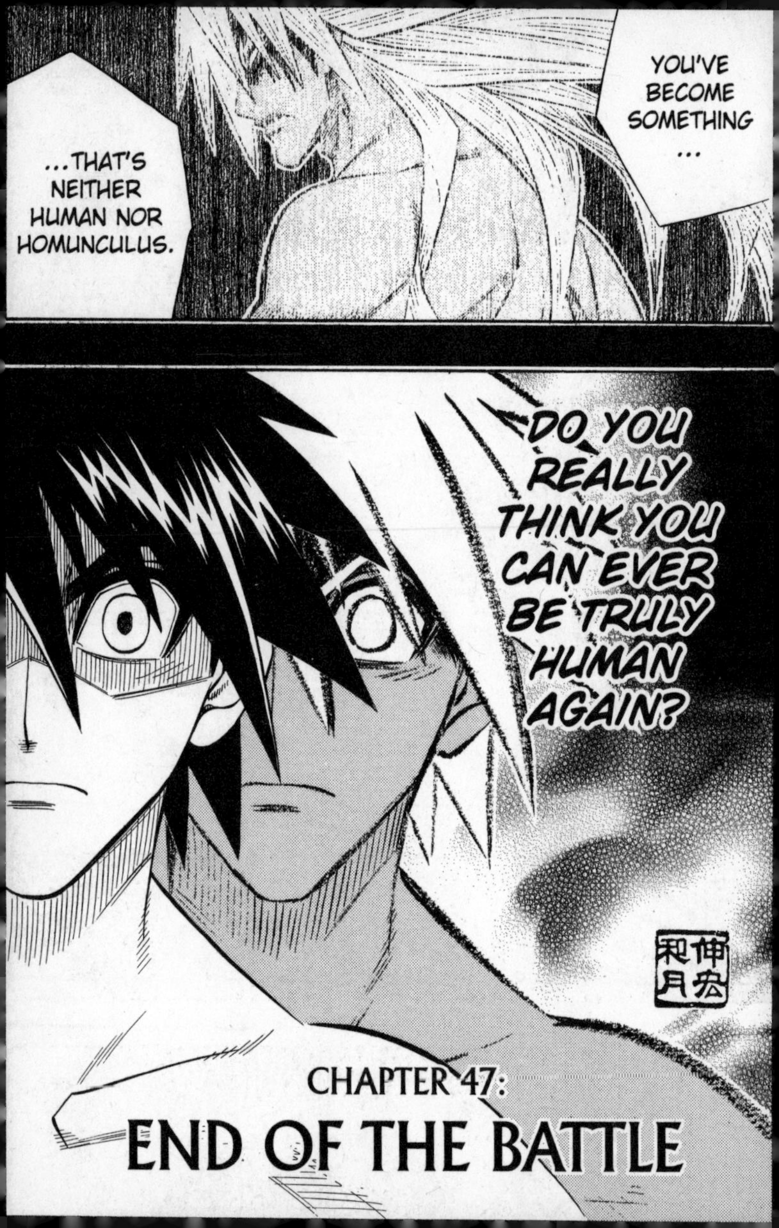
YOU'VE BECOME SOMETHING ...
...THAT'S NEITHER HUMAN NOR HOMUNCULUS.
DO YOU REALLY THINK YOU CAN EVER BE TRULY HUMAN AGAIN?
伸宏和月
CHAPTER 47:
END OF THE BATTLE

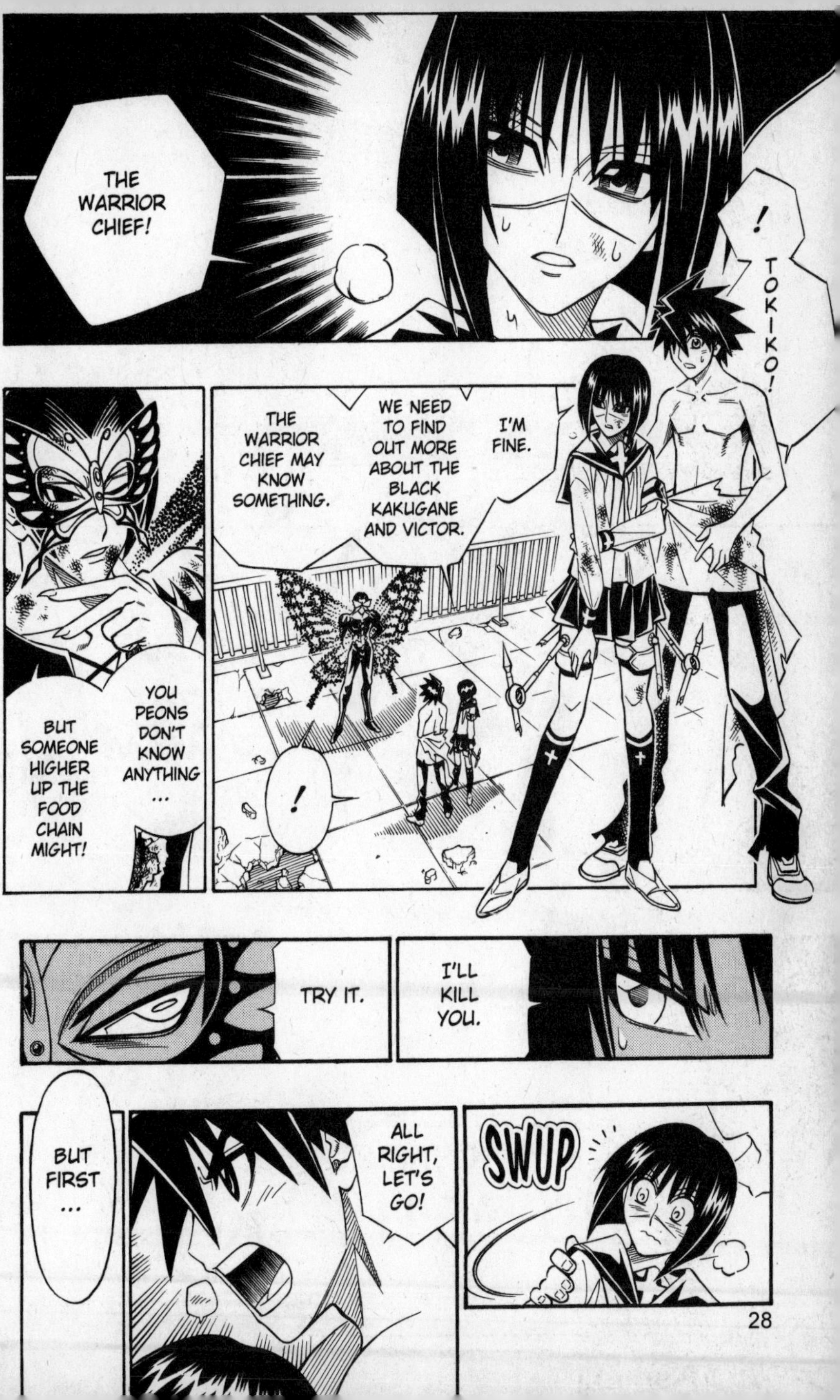

THE WARRIOR CHIEF!
!
TOKIKO!
I'M FINE.
WE NEED TO FIND OUT MORE ABOUT THE BLACK KAKUGANE AND VICTOR.
THE WARRIOR CHIEF MAY KNOW SOMETHING.
!
YOU PEONS DON'T KNOW ANYTHING ...
BUT SOMEONE HIGHER UP THE FOOD CHAIN MIGHT!
I'LL KILL YOU.
TRY IT.
SWUP
ALL RIGHT, LET'S GO!
BUT FIRST ...

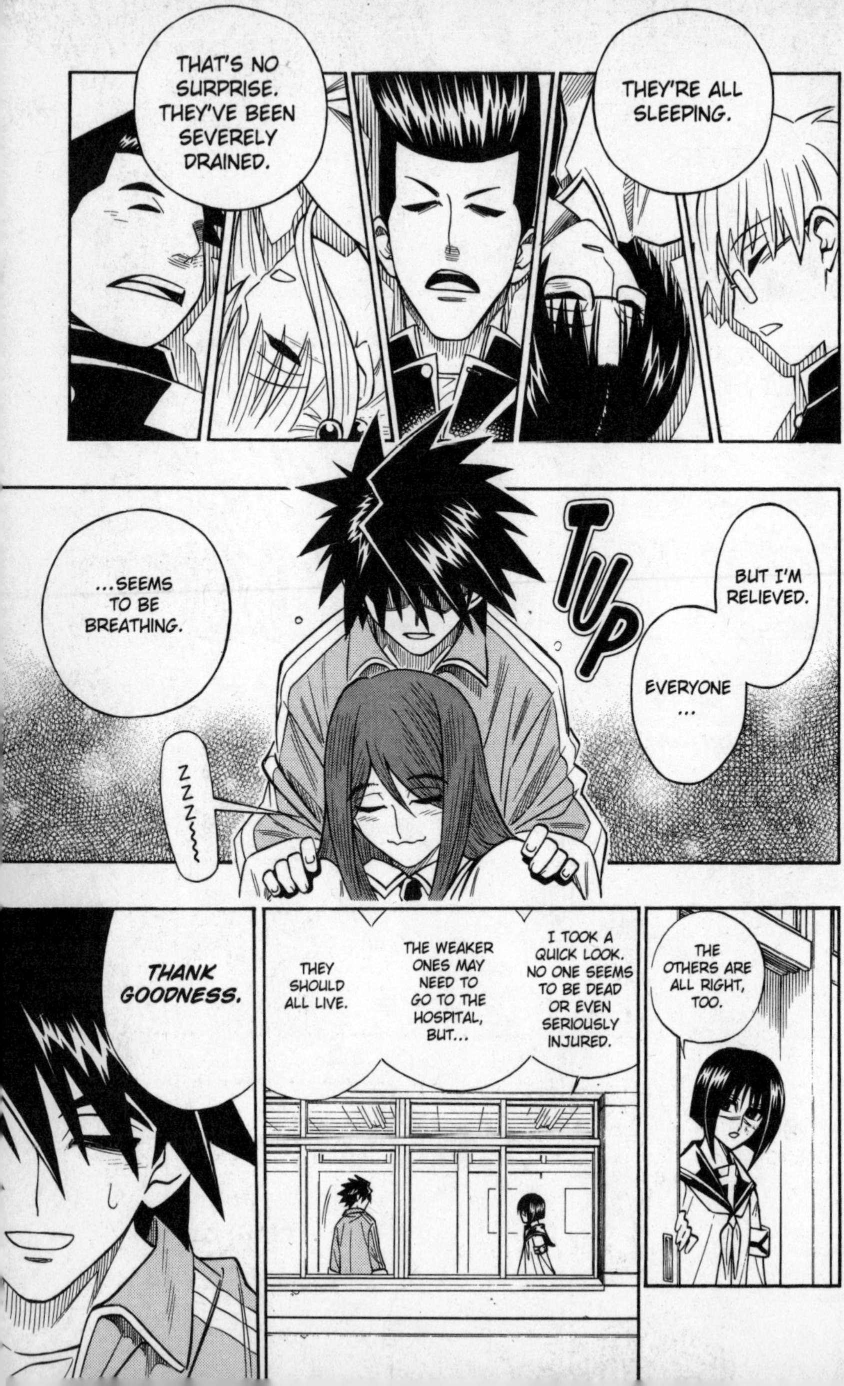
THEY'RE ALL SLEEPING.
THAT'S NO SURPRISE. THEY'VE BEEN SEVERELY DRAINED.
BUT I'M RELIEVED.
EVERYONE ...
TUP
...SEEMS TO BE BREATHING.
ZZZ~~
THE OTHERS ARE ALL RIGHT, TOO.
I TOOK A QUICK LOOK. NO ONE SEEMS TO BE DEAD OR EVEN SERIOUSLY INJURED.
THE WEAKER ONES MAY NEED TO GO TO THE HOSPITAL, BUT...
THEY SHOULD ALL LIVE.
THANK GOODNESS.

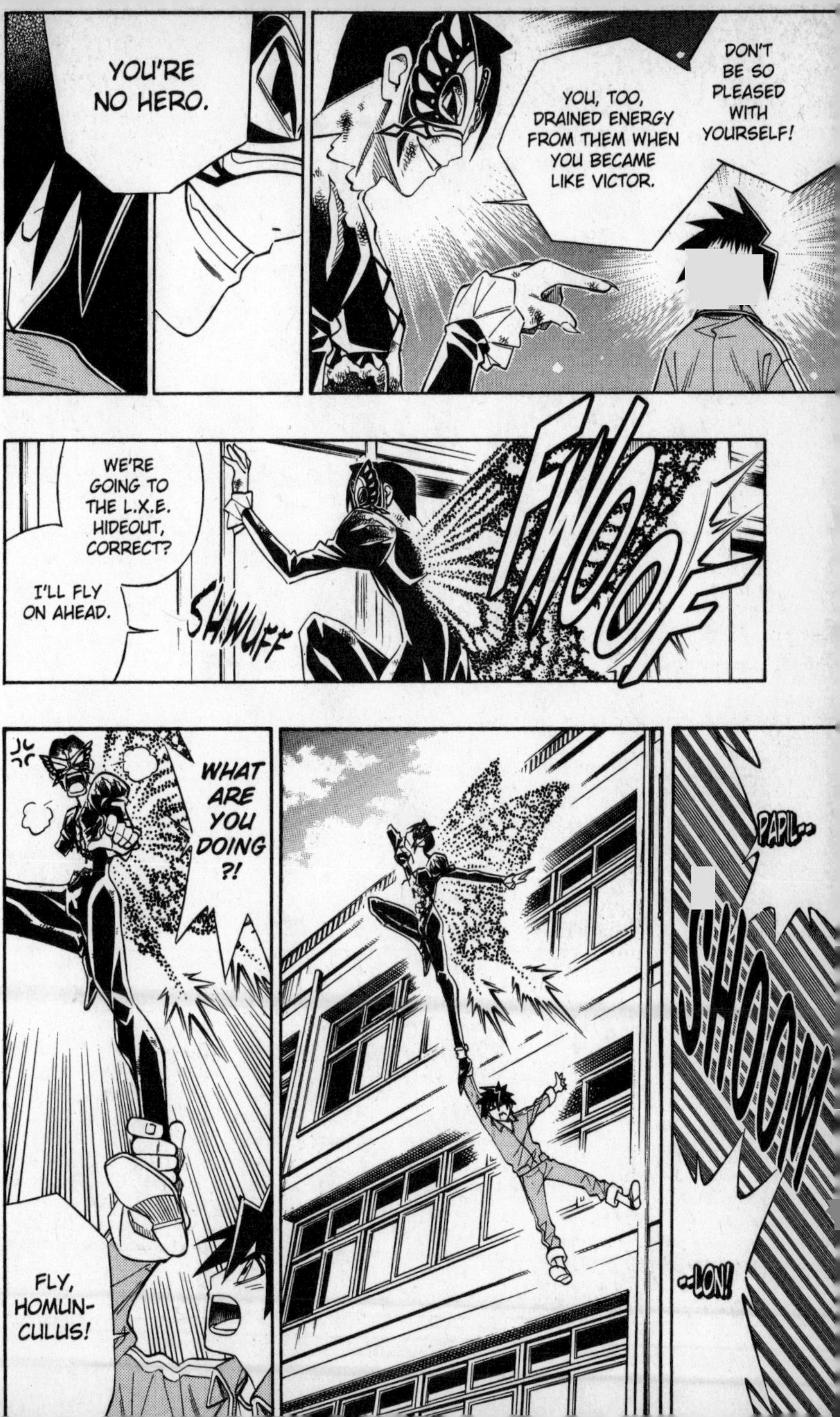
DON'T BE SO PLEASED WITH YOURSELF!
YOU, TOO, DRAINED ENERGY FROM THEM WHEN YOU BECAME LIKE VICTOR.
YOU'RE NO HERO.
FWOOF
WE'RE GOING TO THE L.X.E. HIDEOUT, CORRECT?
I'LL FLY ON AHEAD.
SHWUFF
PAPIL--
SHOOM
--LON!
WHAT ARE YOU DOING ?!
FLY, HOMUN-CULUS!

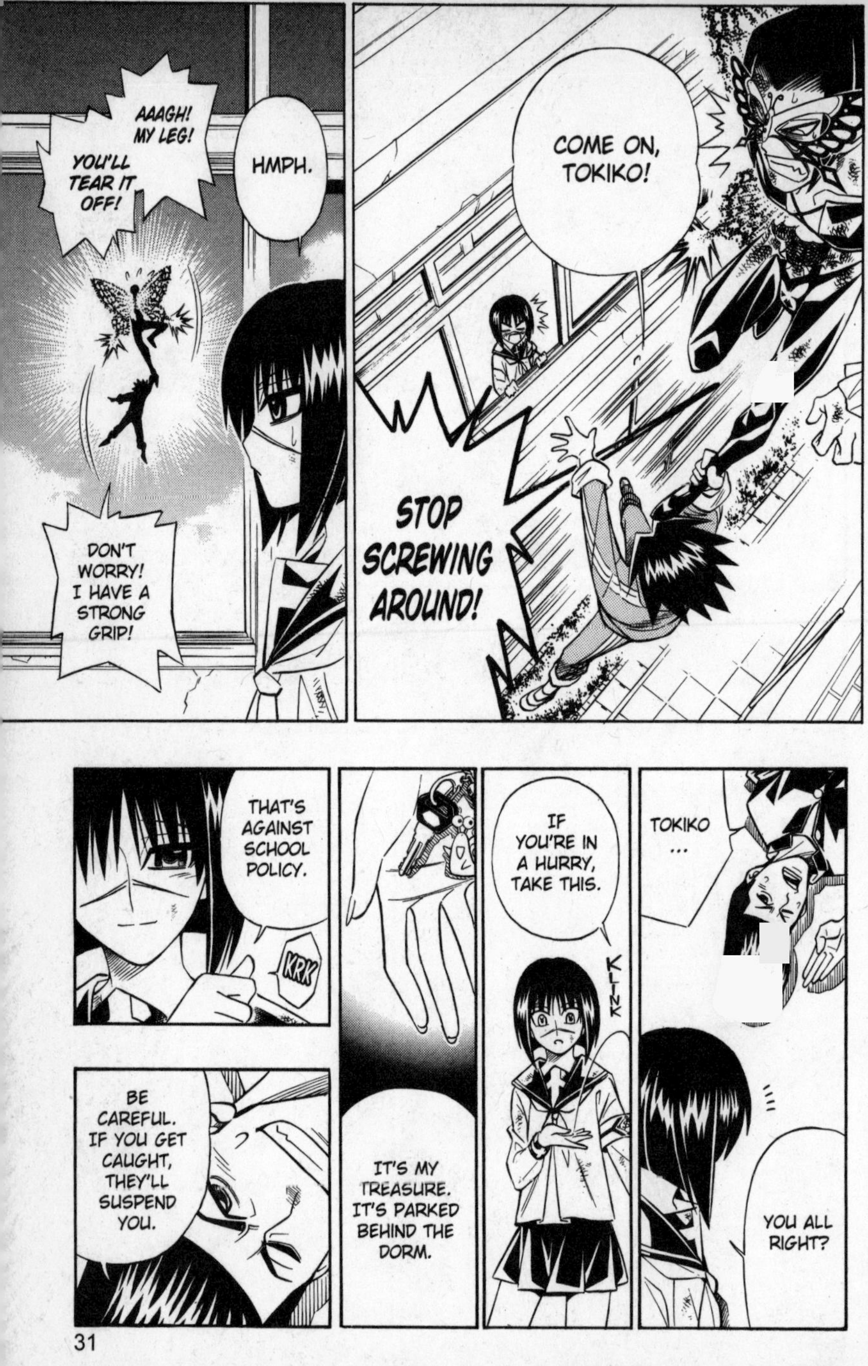
COME ON, TOKIKO!
STOP SCREWING AROUND!
HMPH.
AAAGH! MY LEG!
YOU'LL TEAR IT OFF!
DON'T WORRY! I HAVE A STRONG GRIP!
TOKIKO ...
YOU ALL RIGHT?
IF YOU'RE IN A HURRY, TAKE THIS.
KLINK
IT'S MY TREASURE. IT'S PARKED BEHIND THE DORM.
THAT'S AGAINST SCHOOL POLICY.
KRK
BE CAREFUL. IF YOU GET CAUGHT, THEY'LL SUSPEND YOU.

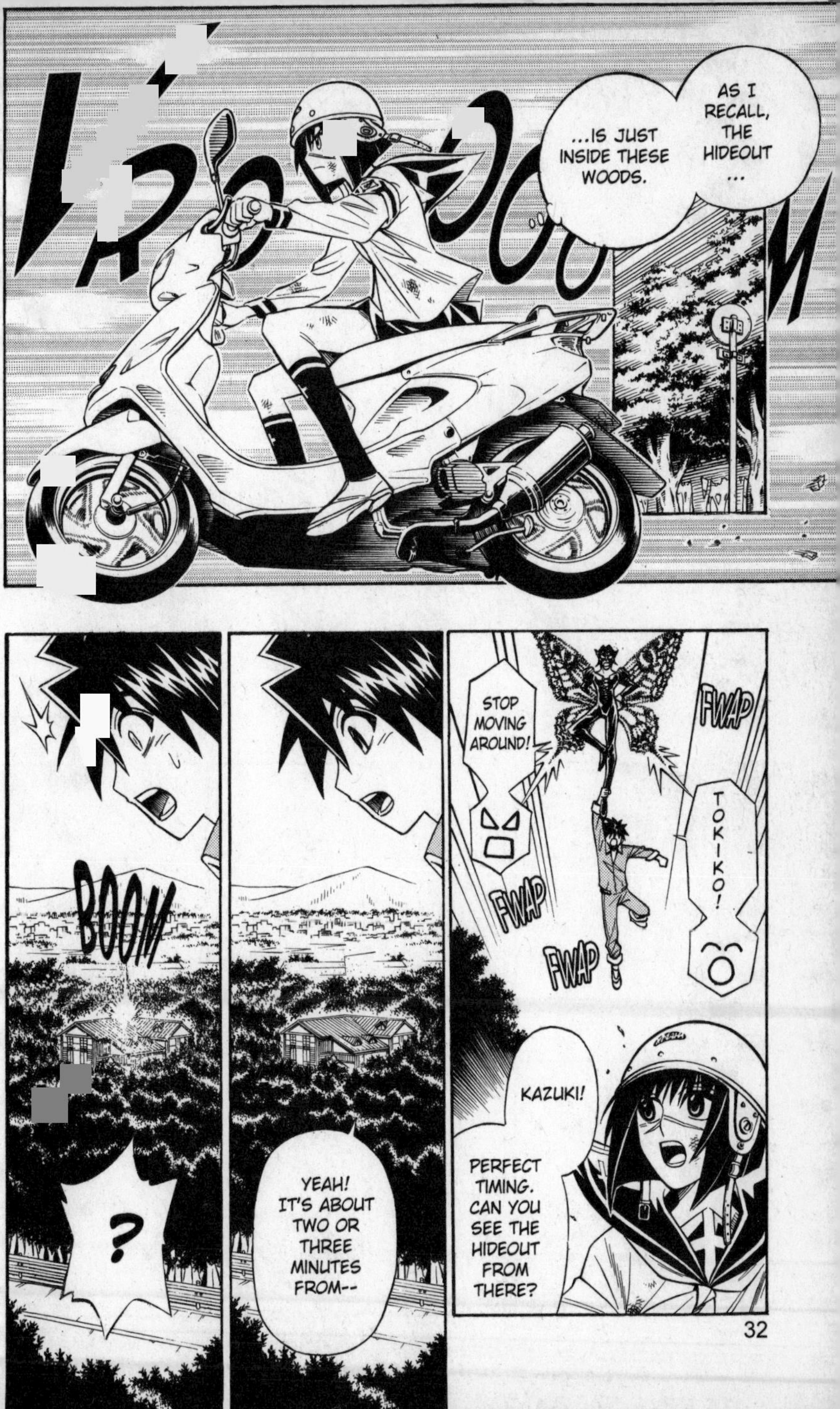
VROOOOM
AS I RECALL, THE HIDEOUT...
...IS JUST INSIDE THESE WOODS.
FWAP
TOKIKO!
STOP MOVING AROUND!
FWAP
FWAP
KAZUKI!
PERFECT TIMING. CAN YOU SEE THE HIDEOUT FROM THERE?
YEAH! IT'S ABOUT TWO OR THREE MINUTES FROM--
BOOM
?

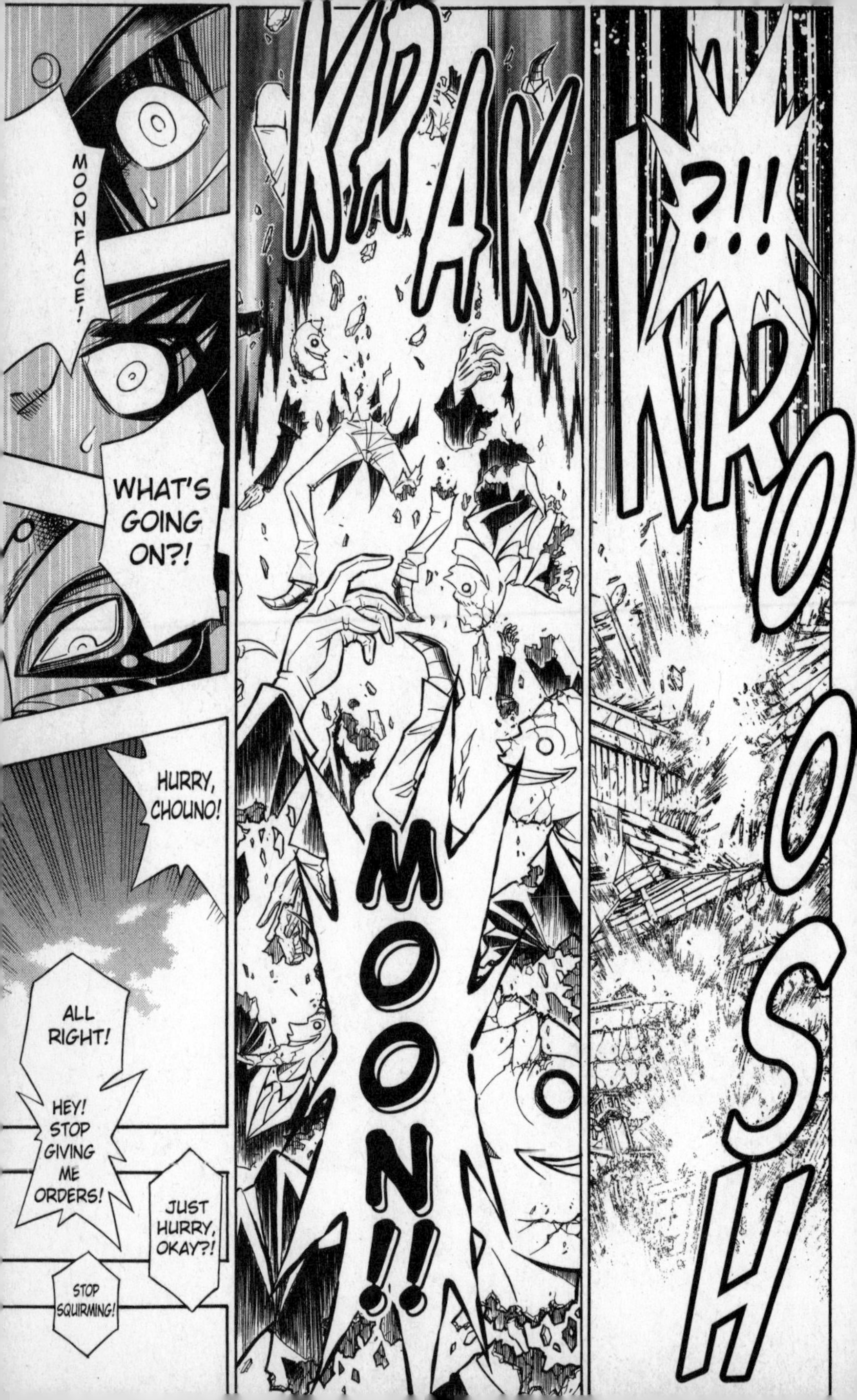
?!!
KROOSH
KRAK
MOOON!!
MOONFACE!
WHAT'S GOING ON?!
HURRY, CHOUNO!
ALL RIGHT!
HEY! STOP GIVING ME ORDERS!
JUST HURRY, OKAY?!
STOP SQUIRMING!

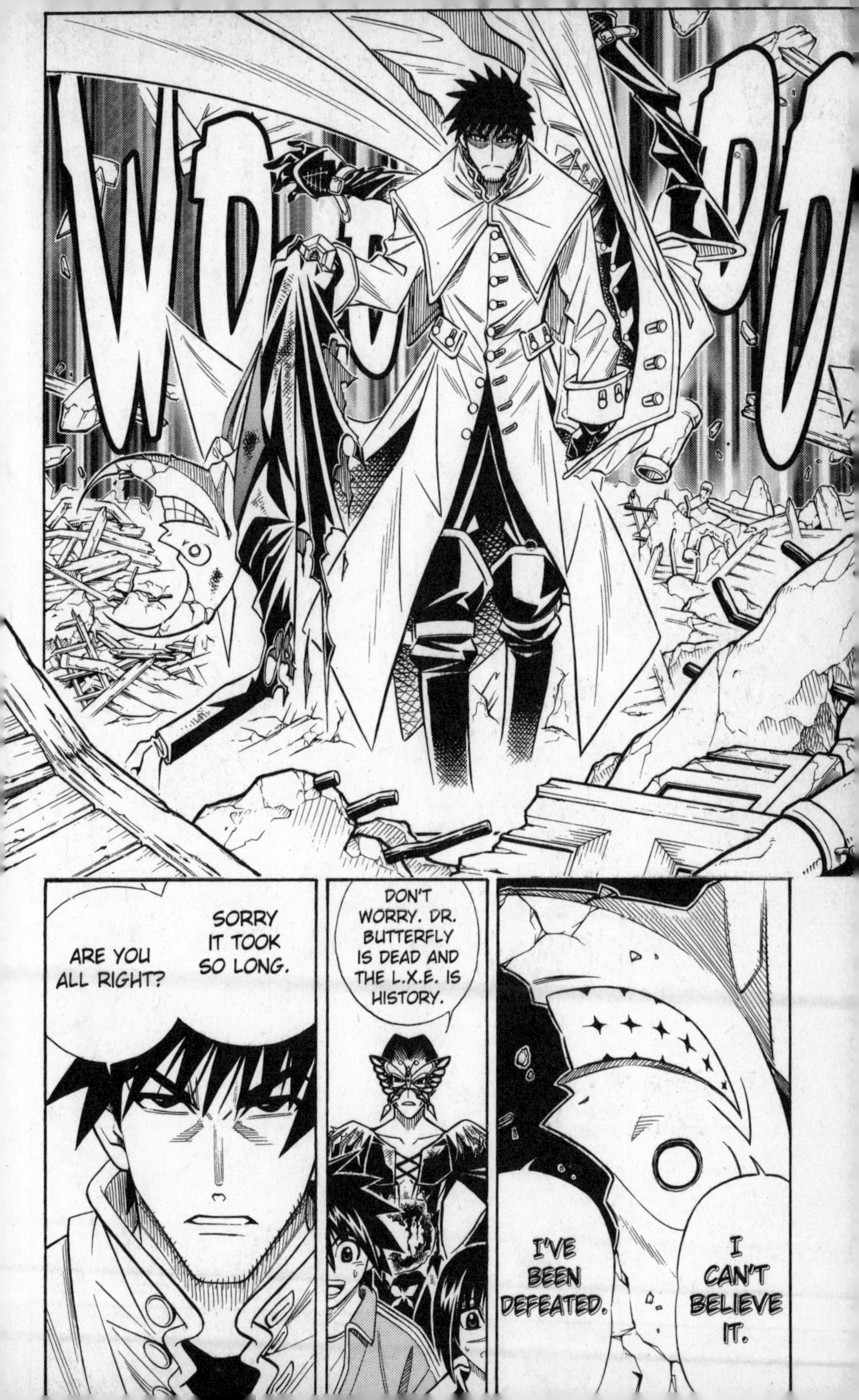
I CAN'T BELIEVE IT.
I'VE BEEN DEFEATED.
DON'T WORRY. DR. BUTTERFLY IS DEAD AND THE L.X.E. IS HISTORY.
SORRY IT TOOK SO LONG.
ARE YOU ALL RIGHT?

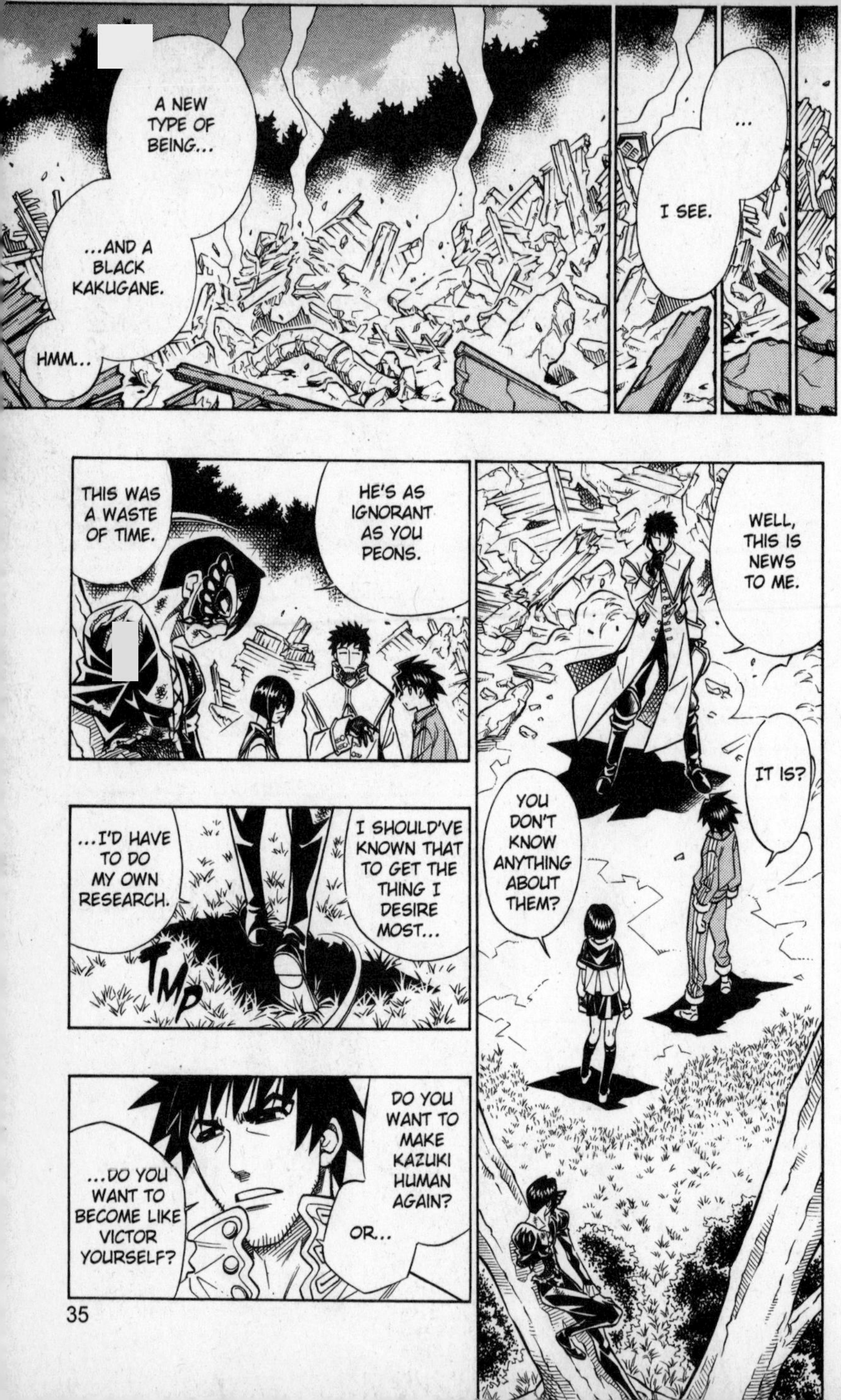
...
I SEE.
A NEW TYPE OF BEING...
...AND A BLACK KAKUGANE.
HMM...
WELL, THIS IS NEWS TO ME.
IT IS?
YOU DON'T KNOW ANYTHING ABOUT THEM?
HE'S AS IGNORANT AS YOU PEONS.
THIS WAS A WASTE OF TIME.
I SHOULD'VE KNOWN THAT TO GET THE THING I DESIRE MOST...
...I'D HAVE TO DO MY OWN RESEARCH.
TMP
DO YOU WANT TO MAKE KAZUKI HUMAN AGAIN?
OR...
...DO YOU WANT TO BECOME LIKE VICTOR YOURSELF?

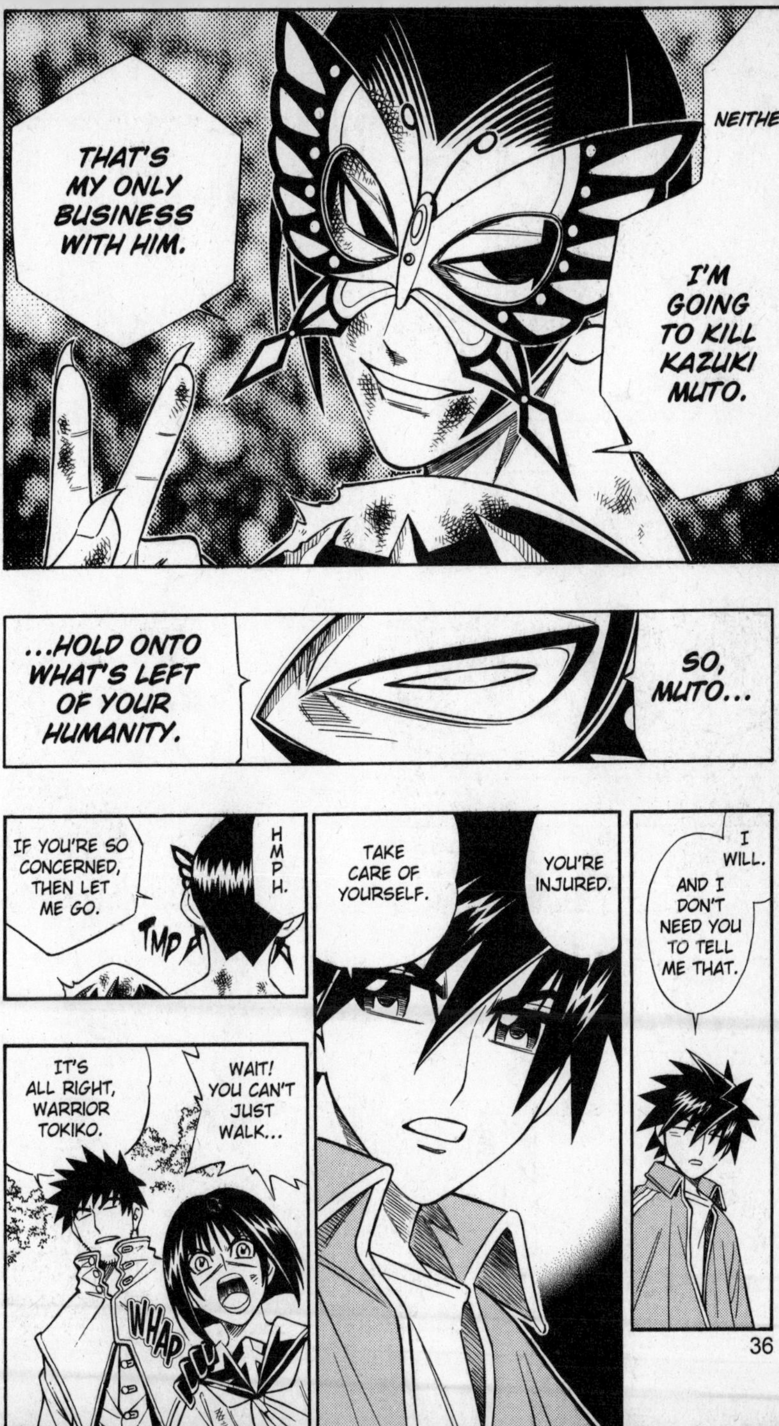
NEITHER.
I'M GOING TO KILL KAZUKI MUTO.
THAT'S MY ONLY BUSINESS WITH HIM.
SO, MUTO...
...HOLD ONTO WHAT'S LEFT OF YOUR HUMANITY.
I WILL.
AND I DON'T NEED YOU TO TELL ME THAT.
YOU'RE INJURED.
TAKE CARE OF YOURSELF.
HMPH.
IF YOU'RE SO CONCERNED, THEN LET ME GO.
TMP
WAIT! YOU CAN'T JUST WALK...
IT'S ALL RIGHT, WARRIOR TOKIKO.
WHAP

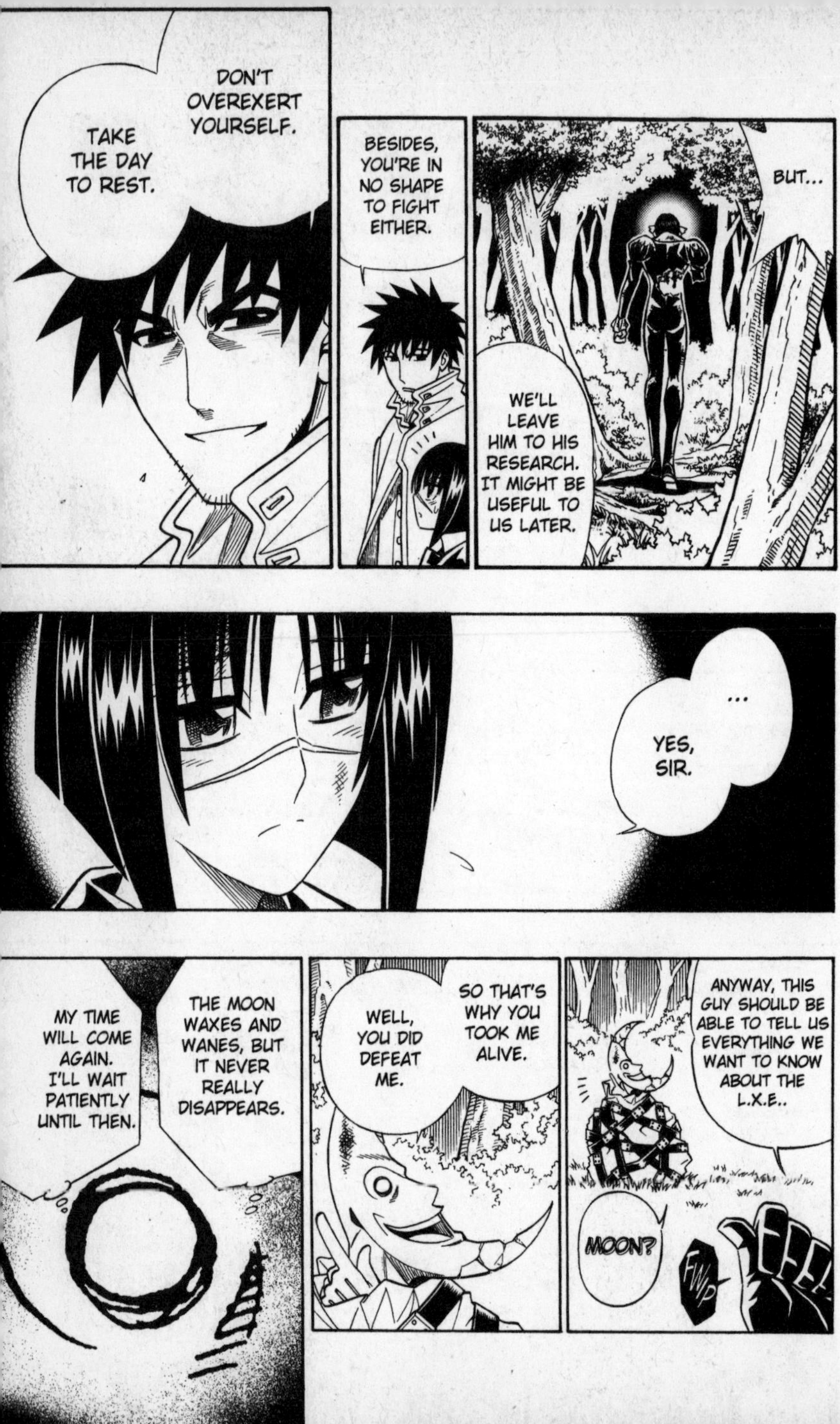
BUT...
WE'LL LEAVE HIM TO HIS RESEARCH. IT MIGHT BE USEFUL TO US LATER.
BESIDES, YOU'RE IN NO SHAPE TO FIGHT EITHER.
DON'T OVEREXERT YOURSELF.
TAKE THE DAY TO REST.
...
YES, SIR.
ANYWAY, THIS GUY SHOULD BE ABLE TO TELL US EVERYTHING WE WANT TO KNOW ABOUT THE L.X.E..
MOON?
FWP
SO THAT'S WHY YOU TOOK ME ALIVE.
WELL, YOU DID DEFEAT ME.
THE MOON WAXES AND WANES, BUT IT NEVER REALLY DISAPPEARS.
MY TIME WILL COME AGAIN. I'LL WAIT PATIENTLY UNTIL THEN.

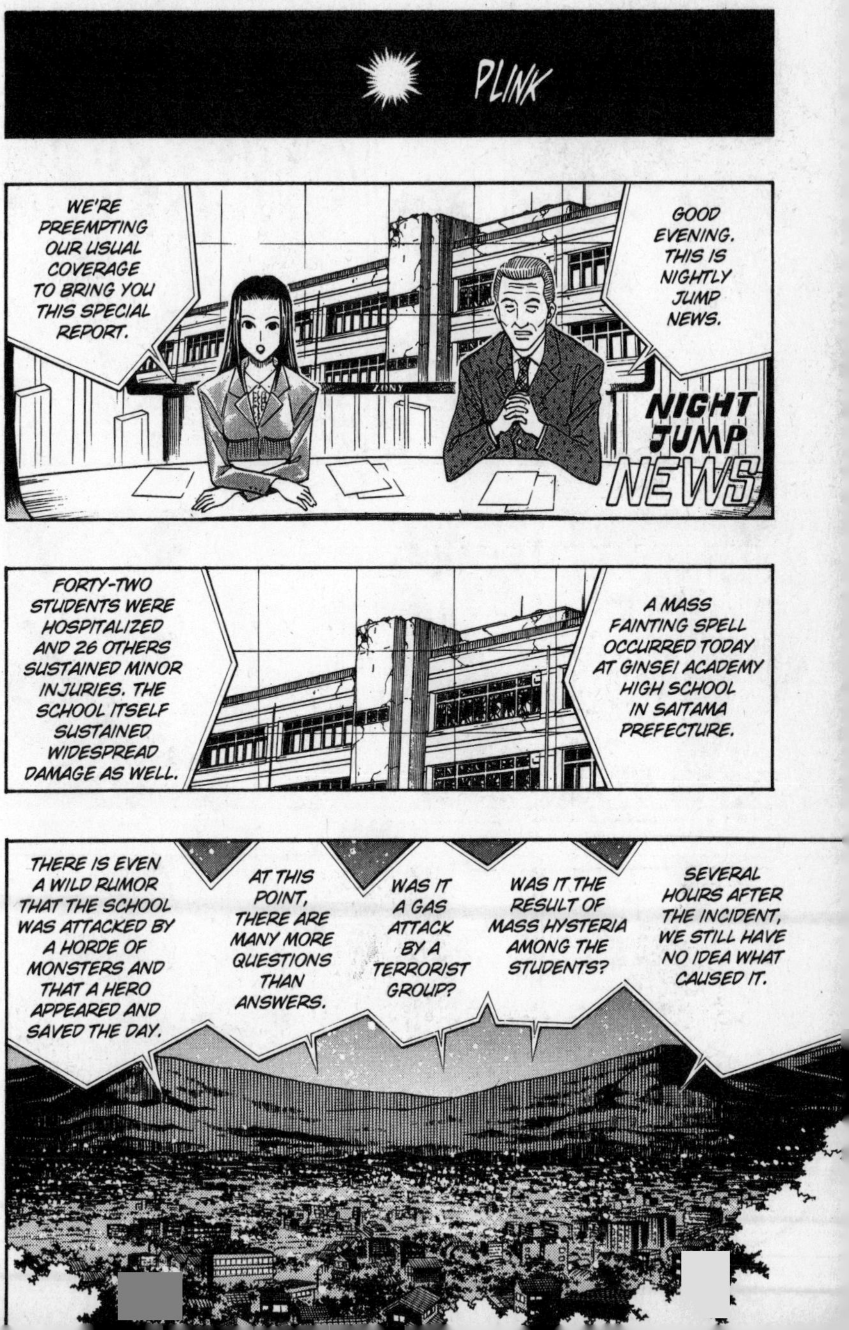
PLINK
GOOD EVENING. THIS IS NIGHTLY JUMP NEWS.
NIGHT JUMP NEWS
WE'RE PREEMPTING OUR USUAL COVERAGE TO BRING YOU THIS SPECIAL REPORT.
ZONY
A MASS FAINTING SPELL OCCURRED TODAY AT GINSEI ACADEMY HIGH SCHOOL IN SAITAMA PREFECTURE.
FORTY-TWO STUDENTS WERE HOSPITALIZED AND 26 OTHERS SUSTAINED MINOR INJURIES. THE SCHOOL ITSELF SUSTAINED WIDESPREAD DAMAGE AS WELL.
SEVERAL HOURS AFTER THE INCIDENT, WE STILL HAVE NO IDEA WHAT CAUSED IT.
WAS IT THE RESULT OF MASS HYSTERIA AMONG THE STUDENTS?
WAS IT A GAS ATTACK BY A TERRORIST GROUP?
AT THIS POINT, THERE ARE MANY MORE QUESTIONS THAN ANSWERS.
THERE IS EVEN A WILD RUMOR THAT THE SCHOOL WAS ATTACKED BY A HORDE OF MONSTERS AND THAT A HERO APPEARED AND SAVED THE DAY.

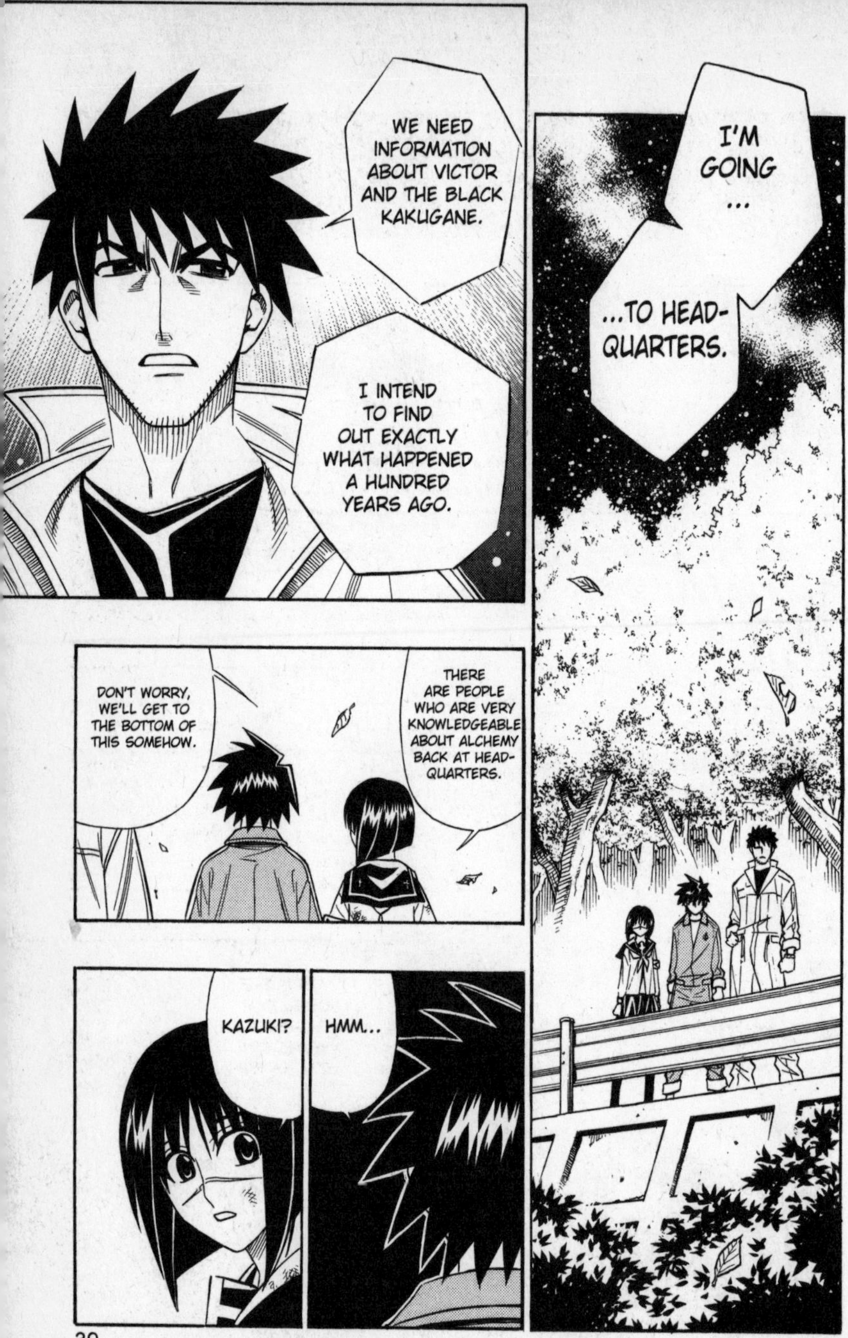
I'M GOING ...
...TO HEAD-QUARTERS.
WE NEED INFORMATION ABOUT VICTOR AND THE BLACK KAKUGANE.
I INTEND TO FIND OUT EXACTLY WHAT HAPPENED A HUNDRED YEARS AGO.
THERE ARE PEOPLE WHO ARE VERY KNOWLEDGEABLE ABOUT ALCHEMY BACK AT HEAD-QUARTERS.
DON'T WORRY, WE'LL GET TO THE BOTTOM OF THIS SOMEHOW.
HMM...
KAZUKI?

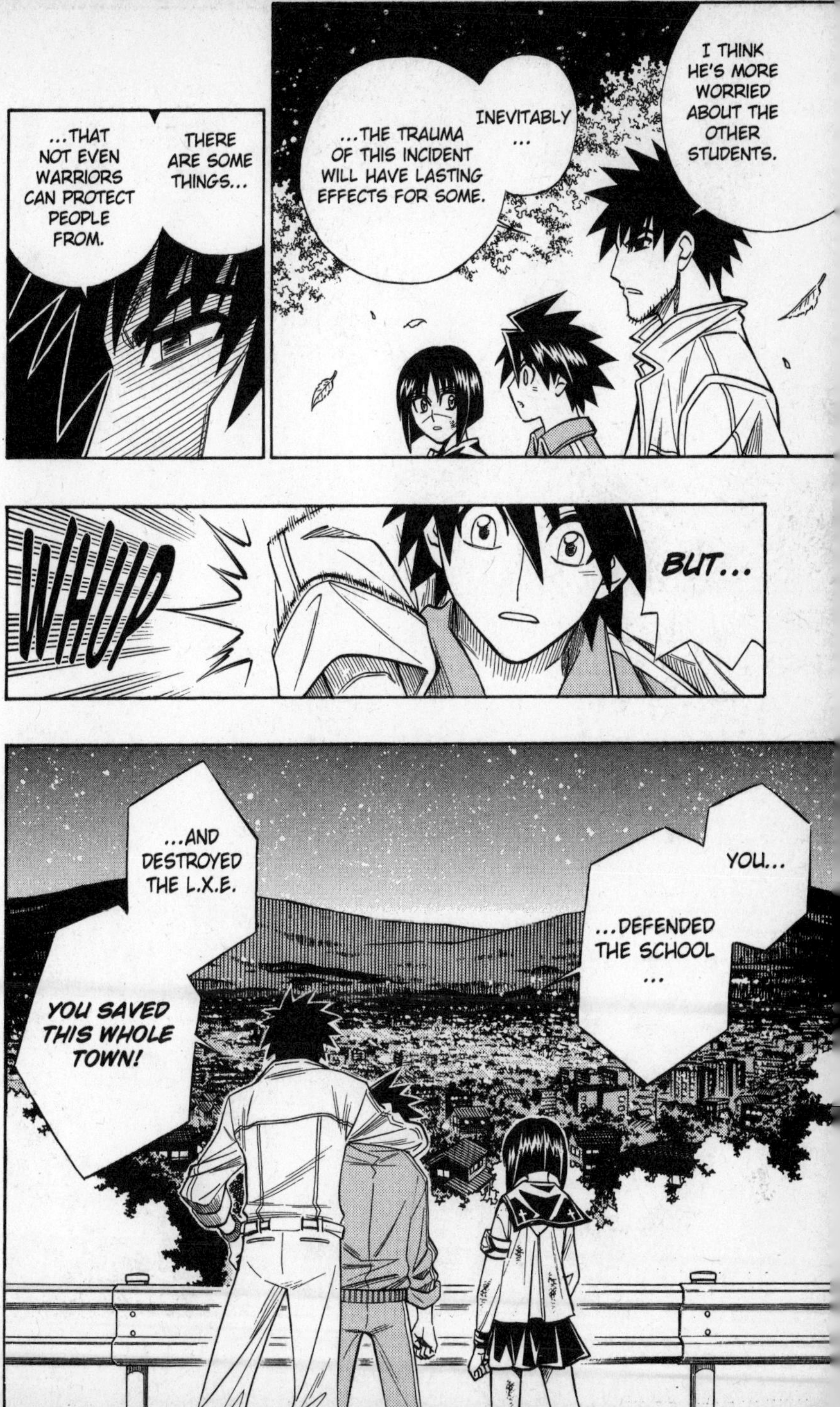
I THINK HE'S MORE WORRIED ABOUT THE OTHER STUDENTS.
INEVITABLY...
...THE TRAUMA OF THIS INCIDENT WILL HAVE LASTING EFFECTS FOR SOME.
THERE ARE SOME THINGS...
...THAT NOT EVEN WARRIORS CAN PROTECT PEOPLE FROM.
BUT...
WHUP
YOU...
...DEFENDED THE SCHOOL ...
...AND DESTROYED THE L.X.E.
YOU SAVED THIS WHOLE TOWN!

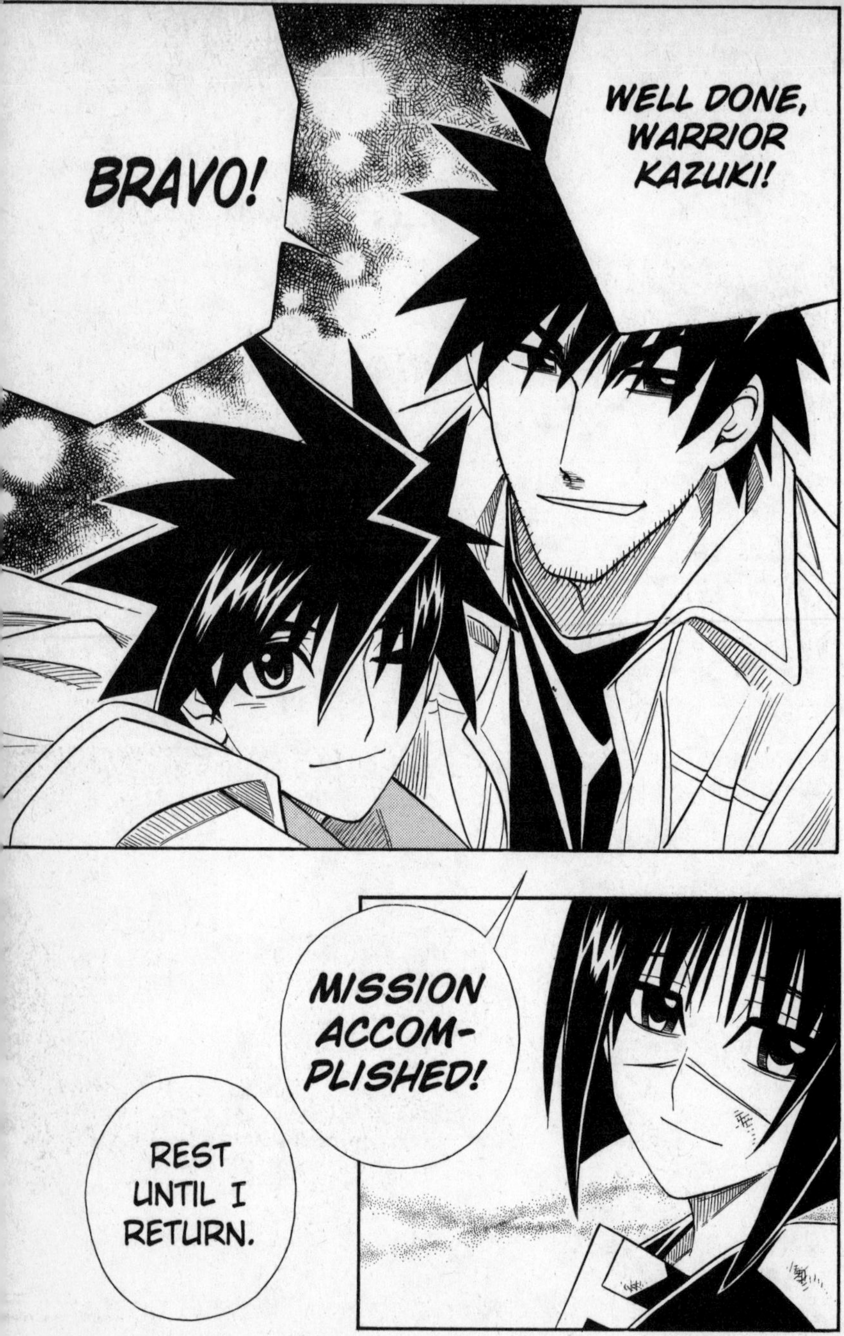
WELL DONE, WARRIOR KAZUKI!
BRAVO!
MISSION ACCOM-PLISHED!
REST UNTIL I RETURN.

- Height: 188cm; Weight: 80kg
- Born: February 2; Aquarius; Blood Type: B, Age: 35
- Likes: The Moon, tsukimi dango (moon-viewing dumplings)
- Dislikes: Clouds that hide the moon, lunar eclipses
- Hobby: Moonbathing, watching the moon
- Special Ability: Somersaults
- Affiliations: L.X.E.

Character File No. 26

MOONFACE

Author's Notes

- This character is based on one of my doodles. He was well received when he first appeared and I took a liking to him. That's how Moonface was born.
- I had a fairly detailed background story written for Moonface, but I couldn't work it into the flow of the main story. He's sort of a presence that's just hanging in the air. Moon... I plan for him to appear again. But, like Victor, his design may change slightly. (Actually, I have a whole other design for his face. And again there is no frontal shot of his face.)
- His real name is Lunare Nikolaev. You may wonder if his name is based on a weapon or something related to combat. Sorry. It's sort of based on a weapon name, but an imaginary one. I got the name from one of the enemy units in *Fang of the Sun Dougram*. I wanted to give his name a Russian flavor and this is what I came up with in my sleep-deprived state. Sorry it's so hard to understand.

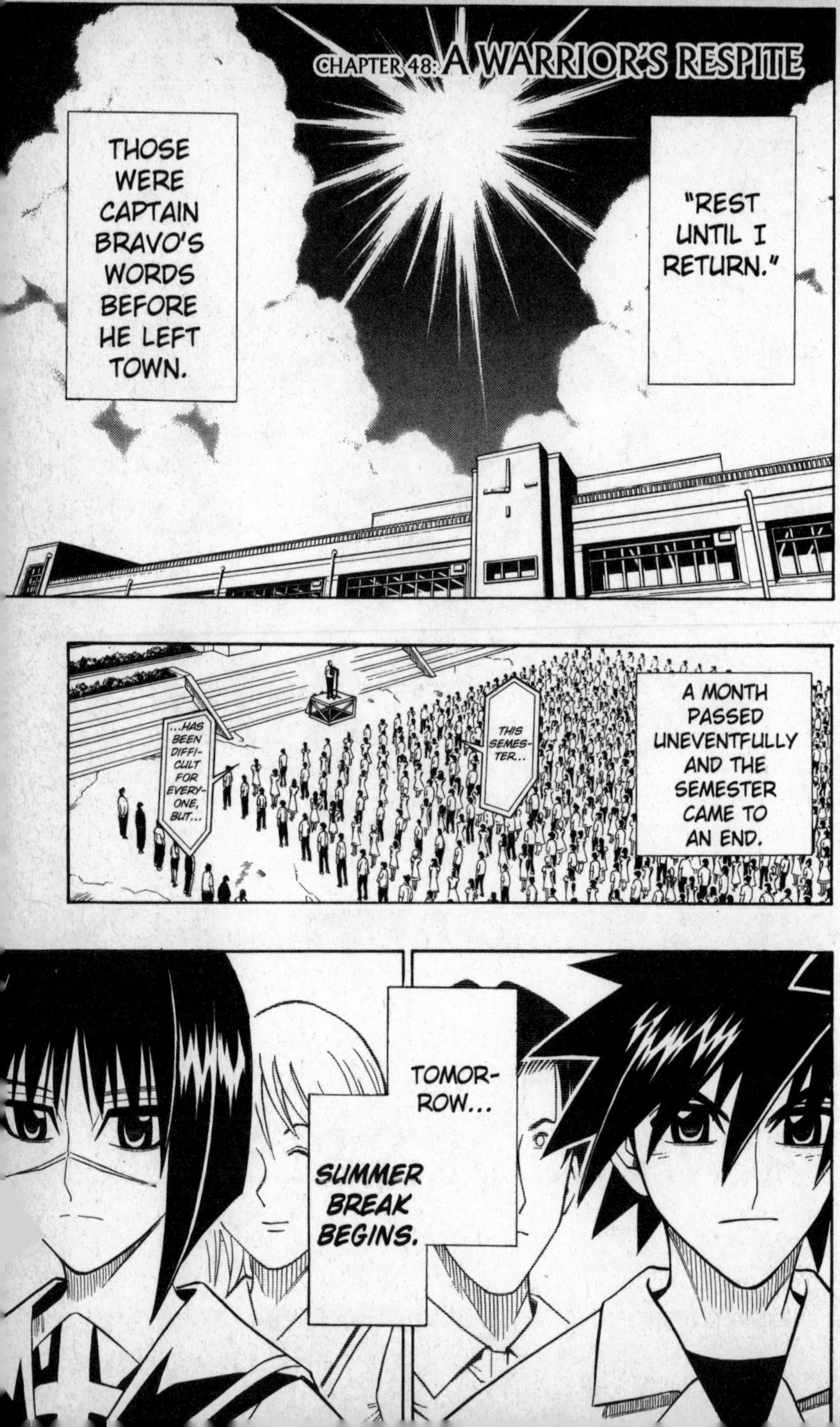
CHAPTER 48: A WARRIOR'S RESPITE
"REST UNTIL I RETURN."
THOSE WERE CAPTAIN BRAVO'S WORDS BEFORE HE LEFT TOWN.
A MONTH PASSED UNEVENTFULLY AND THE SEMESTER CAME TO AN END.
THIS SEMES-TER...
...HAS BEEN DIFFI-CULT FOR EVERY-ONE, BUT...
TOMOR-ROW...
SUMMER BREAK BEGINS.

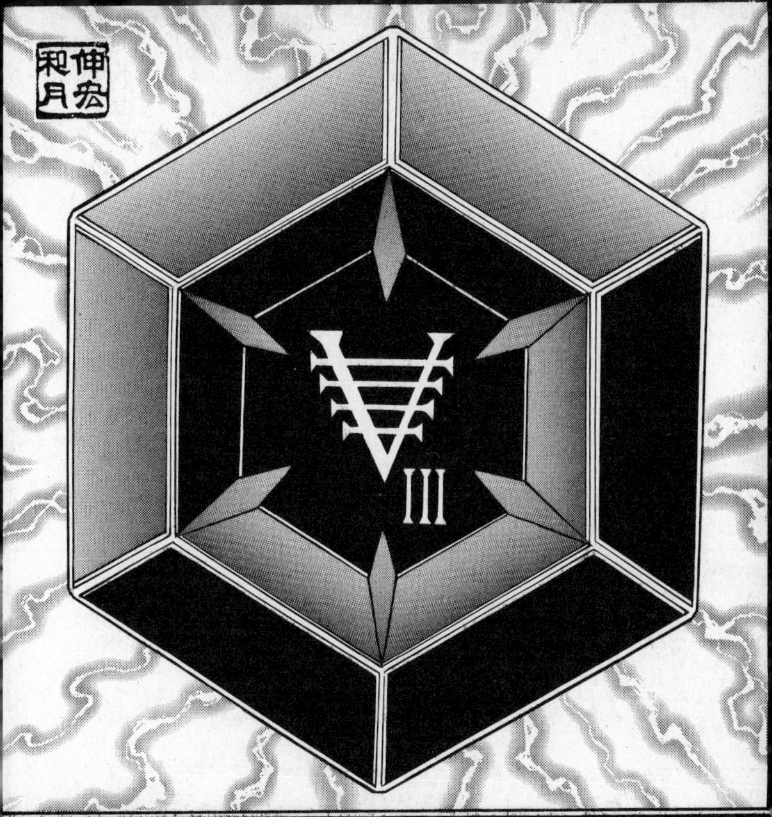
伸宏和月

CHAPTER 48:
A WARRIOR'S RESPITE

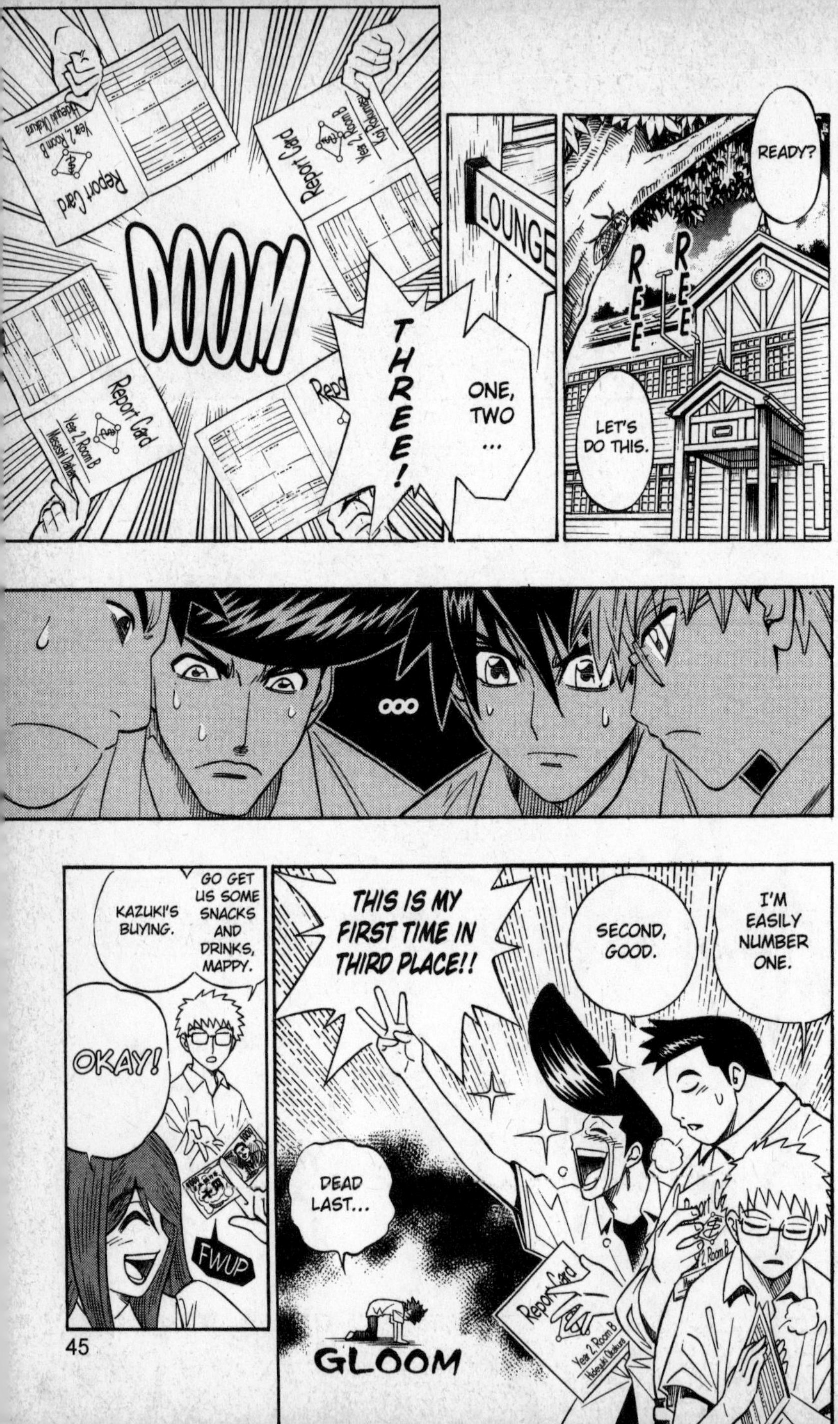
READY?
REE REE
LET'S DO THIS.
LOUNGE
ONE, TWO ...
THREE!
DOOM
Report Card
Year 2, Room B
Report Card
Year 2, Room B
Report Card
Year 2, Room B
...
I'M EASILY NUMBER ONE.
SECOND, GOOD.
THIS IS MY FIRST TIME IN THIRD PLACE!!
DEAD LAST...
GLOOM
Report Card
Year 2, Room B
GO GET US SOME SNACKS AND DRINKS, MAPPY.
KAZUKI'S BUYING.
OKAY!
FWUP

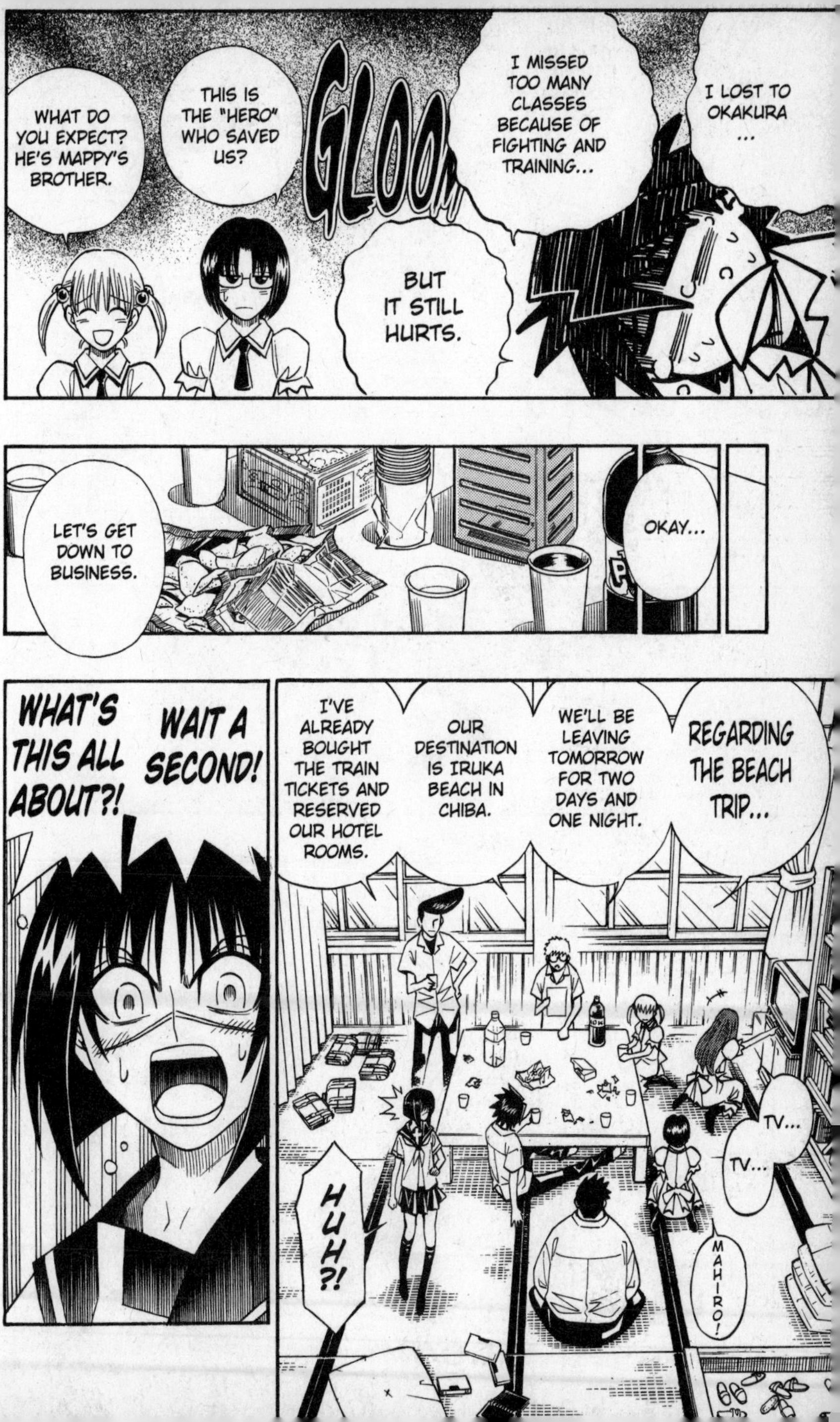
I LOST TO OKAKURA ...
I MISSED TOO MANY CLASSES BECAUSE OF FIGHTING AND TRAINING...
BUT IT STILL HURTS.
GLOO
THIS IS THE "HERO" WHO SAVED US?
WHAT DO YOU EXPECT? HE'S MAPPY'S BROTHER.
OKAY...
LET'S GET DOWN TO BUSINESS.
REGARDING THE BEACH TRIP...
WE'LL BE LEAVING TOMORROW FOR TWO DAYS AND ONE NIGHT.
OUR DESTINATION IS IRUKA BEACH IN CHIBA.
I'VE ALREADY BOUGHT THE TRAIN TICKETS AND RESERVED OUR HOTEL ROOMS.
TV...
TV...
MAHIRO!
HUH?!
WAIT A SECOND!
WHAT'S THIS ALL ABOUT?!

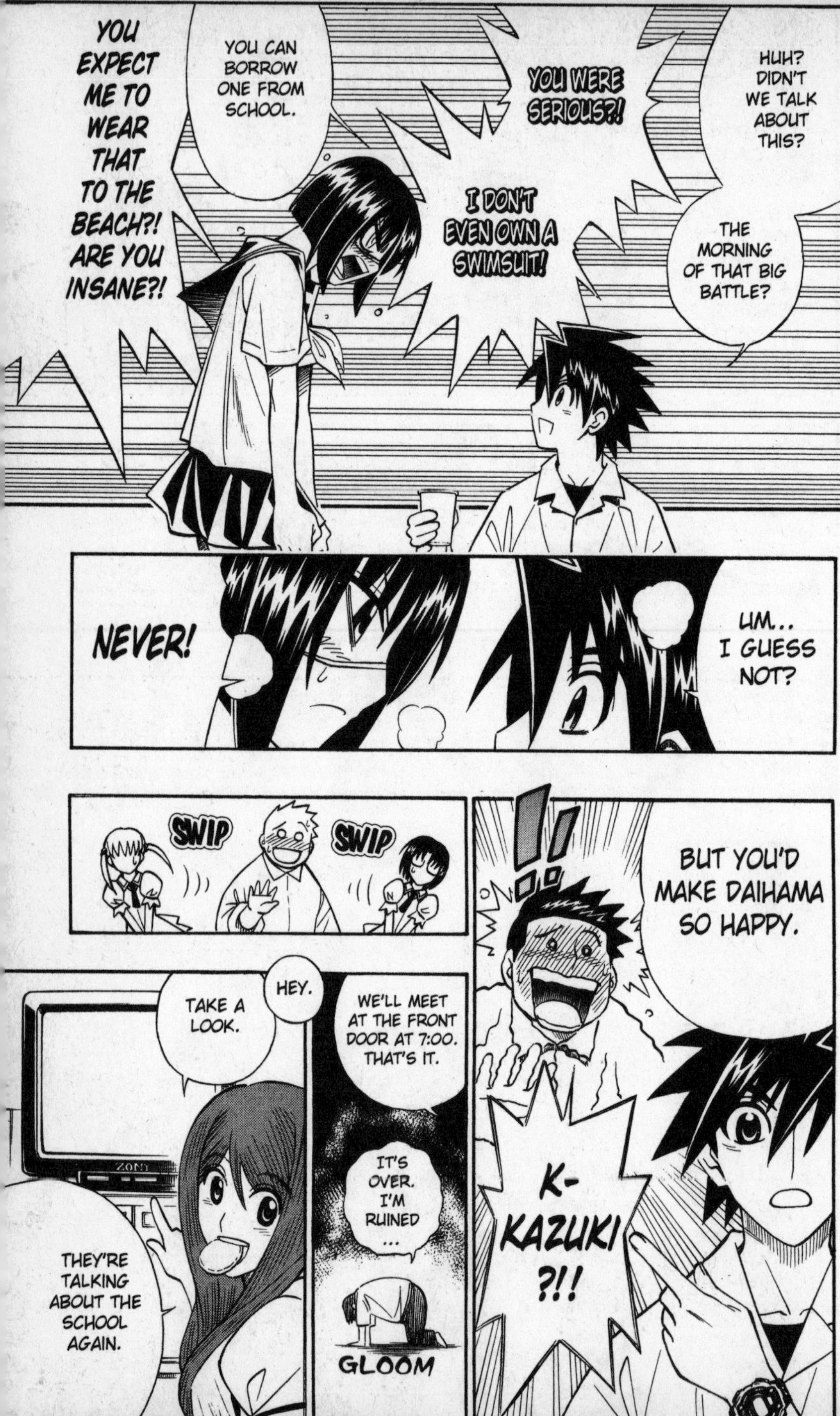
HUH? DIDN'T WE TALK ABOUT THIS?
THE MORNING OF THAT BIG BATTLE?
YOU WERE SERIOUS?!
I DON'T EVEN OWN A SWIMSUIT!
YOU CAN BORROW ONE FROM SCHOOL.
YOU EXPECT ME TO WEAR THAT TO THE BEACH?! ARE YOU INSANE?!
UM... I GUESS NOT?
NEVER!
BUT YOU'D MAKE DAIHAMA SO HAPPY.
K-KAZUKI ?!!
SWIP
SWIP
WE'LL MEET AT THE FRONT DOOR AT 7:00. THAT'S IT.
IT'S OVER. I'M RUINED ...
GLOOM
HEY.
TAKE A LOOK.
THEY'RE TALKING ABOUT THE SCHOOL AGAIN.

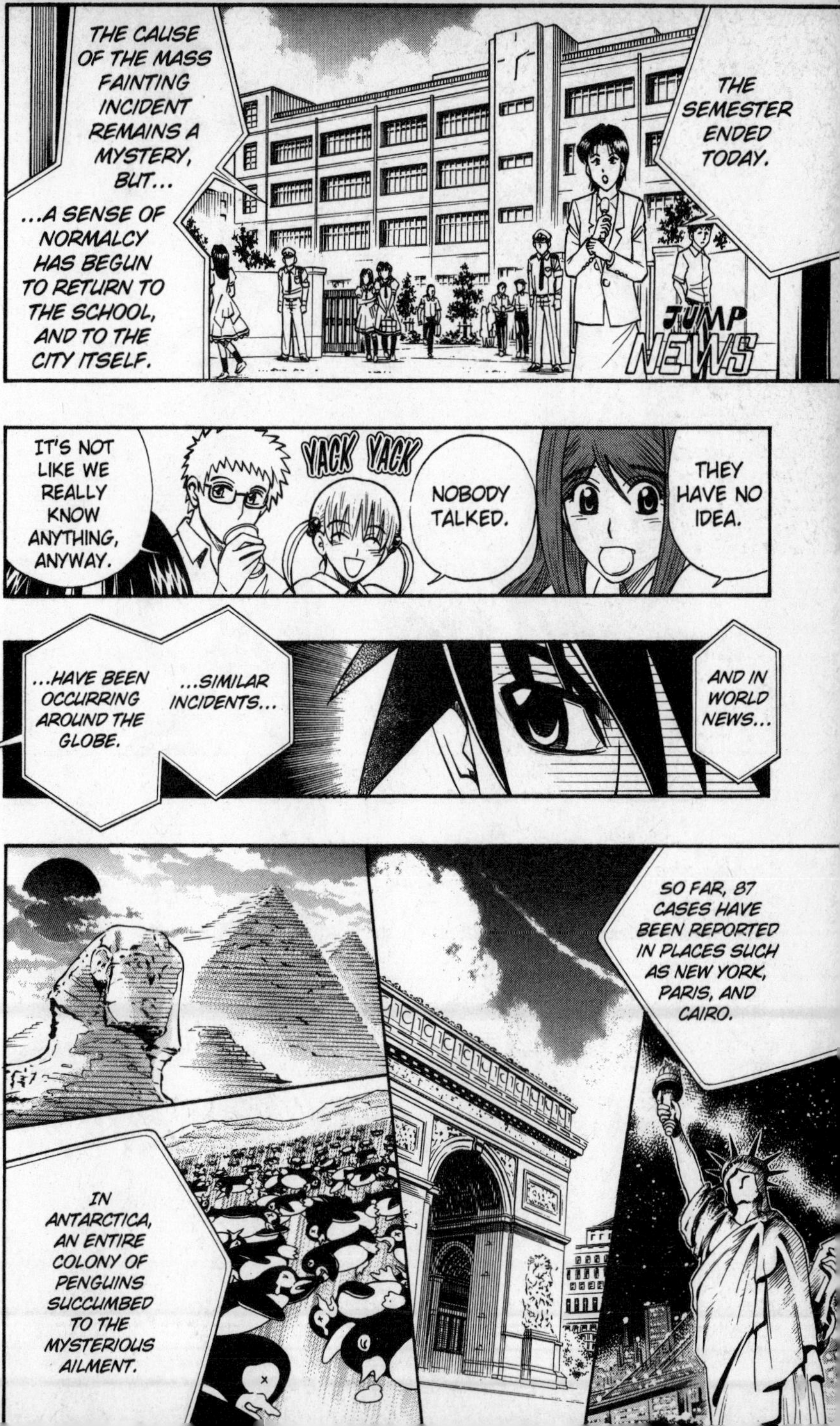
THE SEMESTER ENDED TODAY.
THE CAUSE OF THE MASS FAINTING INCIDENT REMAINS A MYSTERY, BUT...
...A SENSE OF NORMALCY HAS BEGUN TO RETURN TO THE SCHOOL, AND TO THE CITY ITSELF.
JUMP NEWS
THEY HAVE NO IDEA.
NOBODY TALKED.
YACK YACK
IT'S NOT LIKE WE REALLY KNOW ANYTHING, ANYWAY.
AND IN WORLD NEWS...
...SIMILAR INCIDENTS...
...HAVE BEEN OCCURRING AROUND THE GLOBE.
SO FAR, 87 CASES HAVE BEEN REPORTED IN PLACES SUCH AS NEW YORK, PARIS, AND CAIRO.
IN ANTARCTICA, AN ENTIRE COLONY OF PENGUINS SUCCUMBED TO THE MYSTERIOUS AILMENT.

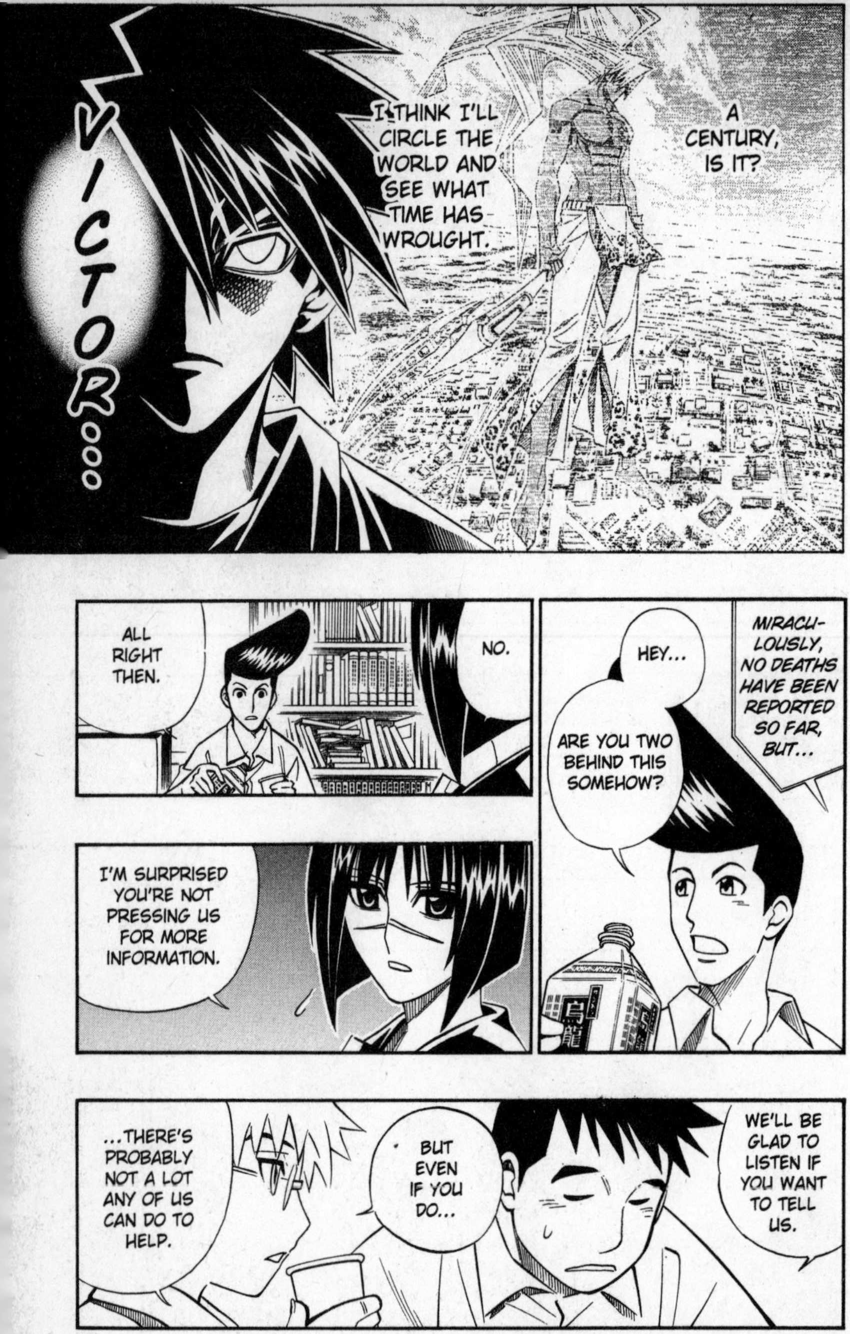
A CENTURY, IS IT?
I THINK I'LL CIRCLE THE WORLD AND SEE WHAT TIME HAS WROUGHT.
VICTOR...
MIRACULOUSLY, NO DEATHS HAVE BEEN REPORTED SO FAR, BUT...
HEY...
ARE YOU TWO BEHIND THIS SOMEHOW?
NO.
ALL RIGHT THEN.
I'M SURPRISED YOU'RE NOT PRESSING US FOR MORE INFORMATION.
WE'LL BE GLAD TO LISTEN IF YOU WANT TO TELL US.
BUT EVEN IF YOU DO...
...THERE'S PROBABLY NOT A LOT ANY OF US CAN DO TO HELP.

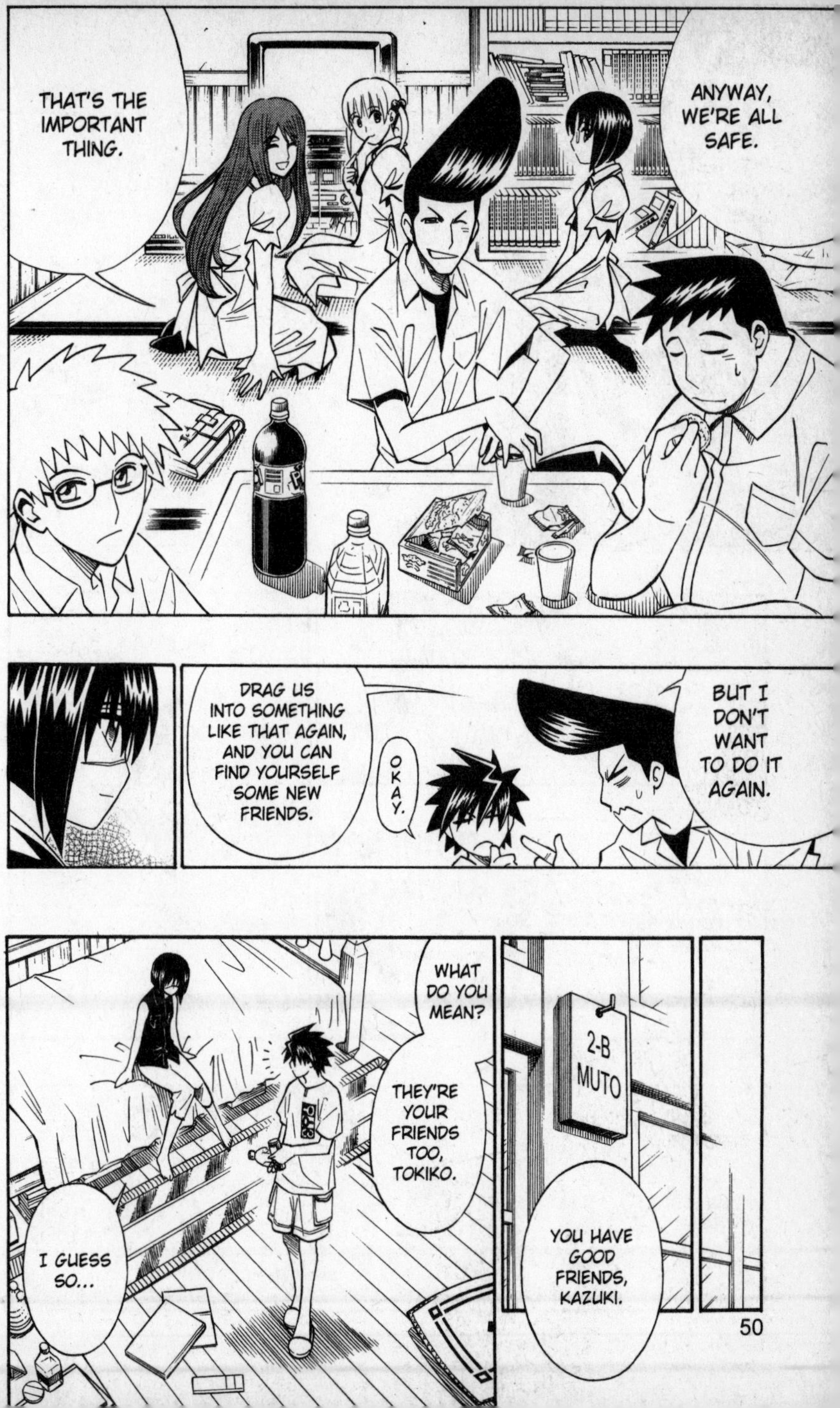
ANYWAY, WE'RE ALL SAFE.
THAT'S THE IMPORTANT THING.
BUT I DON'T WANT TO DO IT AGAIN.
OKAY.
DRAG US INTO SOMETHING LIKE THAT AGAIN, AND YOU CAN FIND YOURSELF SOME NEW FRIENDS.
2-B MUTO
YOU HAVE GOOD FRIENDS, KAZUKI.
WHAT DO YOU MEAN?
THEY'RE YOUR FRIENDS TOO, TOKIKO.
I GUESS SO...

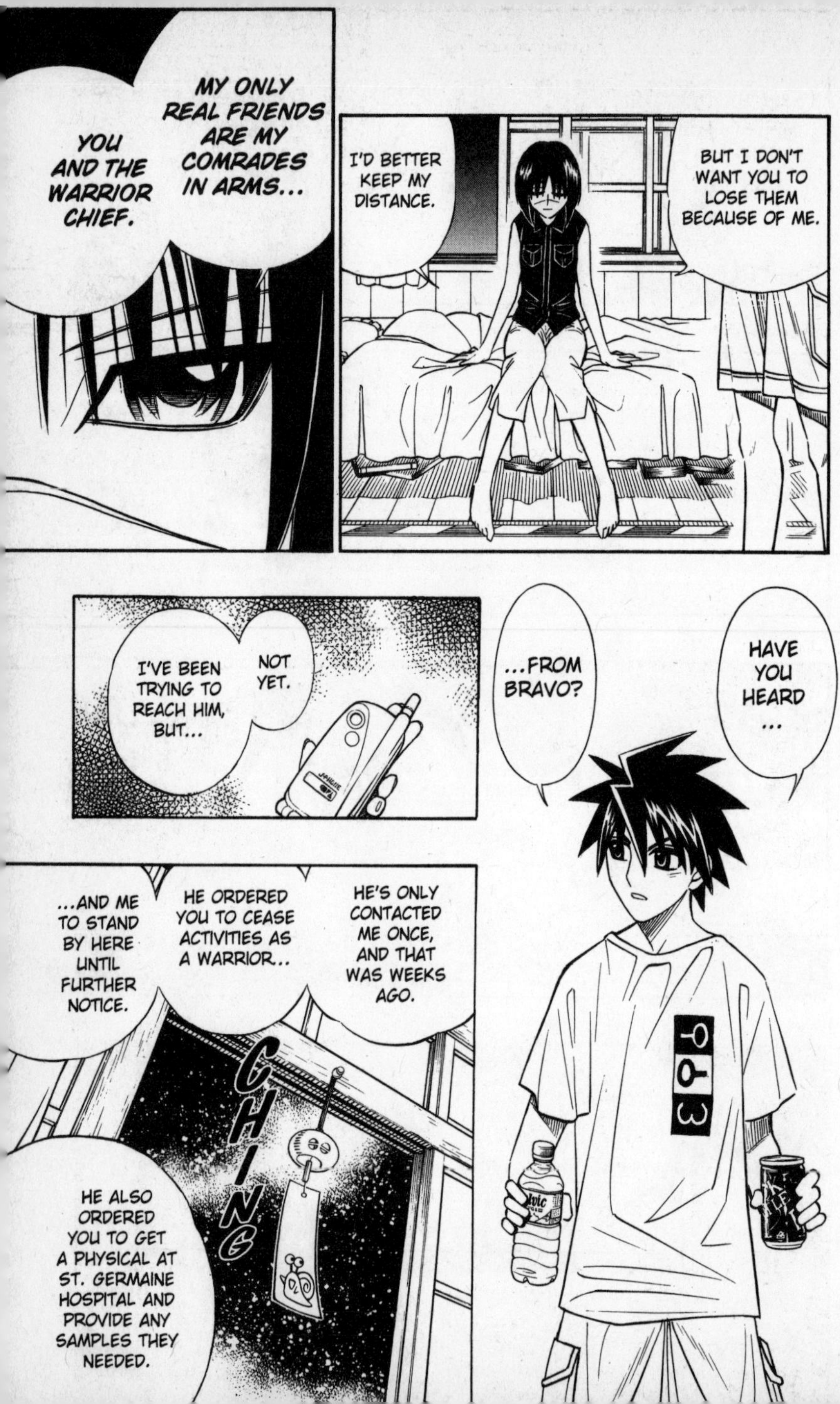
BUT I DON'T WANT YOU TO LOSE THEM BECAUSE OF ME.
I'D BETTER KEEP MY DISTANCE.
MY ONLY REAL FRIENDS ARE MY COMRADES IN ARMS...
YOU AND THE WARRIOR CHIEF.
HAVE YOU HEARD...
...FROM BRAVO?
NOT YET.
I'VE BEEN TRYING TO REACH HIM, BUT...
HE'S ONLY CONTACTED ME ONCE, AND THAT WAS WEEKS AGO.
HE ORDERED YOU TO CEASE ACTIVITIES AS A WARRIOR...
...AND ME TO STAND BY HERE UNTIL FURTHER NOTICE.
CHING
HE ALSO ORDERED YOU TO GET A PHYSICAL AT ST. GERMAINE HOSPITAL AND PROVIDE ANY SAMPLES THEY NEEDED.

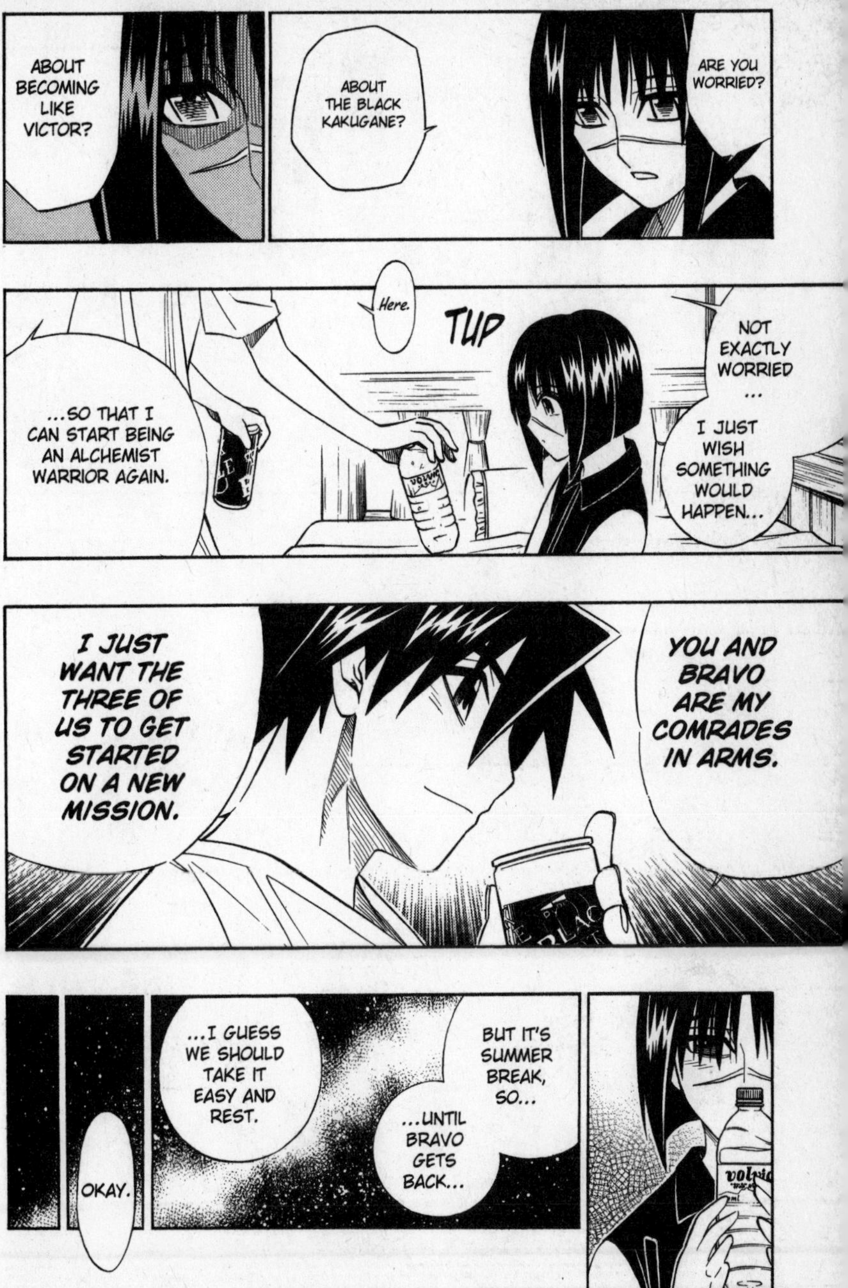
ARE YOU WORRIED?
ABOUT THE BLACK KAKUGANE?
ABOUT BECOMING LIKE VICTOR?
NOT EXACTLY WORRIED ... I JUST WISH SOMETHING WOULD HAPPEN...
Here.
TUP
...SO THAT I CAN START BEING AN ALCHEMIST WARRIOR AGAIN.
YOU AND BRAVO ARE MY COMRADES IN ARMS.
I JUST WANT THE THREE OF US TO GET STARTED ON A NEW MISSION.
BUT IT'S SUMMER BREAK, SO...
...UNTIL BRAVO GETS BACK...
...I GUESS WE SHOULD TAKE IT EASY AND REST.
OKAY.

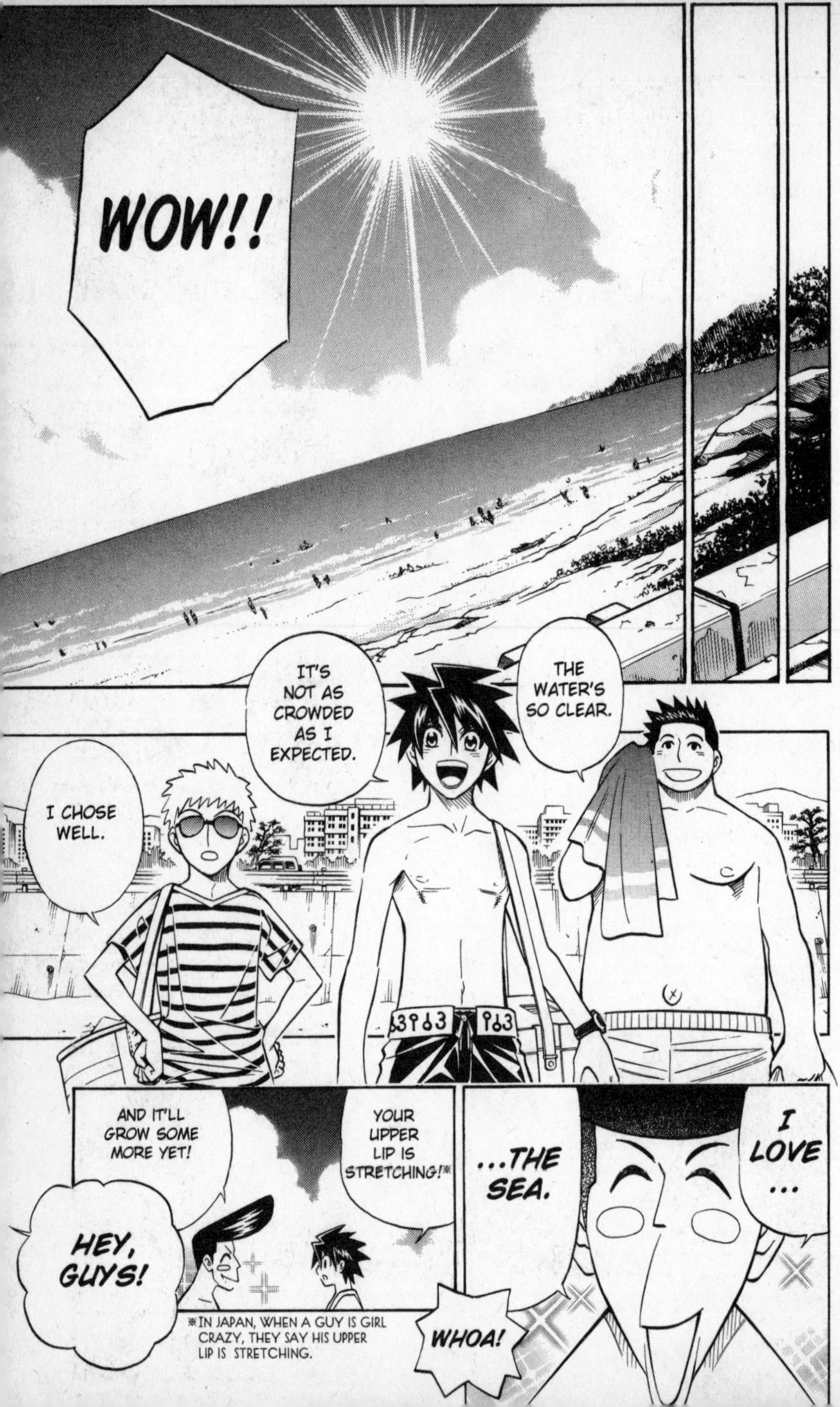
WOW!!
THE WATER'S SO CLEAR.
IT'S NOT AS CROWDED AS I EXPECTED.
I CHOSE WELL.
I LOVE...
...THE SEA.
WHOA!
YOUR UPPER LIP IS STRETCHING!※
AND IT'LL GROW SOME MORE YET!
HEY, GUYS!

※IN JAPAN, WHEN A GUY IS GIRL CRAZY, THEY SAY HIS UPPER LIP IS STRETCHING.

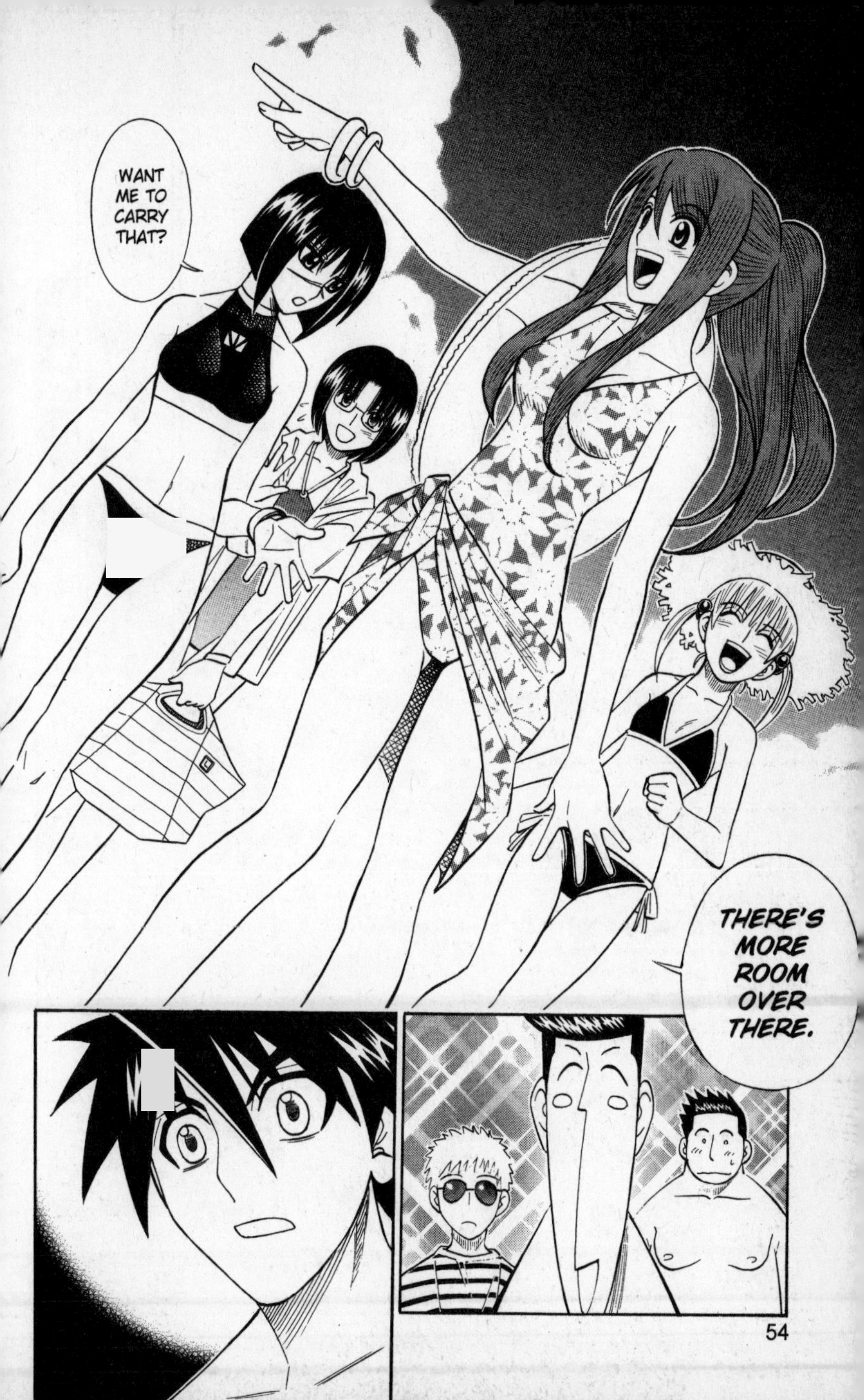
THERE'S MORE ROOM OVER THERE.
WANT ME TO CARRY THAT?

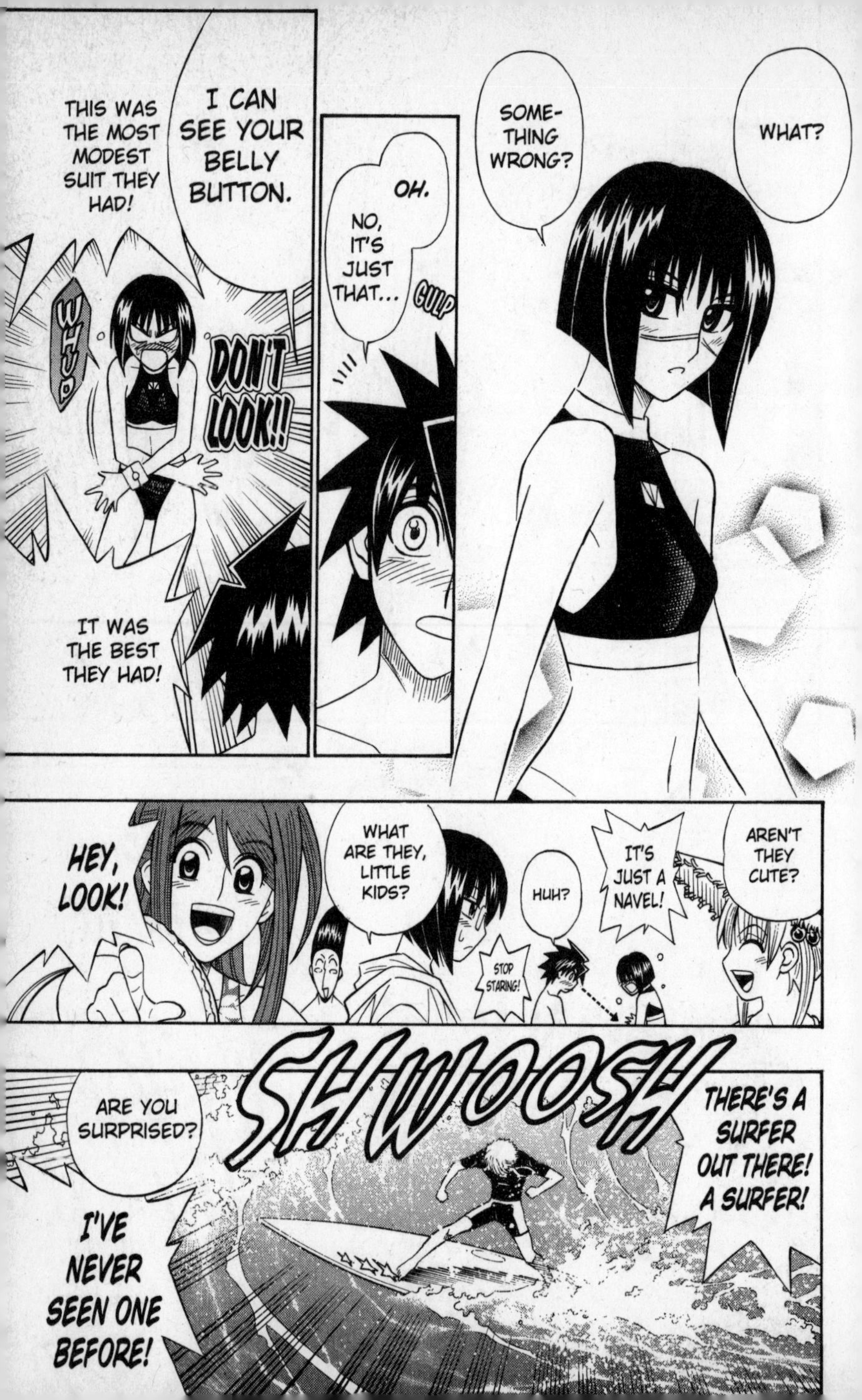
WHAT?
SOME-THING WRONG?
OH.
NO, IT'S JUST THAT...
GULP
I CAN SEE YOUR BELLY BUTTON.
THIS WAS THE MOST MODEST SUIT THEY HAD!
DON'T LOOK!!
WHUD
IT WAS THE BEST THEY HAD!
AREN'T THEY CUTE?
IT'S JUST A NAVEL!
HUH?
STOP STARING!
WHAT ARE THEY, LITTLE KIDS?
HEY, LOOK!
SHWOOSH
THERE'S A SURFER OUT THERE! A SURFER!
ARE YOU SURPRISED?
I'VE NEVER SEEN ONE BEFORE!

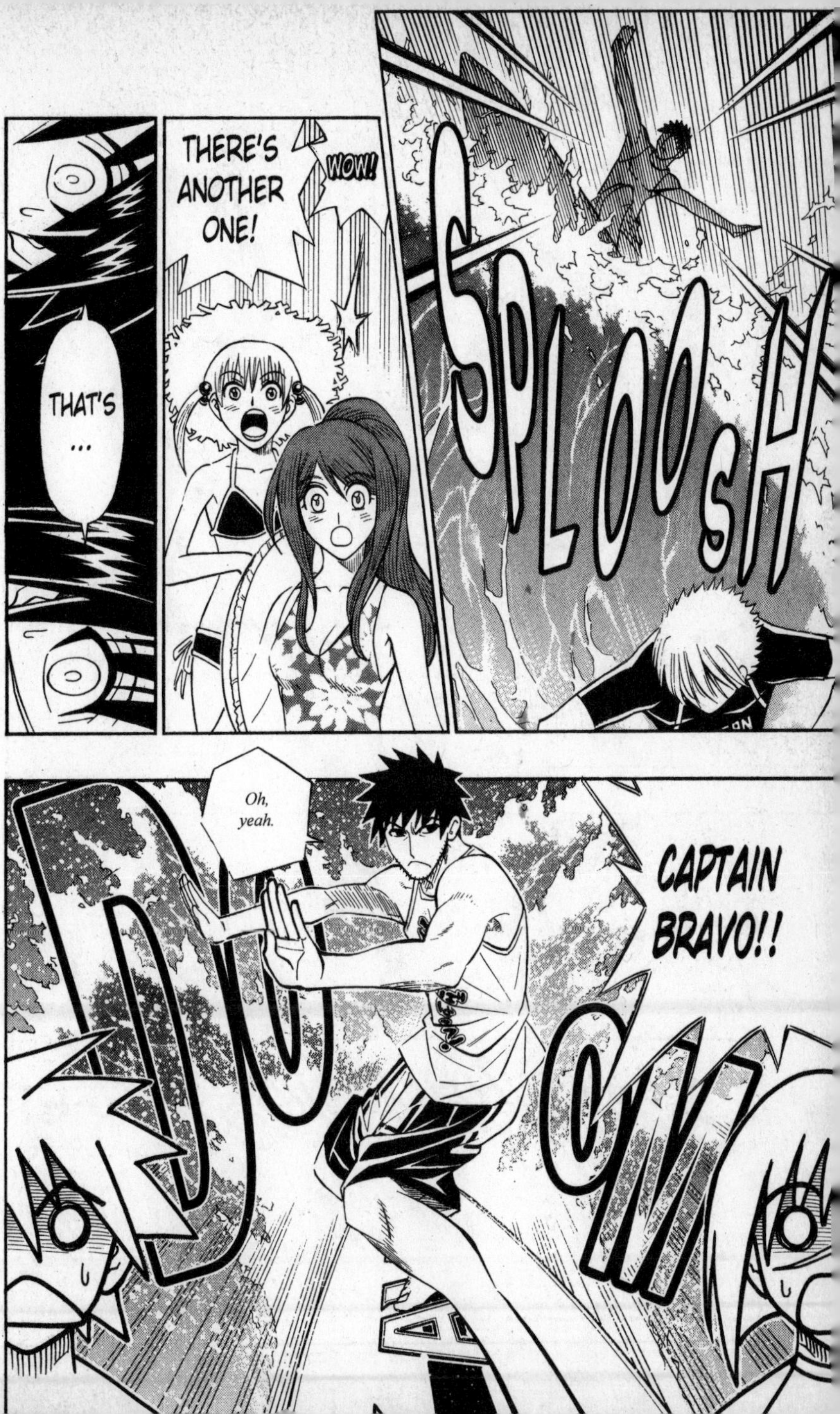
SPLOOSH
THERE'S ANOTHER ONE!
WOW!
THAT'S ...
CAPTAIN BRAVO!!
Oh, yeah.
DOOM

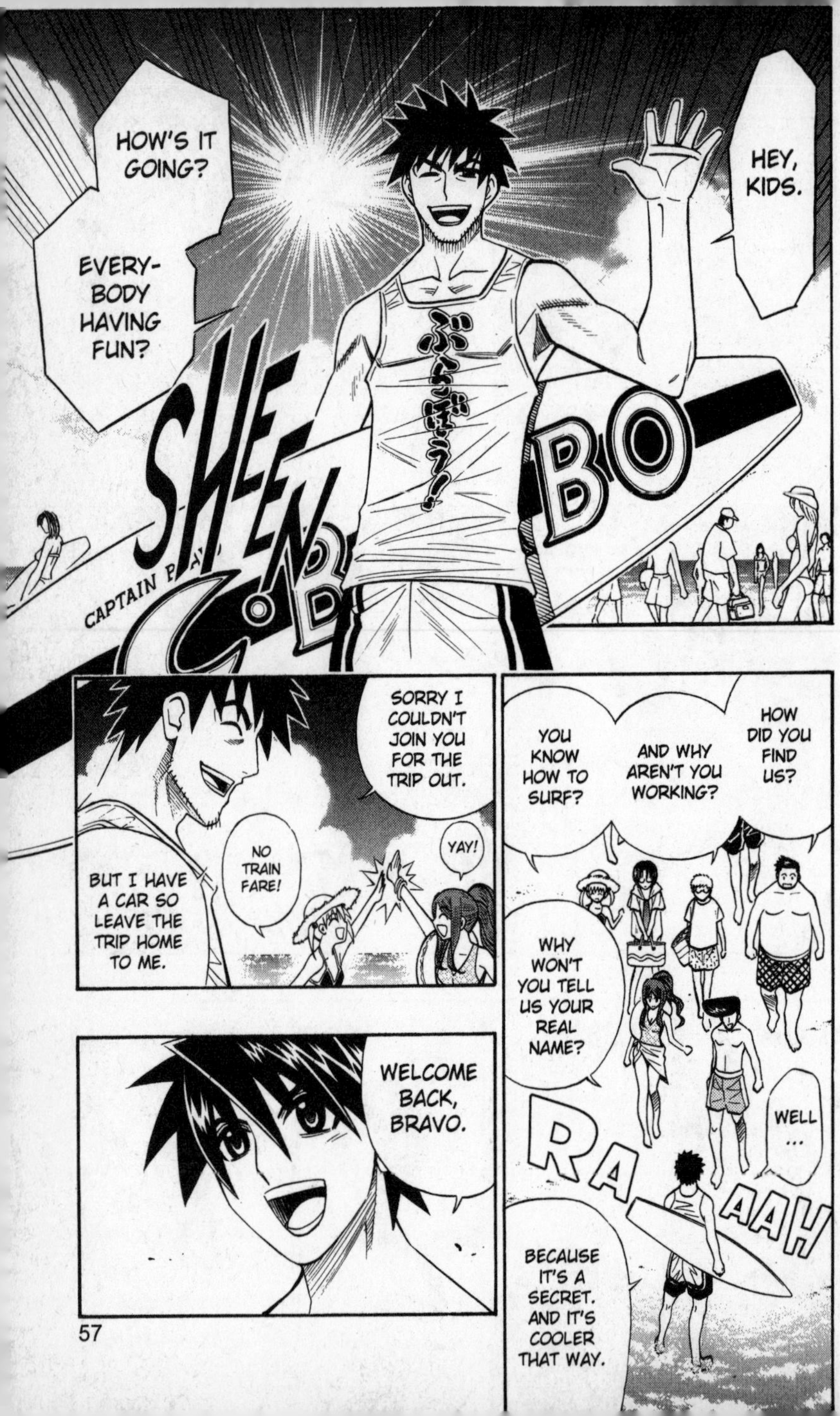
HEY, KIDS.
HOW'S IT GOING?
EVERY-BODY HAVING FUN?
SHEEN
BO
HOW DID YOU FIND US?
AND WHY AREN'T YOU WORKING?
YOU KNOW HOW TO SURF?
WHY WON'T YOU TELL US YOUR REAL NAME?
WELL ...
RAAAH
BECAUSE IT'S A SECRET. AND IT'S COOLER THAT WAY.
SORRY I COULDN'T JOIN YOU FOR THE TRIP OUT.
BUT I HAVE A CAR SO LEAVE THE TRIP HOME TO ME.
YAY!
NO TRAIN FARE!
WELCOME BACK, BRAVO.

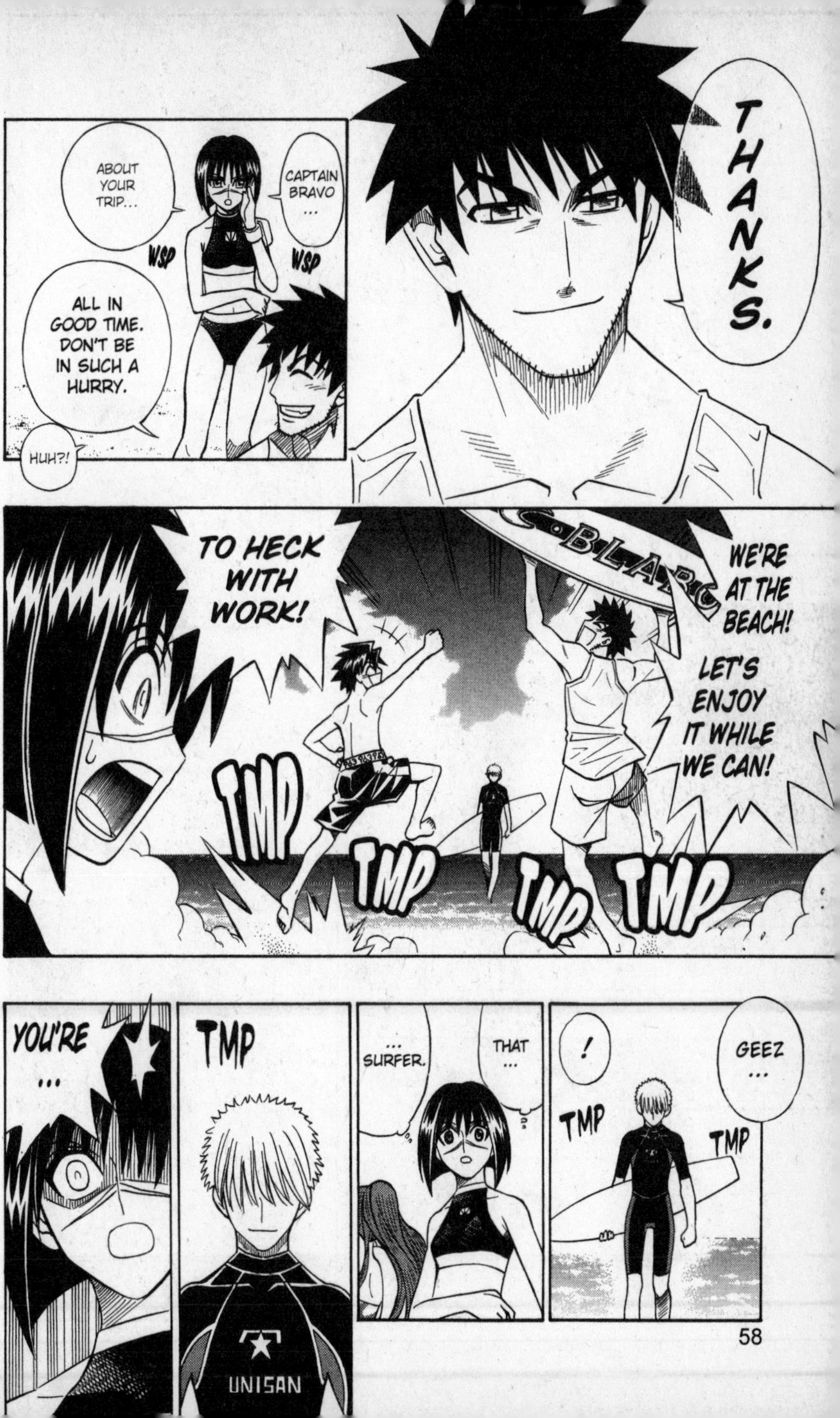
THANKS.
CAPTAIN BRAVO ...
WSP
ABOUT YOUR TRIP...
WSP
ALL IN GOOD TIME. DON'T BE IN SUCH A HURRY.
HUH?!
C-BLARC
WE'RE AT THE BEACH!
LET'S ENJOY IT WHILE WE CAN!
TO HECK WITH WORK!
TMP TMP TMP TMP
GEEZ ...
!
TMP
TMP
THAT ...
... SURFER.
TMP
UNISAN
YOU'RE ...

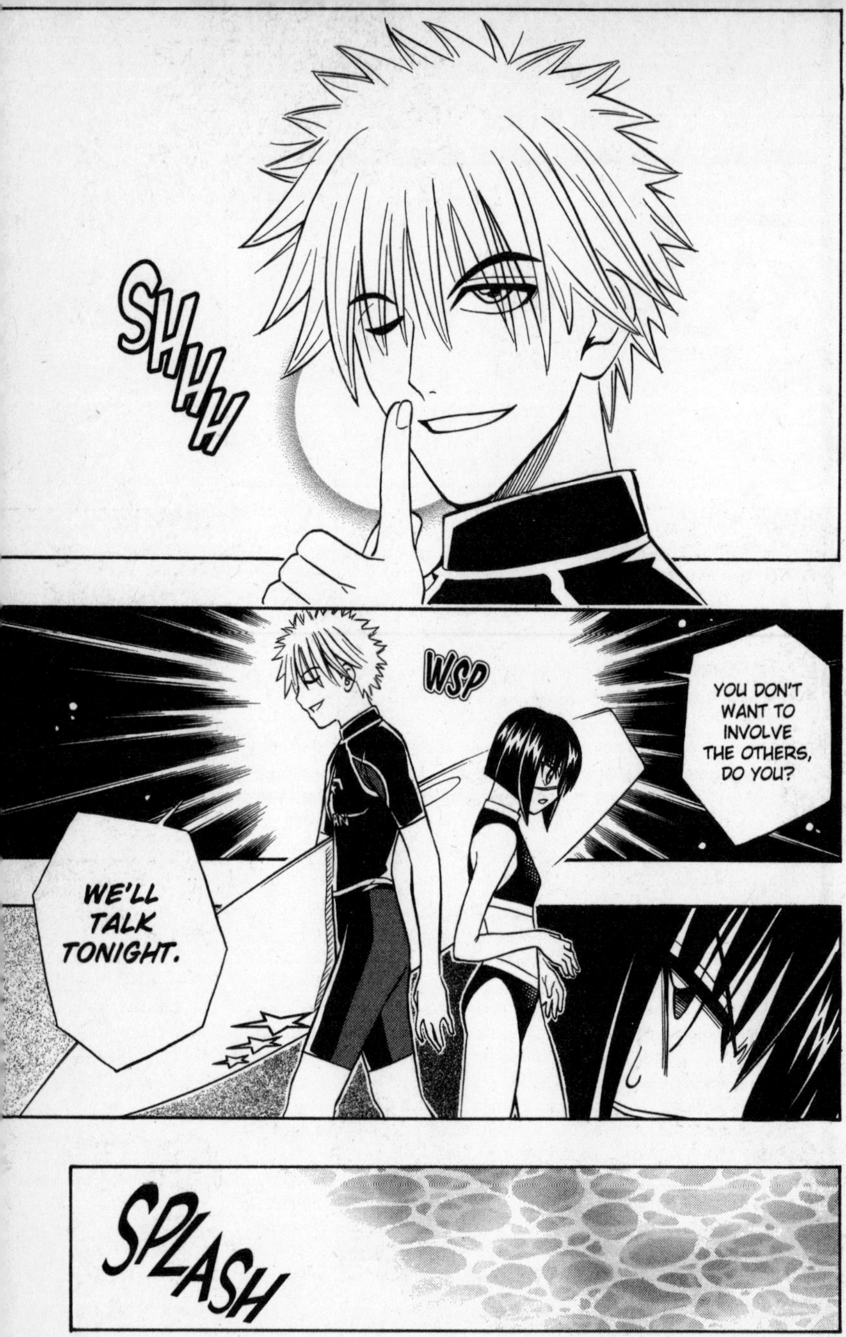
SHHH
WSP
YOU DON'T WANT TO INVOLVE THE OTHERS, DO YOU?
WE'LL TALK TONIGHT.
SPLASH

You cut with a sword.
Remember that.

Buso Renkin File No. 6

ソード
サムライX

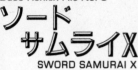

SWORD SAMURAI X

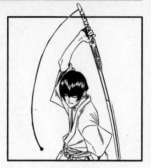

- Kakugane Serial Number: XXIII (23)
- Creator: Shusui Hayasaka
- Form: Japanese Sword
- Main Color: Cobalt Blue
- Special Abilities: · Totally neutralizes energy-based attacks.
- Special Traits:
  - Able to absorb energy and use it against an opponent.
  - Unable to absorb kinetic energy from physical attacks. Against kinetic attacks, it's just a normal sword.
  - Its use as a blade weapon is limited. Its effectiveness is entirely dependent upon the swordsmanship of the wielder.
- Author's Notes:

· The name comes from the title of the English language version of my previous work, *Ruroni Kenshin*. I liked the name so much that I used it for this.

· I don't like it when blades emit beams or any kind of ranged attack. (A lot of combat video games have swords like that, but I don't like it when swords aren't used to cut and slash. It defeats the whole purpose of a blade.) That's what led me to give the Sword Samurai X the ability to defeat such attacks.

· The main reason that I came up with this weapon was to show the development of Kazuki's Buso Renkin. Although that purpose has already been achieved, I'd still like to showcase Samurai X's abilities further in the future.

· The design is based on a samurai sword, obviously. There's something about a katana that sends shivers up your spine when you hold one. It's so cool.

· It looked a bit plain for a Buso Renkin, so I added the cord and the ring.

SWORD SAMURAI X

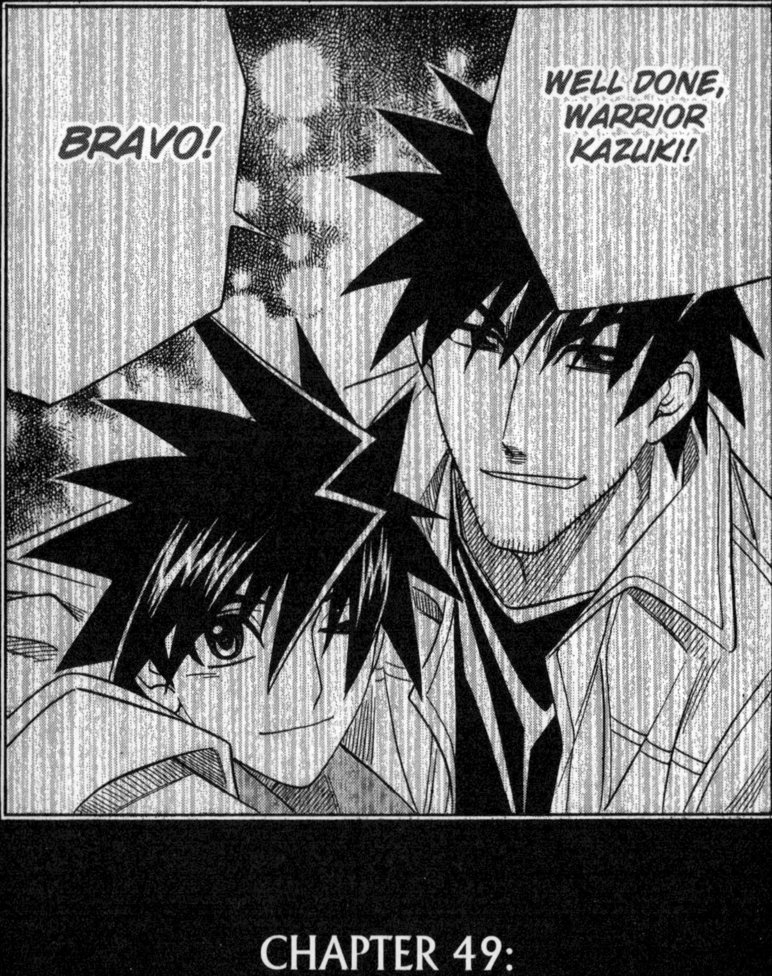
WELL DONE, WARRIOR KAZUKI!
BRAVO!

CHAPTER 49:
A NEW MISSION

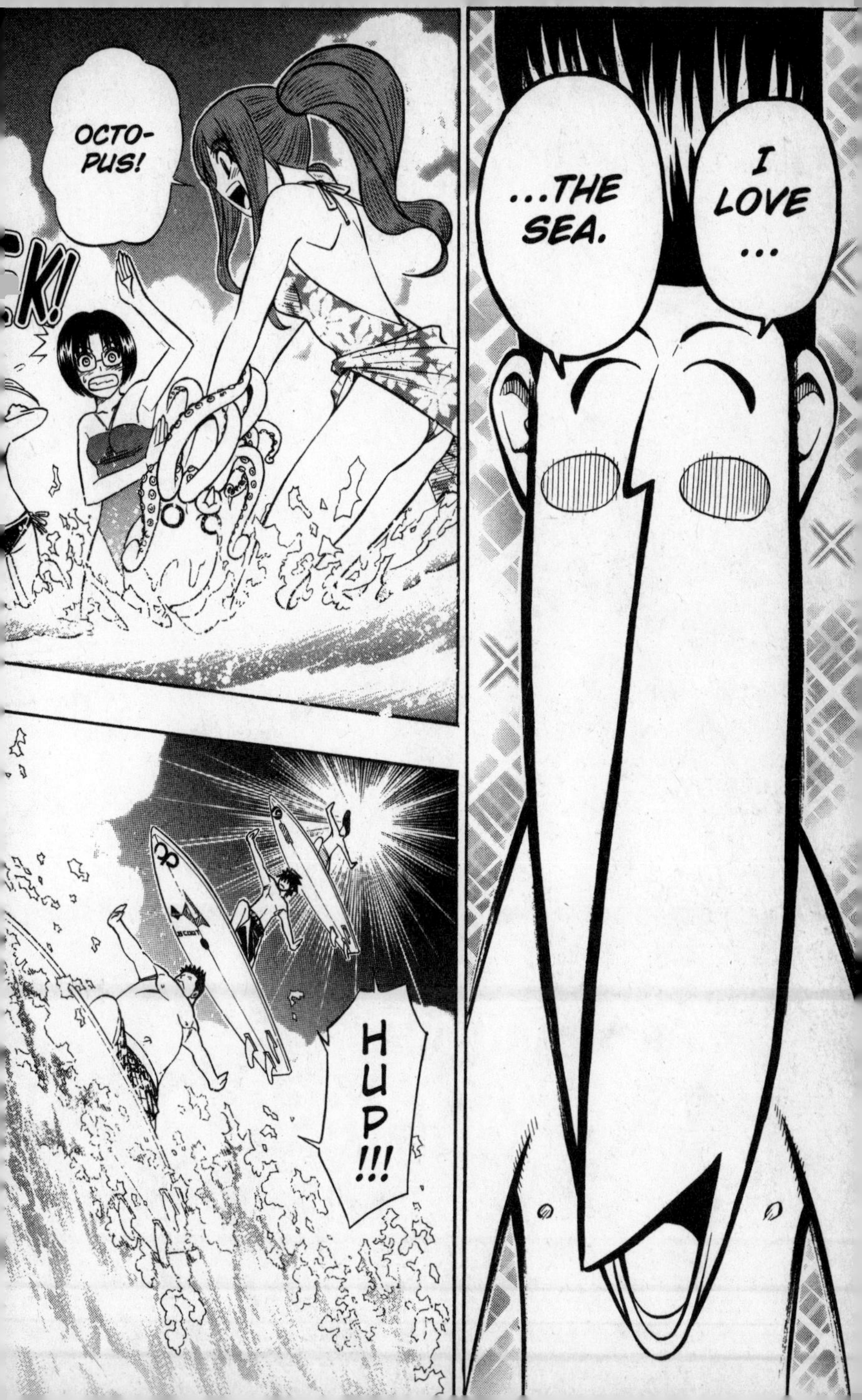
I LOVE ...
...THE SEA.
OCTO-PUS!
HUP!!!

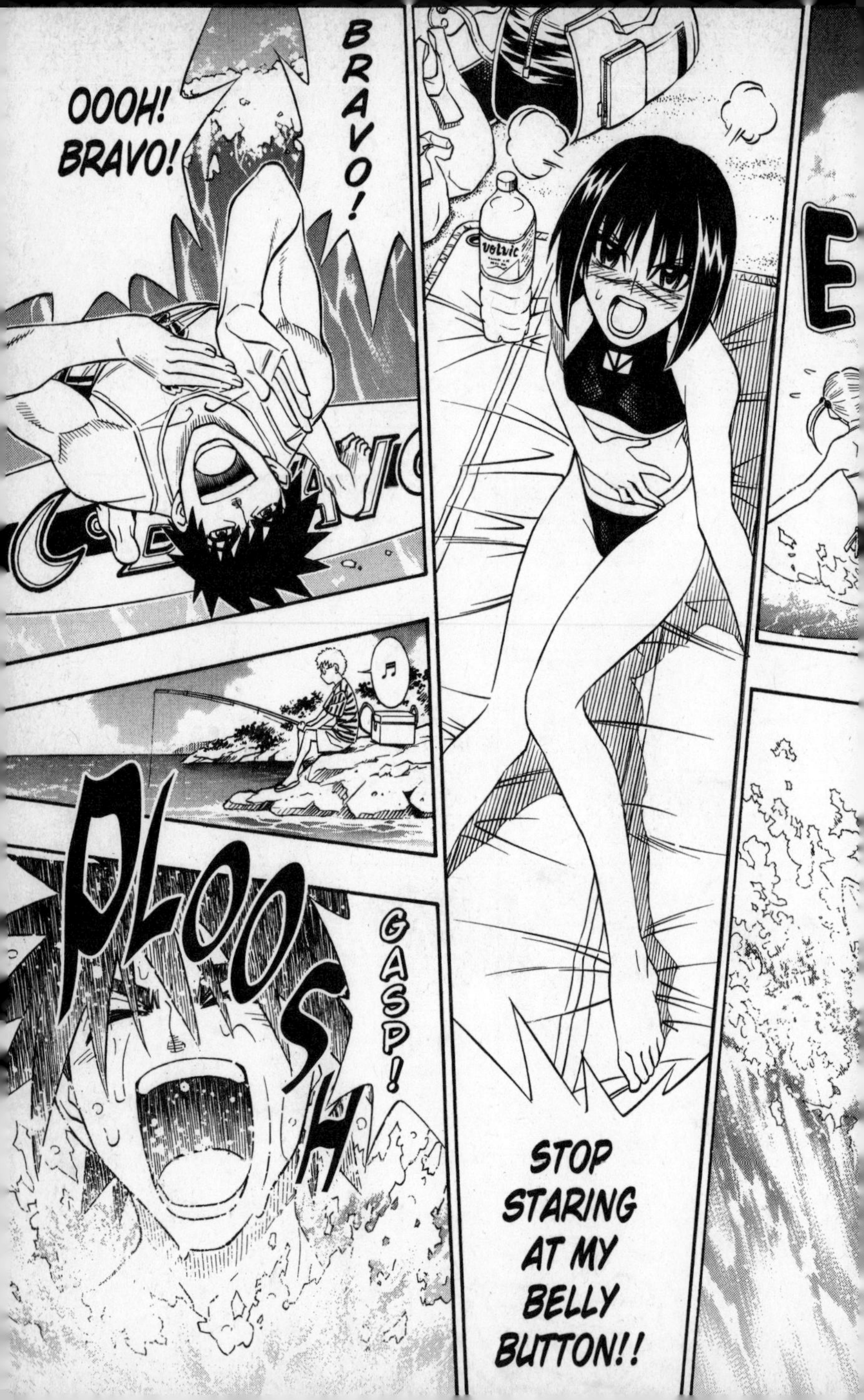
E
volvic
STOP STARING AT MY BELLY BUTTON!!
BRAVO!
OOOH! BRAVO!
♪
GASP!
PLOOSH

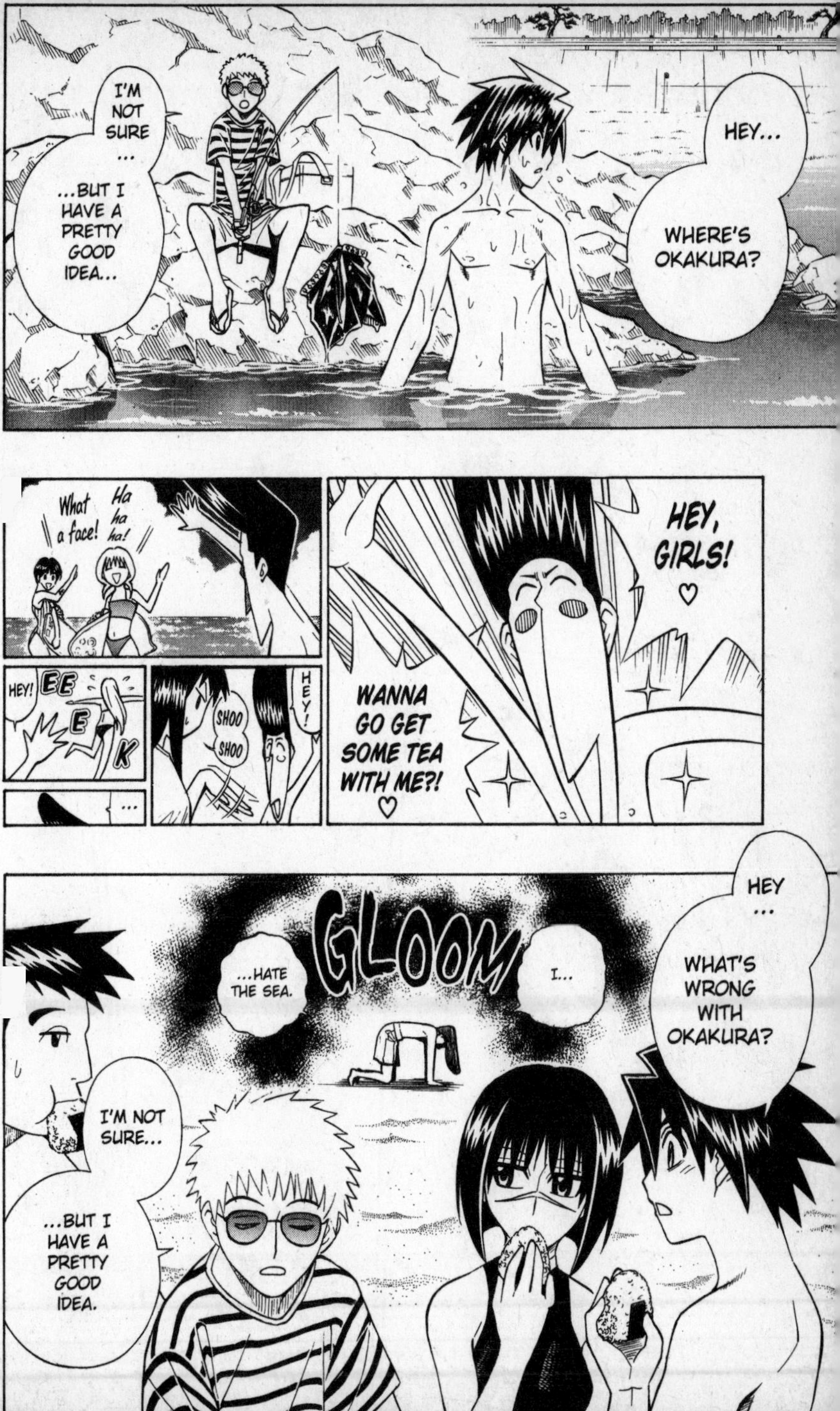
HEY... WHERE'S OKAKURA?
I'M NOT SURE ...
...BUT I HAVE A PRETTY GOOD IDEA...
HEY, GIRLS! ♡
WANNA GO GET SOME TEA WITH ME?! ♡
Ha ha ha!
What a face!
HEY!
SHOO SHOO
HEY!
EEEK
...
HEY ... WHAT'S WRONG WITH OKAKURA?
I...
GLOOM
...HATE THE SEA.
I'M NOT SURE...
...BUT I HAVE A PRETTY GOOD IDEA.

READ THIS WAY

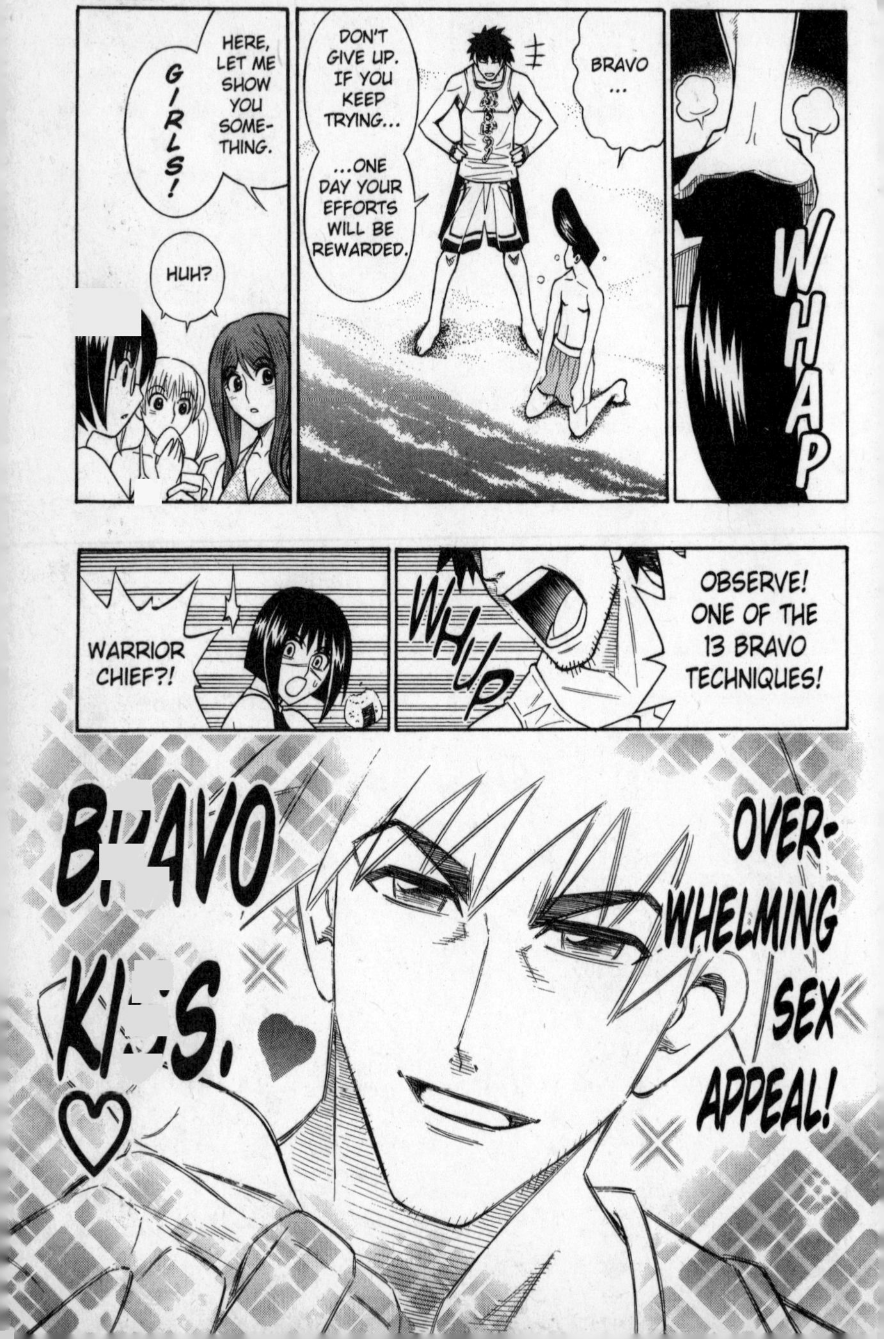
WHAP
BRAVO ...
DON'T GIVE UP. IF YOU KEEP TRYING...
...ONE DAY YOUR EFFORTS WILL BE REWARDED.
HERE, LET ME SHOW YOU SOMETHING.
GIRLS!
HUH?
OBSERVE! ONE OF THE 13 BRAVO TECHNIQUES!
WHUP
WARRIOR CHIEF?!
OVER-WHELMING SEX APPEAL!

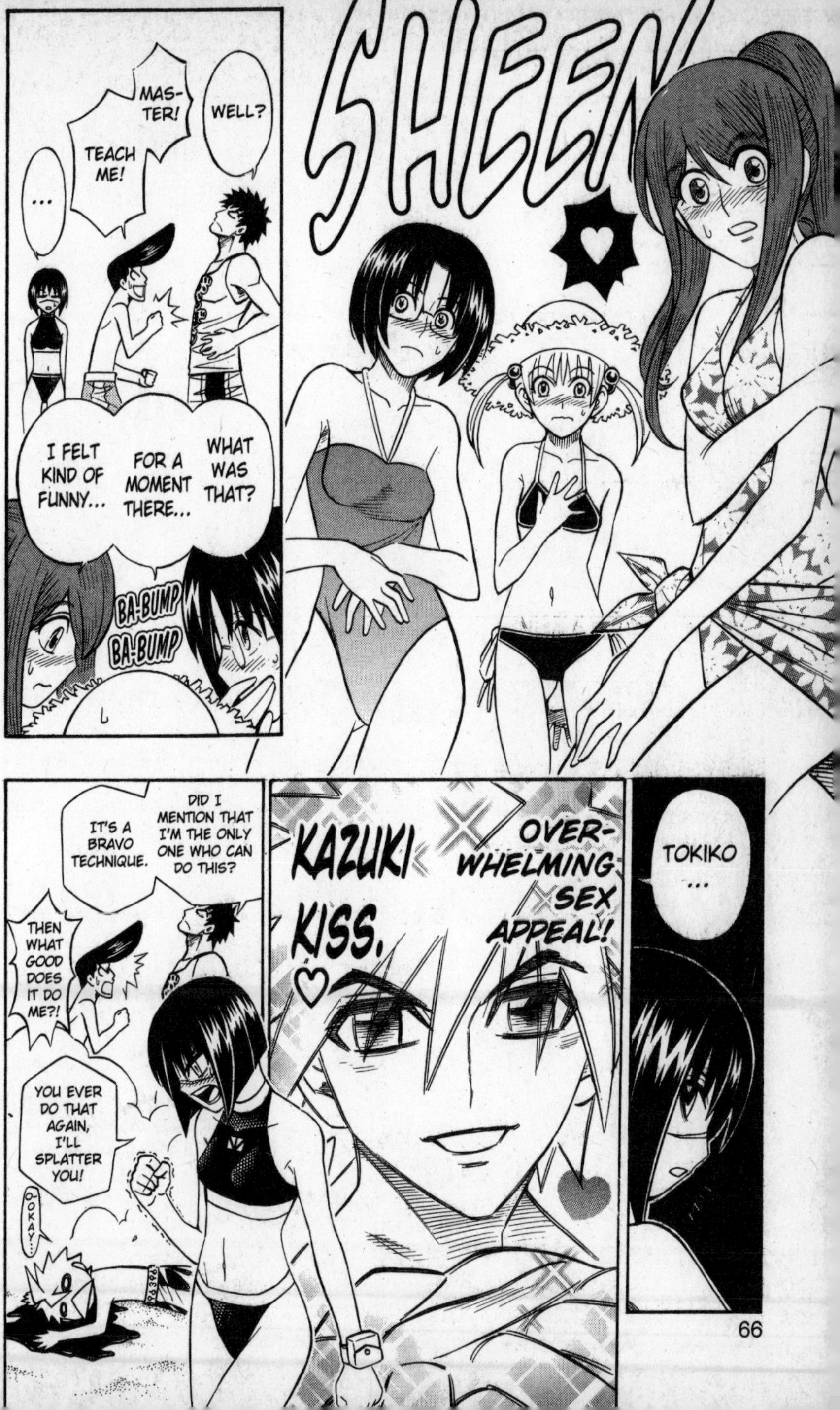
SHEEN
WELL?
MASTER! TEACH ME!
...
WHAT WAS THAT?
FOR A MOMENT THERE...
I FELT KIND OF FUNNY...
BA-BUMP BA-BUMP
TOKIKO ...
OVERWHELMING SEX APPEAL!
KAZUKI KISS.
DID I MENTION THAT I'M THE ONLY ONE WHO CAN DO THIS?
IT'S A BRAVO TECHNIQUE.
THEN WHAT GOOD DOES IT DO ME?!
YOU EVER DO THAT AGAIN, I'LL SPLATTER YOU!
O-OKAY...

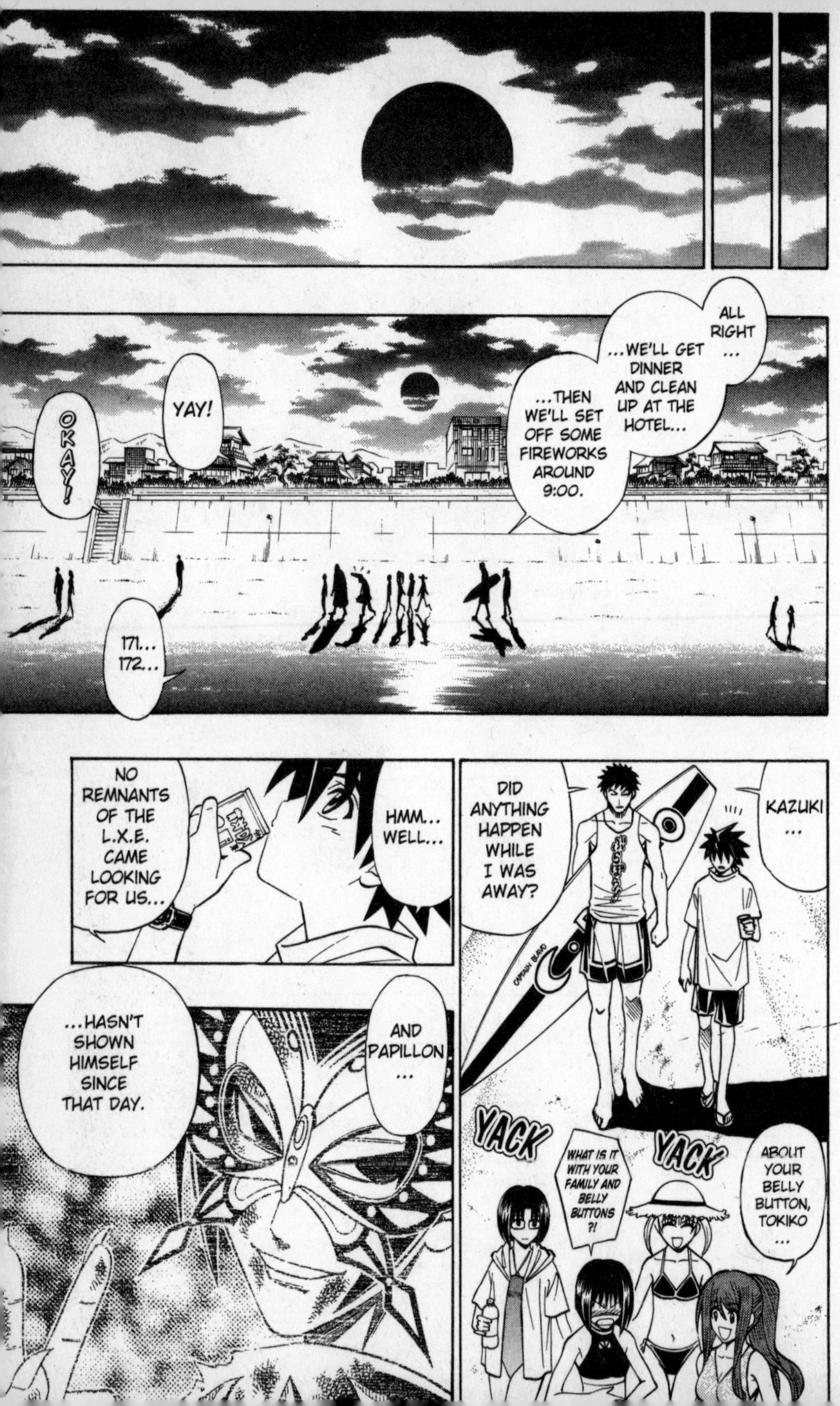
ALL RIGHT ...
...WE'LL GET DINNER AND CLEAN UP AT THE HOTEL...
...THEN WE'LL SET OFF SOME FIREWORKS AROUND 9:00.
YAY!
OKAY!
171... 172...
KAZUKI ...
DID ANYTHING HAPPEN WHILE I WAS AWAY?
CAPTAIN BRAVO
ABOUT YOUR BELLY BUTTON, TOKIKO ...
YACK
WHAT IS IT WITH YOUR FAMILY AND BELLY BUTTONS ?!
YACK
HMM... WELL...
NO REMNANTS OF THE L.X.E. CAME LOOKING FOR US...
AND PAPILLON ...
...HASN'T SHOWN HIMSELF SINCE THAT DAY.

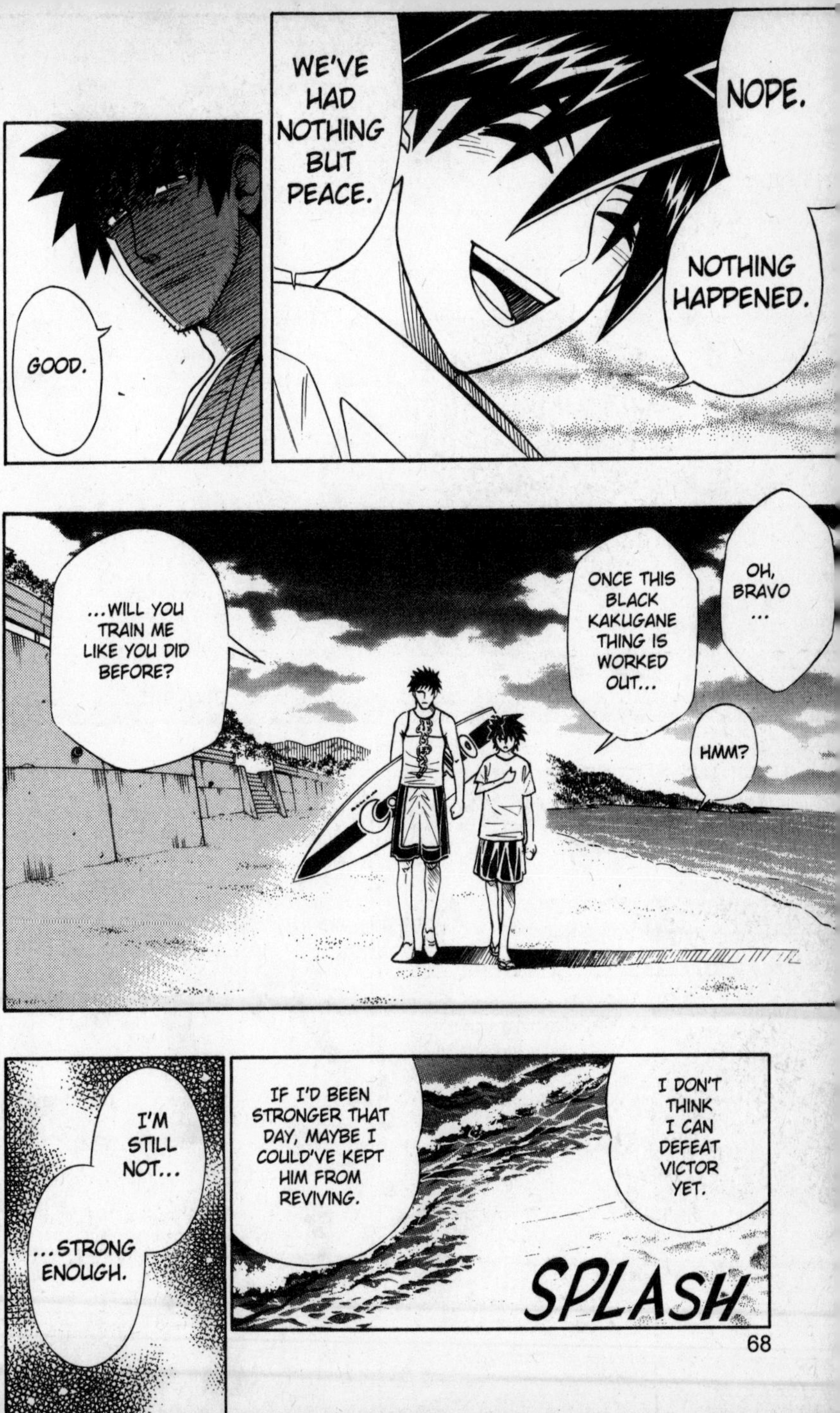
NOPE.
NOTHING HAPPENED.
WE'VE HAD NOTHING BUT PEACE.
GOOD.
OH, BRAVO ...
ONCE THIS BLACK KAKUGANE THING IS WORKED OUT...
HMM?
...WILL YOU TRAIN ME LIKE YOU DID BEFORE?
I DON'T THINK I CAN DEFEAT VICTOR YET.
IF I'D BEEN STRONGER THAT DAY, MAYBE I COULD'VE KEPT HIM FROM REVIVING.
SPLASH
I'M STILL NOT...
...STRONG ENOUGH.

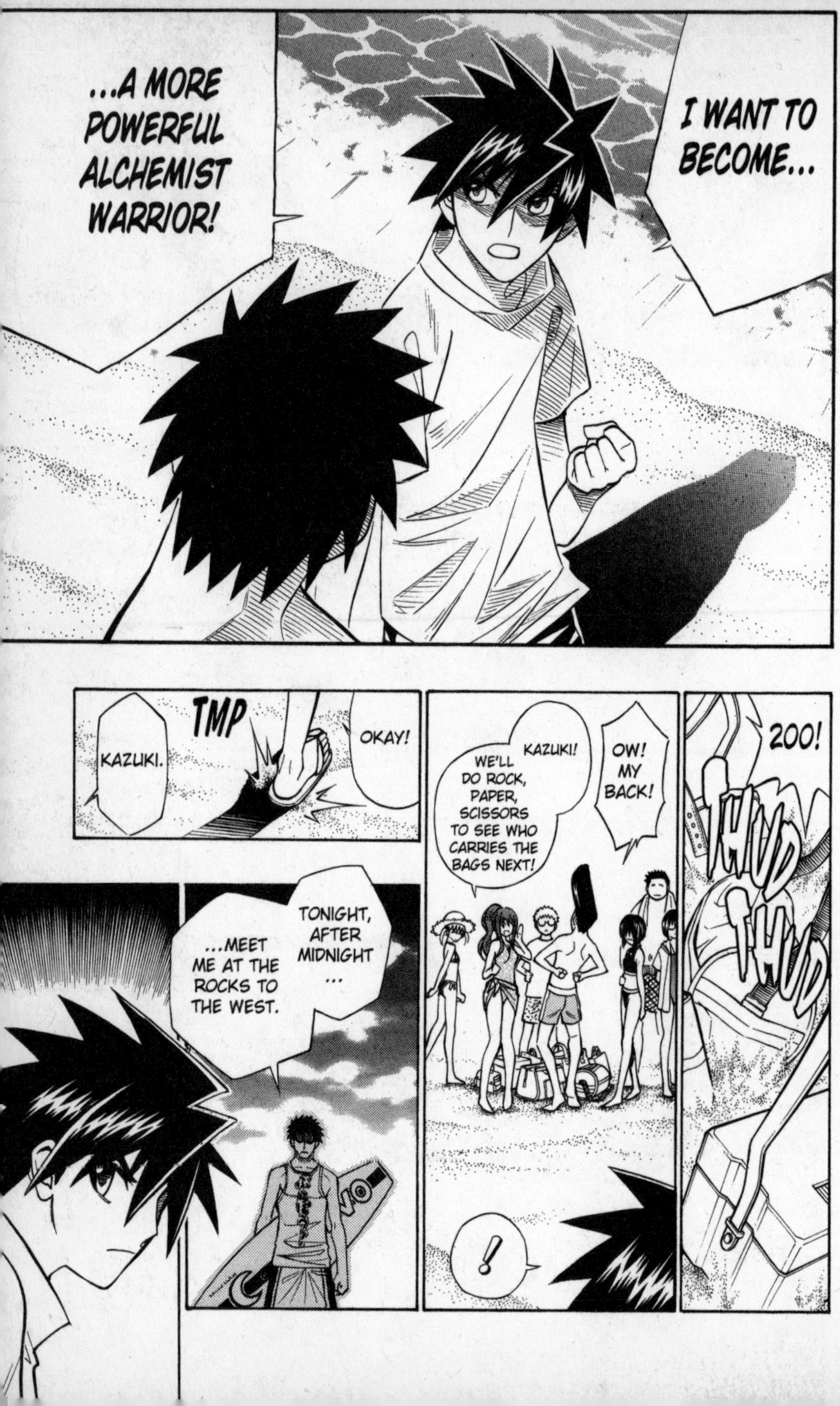
I WANT TO BECOME...
...A MORE POWERFUL ALCHEMIST WARRIOR!
200!
THUD THUD
OW! MY BACK!
KAZUKI! WE'LL DO ROCK, PAPER, SCISSORS TO SEE WHO CARRIES THE BAGS NEXT!
!
OKAY!
TMP
KAZUKI.
TONIGHT, AFTER MIDNIGHT...
...MEET ME AT THE ROCKS TO THE WEST.

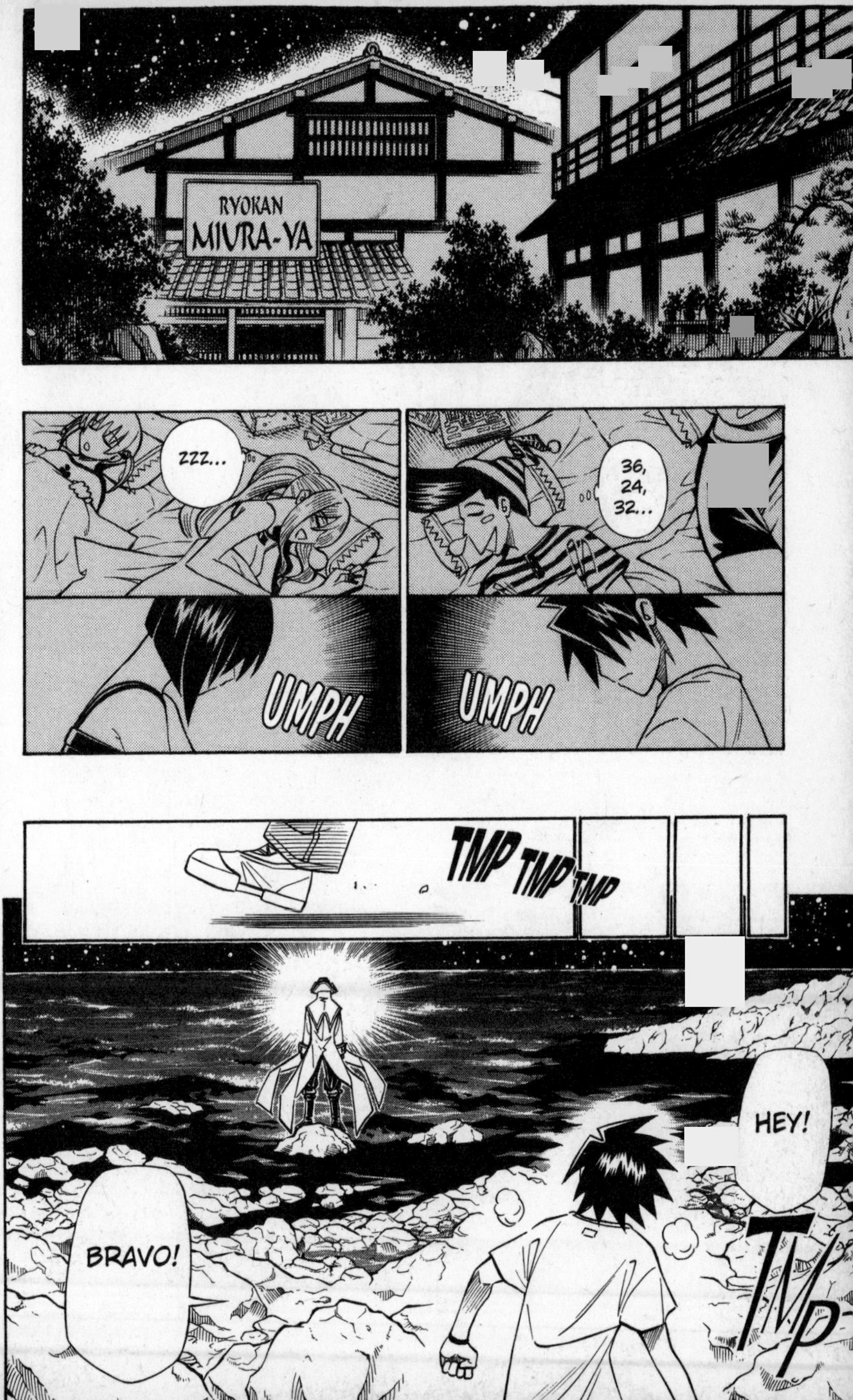
RYOKAN
MIURA-YA
36, 24, 32...
ZZZ...
UMPH
UMPH
TMP TMP TMP
HEY!
TMP
BRAVO!

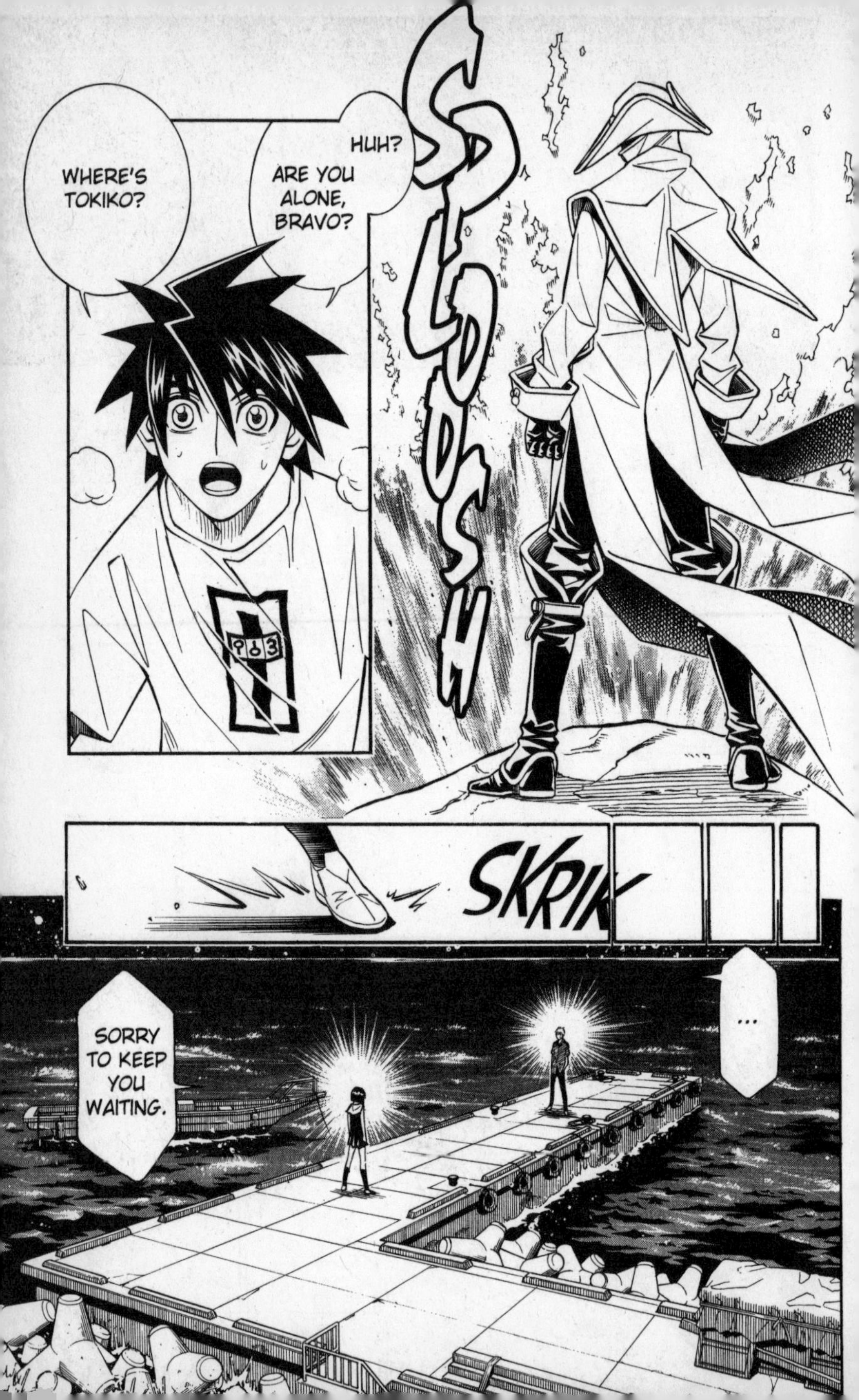
SPLOOSH
HUH? ARE YOU ALONE, BRAVO?
WHERE'S TOKIKO?
SKRIK
...
SORRY TO KEEP YOU WAITING.

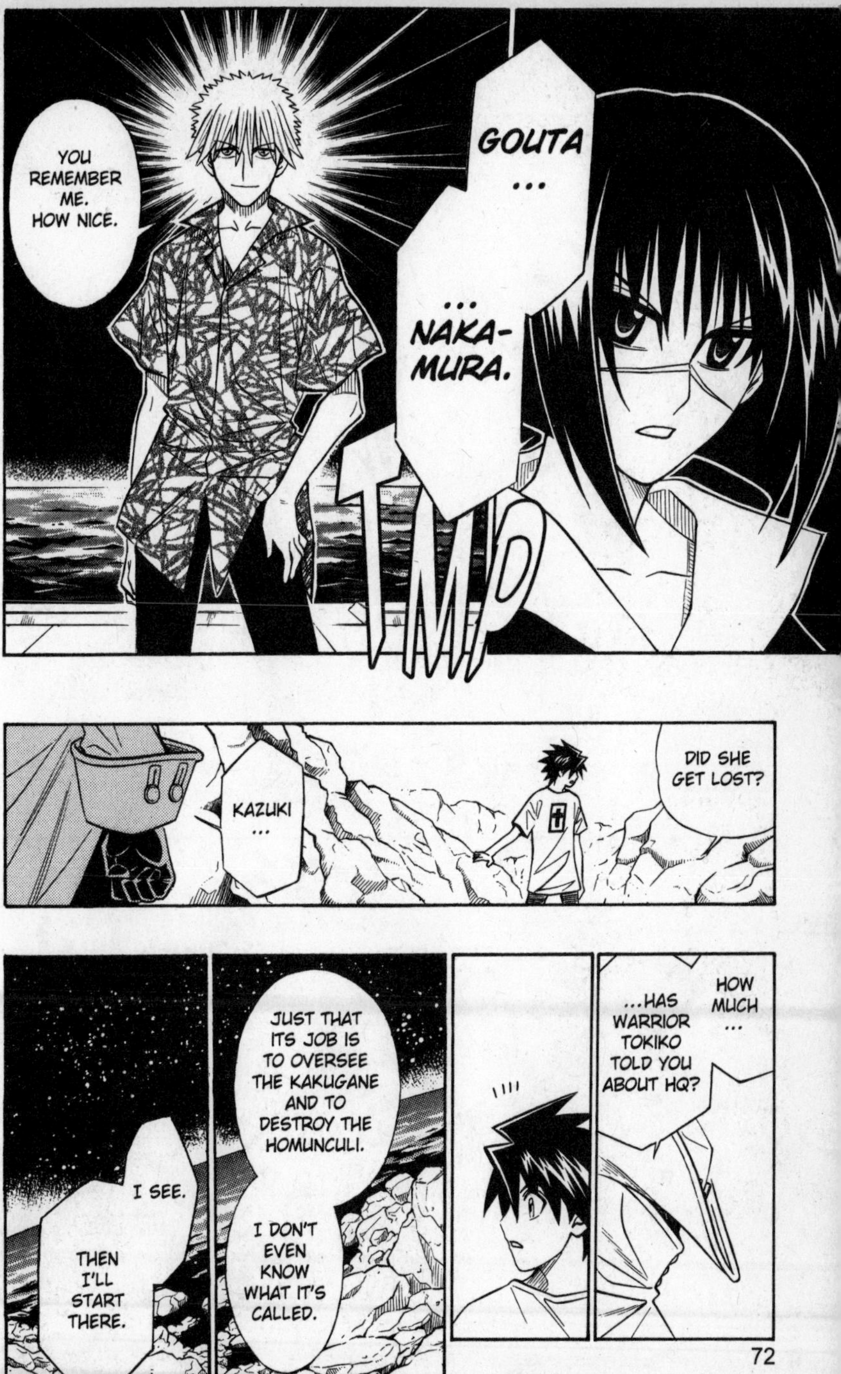
GOUTA ...
... NAKA-MURA.
TMP
YOU REMEMBER ME. HOW NICE.
DID SHE GET LOST?
KAZUKI ...
HOW MUCH ...
...HAS WARRIOR TOKIKO TOLD YOU ABOUT HQ?
!!!
JUST THAT ITS JOB IS TO OVERSEE THE KAKUGANE AND TO DESTROY THE HOMUNCULI.
I DON'T EVEN KNOW WHAT IT'S CALLED.
I SEE.
THEN I'LL START THERE.

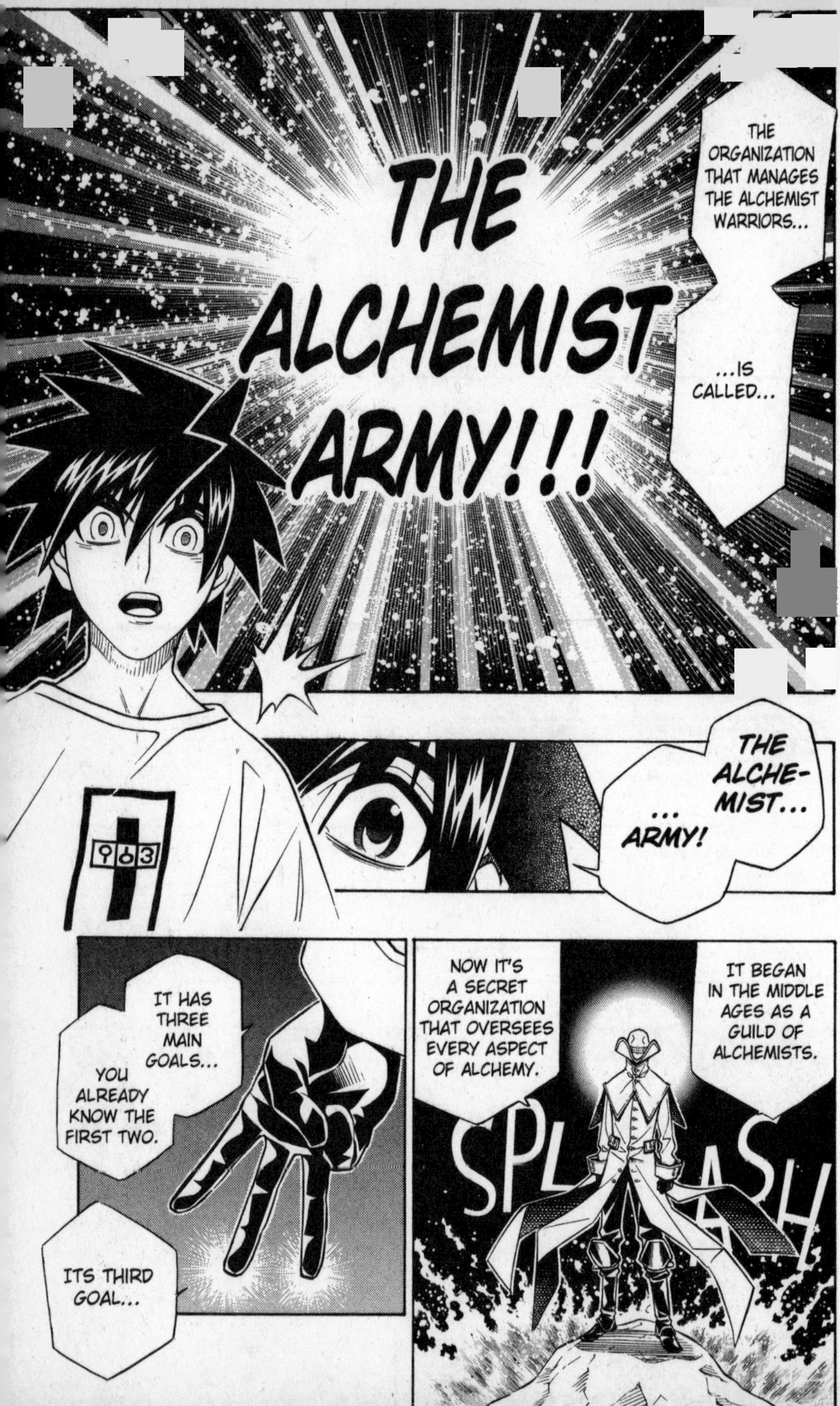
THE ORGANIZATION THAT MANAGES THE ALCHEMIST WARRIORS...
...IS CALLED...
THE ALCHEMIST ARMY!!!
THE ALCHE-MIST...
...ARMY!
IT BEGAN IN THE MIDDLE AGES AS A GUILD OF ALCHEMISTS.
NOW IT'S A SECRET ORGANIZATION THAT OVERSEES EVERY ASPECT OF ALCHEMY.
SPLASH
IT HAS THREE MAIN GOALS...
YOU ALREADY KNOW THE FIRST TWO.
ITS THIRD GOAL...

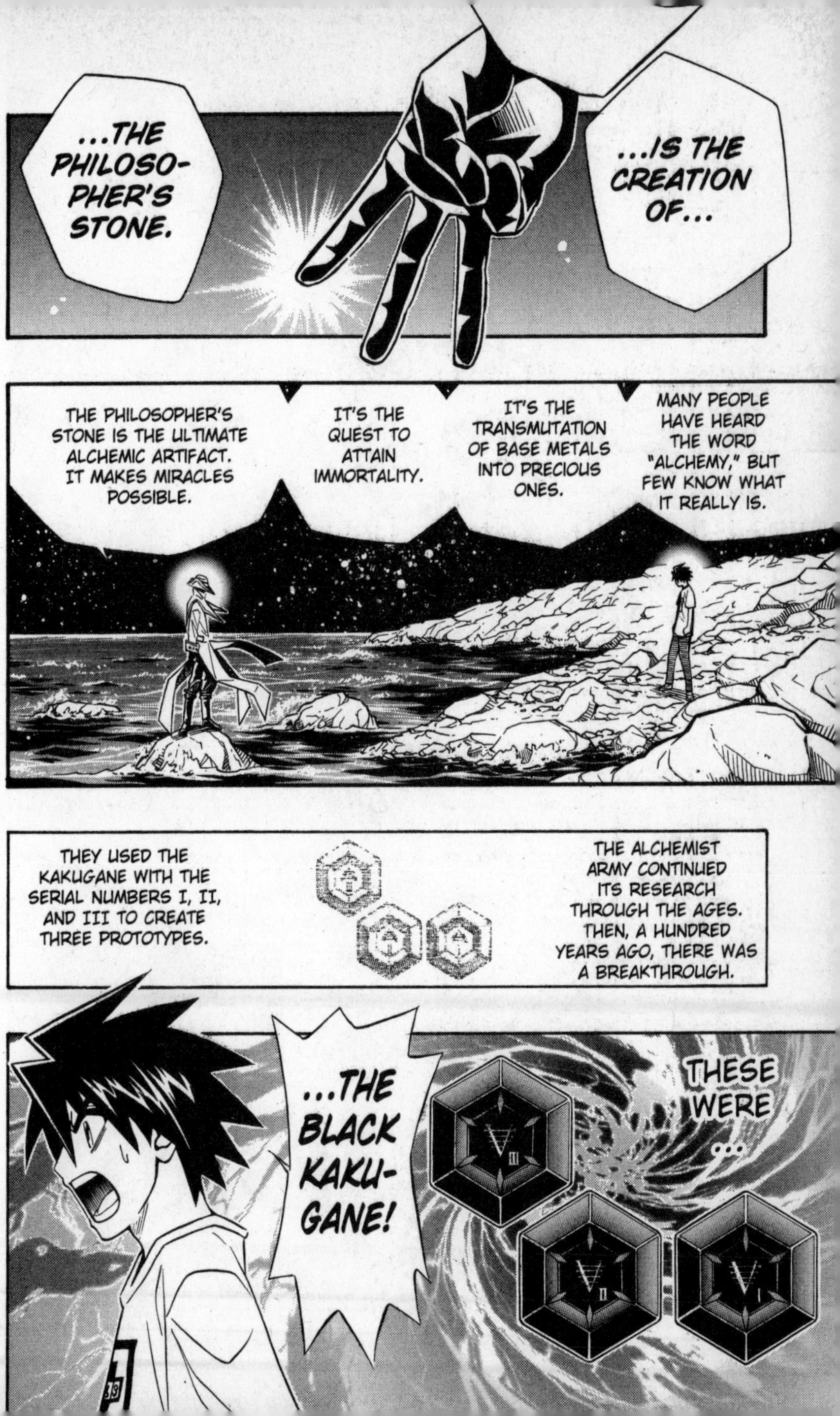
...IS THE CREATION OF...
...THE PHILOSOPHER'S STONE.
MANY PEOPLE HAVE HEARD THE WORD "ALCHEMY," BUT FEW KNOW WHAT IT REALLY IS.
IT'S THE TRANSMUTATION OF BASE METALS INTO PRECIOUS ONES.
IT'S THE QUEST TO ATTAIN IMMORTALITY.
THE PHILOSOPHER'S STONE IS THE ULTIMATE ALCHEMIC ARTIFACT. IT MAKES MIRACLES POSSIBLE.
THE ALCHEMIST ARMY CONTINUED ITS RESEARCH THROUGH THE AGES. THEN, A HUNDRED YEARS AGO, THERE WAS A BREAKTHROUGH.
THEY USED THE KAKUGANE WITH THE SERIAL NUMBERS I, II, AND III TO CREATE THREE PROTOTYPES.
THESE WERE...
...THE BLACK KAKUGANE!

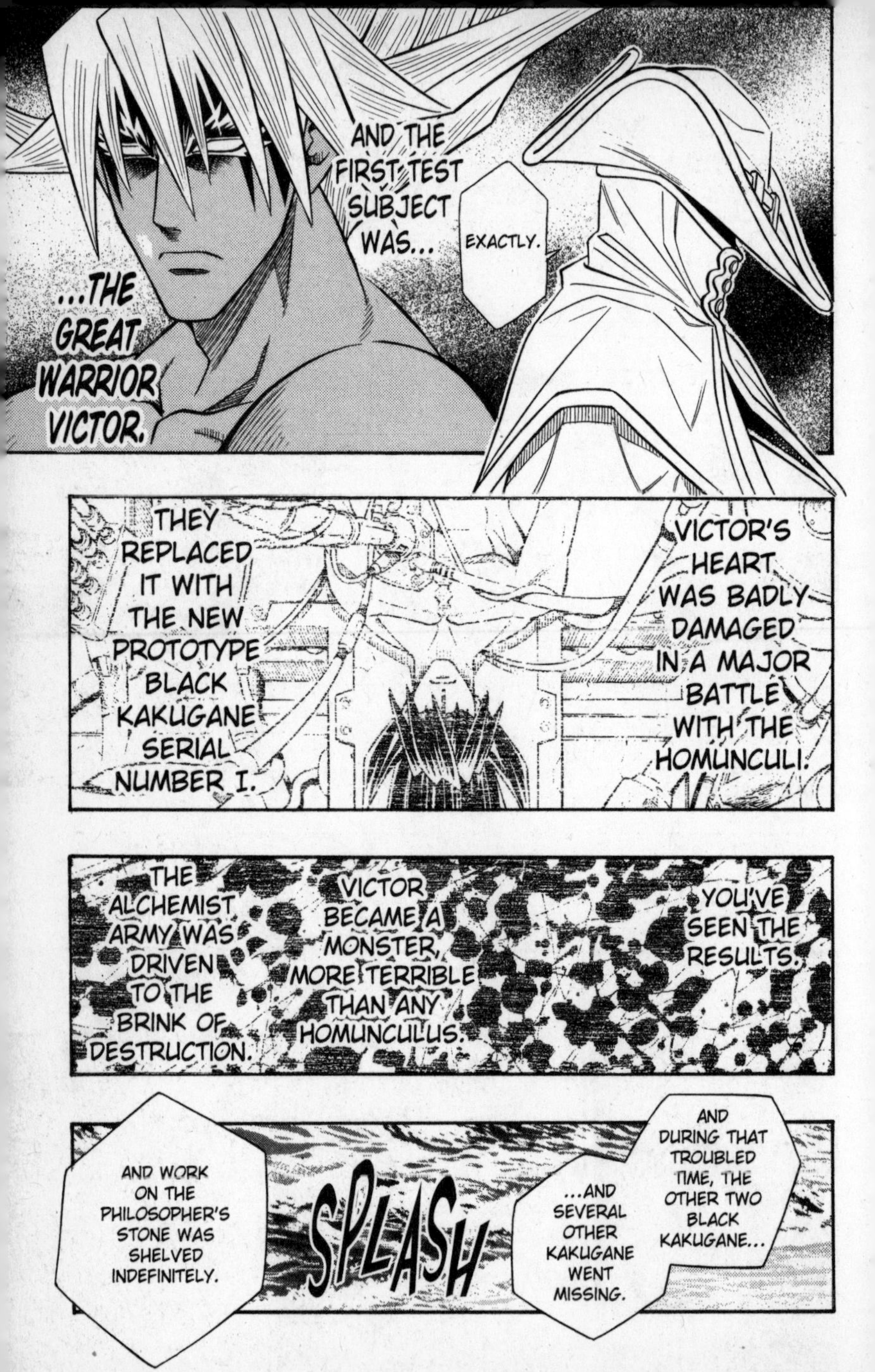
AND THE FIRST TEST SUBJECT WAS...
...THE GREAT WARRIOR VICTOR.
EXACTLY.
VICTOR'S HEART WAS BADLY DAMAGED IN A MAJOR BATTLE WITH THE HOMUNCULI.
THEY REPLACED IT WITH THE NEW PROTOTYPE BLACK KAKUGANE SERIAL NUMBER I.
YOU'VE SEEN THE RESULTS.
VICTOR BECAME A MONSTER, MORE TERRIBLE THAN ANY HOMUNCULUS.
THE ALCHEMIST ARMY WAS DRIVEN TO THE BRINK OF DESTRUCTION.
AND DURING THAT TROUBLED TIME, THE OTHER TWO BLACK KAKUGANE...
...AND SEVERAL OTHER KAKUGANE WENT MISSING.
SPLASH
AND WORK ON THE PHILOSOPHER'S STONE WAS SHELVED INDEFINITELY.

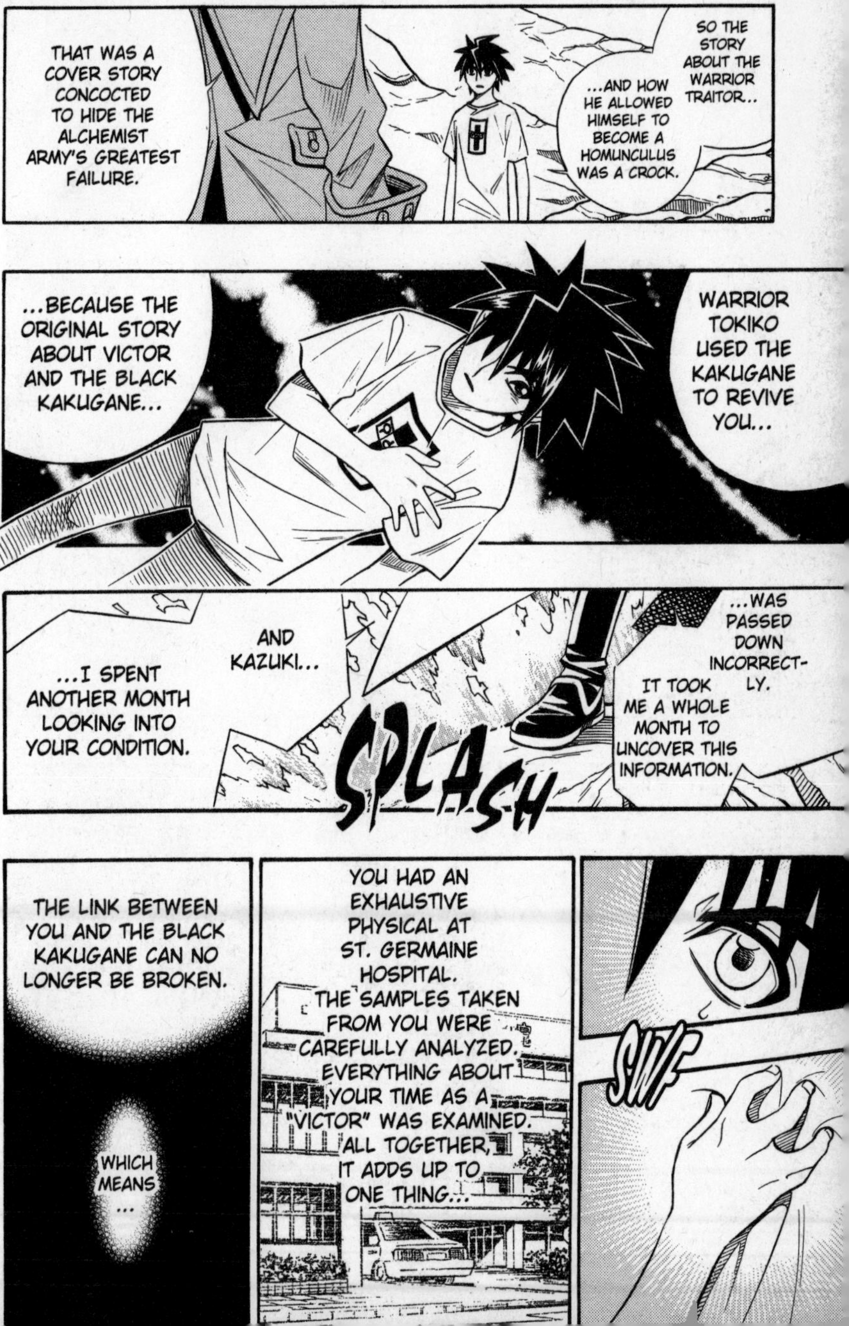
SO THE STORY ABOUT THE WARRIOR TRAITOR...
...AND HOW HE ALLOWED HIMSELF TO BECOME A HOMUNCULUS WAS A CROCK.
THAT WAS A COVER STORY CONCOCTED TO HIDE THE ALCHEMIST ARMY'S GREATEST FAILURE.
WARRIOR TOKIKO USED THE KAKUGANE TO REVIVE YOU...
...BECAUSE THE ORIGINAL STORY ABOUT VICTOR AND THE BLACK KAKUGANE...
...WAS PASSED DOWN INCORRECT-LY.
IT TOOK ME A WHOLE MONTH TO UNCOVER THIS INFORMATION.
SPLASH
AND KAZUKI...
...I SPENT ANOTHER MONTH LOOKING INTO YOUR CONDITION.
YOU HAD AN EXHAUSTIVE PHYSICAL AT ST. GERMAINE HOSPITAL. THE SAMPLES TAKEN FROM YOU WERE CAREFULLY ANALYZED. EVERYTHING ABOUT YOUR TIME AS A "VICTOR" WAS EXAMINED. ALL TOGETHER, IT ADDS UP TO ONE THING...
THE LINK BETWEEN YOU AND THE BLACK KAKUGANE CAN NO LONGER BE BROKEN.
WHICH MEANS ...

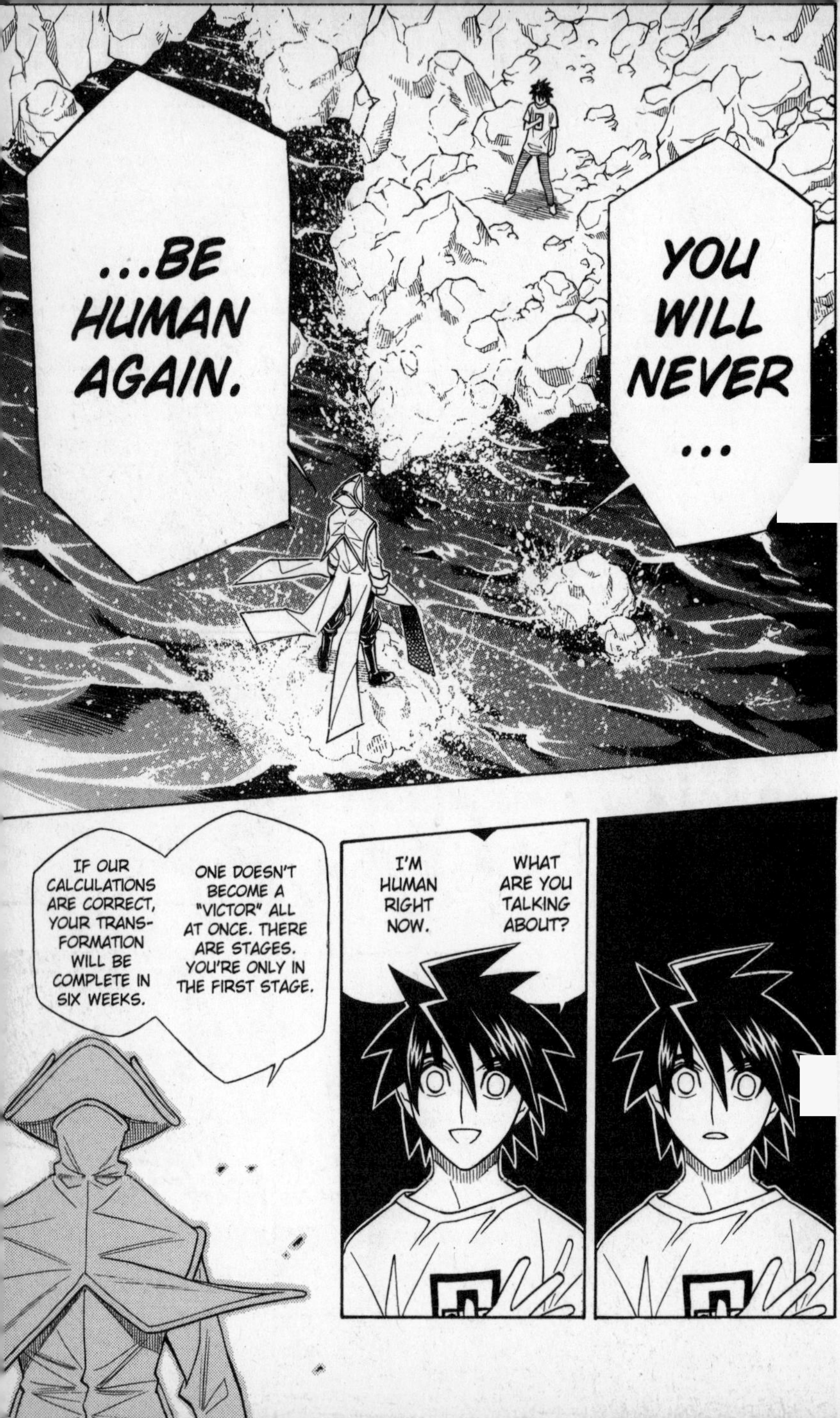
YOU WILL NEVER...
...BE HUMAN AGAIN.
WHAT ARE YOU TALKING ABOUT?
I'M HUMAN RIGHT NOW.
ONE DOESN'T BECOME A "VICTOR" ALL AT ONCE. THERE ARE STAGES. YOU'RE ONLY IN THE FIRST STAGE.
IF OUR CALCULATIONS ARE CORRECT, YOUR TRANSFORMATION WILL BE COMPLETE IN SIX WEEKS.

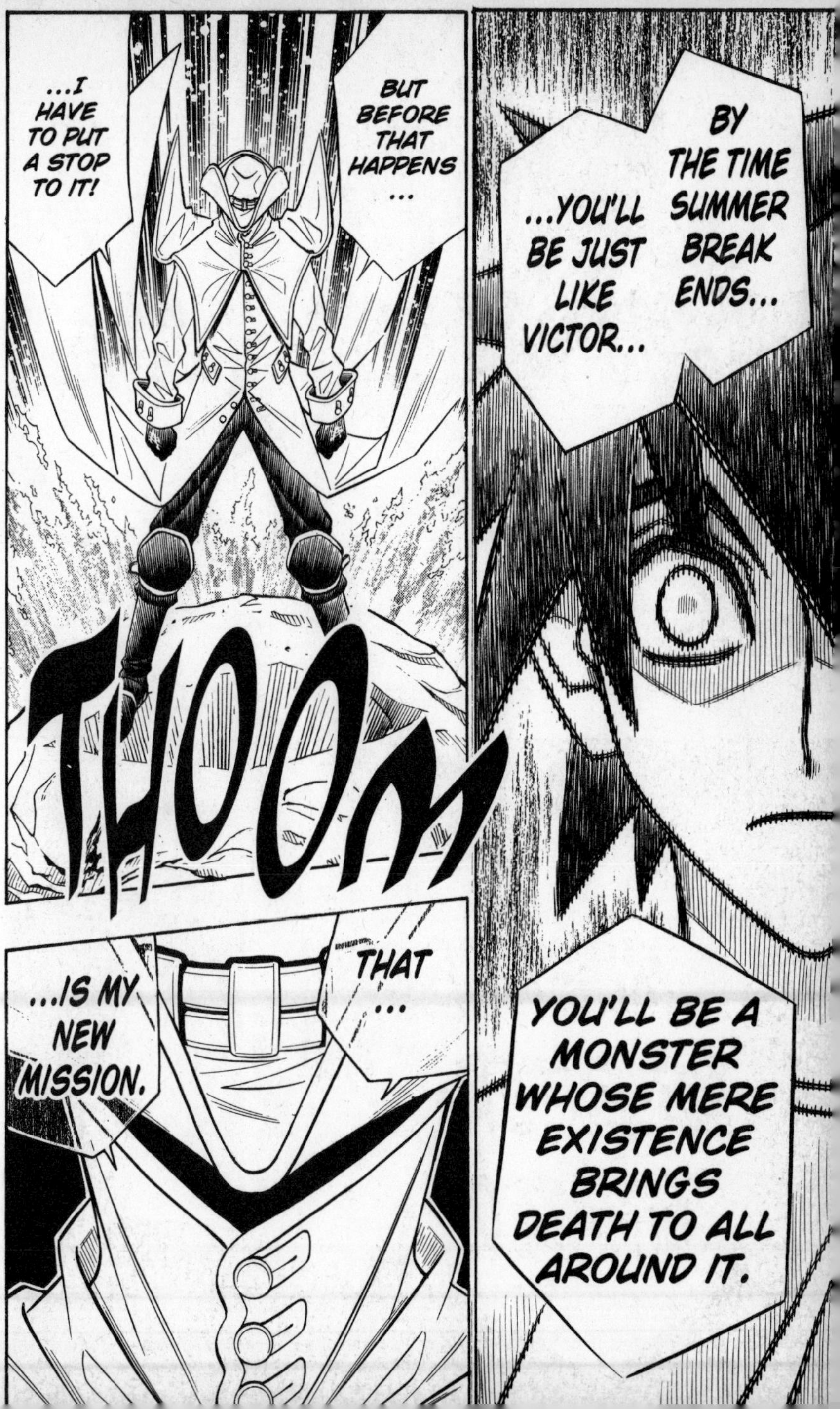
BY THE TIME SUMMER BREAK ENDS...
...YOU'LL BE JUST LIKE VICTOR...
YOU'LL BE A MONSTER WHOSE MERE EXISTENCE BRINGS DEATH TO ALL AROUND IT.
BUT BEFORE THAT HAPPENS...
...I HAVE TO PUT A STOP TO IT!
THOOM
THAT...
...IS MY NEW MISSION.

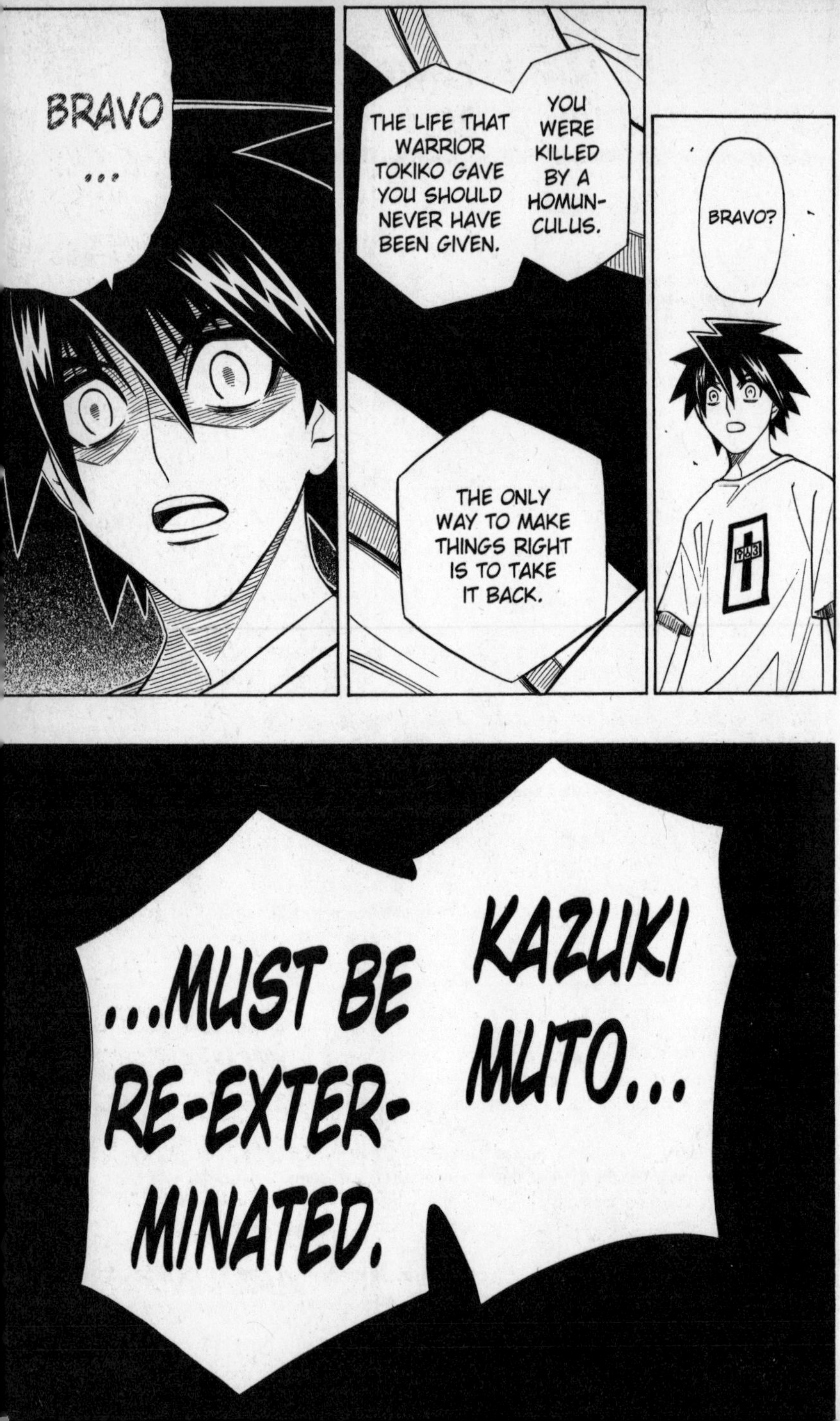
BRAVO?
YOU WERE KILLED BY A HOMUNCULUS.
THE LIFE THAT WARRIOR TOKIKO GAVE YOU SHOULD NEVER HAVE BEEN GIVEN.
THE ONLY WAY TO MAKE THINGS RIGHT IS TO TAKE IT BACK.
BRAVO ...
KAZUKI MUTO...
...MUST BE RE-EXTER-MINATED.

What are the arrows loosed by a laughing angel?

Buso Renkin File No. 7

エンゼル御前

ANGEL GOZEN

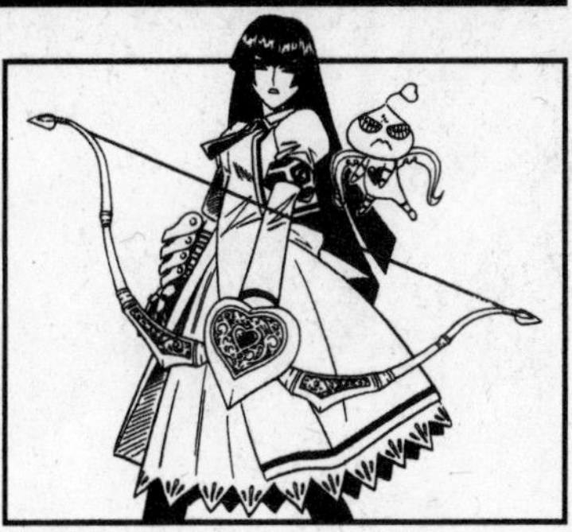

- Kakugane Serial Number: XXII (22)
- Creator: Ouka Hayasaka
- Form: Bow and Arrows
- Main Color: Pearl Pink and Ruby Red
- Special Abilities:
  - Extreme Accuracy made possible by an automaton.
  - The Heart Arrows created by the right gauntlet have the ability to absorb another's injuries and transfer it to the archer.
- Special Traits:
  - Gozen, the automaton, shares its consciousness with Ouka Hayasaka. It becomes Ouka's alter ego.
  - It has many useful abilities, including the creation of Heart Arrows, speech, video broadcasting, and other forms of communication. It also has the rather less useful ability to pee itself. Few Buso Renkin are so versatile.
  - The damage transfer power of the Heart Arrows is limited to physical injuries and weariness. It can't transfer serious injuries such as a lost limb. Also, if the person taking on the damage lacks the corresponding body part, the damage can't be transferred.
  - Diseases and death cannot be transferred.
- Author's Notes:

· The name of this weapon came from Kaoru Kurosaki. I was hard up for ideas and he suggested "Cupid Gozen." I thought, "Oh, come on!" But since I was using Sword Samurai X myself, I changed "Cupid" to "Angel" and went with it.

· I'd been thinking of creating a mascot character for this series and all I had so far was a failed turtle Homunculus. After a series of permutations, Angel Gozen was born. I'm very pleased with the results.

· The basic design motif is the heart. The bow and arrows were designed by one of my assistants and I'm very happy with them.

· Gozen's expressions are created using only the simple mechanical parts of his face. Making up different expressions has been a chore, but I'll keep coming up with new ones.

ANGEL GOZEN

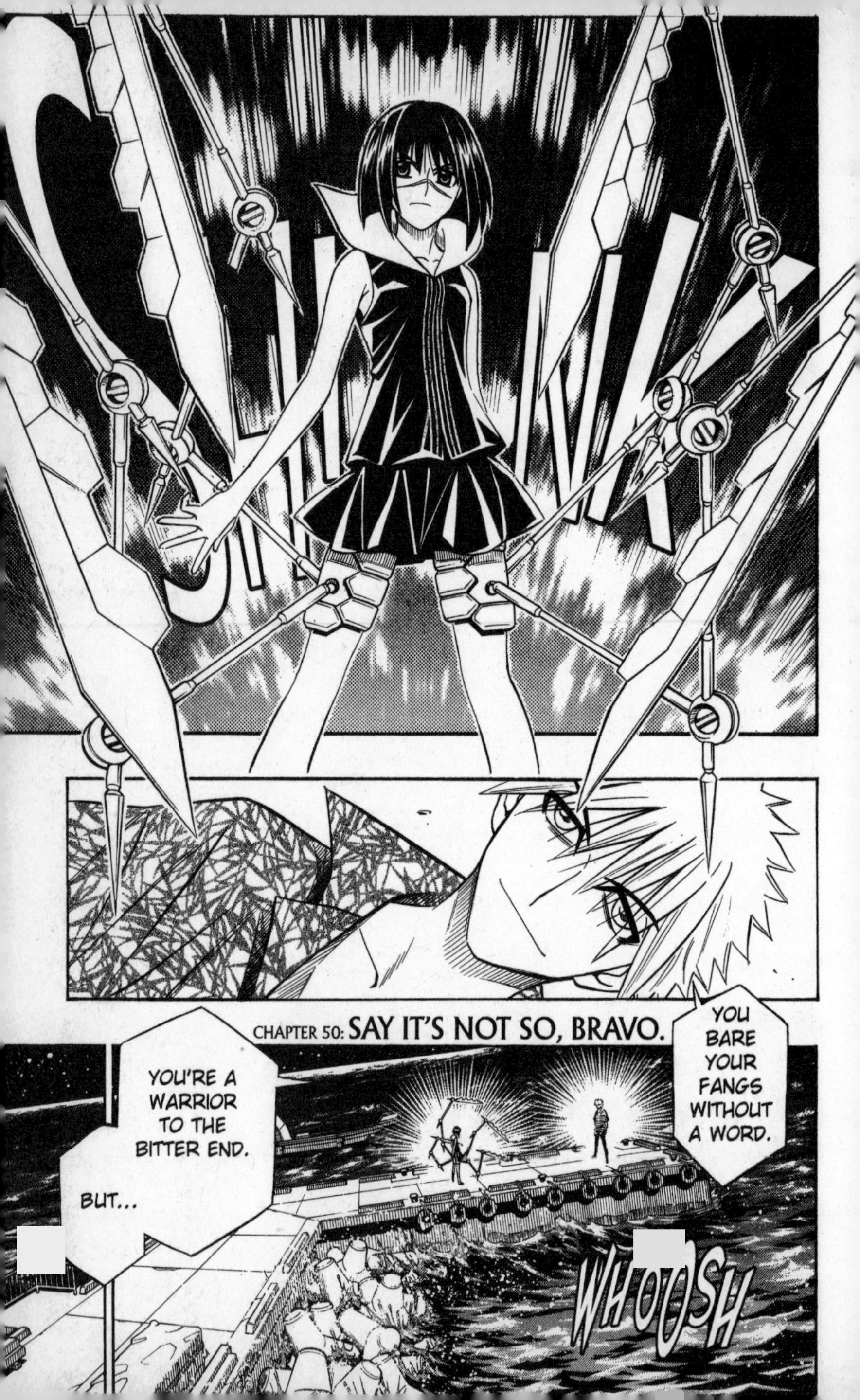
CHAPTER 50: SAY IT'S NOT SO, BRAVO.
YOU BARE YOUR FANGS WITHOUT A WORD.
WHOOSH
YOU'RE A WARRIOR TO THE BITTER END.
BUT...

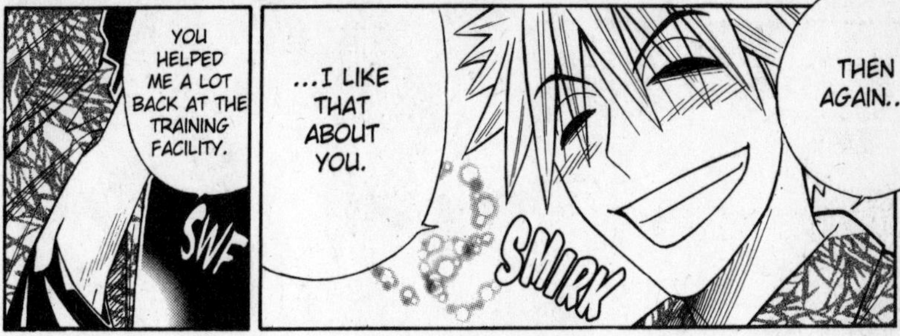
THEN AGAIN...
...I LIKE THAT ABOUT YOU.
SMIRK
YOU HELPED ME A LOT BACK AT THE TRAINING FACILITY.
SWF

CHAPTER 50:

SAY IT'S NOT SO, BRAVO.

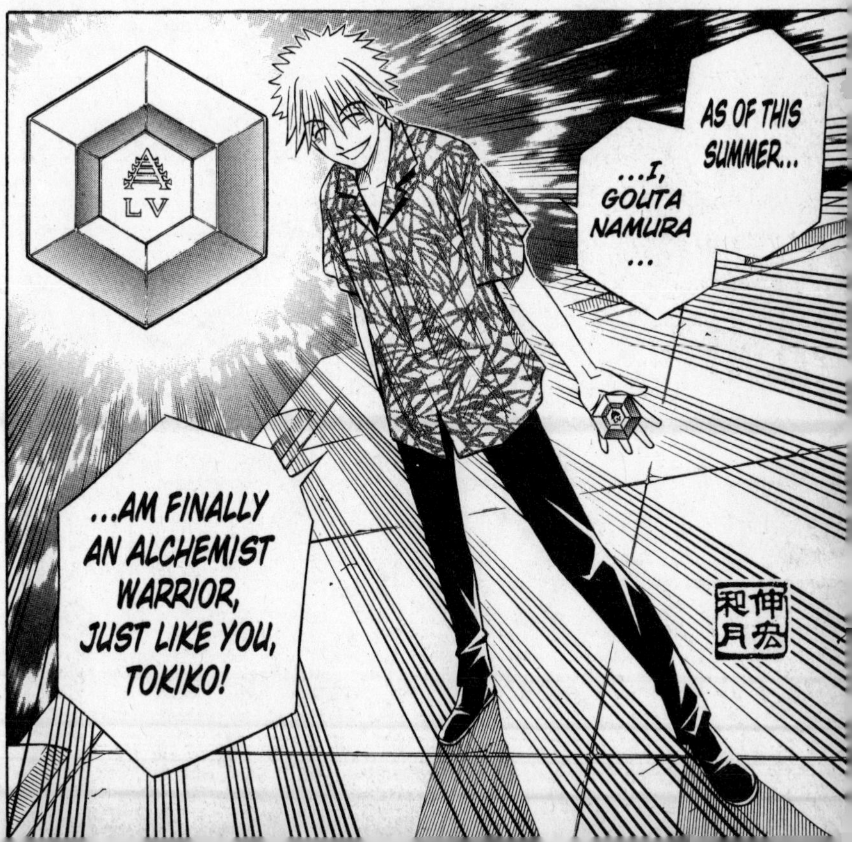
AS OF THIS SUMMER...
...I, GOUTA NAMURA...
LV
...AM FINALLY AN ALCHEMIST WARRIOR, JUST LIKE YOU, TOKIKO!
伸宏和月

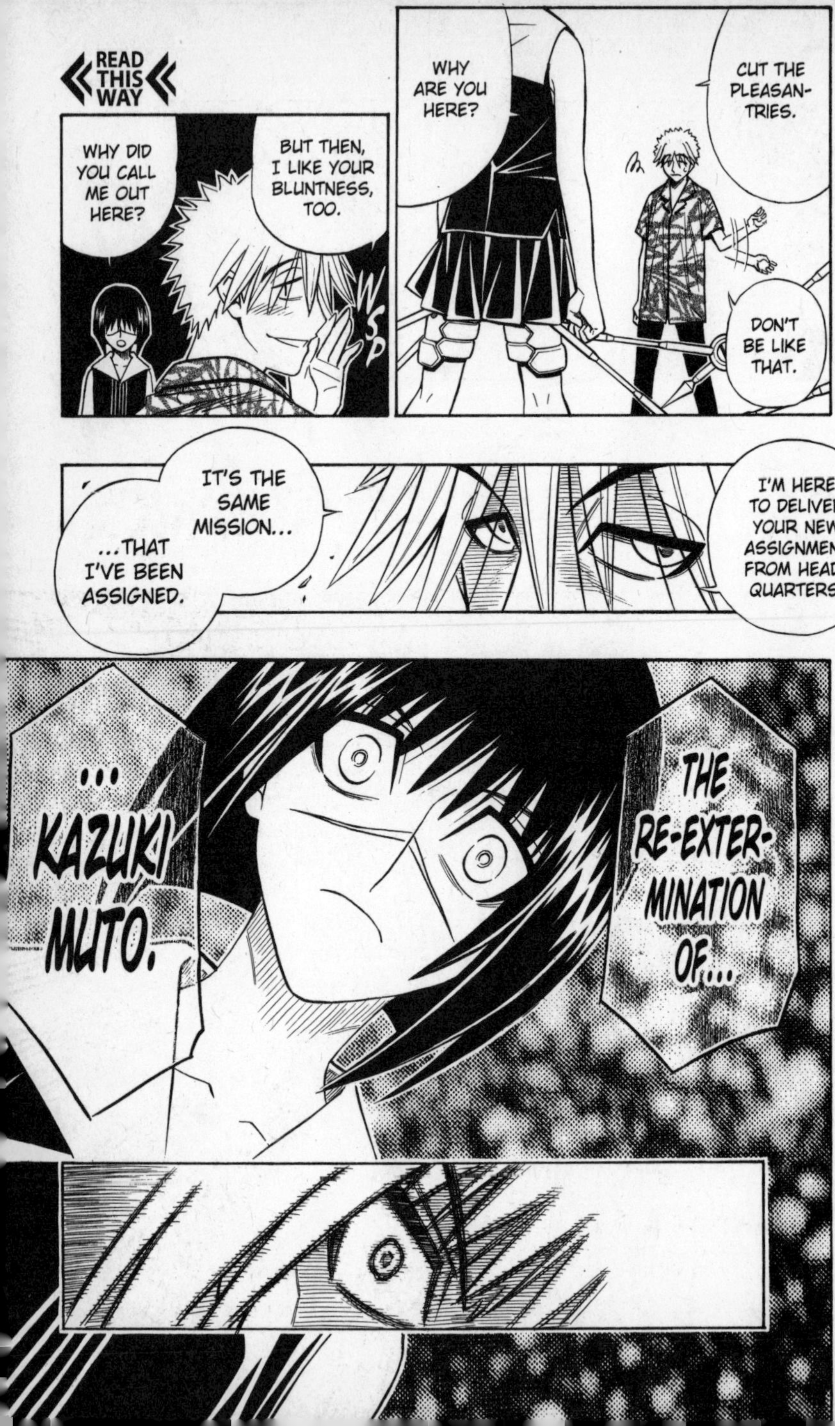
READ THIS WAY
CUT THE PLEASAN-TRIES.
WHY ARE YOU HERE?
DON'T BE LIKE THAT.
BUT THEN, I LIKE YOUR BLUNTNESS, TOO.
WSP
WHY DID YOU CALL ME OUT HERE?
I'M HERE TO DELIVER YOUR NEW ASSIGNMENT FROM HEAD-QUARTERS.
IT'S THE SAME MISSION...
...THAT I'VE BEEN ASSIGNED.
THE RE-EXTER-MINATION OF...
...KAZUKI MUTO.

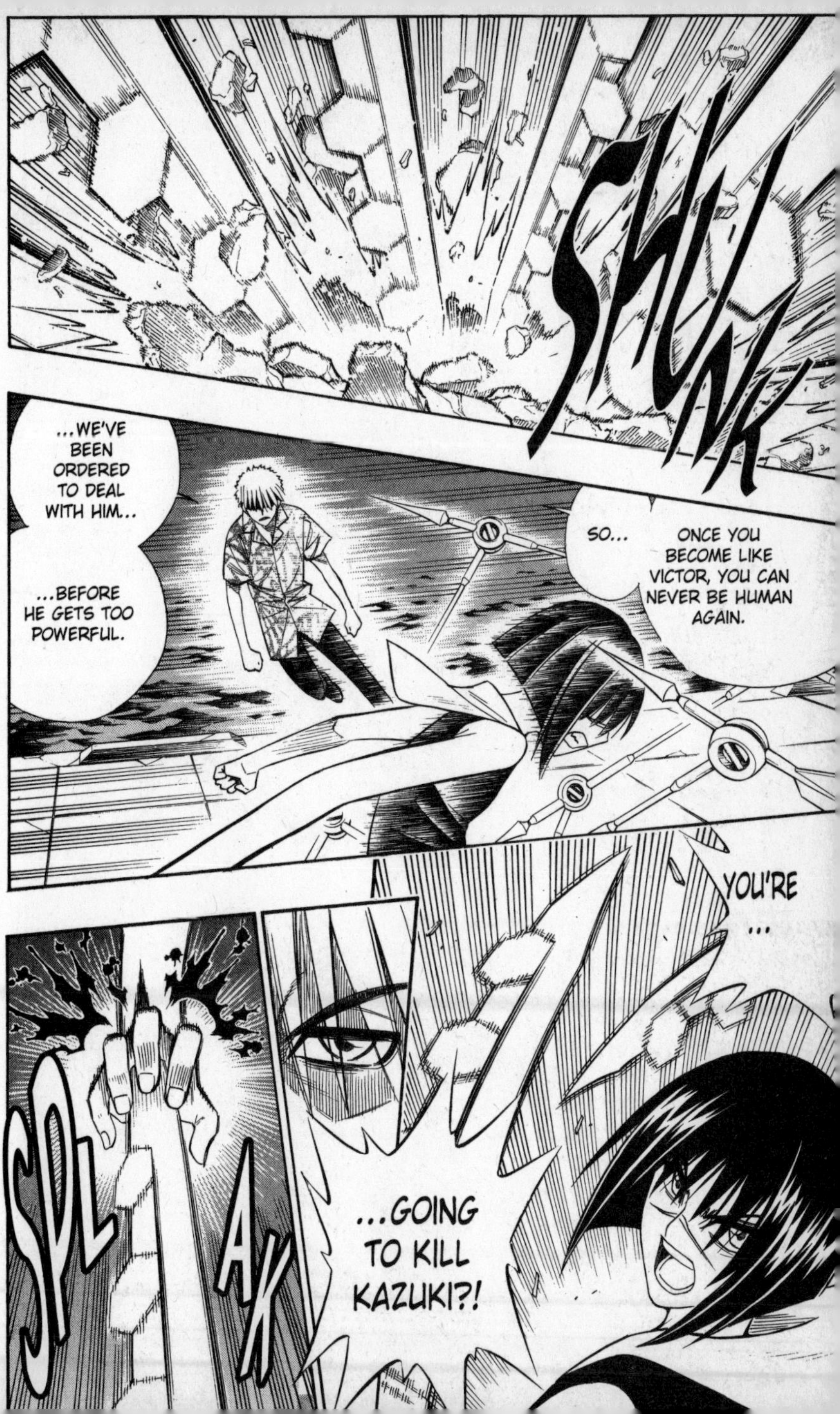
SHUNK
SO...
ONCE YOU BECOME LIKE VICTOR, YOU CAN NEVER BE HUMAN AGAIN.
...WE'VE BEEN ORDERED TO DEAL WITH HIM...
...BEFORE HE GETS TOO POWERFUL.
YOU'RE ...
...GOING TO KILL KAZUKI?!
SPLAK

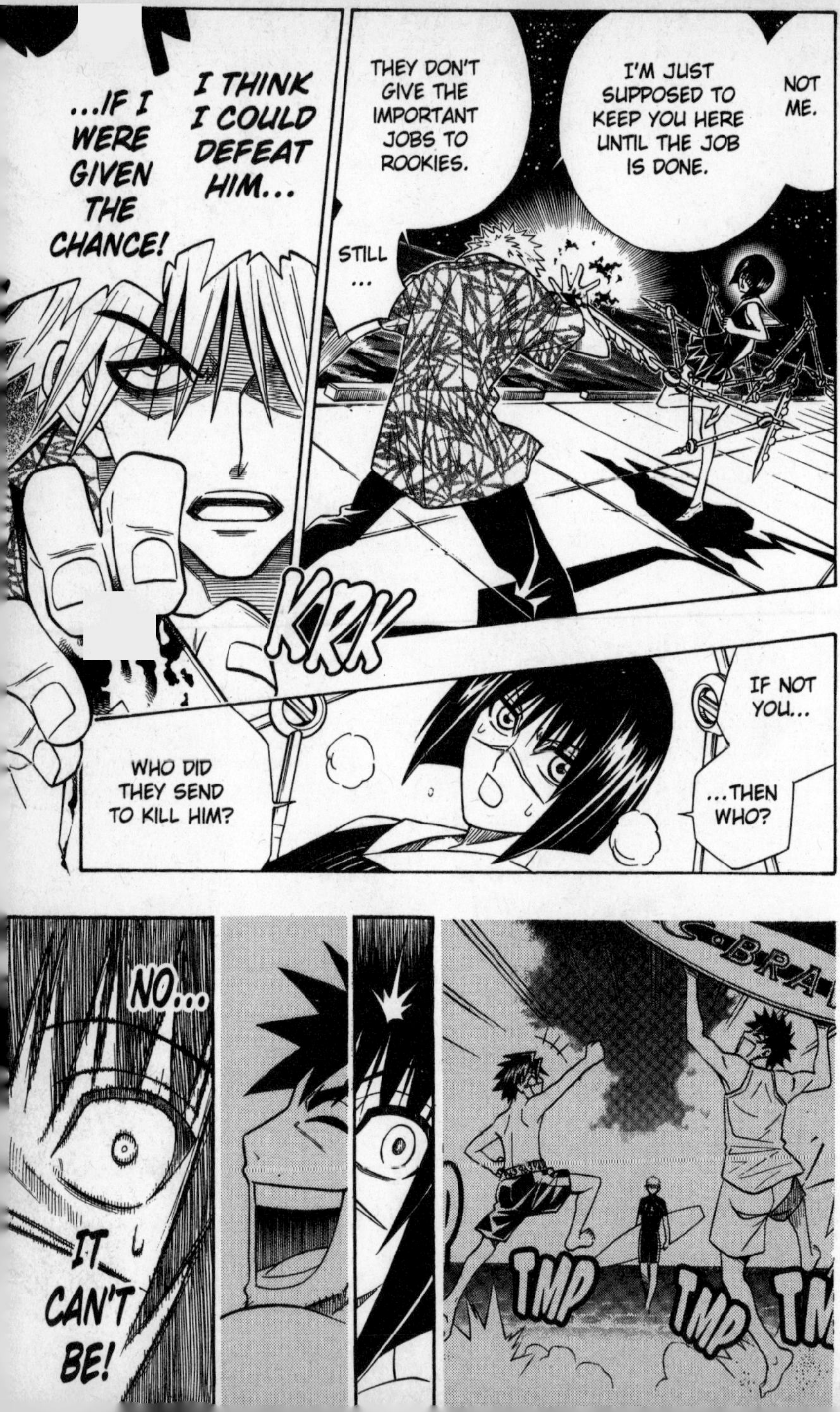
NOT ME.
I'M JUST SUPPOSED TO KEEP YOU HERE UNTIL THE JOB IS DONE.
THEY DON'T GIVE THE IMPORTANT JOBS TO ROOKIES.
STILL...
I THINK I COULD DEFEAT HIM...
...IF I WERE GIVEN THE CHANCE!
KRK
IF NOT YOU...
...THEN WHO?
WHO DID THEY SEND TO KILL HIM?
TMP
TMP
NO...
IT CAN'T BE!

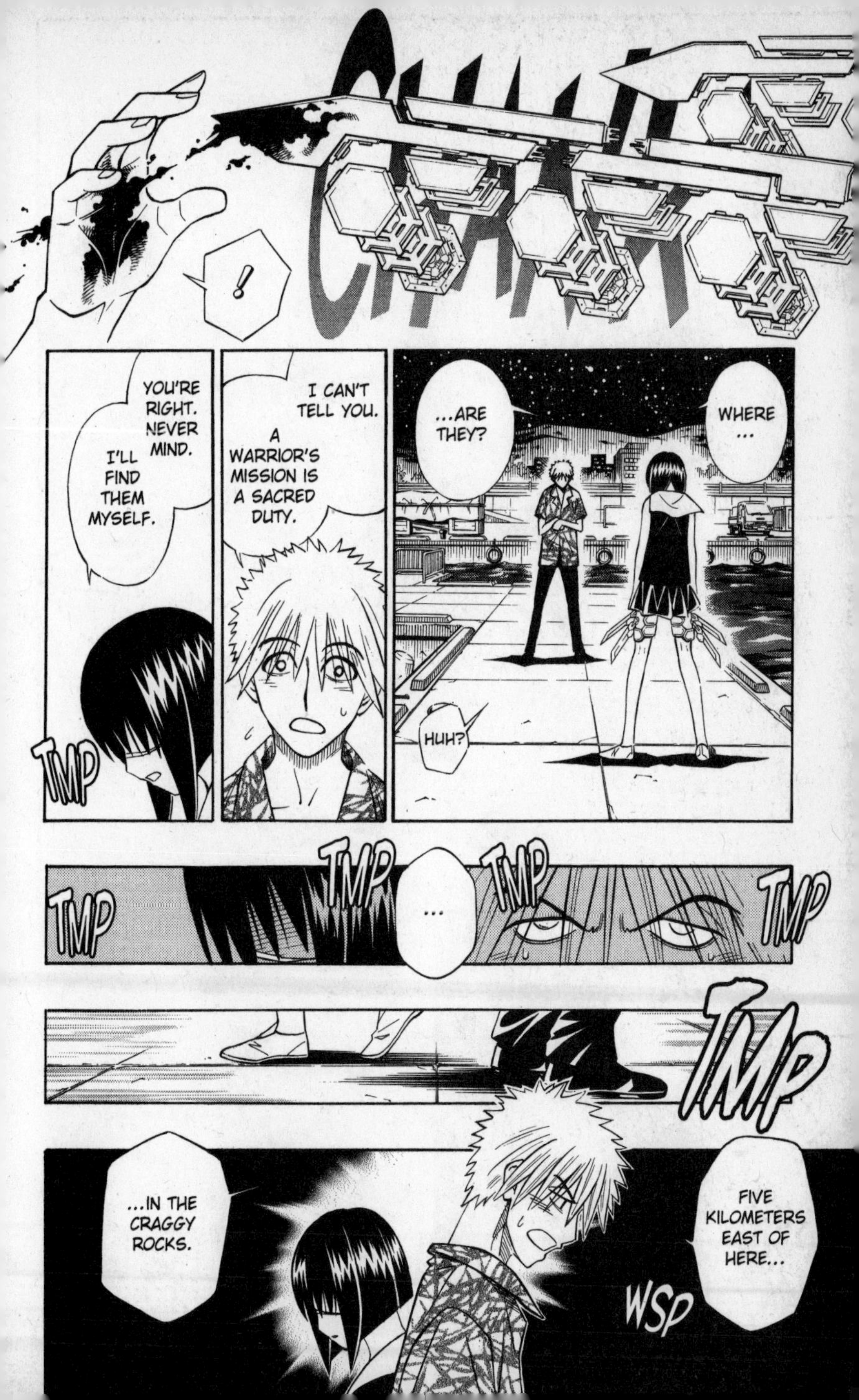
CHAK
!
WHERE...
...ARE THEY?
HUH?
I CAN'T TELL YOU.
A WARRIOR'S MISSION IS A SACRED DUTY.
YOU'RE RIGHT. NEVER MIND.
I'LL FIND THEM MYSELF.
TMP
TMP
TMP
...
TMP
TMP
FIVE KILOMETERS EAST OF HERE...
WSP
...IN THE CRAGGY ROCKS.

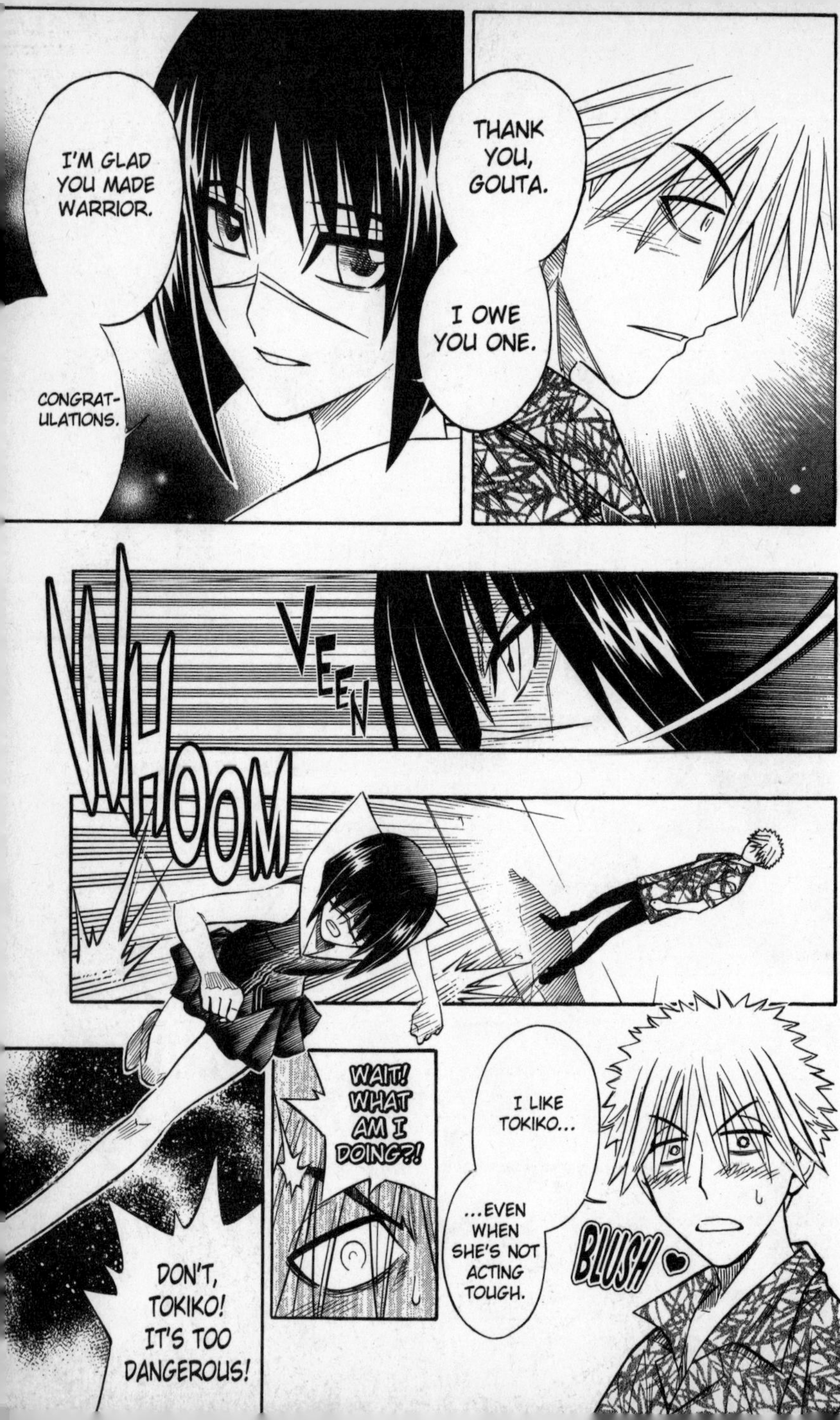
THANK YOU, GOUTA.
I OWE YOU ONE.
I'M GLAD YOU MADE WARRIOR.
CONGRAT-ULATIONS.
VEEN
WHOOM
I LIKE TOKIKO...
...EVEN WHEN SHE'S NOT ACTING TOUGH.
BLUSH
WAIT! WHAT AM I DOING?!
DON'T, TOKIKO! IT'S TOO DANGEROUS!

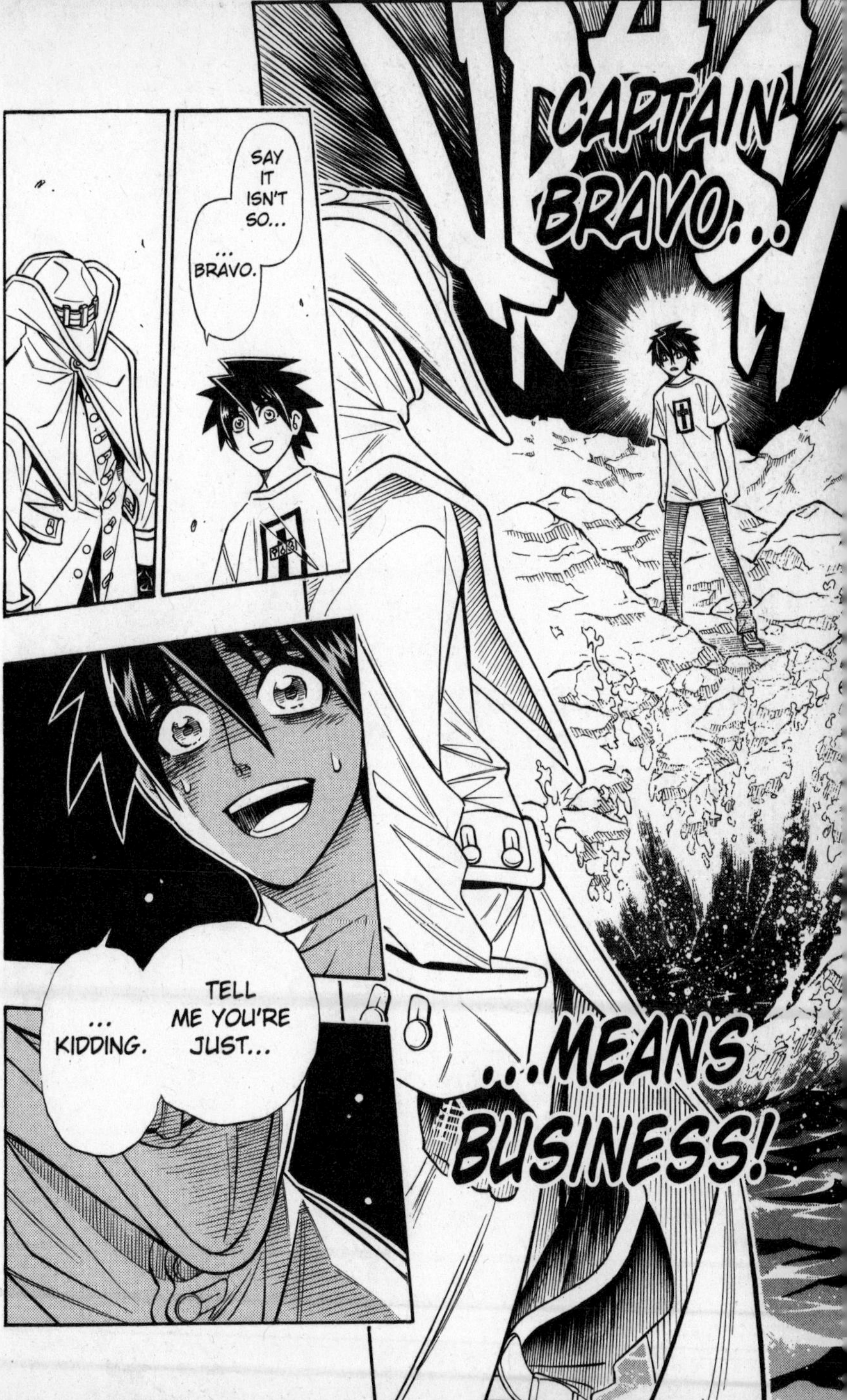
CAPTAIN BRAVO...
...MEANS BUSINESS!
SAY IT ISN'T SO... ...BRAVO.
TELL ME YOU'RE JUST...
...KIDDING.

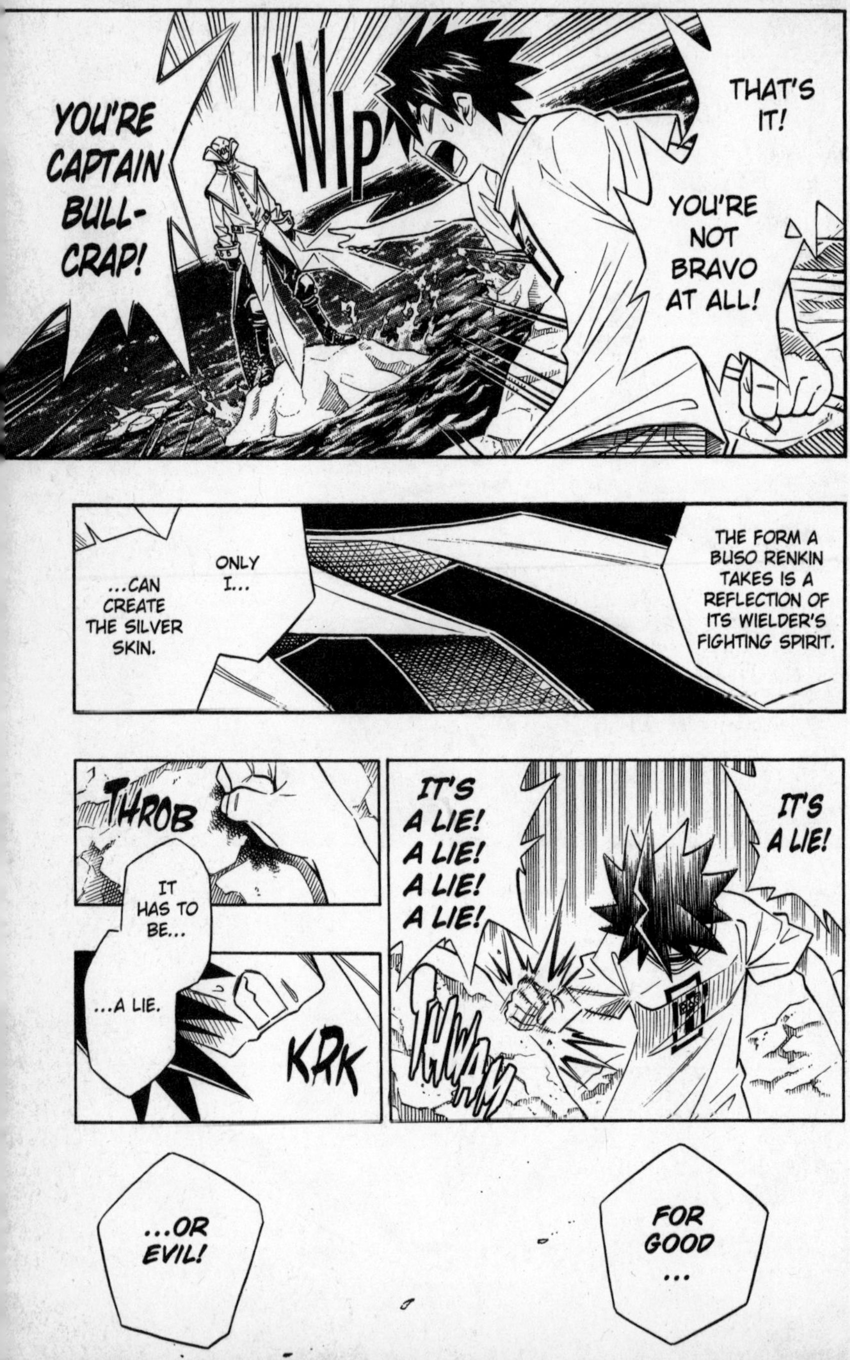
THAT'S IT!
YOU'RE NOT BRAVO AT ALL!
WIP
YOU'RE CAPTAIN BULL-CRAP!
THE FORM A BUSO RENKIN TAKES IS A REFLECTION OF ITS WIELDER'S FIGHTING SPIRIT.
ONLY I...
...CAN CREATE THE SILVER SKIN.
IT'S A LIE!
IT'S A LIE! A LIE! A LIE! A LIE!
THWAM
THROB
IT HAS TO BE...
...A LIE.
KRK
FOR GOOD...
...OR EVIL!

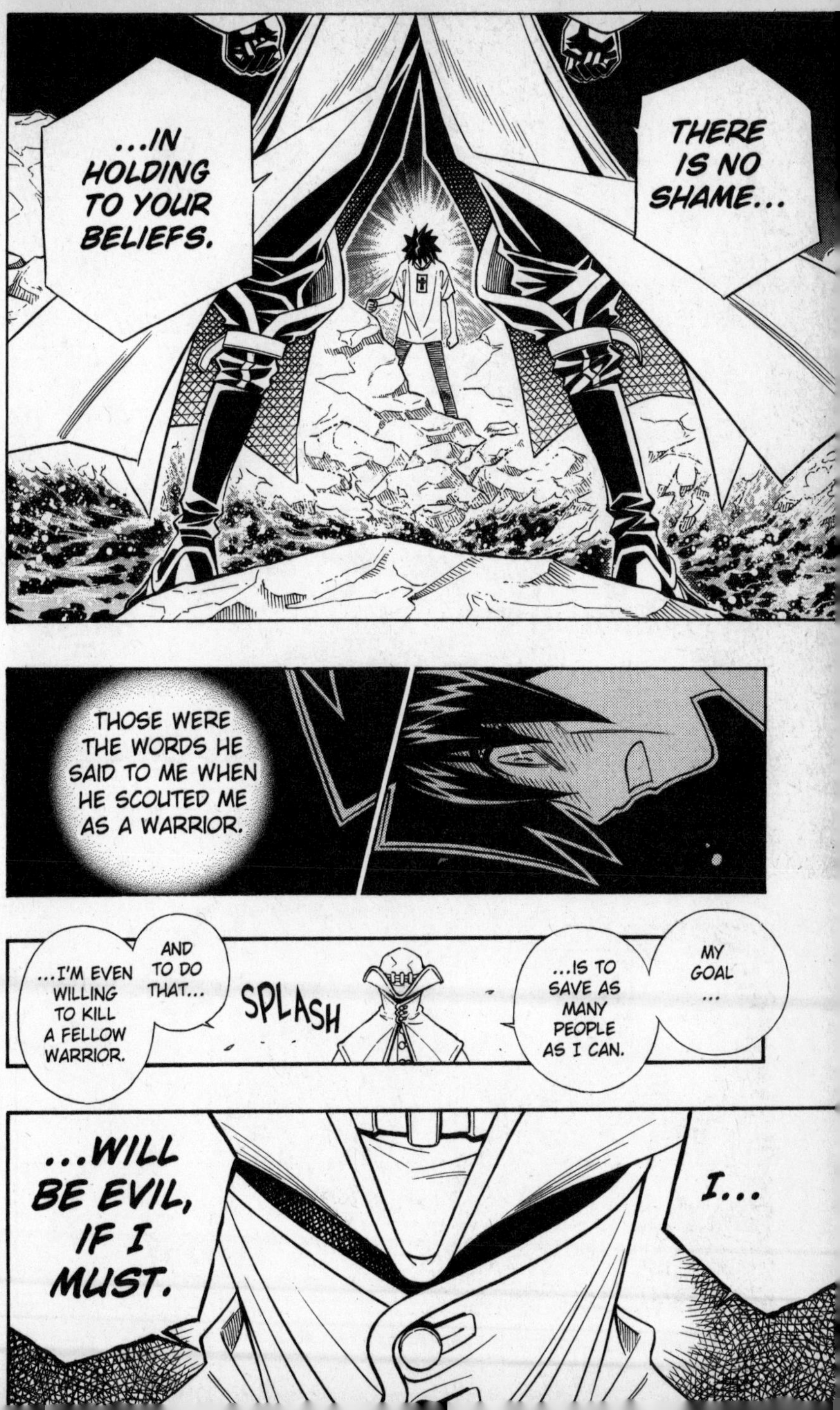
THERE IS NO SHAME...
...IN HOLDING TO YOUR BELIEFS.
THOSE WERE THE WORDS HE SAID TO ME WHEN HE SCOUTED ME AS A WARRIOR.
MY GOAL ...
...IS TO SAVE AS MANY PEOPLE AS I CAN.
SPLASH
AND TO DO THAT...
...I'M EVEN WILLING TO KILL A FELLOW WARRIOR.
I...
...WILL BE EVIL, IF I MUST.

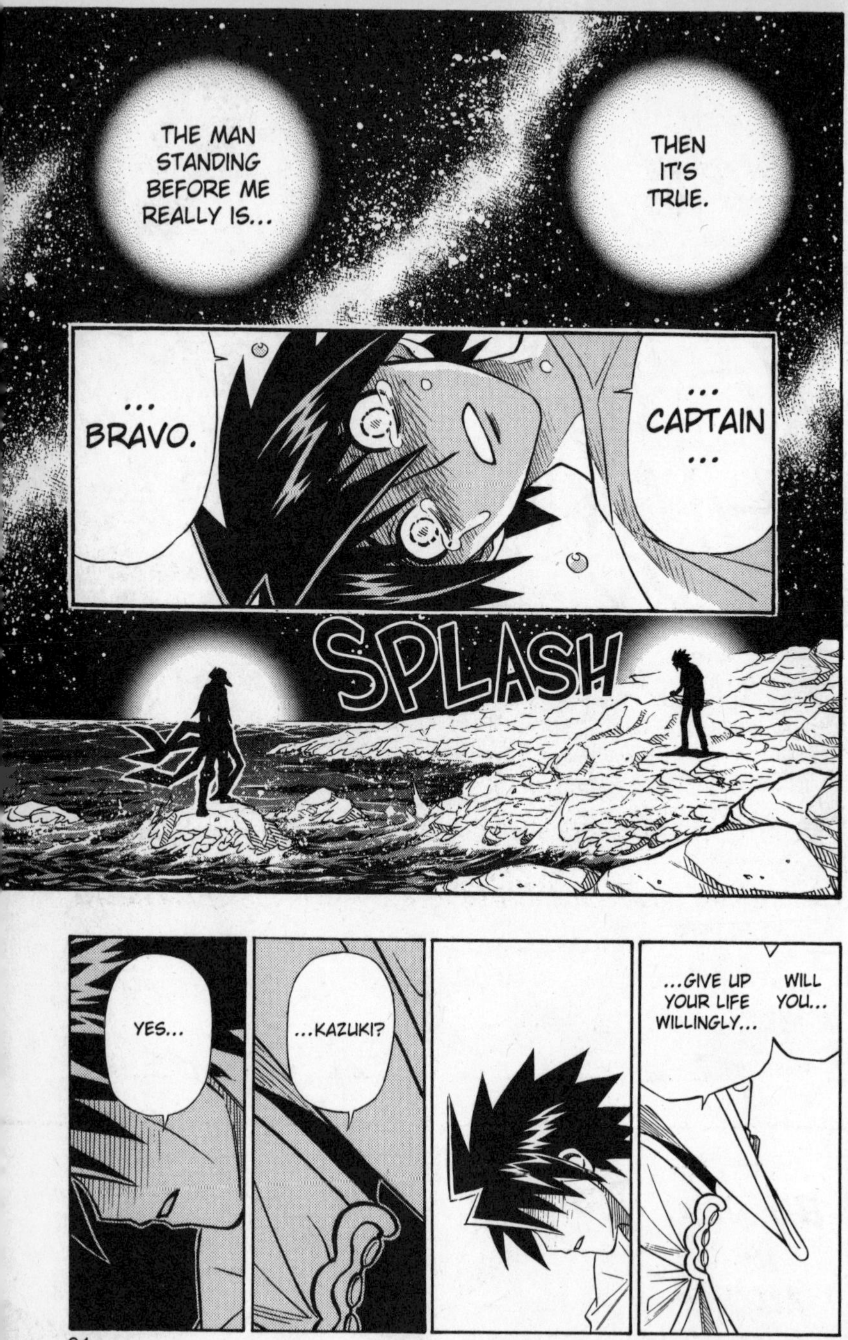
THEN IT'S TRUE.
THE MAN STANDING BEFORE ME REALLY IS...
... CAPTAIN ...
... BRAVO.
SPLASH
WILL YOU... ...GIVE UP YOUR LIFE WILLINGLY...
...KAZUKI?
YES...

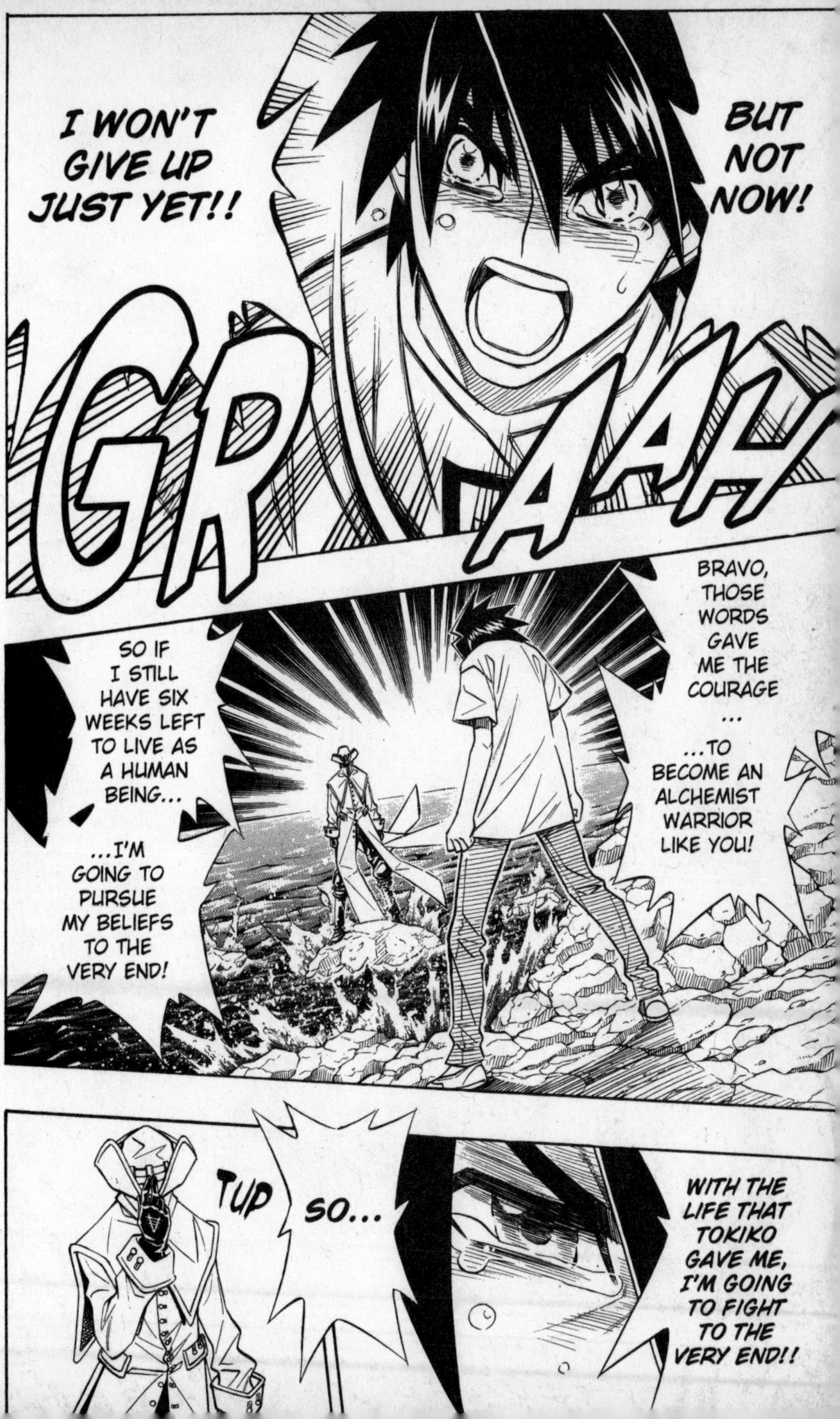
BUT NOT NOW!
I WON'T GIVE UP JUST YET!!
GRAAH
BRAVO, THOSE WORDS GAVE ME THE COURAGE...
...TO BECOME AN ALCHEMIST WARRIOR LIKE YOU!
SO IF I STILL HAVE SIX WEEKS LEFT TO LIVE AS A HUMAN BEING...
...I'M GOING TO PURSUE MY BELIEFS TO THE VERY END!
WITH THE LIFE THAT TOKIKO GAVE ME, I'M GOING TO FIGHT TO THE VERY END!!
SO...
TUP

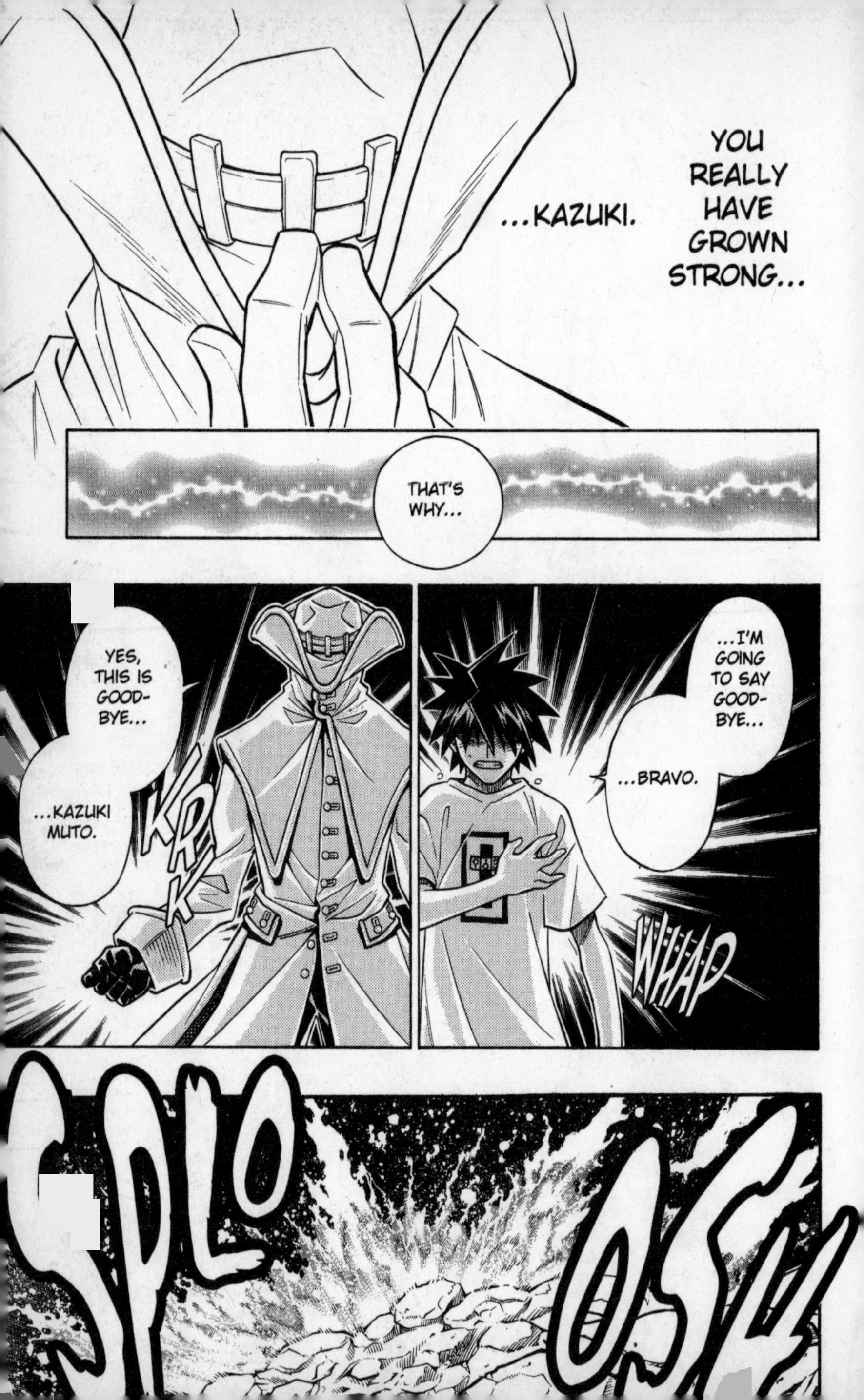
YOU REALLY HAVE GROWN STRONG...
...KAZUKI.
THAT'S WHY...
...I'M GOING TO SAY GOOD-BYE...
...BRAVO.
WHAP
YES, THIS IS GOOD-BYE...
...KAZUKI MUTO.
KRAK
SPLOOSH

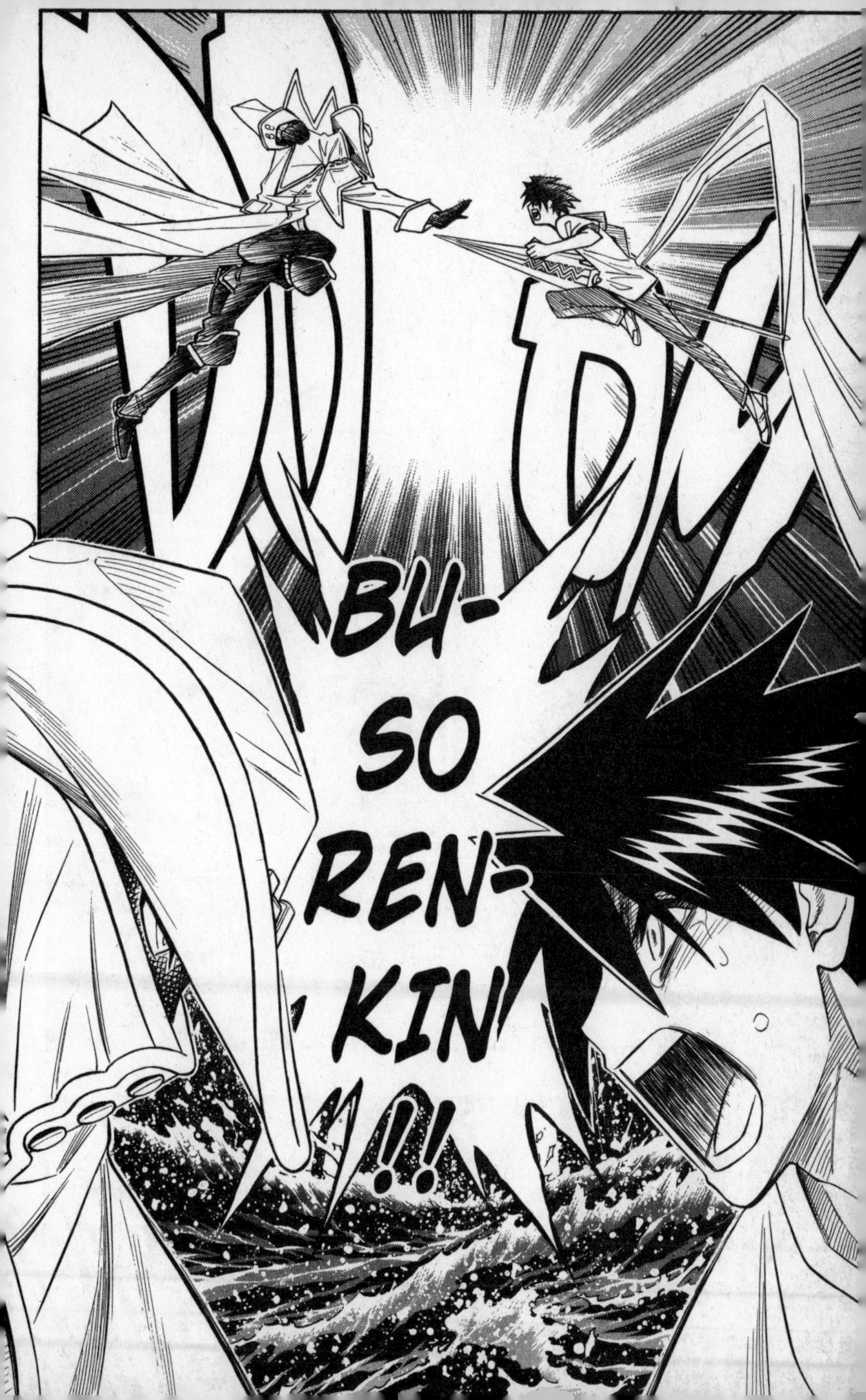
BU-
SO
REN-
KIN!!

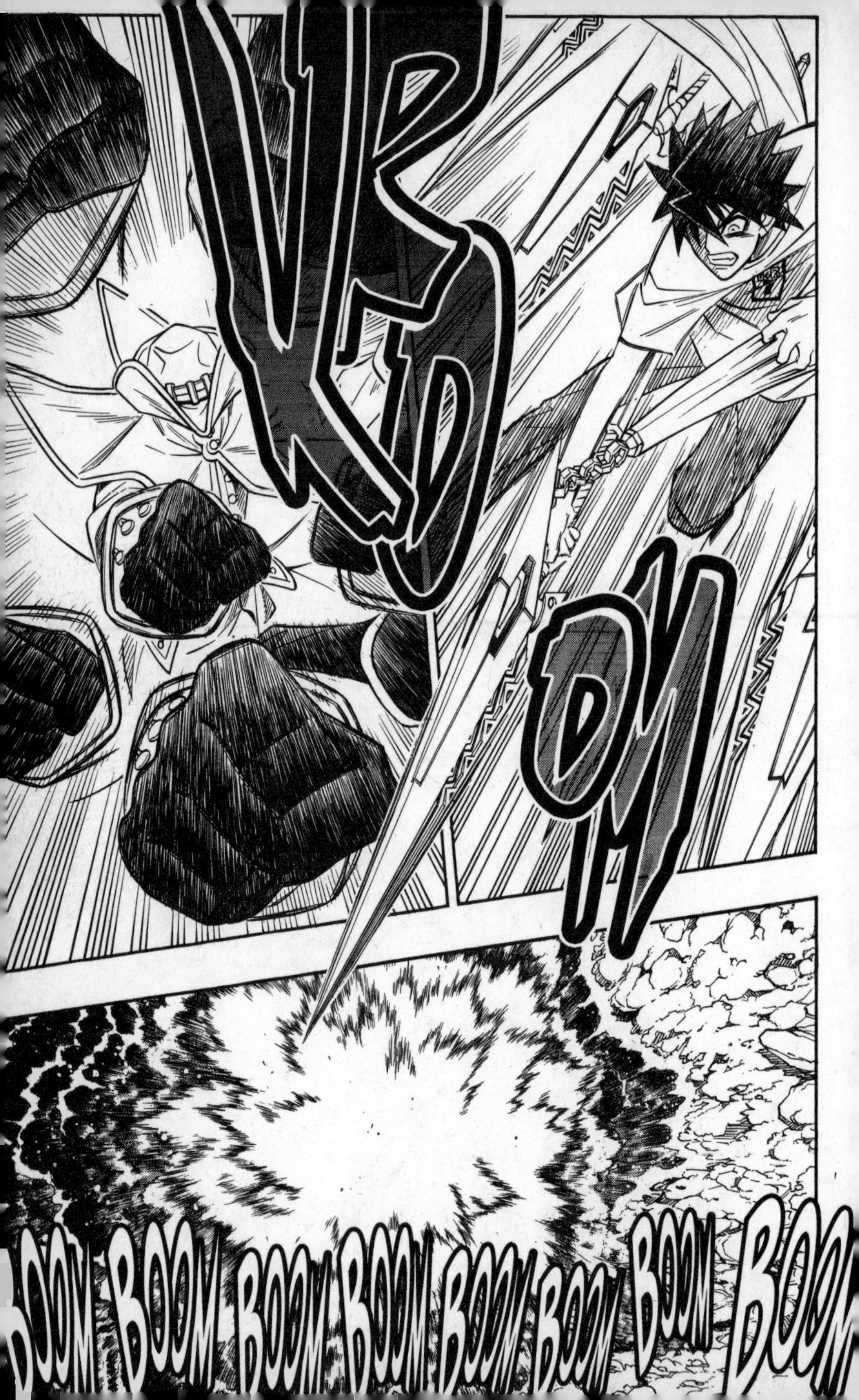
OOM BOOM BOOM BOOM BOOM BOOM BOOM BOO

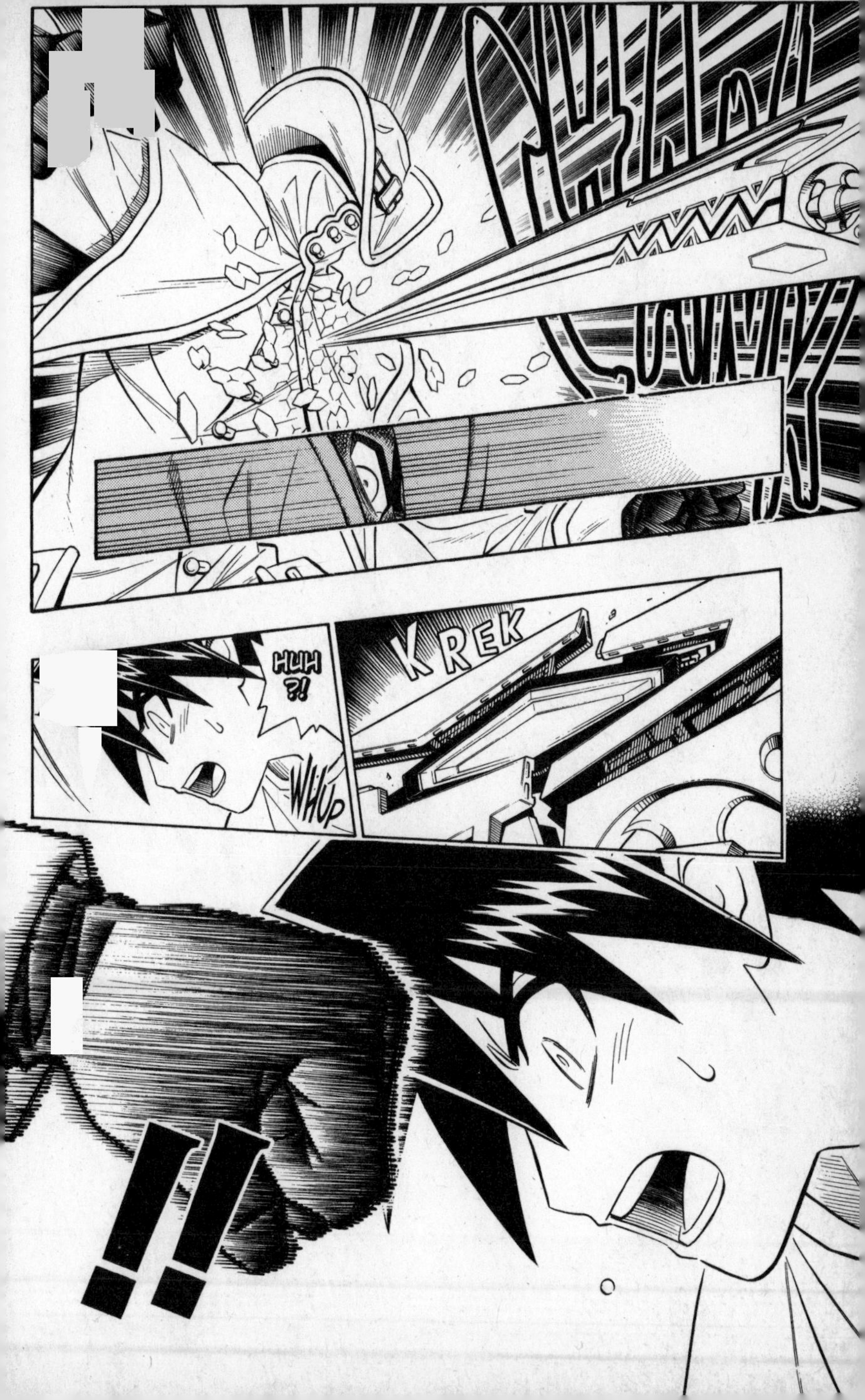
KREK
HUH ?!
WHUP
!!

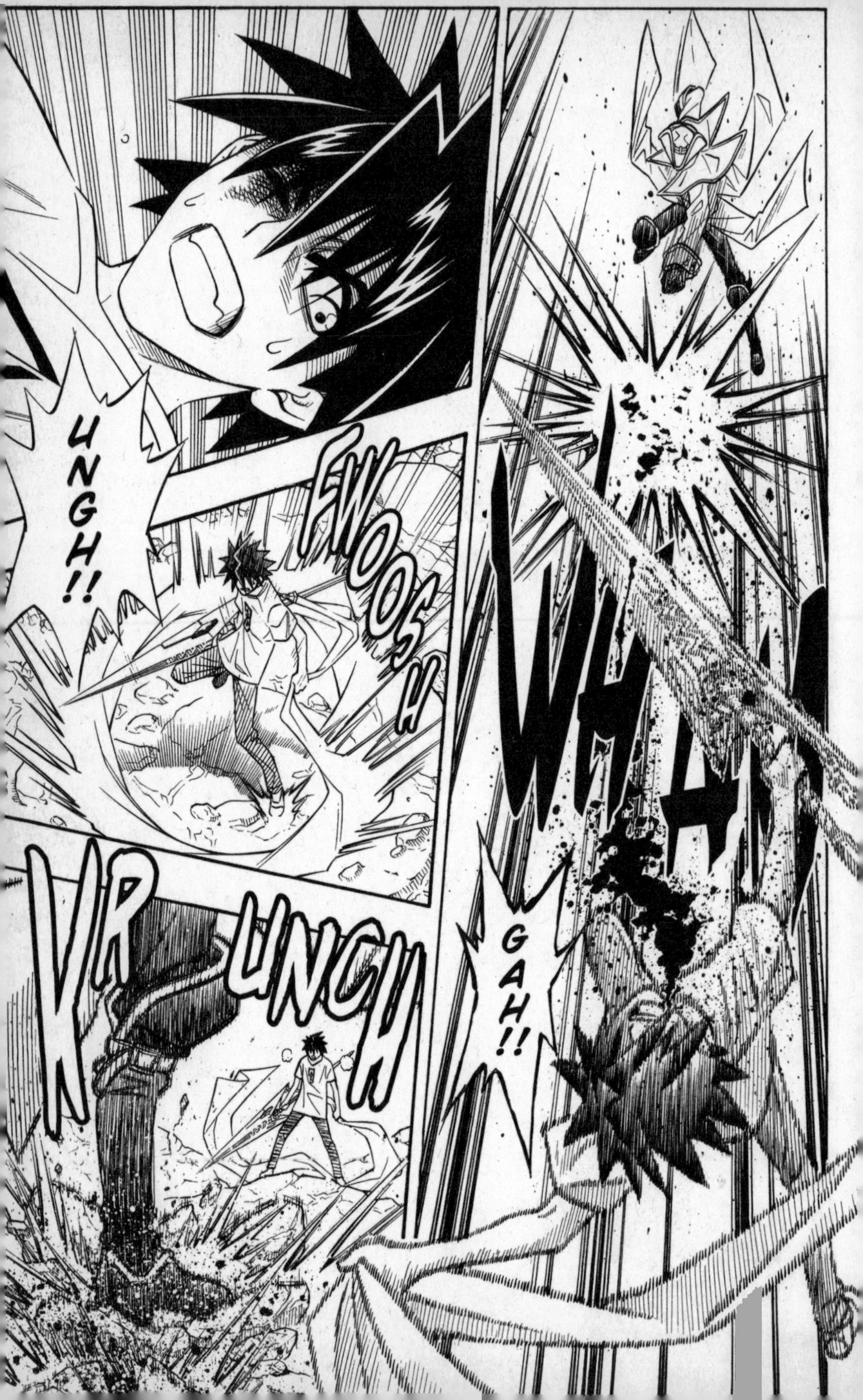
WHAM
GAH!!
UNGH!!
FWOOSH!!
KRUNCH

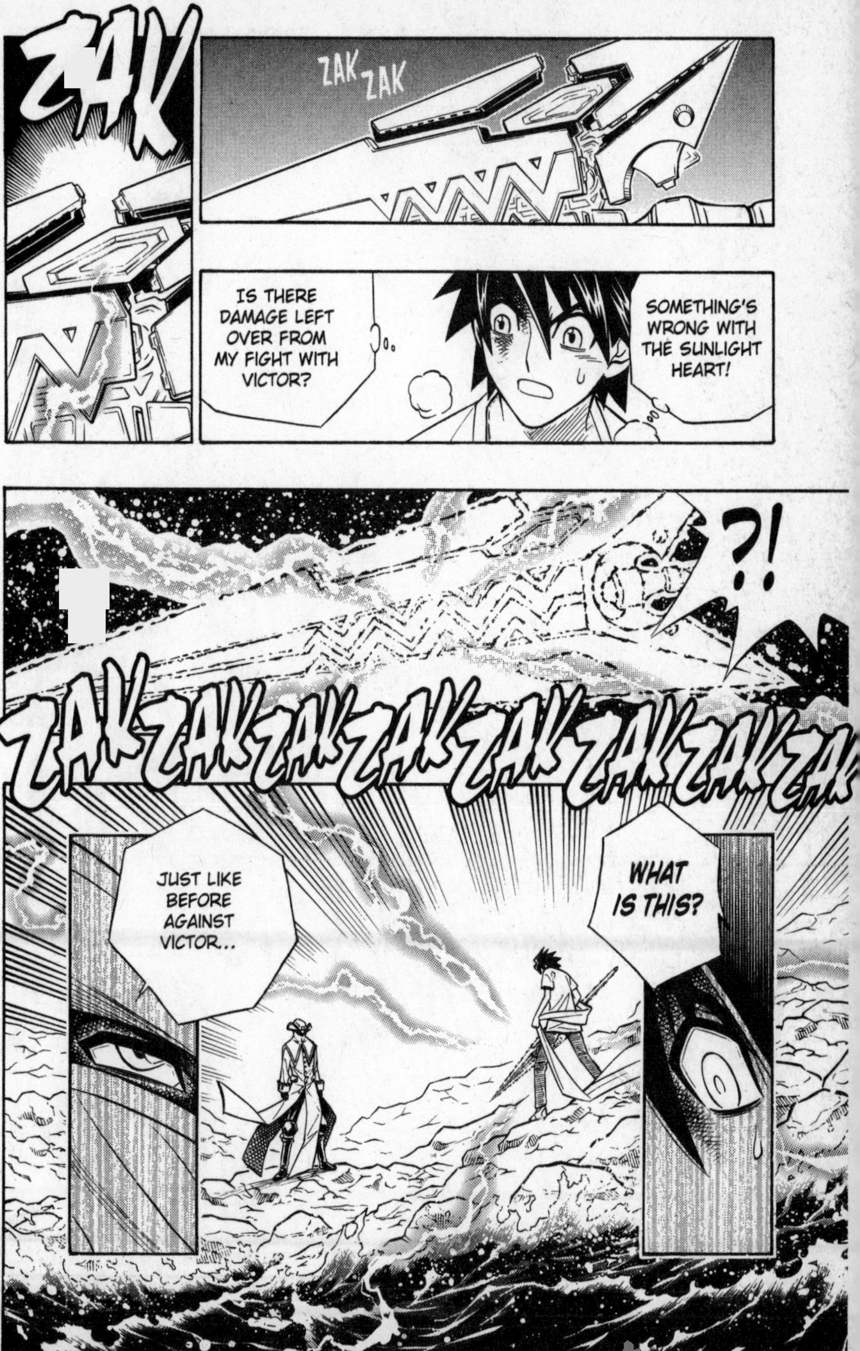

ZAK ZAK
SOMETHING'S WRONG WITH THE SUNLIGHT HEART!
IS THERE DAMAGE LEFT OVER FROM MY FIGHT WITH VICTOR?
ZAK
?!
ZAK ZAK ZAK ZAK ZAK ZAK ZAK ZAK
WHAT IS THIS?
JUST LIKE BEFORE AGAINST VICTOR...

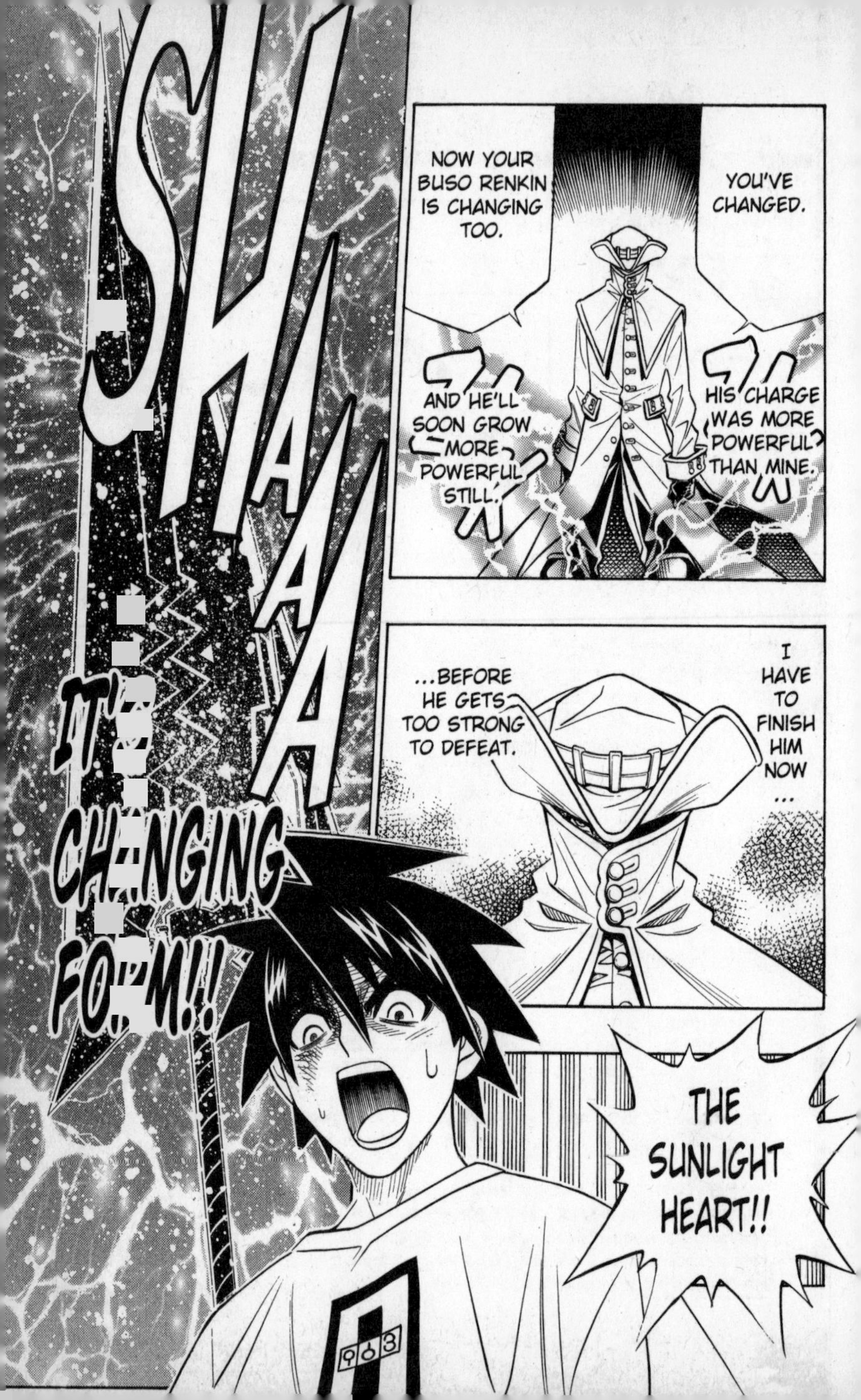
YOU'VE CHANGED.
NOW YOUR BUSO RENKIN IS CHANGING TOO.
HIS CHARGE WAS MORE POWERFUL THAN MINE.
AND HE'LL SOON GROW MORE POWERFUL STILL.
I HAVE TO FINISH HIM NOW...
...BEFORE HE GETS TOO STRONG TO DEFEAT.
THE SUNLIGHT HEART!!
SHAAAA
IT'S... CHANGING FORM!!

The Moon has many faces.

Buso Renkin File No. 8

サテライト 30

SATELLITE THIRTY

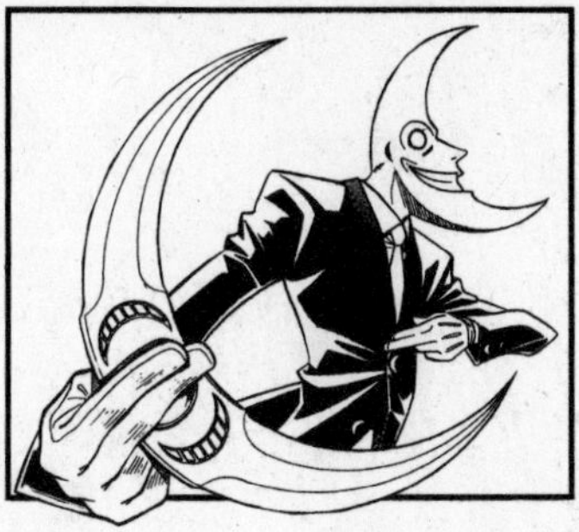

- ○Kakugane Serial Number: XXX (30)
- ○Creator: Moonface
- ○Form: Moon Fang
- ○Main Color: Silver and Yellow
- ○Special Abilities: · It can split its creator into as many as 30 bodies that can fight as a unit.
- ○Special Traits: · Each of the bodies is the same as the original. If even one remains, it can be divided into 30 bodies again. However, this requires a huge amount of energy so only a Homunculus with its nearly immortal body can use this weapon to its full potential.
  - · Because it has only one consciousness, complex combo attacks become more difficult with each additional body.
  - · There is no symbolism behind the different heads, but different aspects of Moonface's personality are reflected in his duplicates.

○Author's Notes:

- · The idea for this weapon came from Agent Smith in *Matrix Reloaded*. When I first saw it, I thought to myself, "This is a joke, right?" So I had to use it myself.
- · I wasn't able to find the names for the various phases of moon when I first did that chapter. Thankfully, my editor found them for me in time for publication.
- · The Moon Fang refers to a type of blade found on several Chinese weapons and is not the proper name of a weapon. The houtengeki, goshukou, and shiboenouetsu all have moon-shaped blades.
- · It wasn't easy to draw 30 Moonfaces. I really didn't want to use a copy machine, but it was so much work....

SATELLITE THIRTY

CHAPTER 51: CRIMSON OCEAN

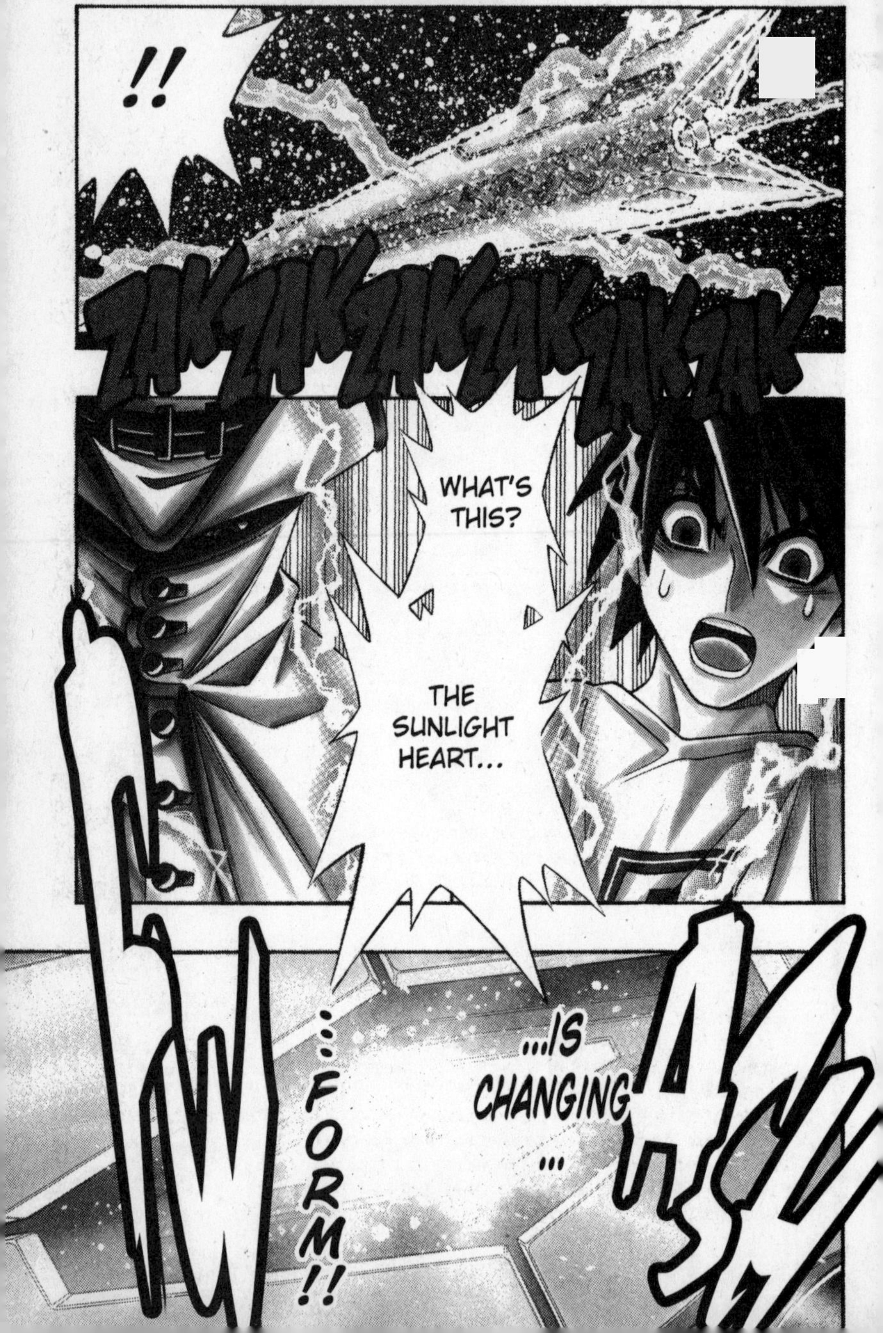
!!
ZAK ZAK ZAK ZAK ZAK ZAK
WHAT'S THIS?
THE SUNLIGHT HEART...
...IS CHANGING...
...FORM!!

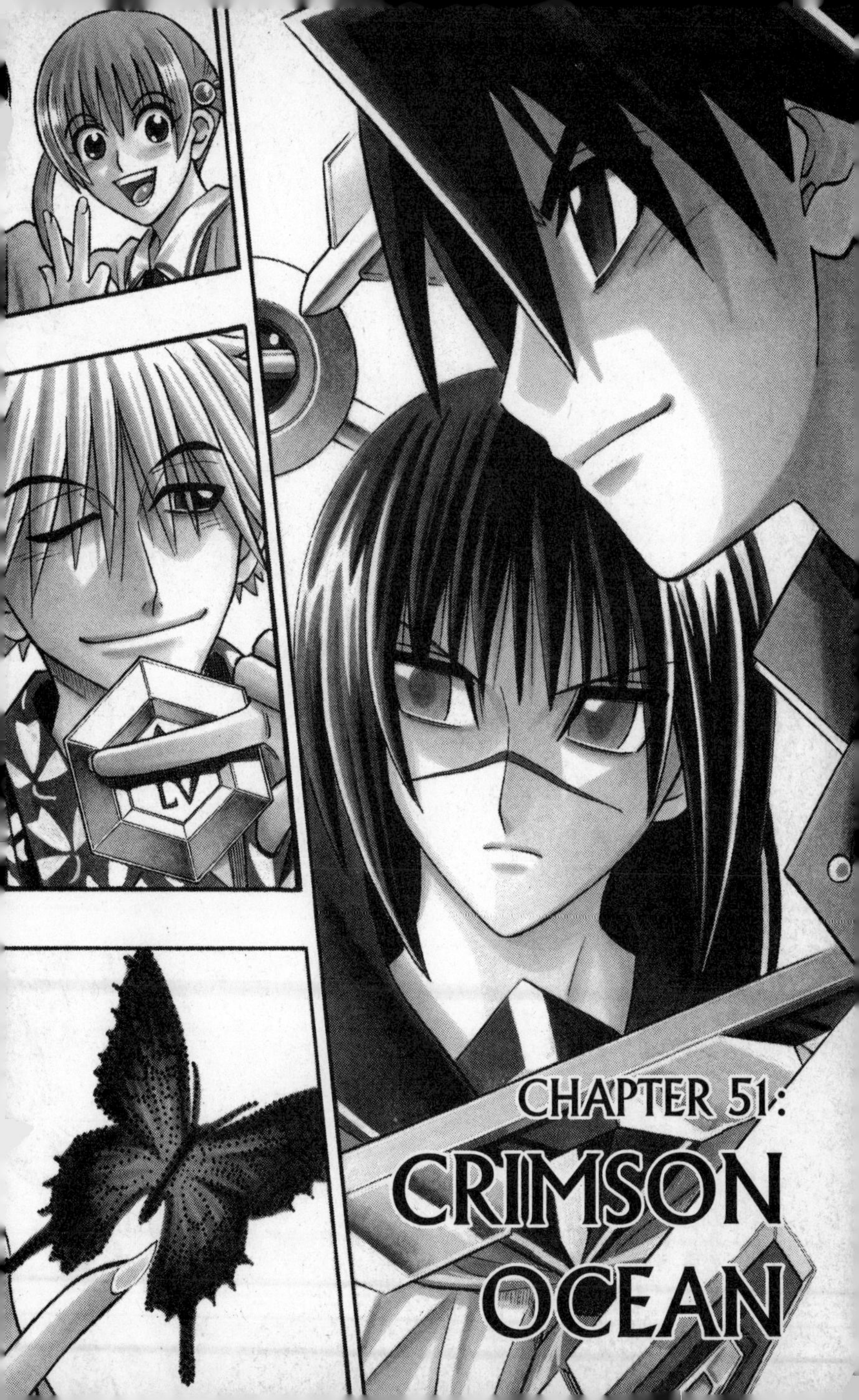
CHAPTER 51:
CRIMSON OCEAN

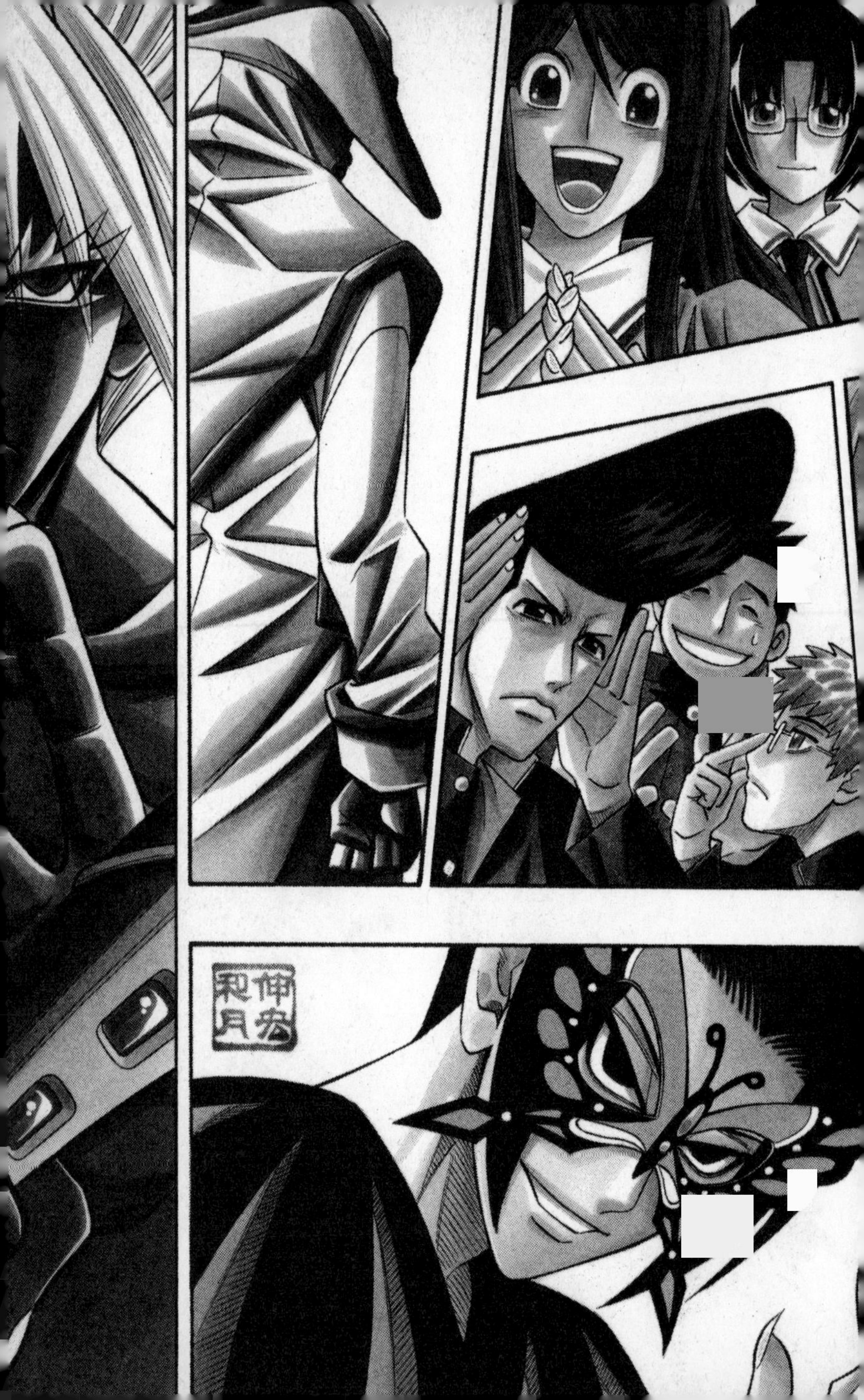
伸宏
和月

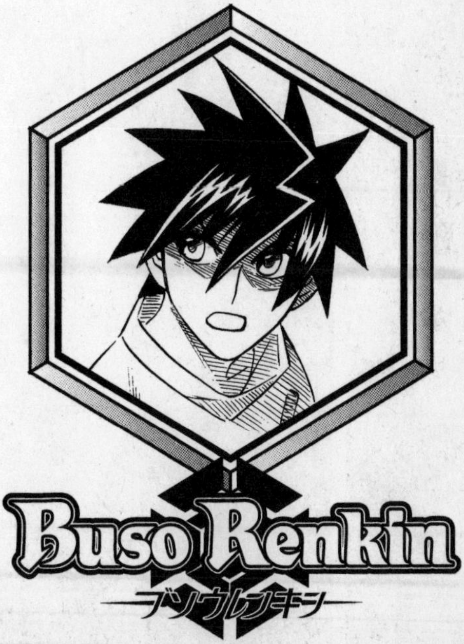
Buso Renkin
ブソウレンキン

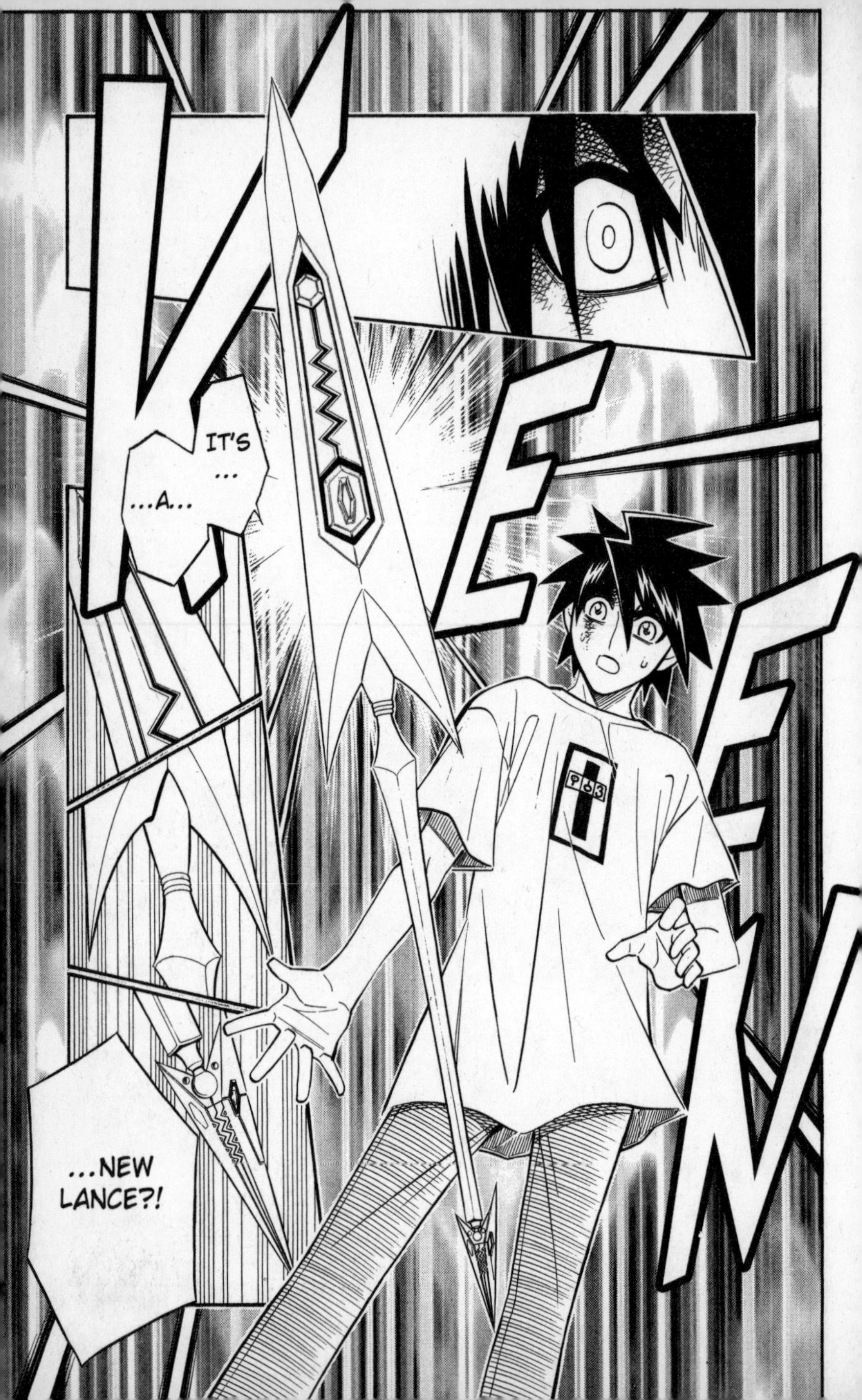
IT'S ... ...A...
...NEW LANCE?!

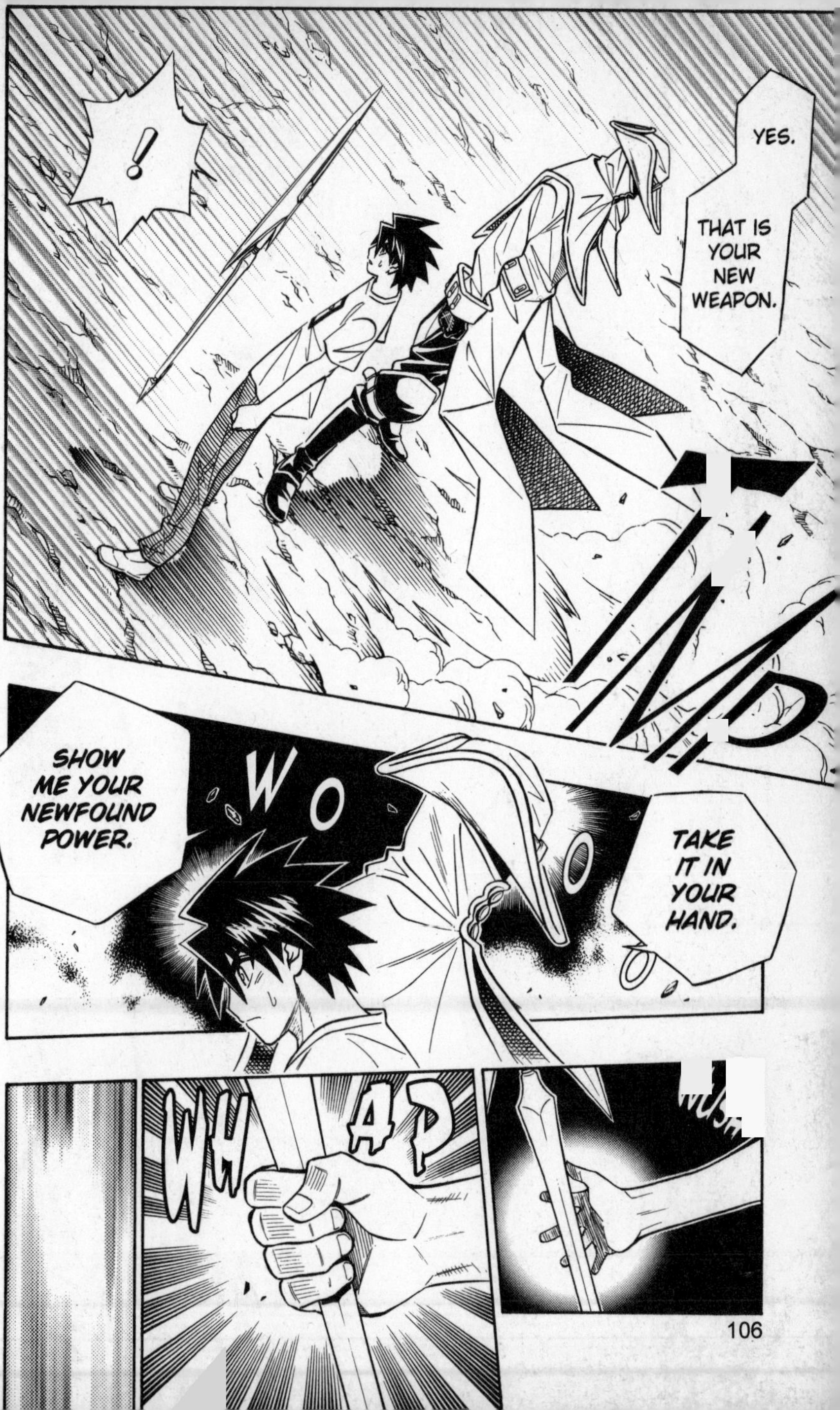
YES.
THAT IS YOUR NEW WEAPON.
!
TAKE IT IN YOUR HAND.
SHOW ME YOUR NEWFOUND POWER.
WHAP

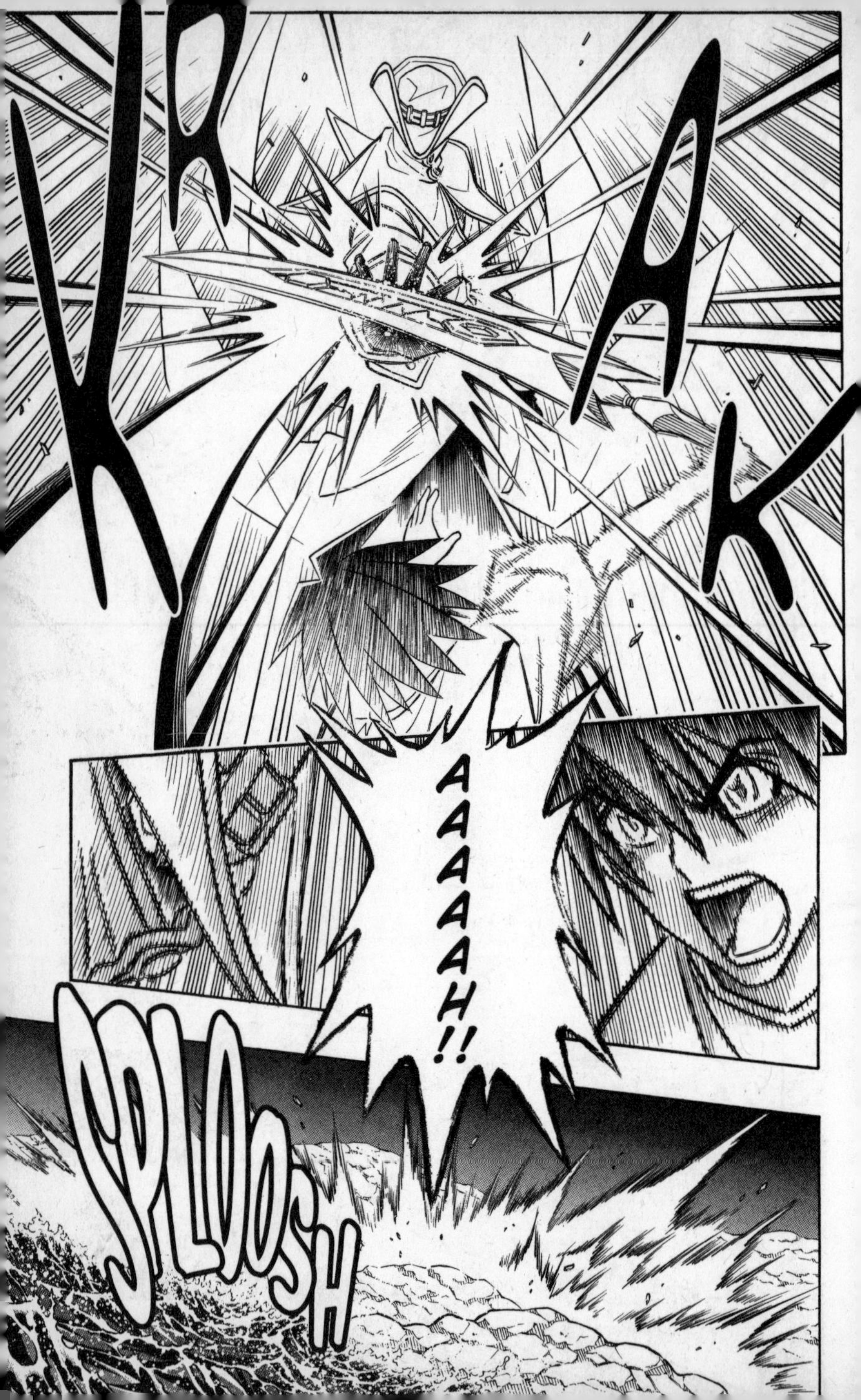
KRAAK
AAAAAAH!!
SPLOOSH

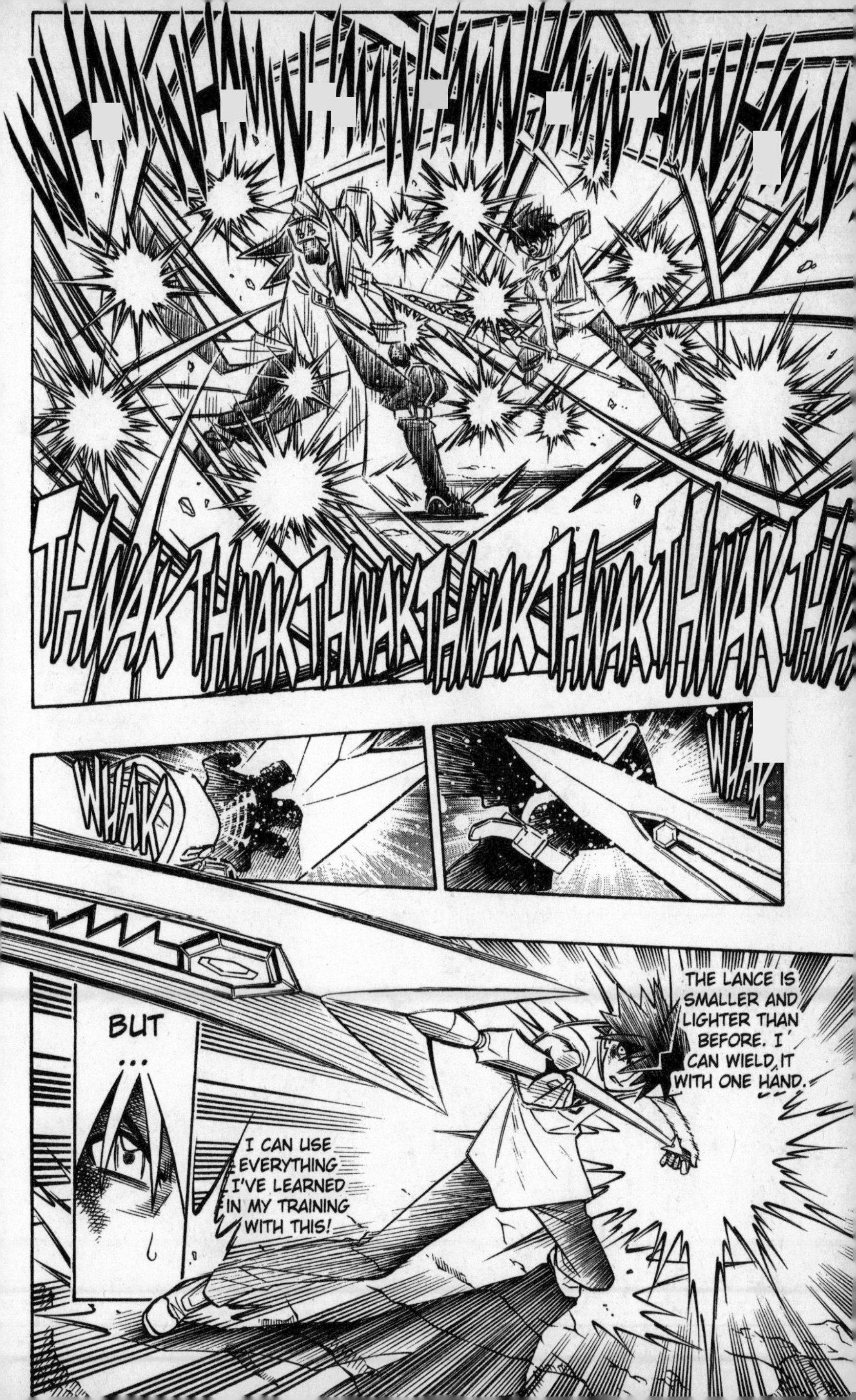
THWAK THWAK THWAK THWAK THWAK
WHAK
WHAK
THE LANCE IS SMALLER AND LIGHTER THAN BEFORE. I CAN WIELD IT WITH ONE HAND.
I CAN USE EVERYTHING I'VE LEARNED IN MY TRAINING WITH THIS!
BUT ...

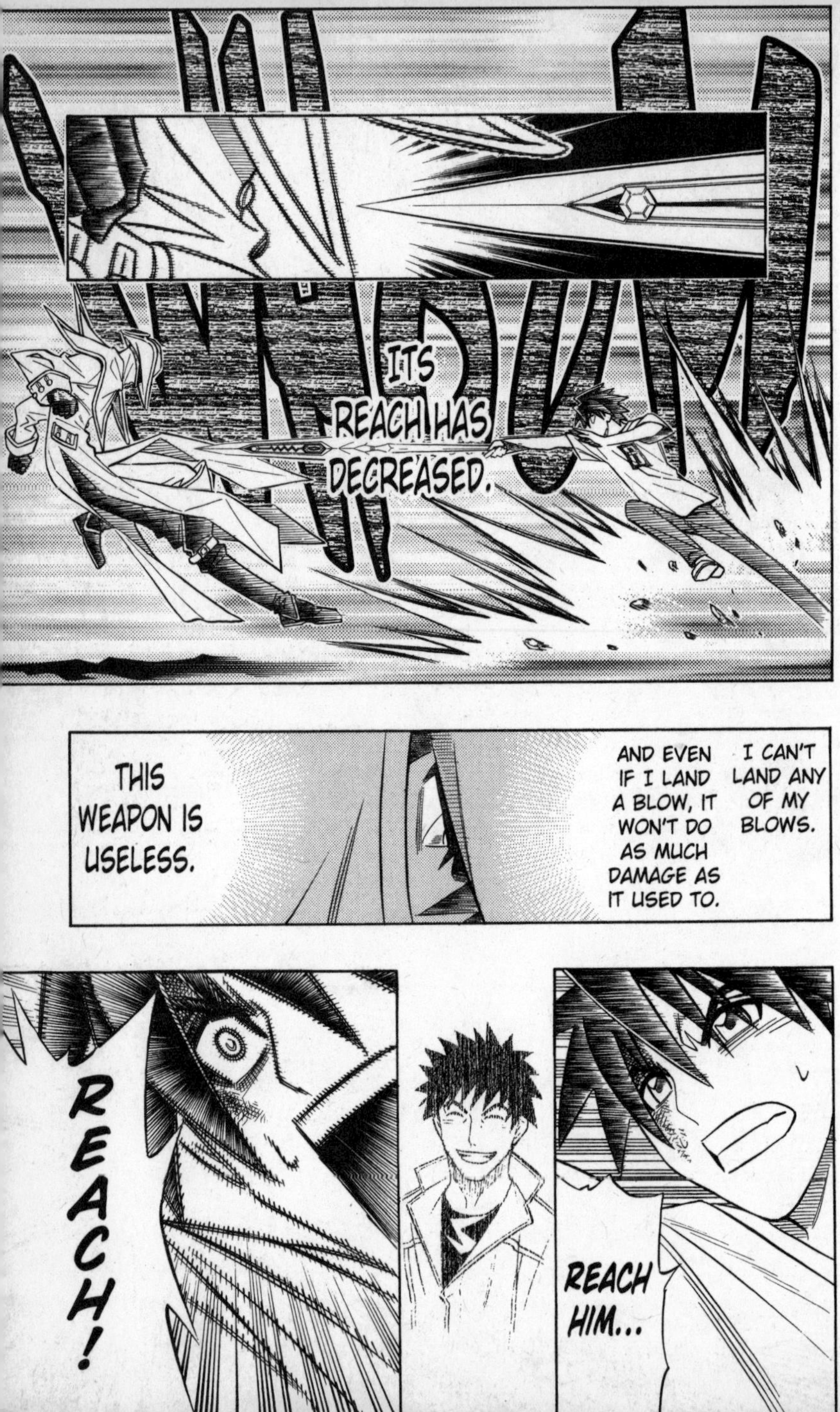
ITS REACH HAS DECREASED.
I CAN'T LAND ANY OF MY BLOWS.
AND EVEN IF I LAND A BLOW, IT WON'T DO AS MUCH DAMAGE AS IT USED TO.
THIS WEAPON IS USELESS.
REACH HIM...
REACH!

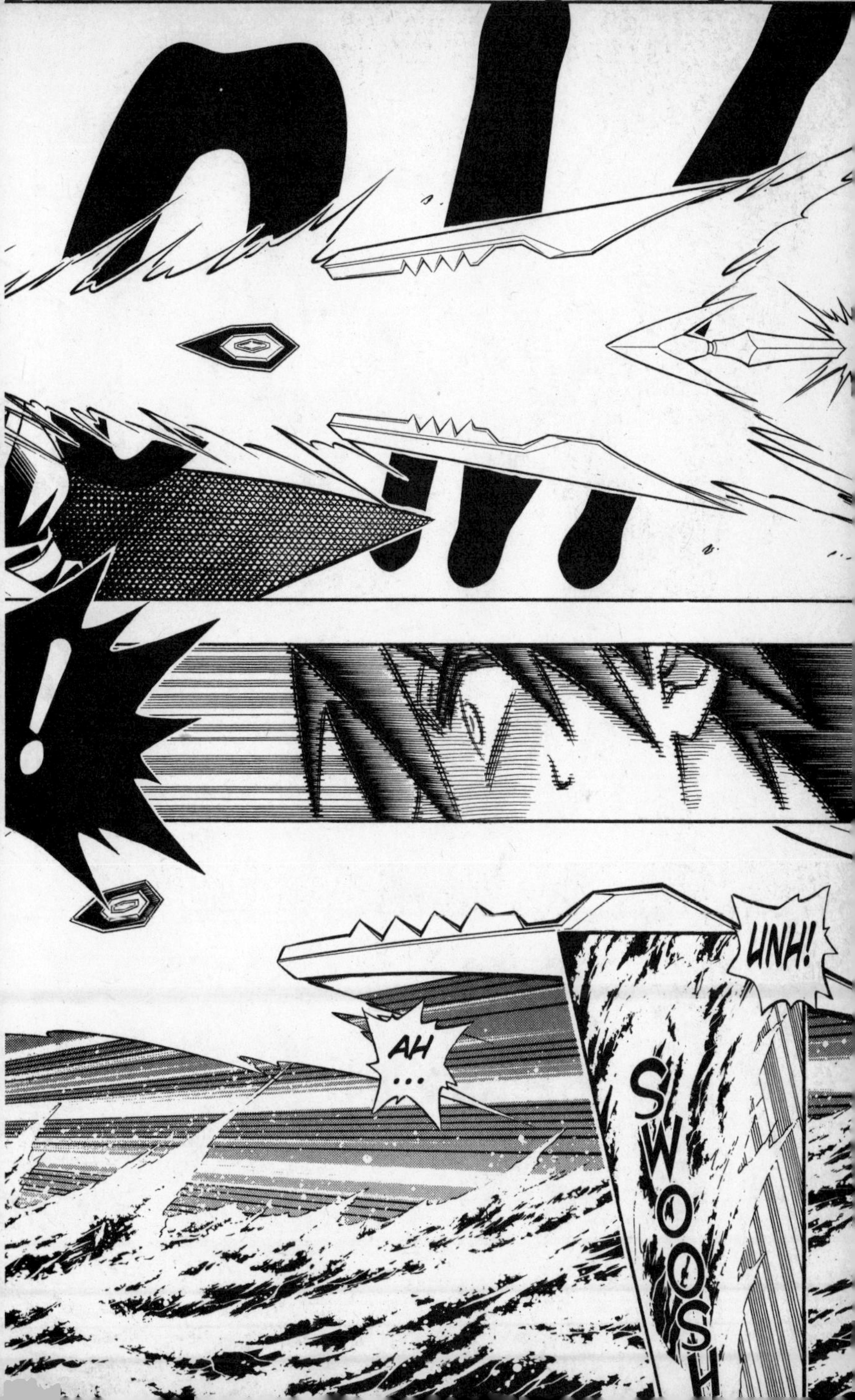
!
UNH!
AH ...
SWOOSH

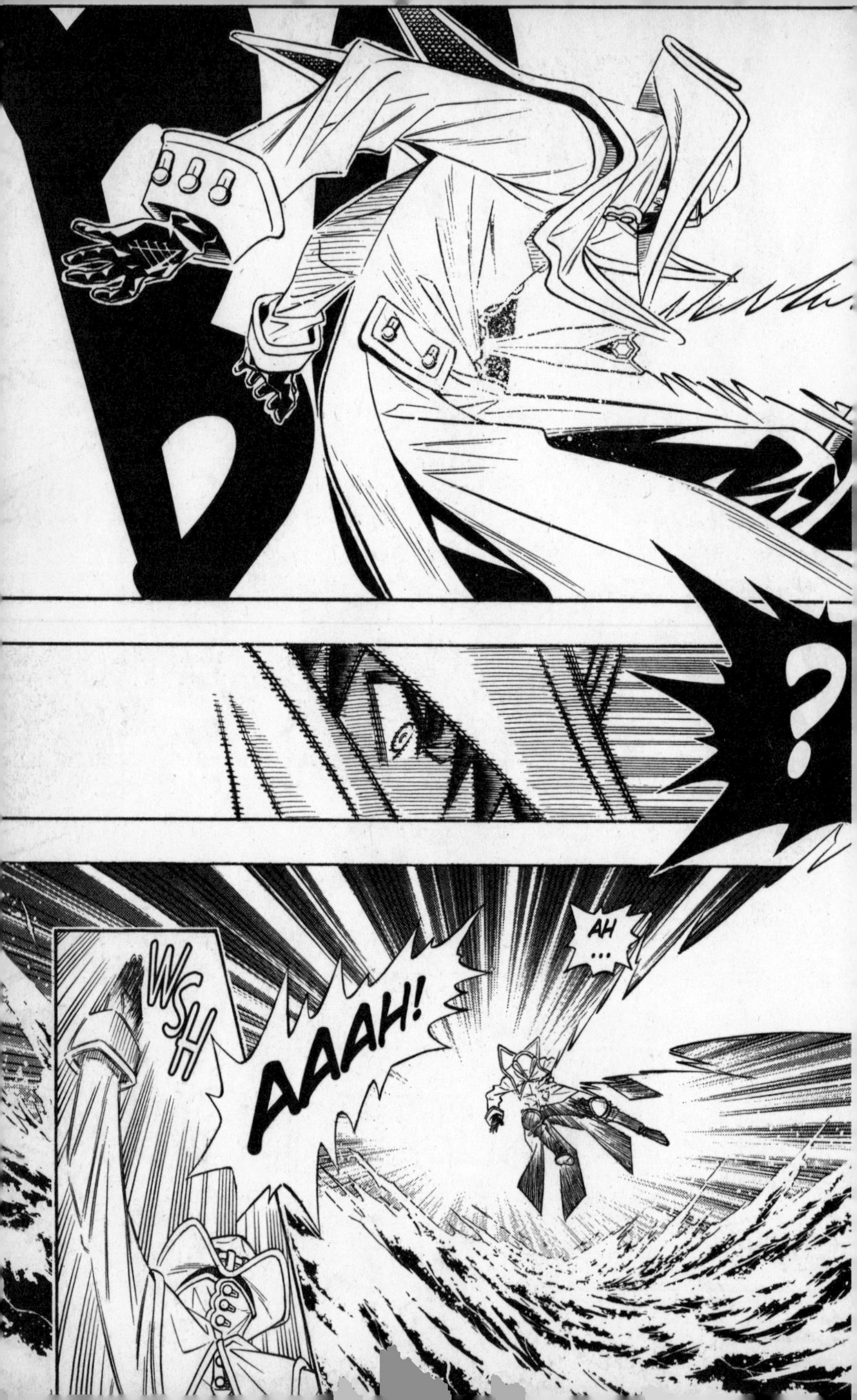
?
AH ...
AAAH!
WSH

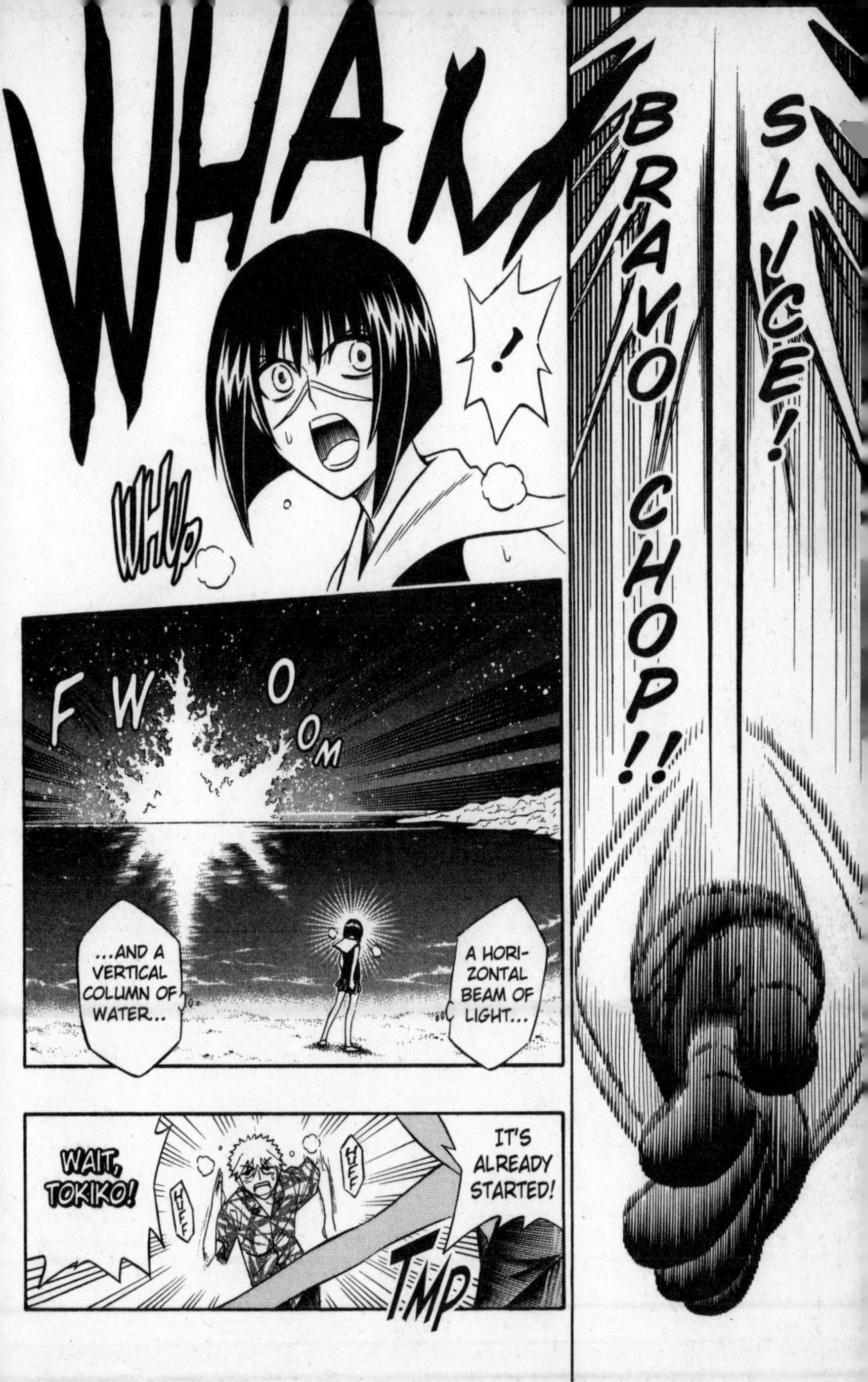
SLICE!
BRAVO CHOP!!
WHAM
!
WHUP
FWOOM
A HORI-ZONTAL BEAM OF LIGHT...
...AND A VERTICAL COLUMN OF WATER...
IT'S ALREADY STARTED!
HUFF
HUFF
TMP
WAIT, TOKIKO!

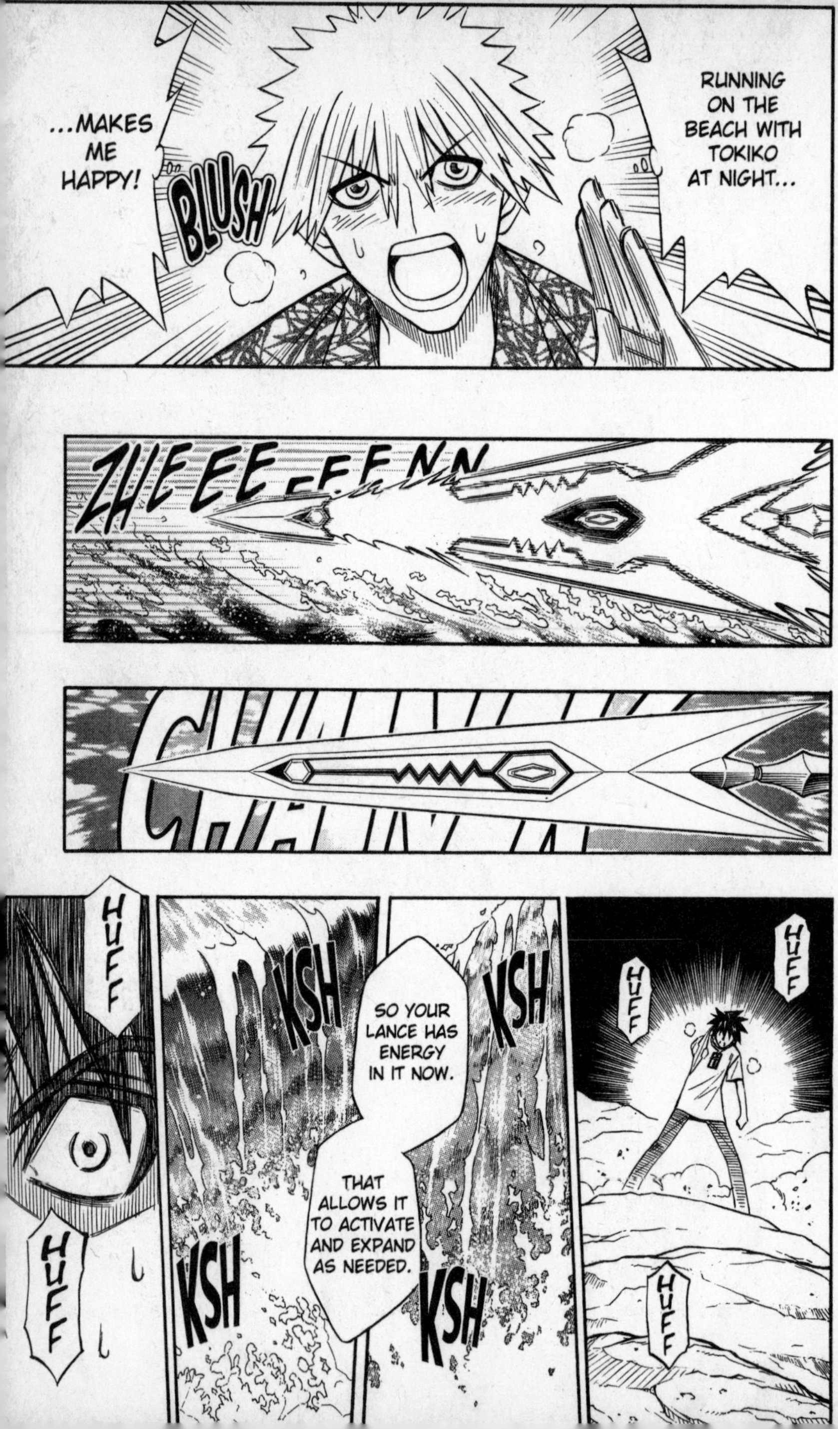
RUNNING ON THE BEACH WITH TOKIKO AT NIGHT...
...MAKES ME HAPPY!
BLUSH
ZHEEEEEENN
HUFF
HUFF
HUFF
KSH
KSH
SO YOUR LANCE HAS ENERGY IN IT NOW.
THAT ALLOWS IT TO ACTIVATE AND EXPAND AS NEEDED.
KSH
KSH
HUFF
HUFF

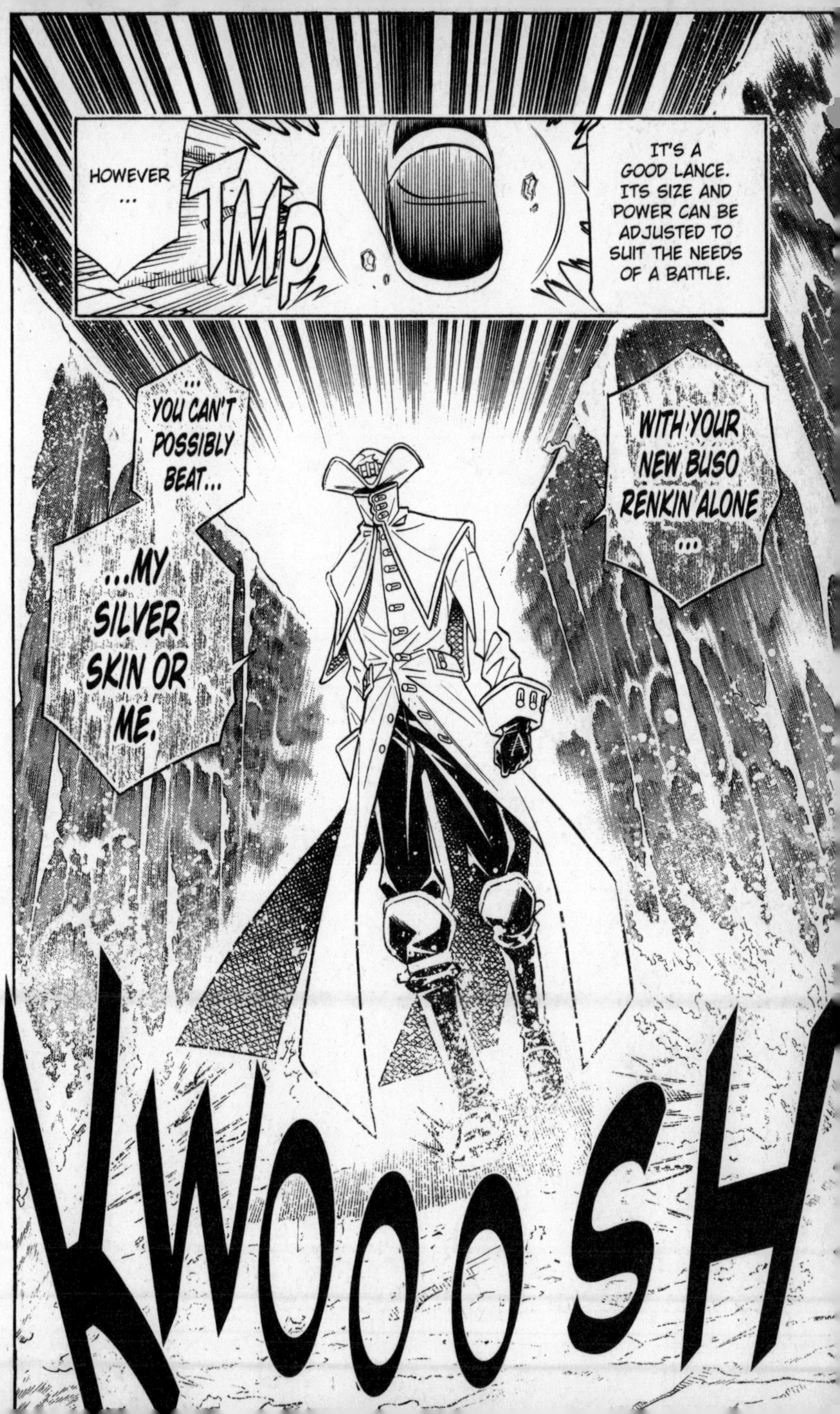
IT'S A GOOD LANCE. ITS SIZE AND POWER CAN BE ADJUSTED TO SUIT THE NEEDS OF A BATTLE.
TMP
HOWEVER ...
WITH YOUR NEW BUSO RENKIN ALONE ...
... YOU CAN'T POSSIBLY BEAT...
...MY SILVER SKIN OR ME.
KWOOOSH

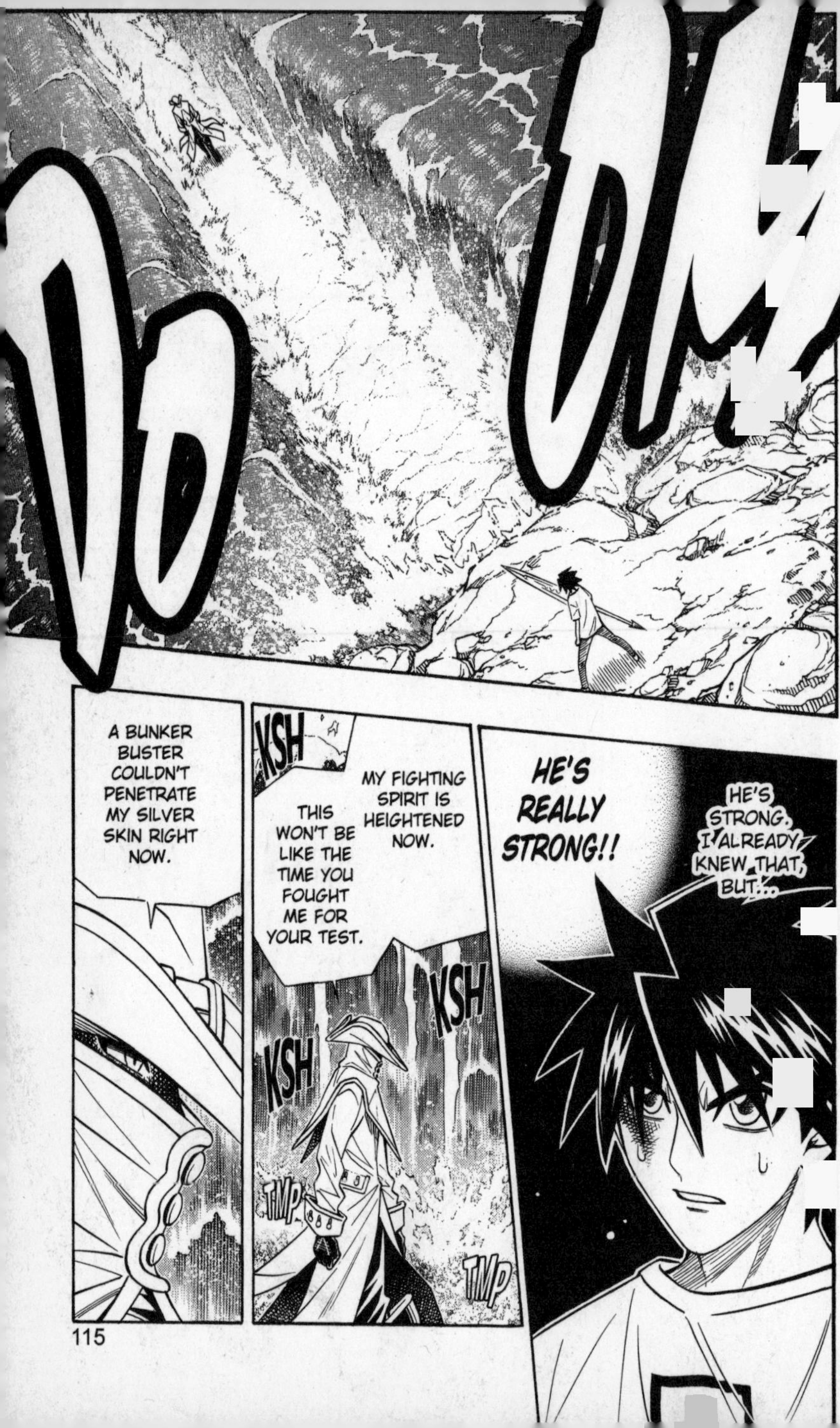
HE'S STRONG. I ALREADY KNEW THAT, BUT...
HE'S REALLY STRONG!!
KSH
MY FIGHTING SPIRIT IS HEIGHTENED NOW.
THIS WON'T BE LIKE THE TIME YOU FOUGHT ME FOR YOUR TEST.
KSH
KSH
TMP
TMP
A BUNKER BUSTER COULDN'T PENETRATE MY SILVER SKIN RIGHT NOW.

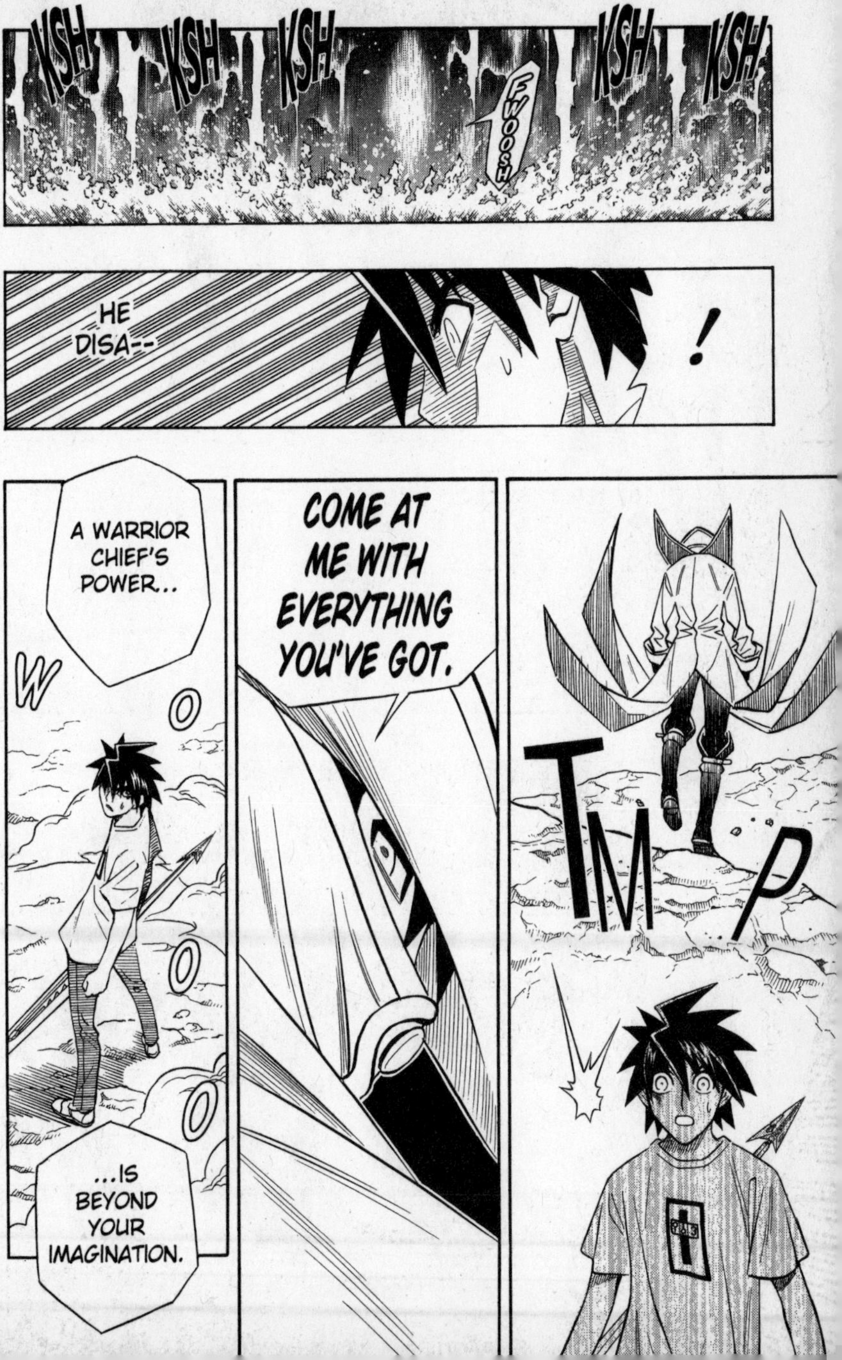
KSH
KSH
FWOOSH
KSH
KSH
KSH
!
HE DISA--
TMP
COME AT ME WITH EVERYTHING YOU'VE GOT.
A WARRIOR CHIEF'S POWER...
WOOOO
...IS BEYOND YOUR IMAGINATION.

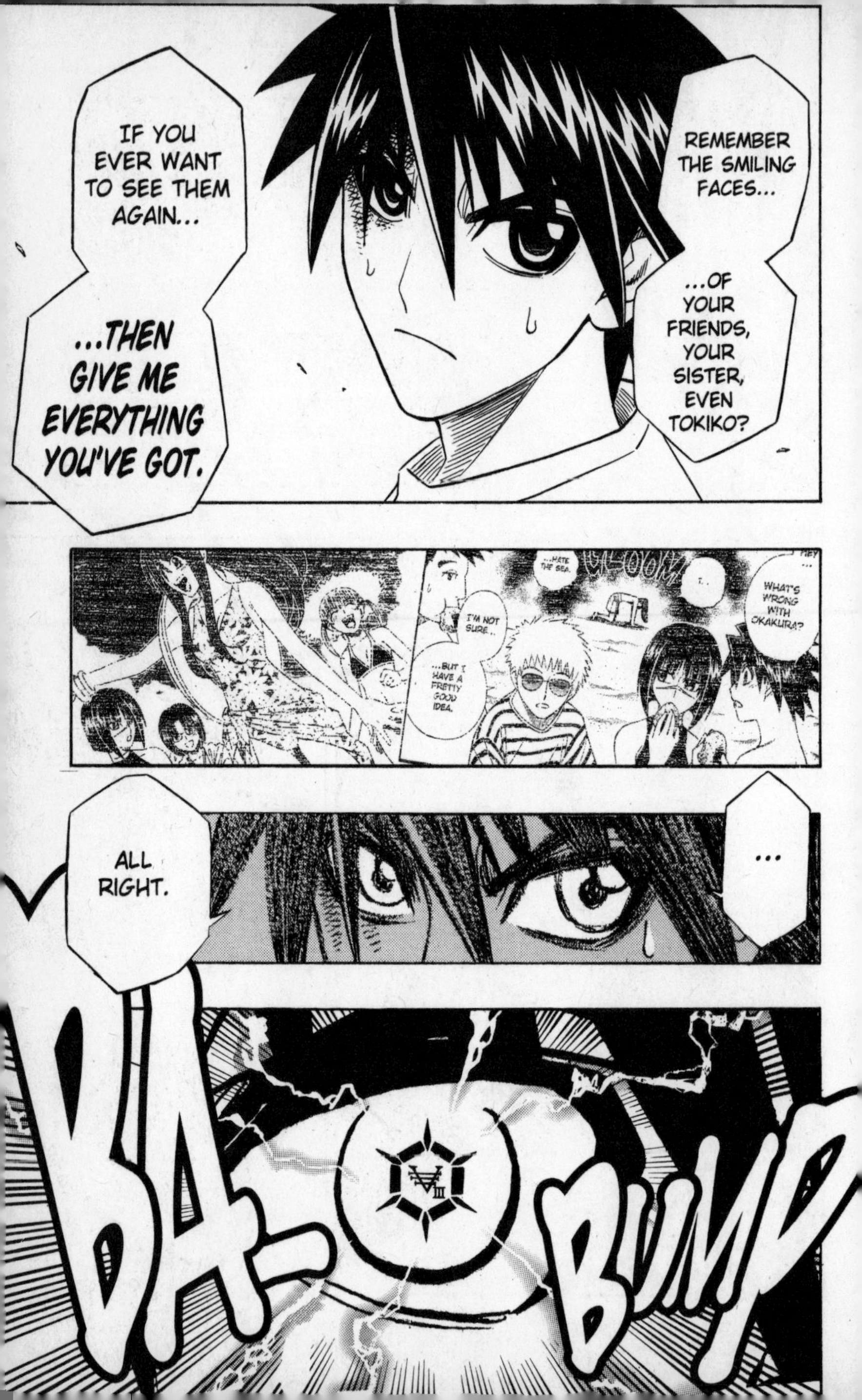
REMEMBER THE SMILING FACES...
...OF YOUR FRIENDS, YOUR SISTER, EVEN TOKIKO?
IF YOU EVER WANT TO SEE THEM AGAIN...
...THEN GIVE ME EVERYTHING YOU'VE GOT.
HEY...
WHAT'S WRONG WITH OKAKURA?
I..
GLOOM
...HATE THE SEA.
I'M NOT SURE..
...BUT I HAVE A PRETTY GOOD IDEA.
...
ALL RIGHT.
BA-BUMP

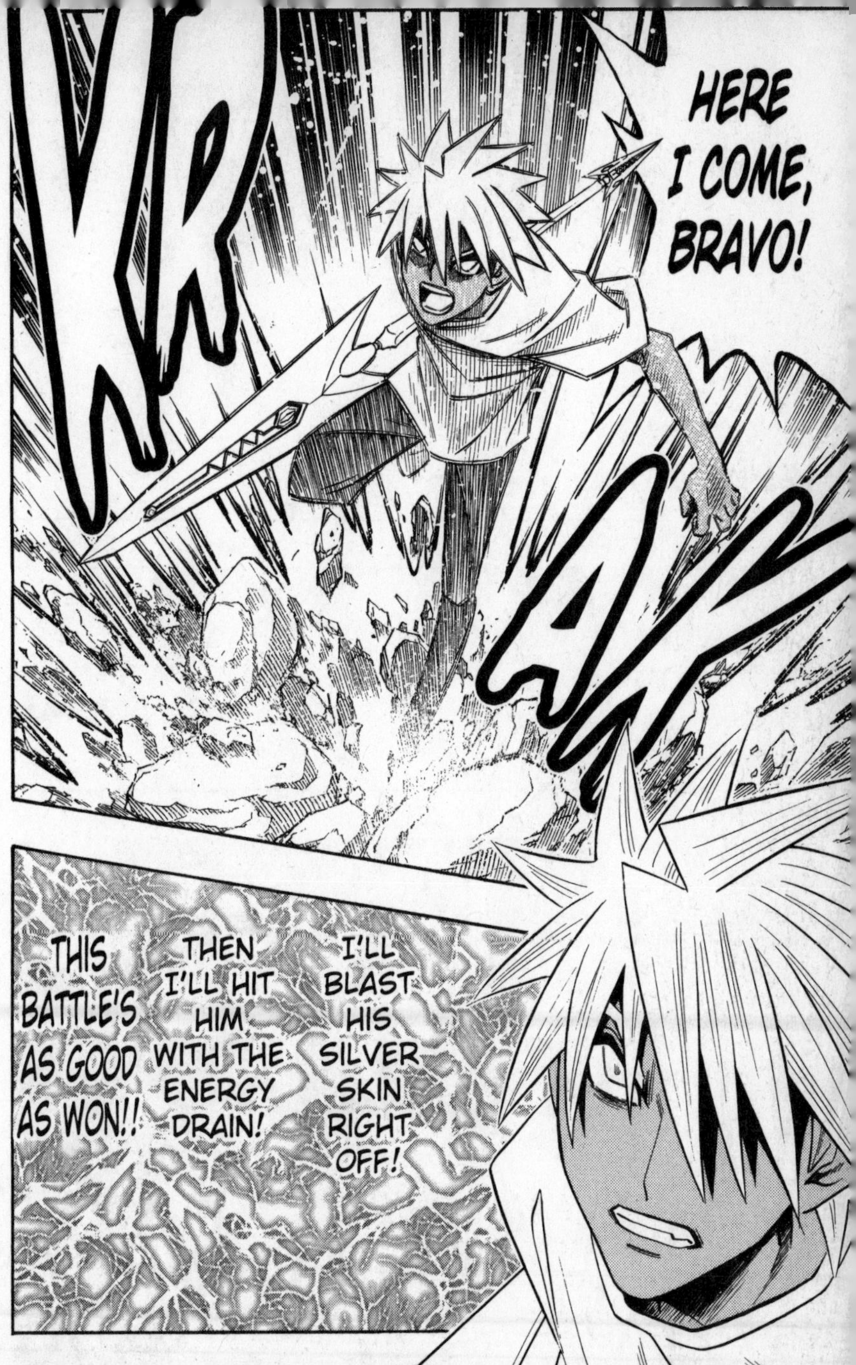
HERE I COME, BRAVO!
I'LL BLAST HIS SILVER SKIN RIGHT OFF!
THEN I'LL HIT HIM WITH THE ENERGY DRAIN!
THIS BATTLE'S AS GOOD AS WON!!

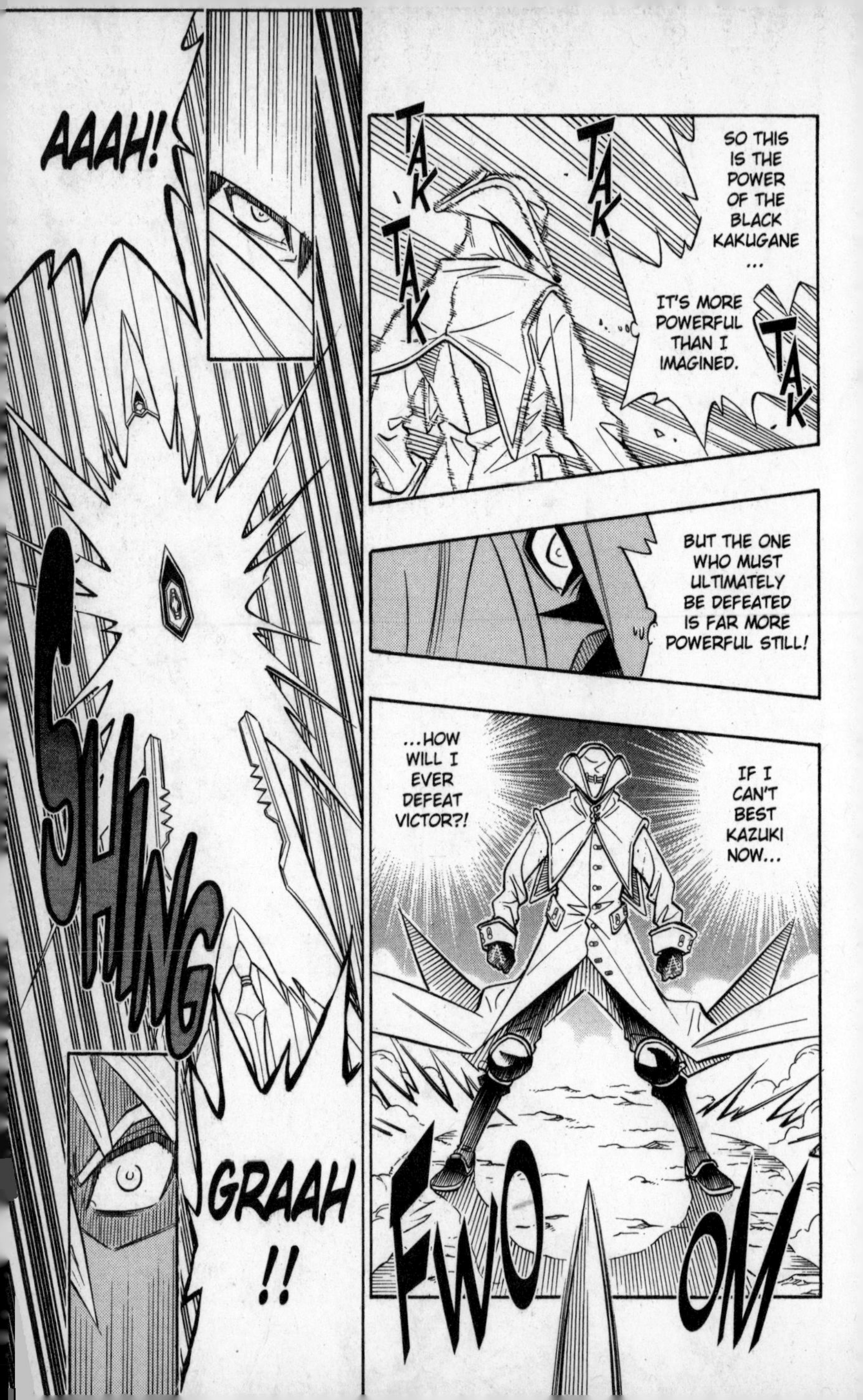
TAK TAK TAK TAK
SO THIS IS THE POWER OF THE BLACK KAKUGANE...
IT'S MORE POWERFUL THAN I IMAGINED.
TAK
BUT THE ONE WHO MUST ULTIMATELY BE DEFEATED IS FAR MORE POWERFUL STILL!
IF I CAN'T BEST KAZUKI NOW...
...HOW WILL I EVER DEFEAT VICTOR?!
FWOOM
AAAH!
SHING
GRAAH!!

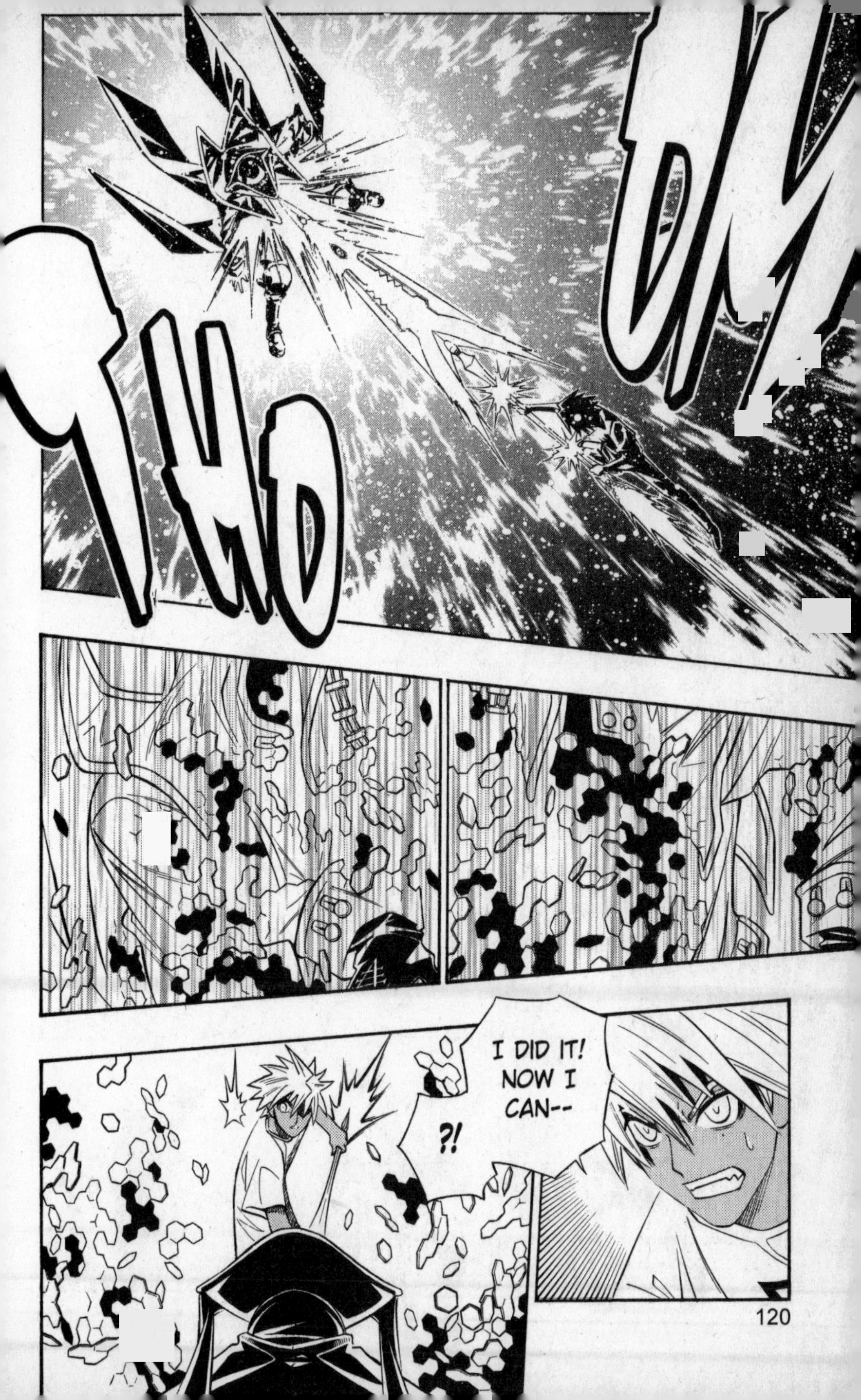
I DID IT! NOW I CAN--
?!

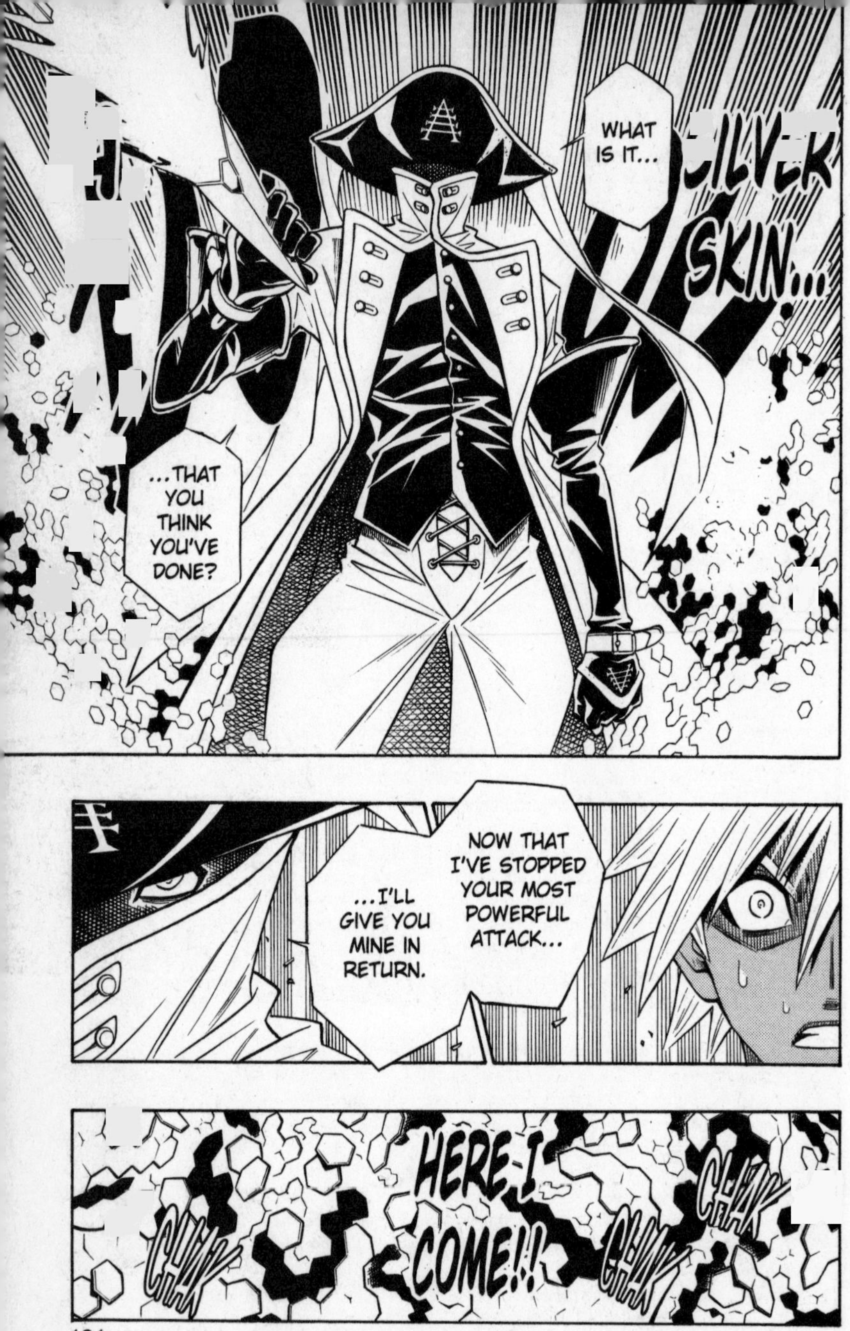
WHAT IS IT...
...THAT YOU THINK YOU'VE DONE?
SKIN...
NOW THAT I'VE STOPPED YOUR MOST POWERFUL ATTACK...
...I'LL GIVE YOU MINE IN RETURN.
CHAK
CHAK
HERE I COME!!
CHAK

"Happiness is found at the verge of death!"♡

Buso Renkin File No. 8

ニアデス ハピネス

NEAR-DEATH HAPPINESS

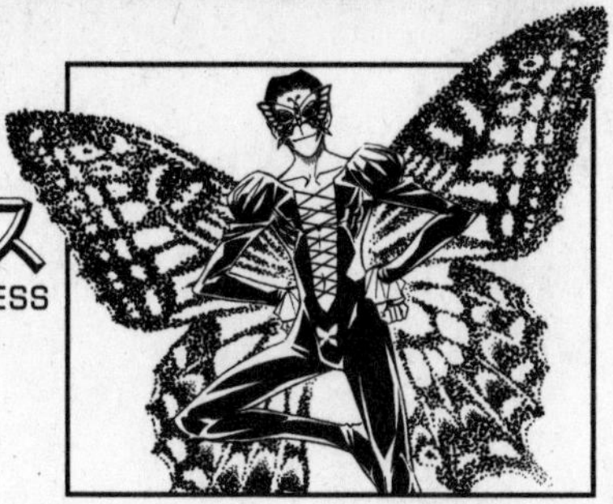

- Kakugane Serial Number: LXI (61)
- Creator: Koushaku Chouno (Papillon)
- Form: Gunpowder
- Main Color: Black
- Special Abilities: · Black gunpowder that can assume any form and be detonated remotely.
- Special Traits:
  - · The gunpowder itself is the Buso Renkin. It takes three days for it to replenish once it's used up.
  - · The maximum distance for remote control is 50 meters. Also, the gunpowder can't be ignited unless it's within its creator's line of sight.
  - · Able to achieve flight by burning some of the gunpowder to generate thrust.
  - · The gunpowder takes the form of a butterfly as a reflection of Papillon's soul. Even if the gunpowder were to take a different form, the abilities would still be the same.

○ Author's Notes:

- · I tried to come up with a kind of Buso Renkin that would best reflect Papillon's personality. For motifs I decided on the color black, a butterfly, and something that would burn away completely. I like this one a lot.
- · The name of this weapon came from the novel *Stacy* by Kenji Otsuki. In the book it was the name of a strange disease.
- · When the story was first printed in the weekly magazine, the name was misprinted as "Near-Death Papiness" and was received better than I expected. I thought about leaving it that way since Papillon is also based on a character from Otsuki's *Spider's Thread*, but I corrected it in the end.
- · Papillon is a useful character to have around so I'm careful not to make his weapons too powerful.

NEARDEATH HAPPINESS

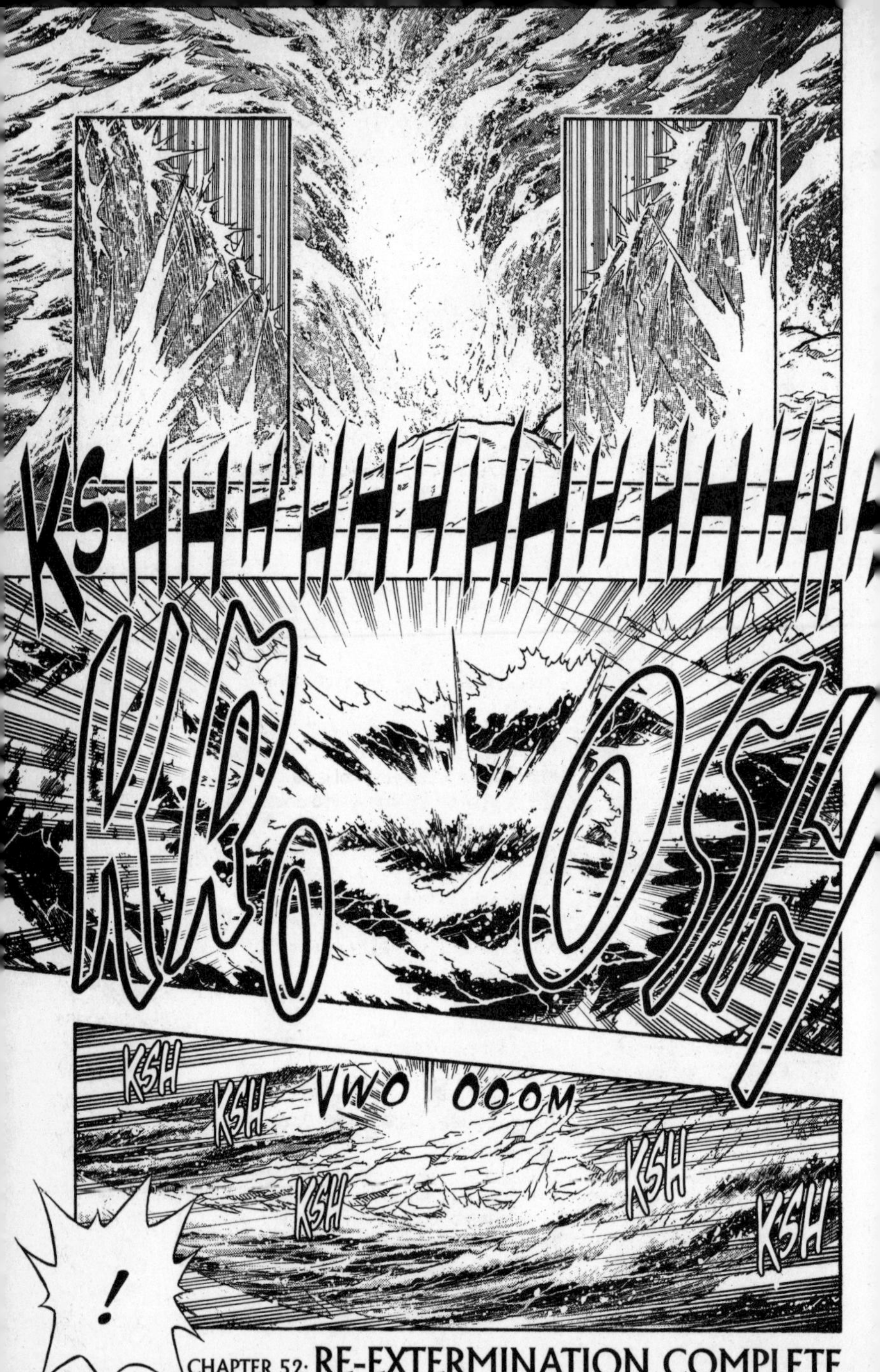
KSHHHHHHHHHHHHHH
KROOSH
KSH
KSH
VWO OOOM
KSH
KSH
KSH
!

CHAPTER 52: RE-EXTERMINATION COMPLETE

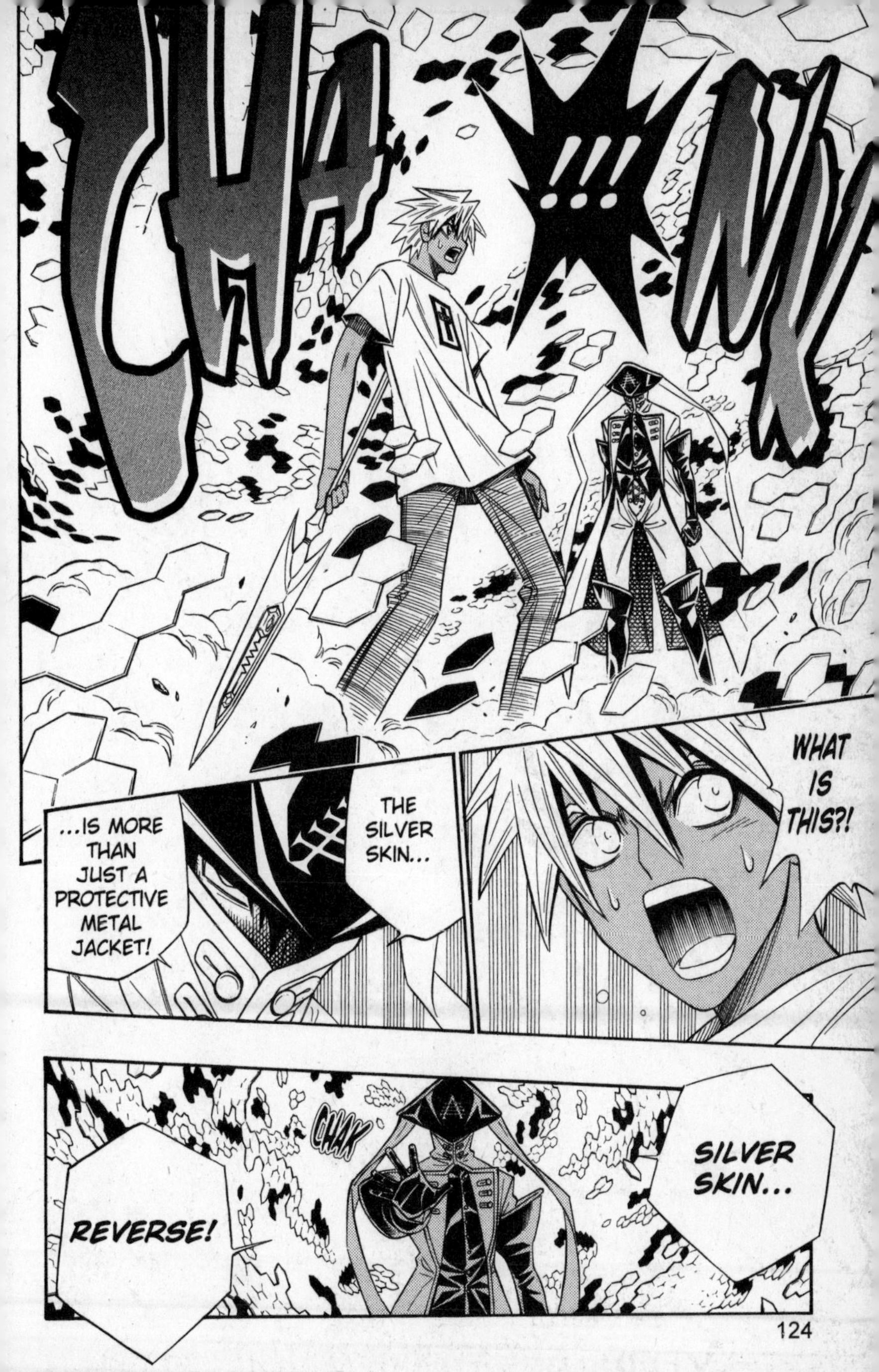
CHA
!!!
NNK
WHAT IS THIS?!
THE SILVER SKIN...
...IS MORE THAN JUST A PROTECTIVE METAL JACKET!
CHAK
SILVER SKIN...
REVERSE!

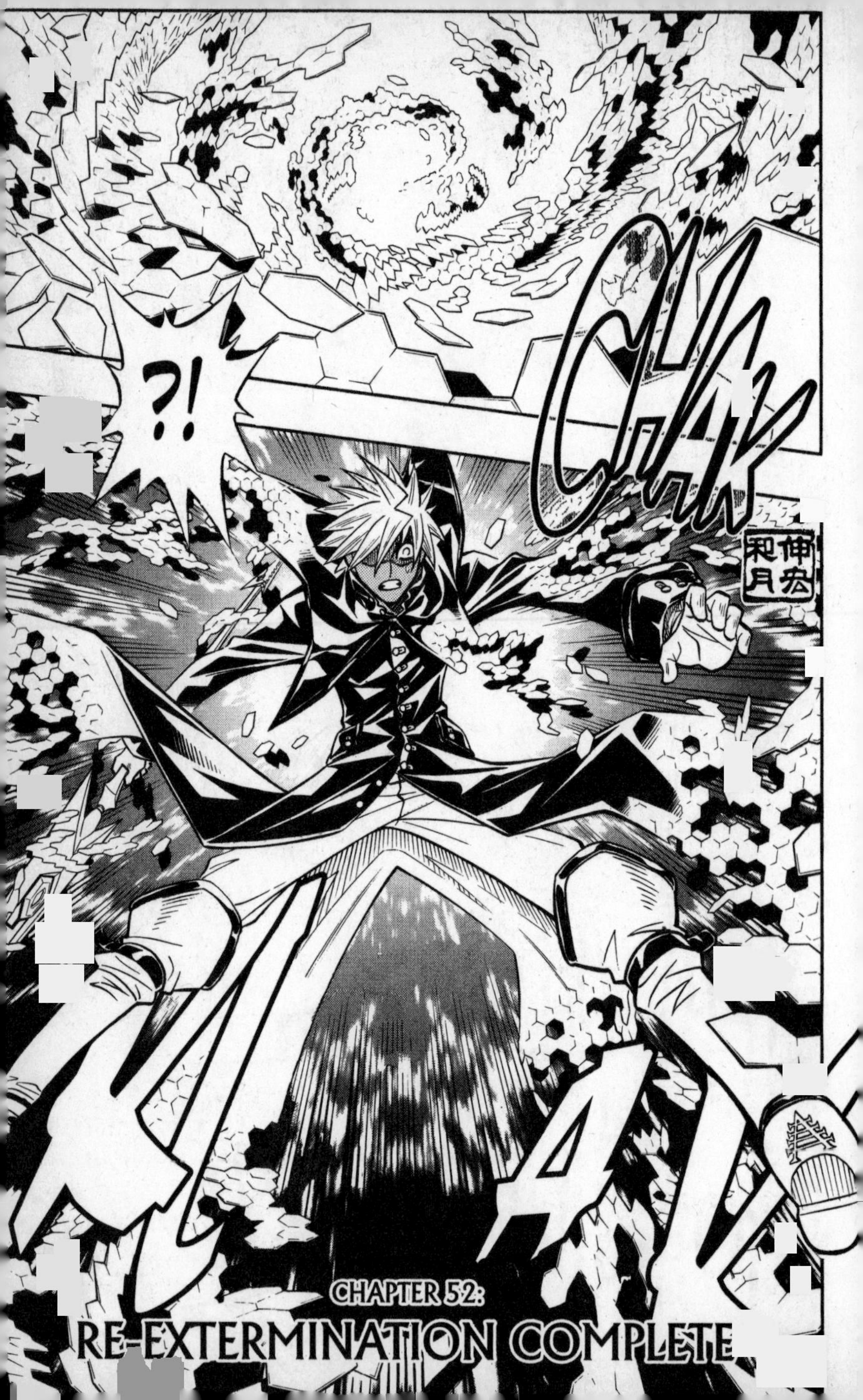
?!
CHAK
和月伸宏

CHAPTER 52: RE-EXTERMINATION COMPLETE

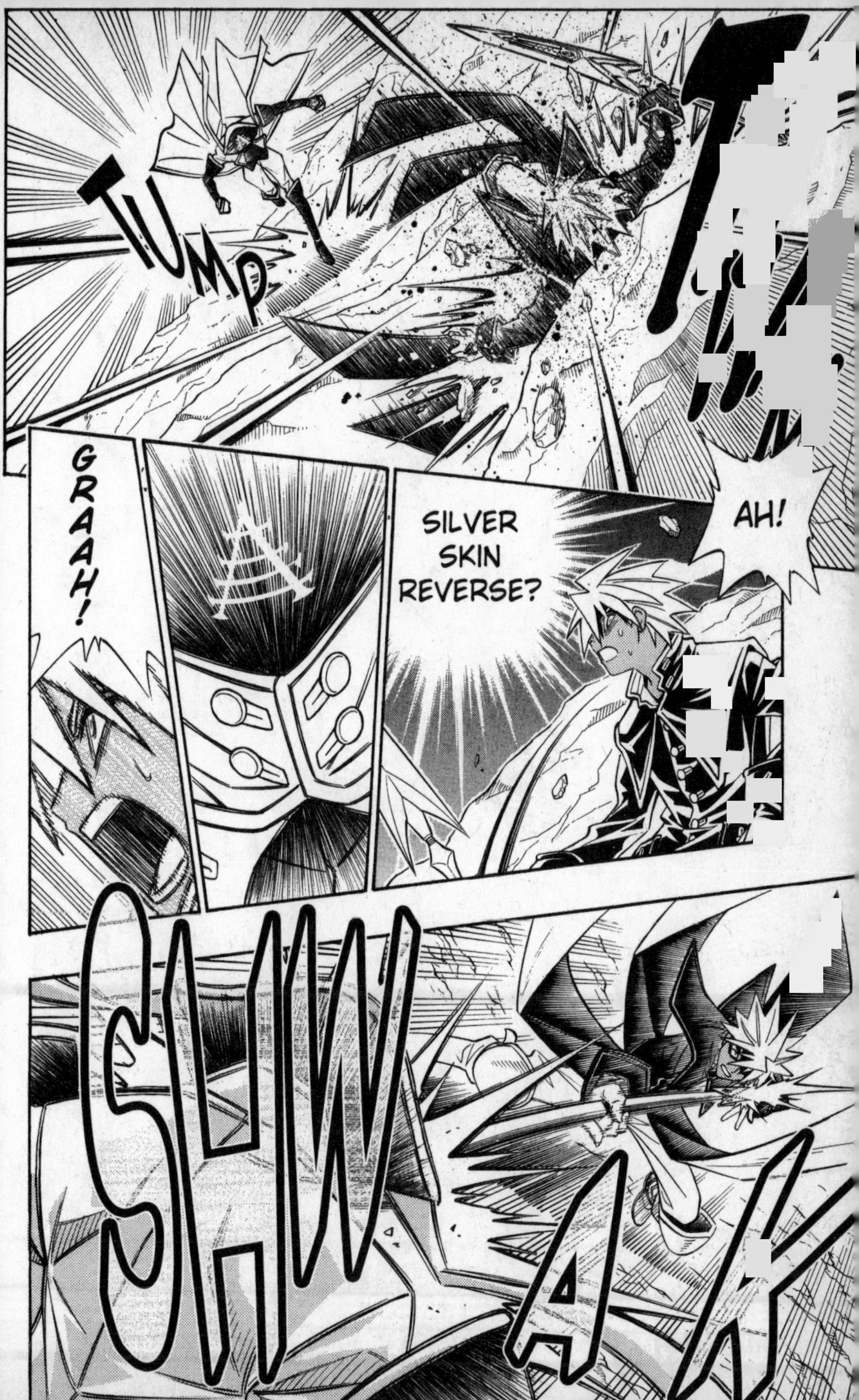
TUMP
AH!
SILVER SKIN REVERSE?
GRAAH!
SHWAK

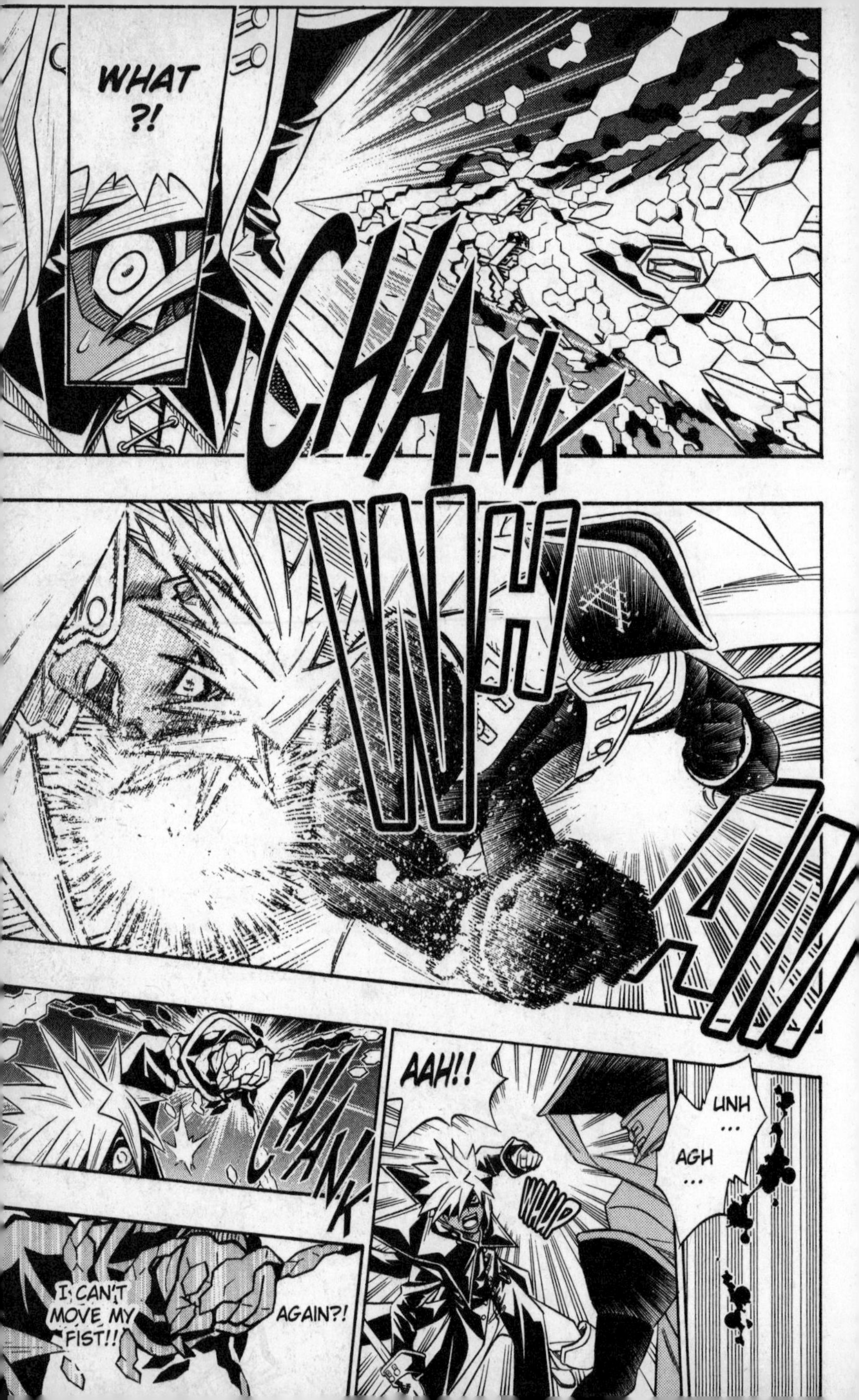
CHANK
WHAT ?!
AAH!!
UNH ... AGH ...
CHANK
AGAIN?!
I CAN'T MOVE MY FIST!!

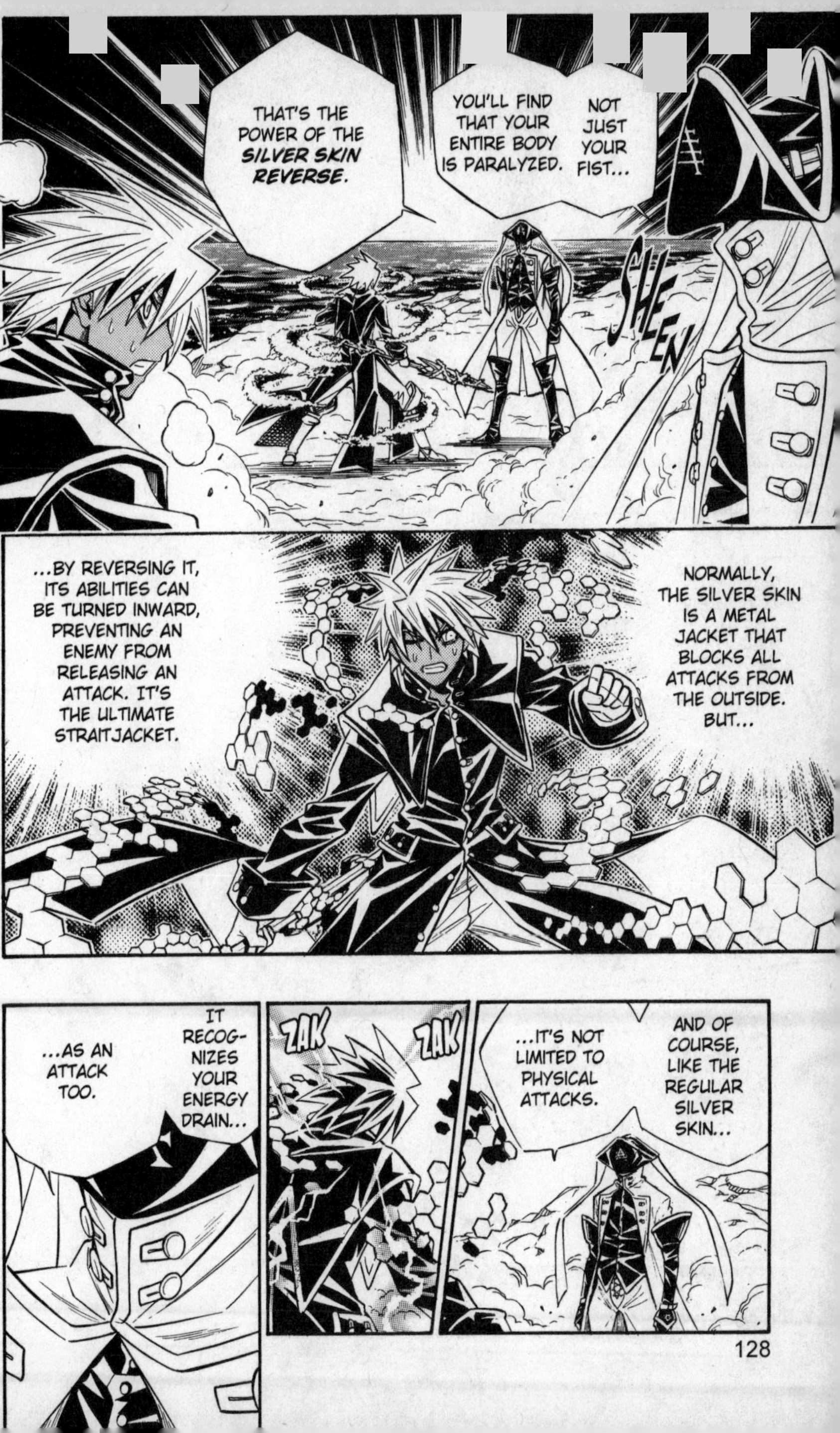
NOT JUST YOUR FIST...
YOU'LL FIND THAT YOUR ENTIRE BODY IS PARALYZED.
THAT'S THE POWER OF THE *SILVER SKIN REVERSE*.
SHEEN
NORMALLY, THE SILVER SKIN IS A METAL JACKET THAT BLOCKS ALL ATTACKS FROM THE OUTSIDE. BUT...
...BY REVERSING IT, ITS ABILITIES CAN BE TURNED INWARD, PREVENTING AN ENEMY FROM RELEASING AN ATTACK. IT'S THE ULTIMATE STRAITJACKET.
AND OF COURSE, LIKE THE REGULAR SILVER SKIN...
...IT'S NOT LIMITED TO PHYSICAL ATTACKS.
ZAK
ZAK
IT RECOG-NIZES YOUR ENERGY DRAIN...
...AS AN ATTACK TOO.

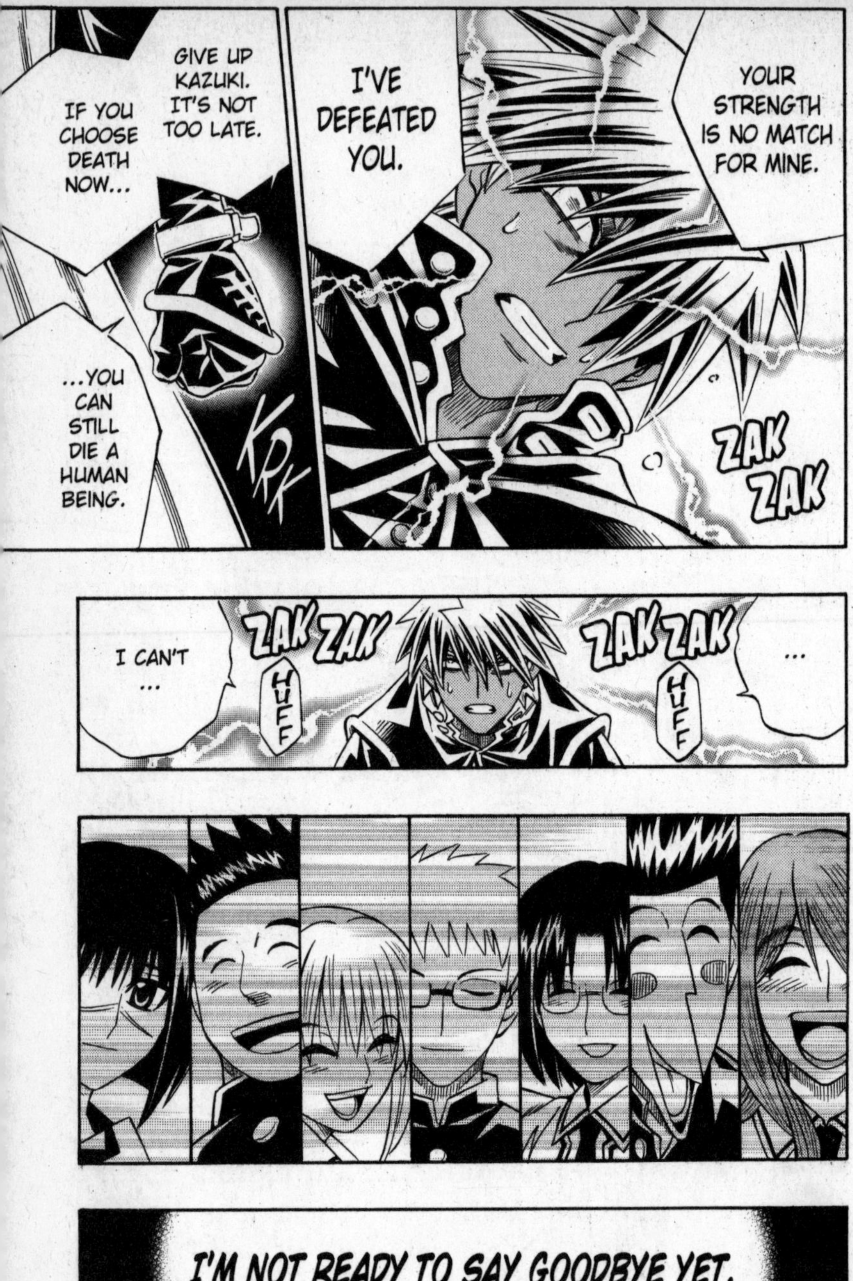
YOUR STRENGTH IS NO MATCH FOR MINE.
I'VE DEFEATED YOU.
ZAK ZAK
GIVE UP KAZUKI. IT'S NOT TOO LATE.
IF YOU CHOOSE DEATH NOW...
KRK
...YOU CAN STILL DIE A HUMAN BEING.
...
ZAK ZAK
HUFF
ZAK ZAK
HUFF
I CAN'T ...
I'M NOT READY TO SAY GOODBYE YET.

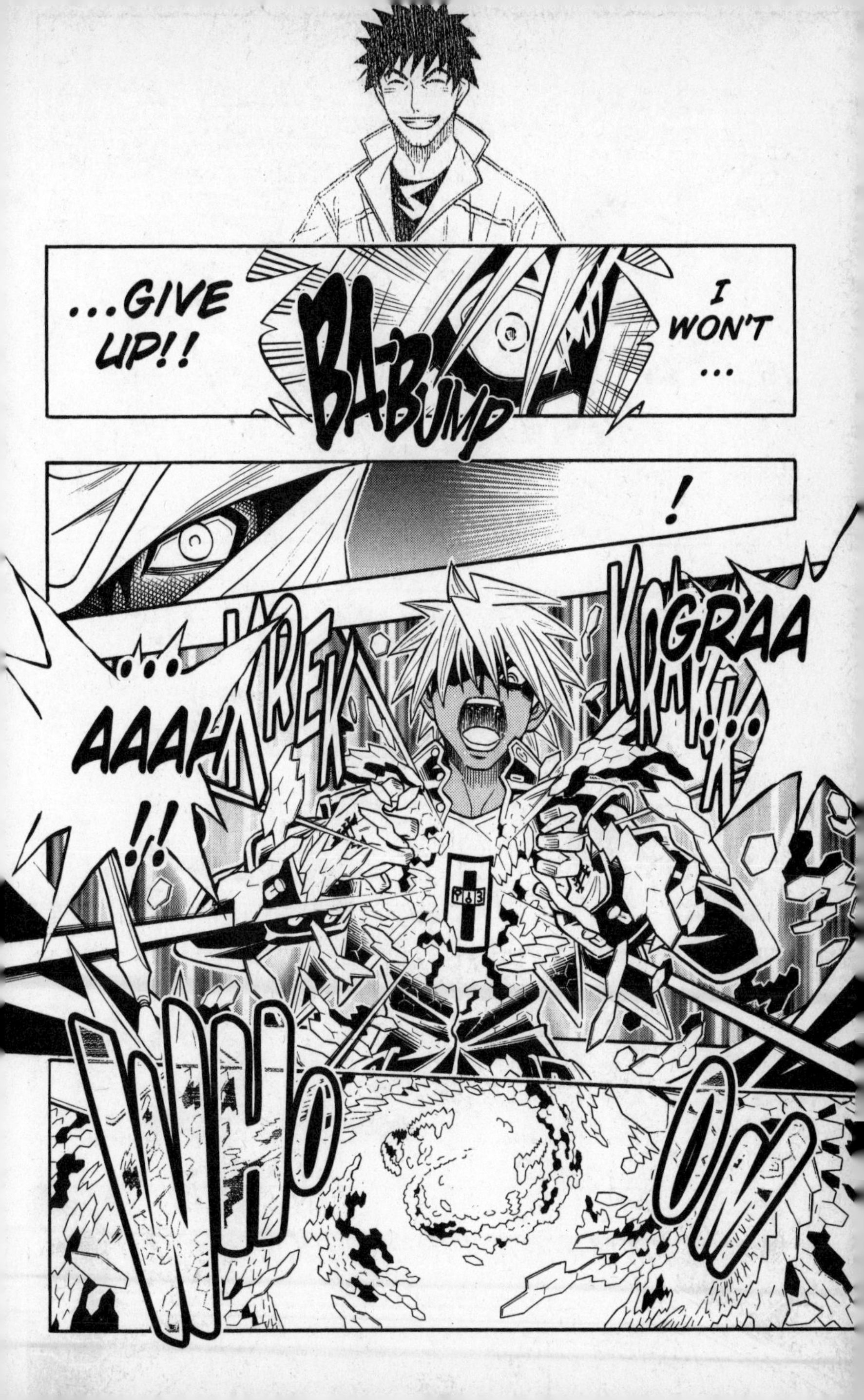
I WON'T ...
BA-BUMP
...GIVE UP!!
!
GRAA
...AAAH!!
KREK
WHOOM

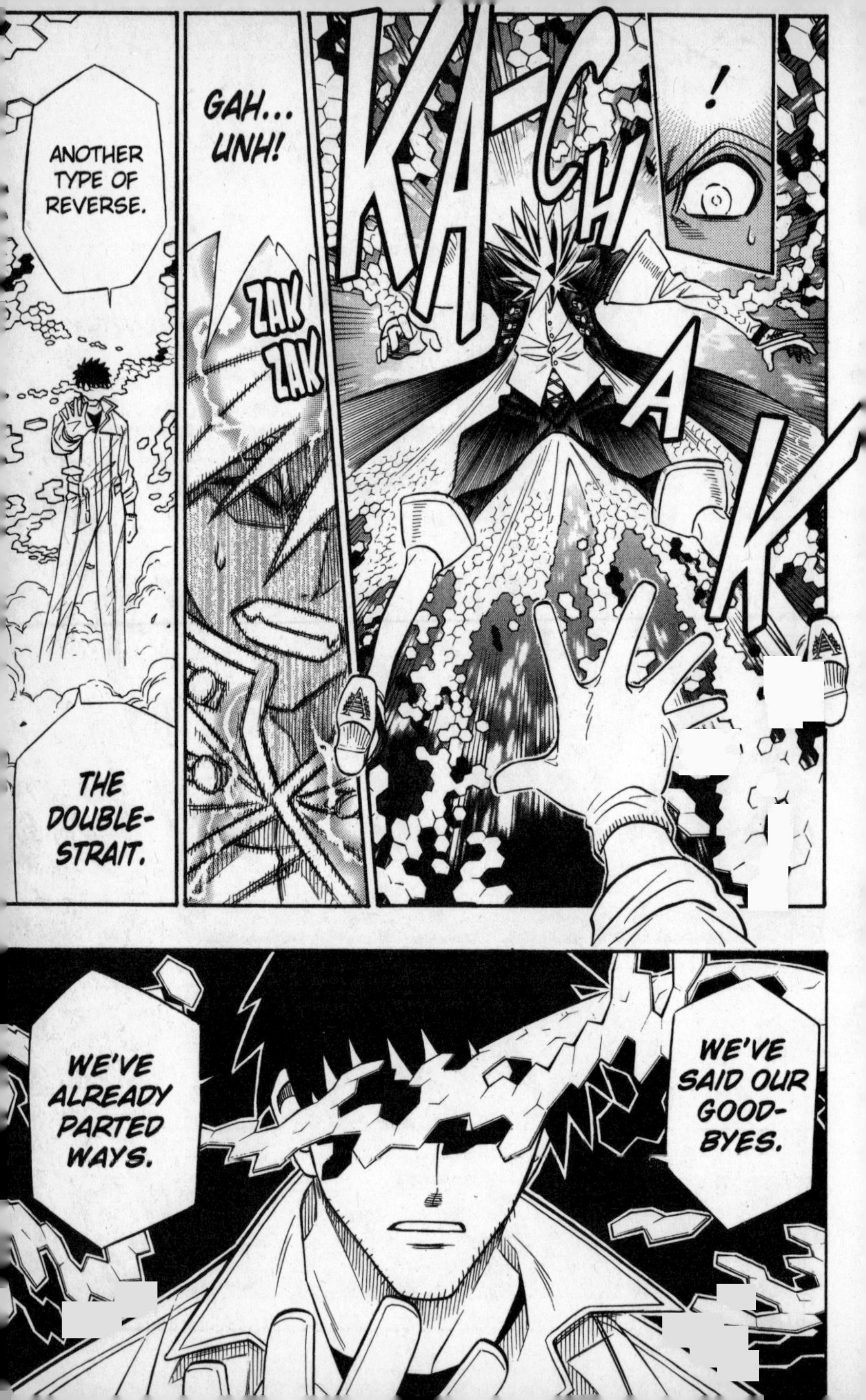
!
KA-CHAK
GAH... UNH!
ZAK ZAK
ANOTHER TYPE OF REVERSE.
THE DOUBLE-STRAIT.
WE'VE SAID OUR GOOD-BYES.
WE'VE ALREADY PARTED WAYS.

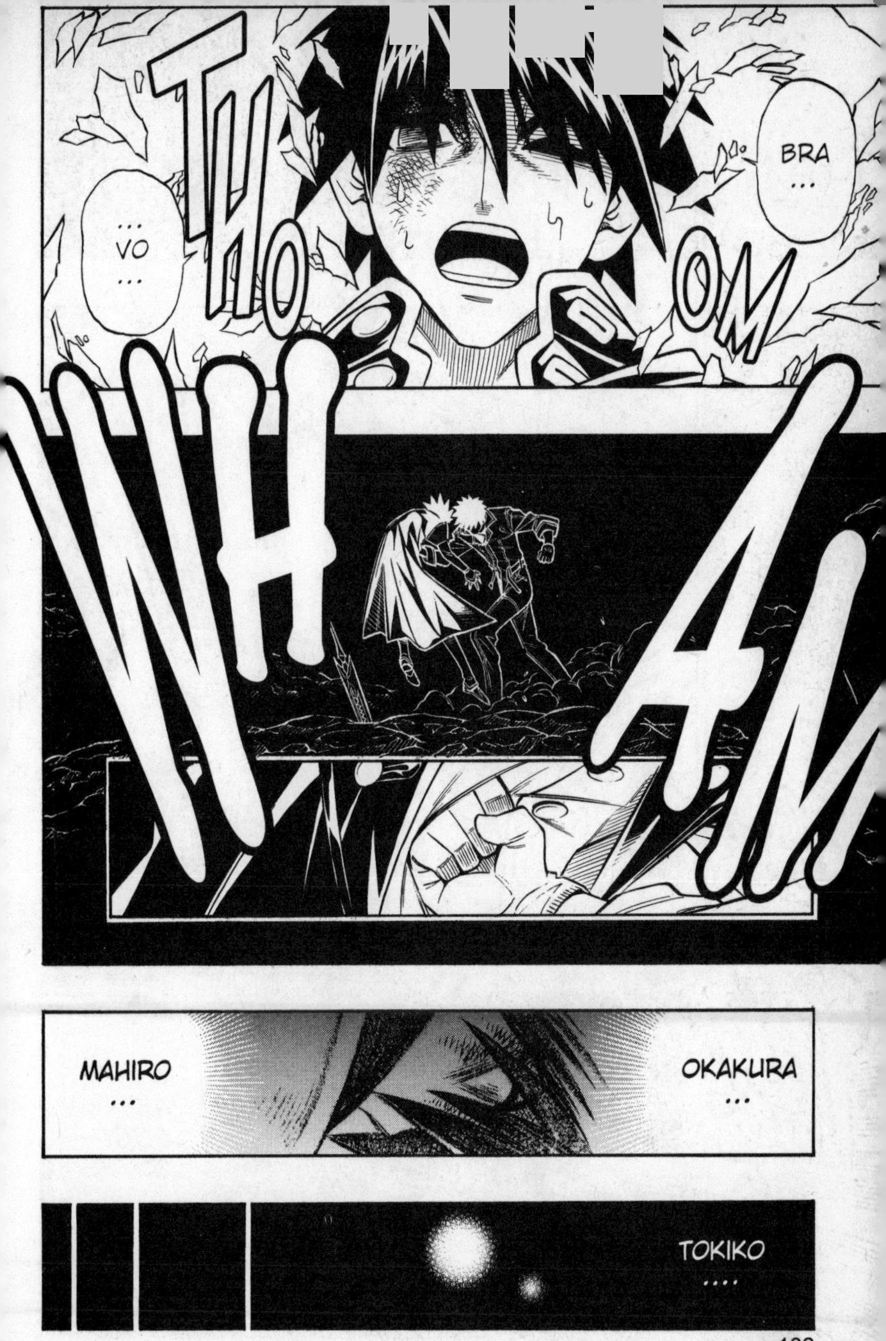
BRA
...
THO
OM
...
VO
...
WH
AM
OKAKURA
...
MAHIRO
...
TOKIKO
....

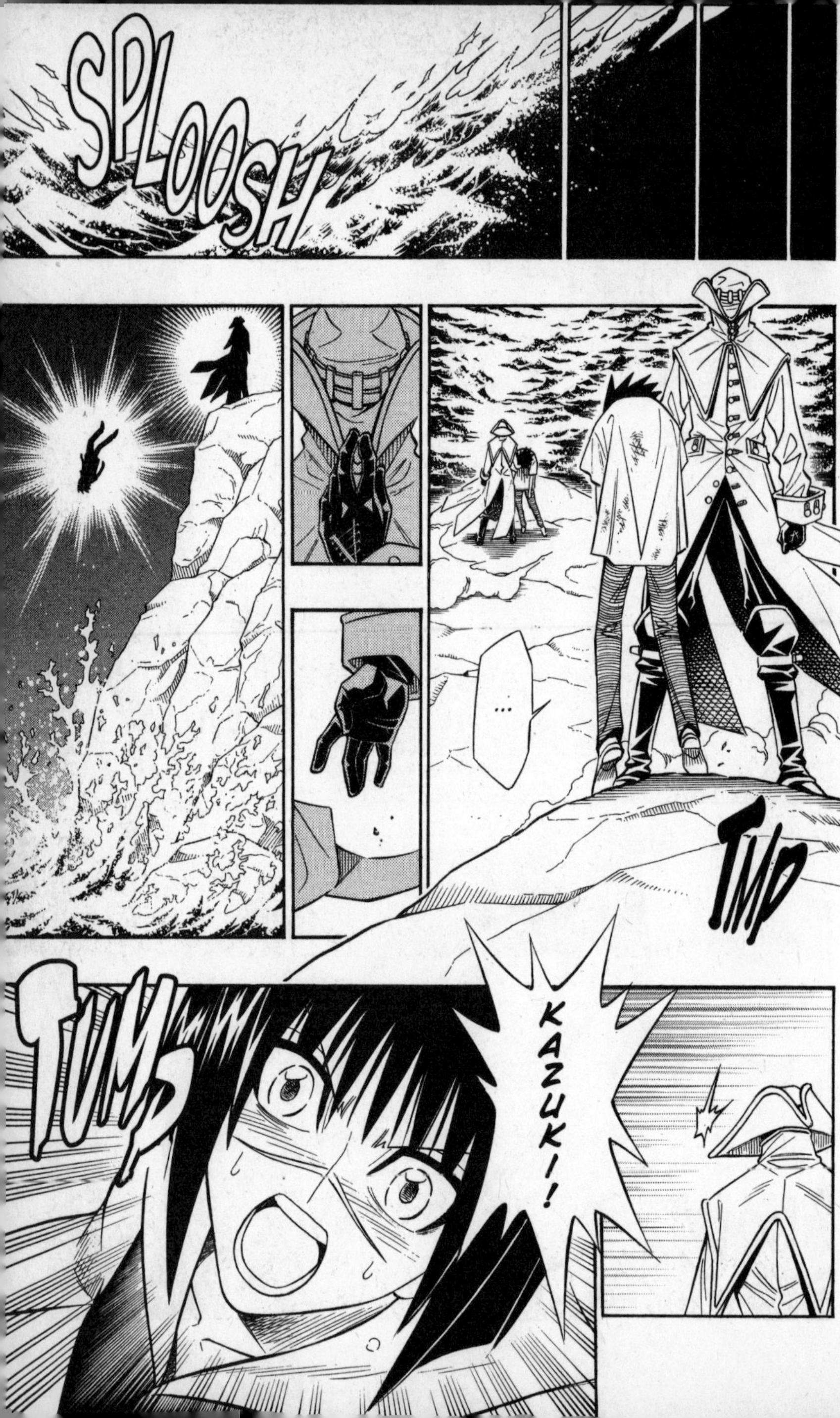
SPLOOSH
...
TMP
KAZUKI!
TUMP

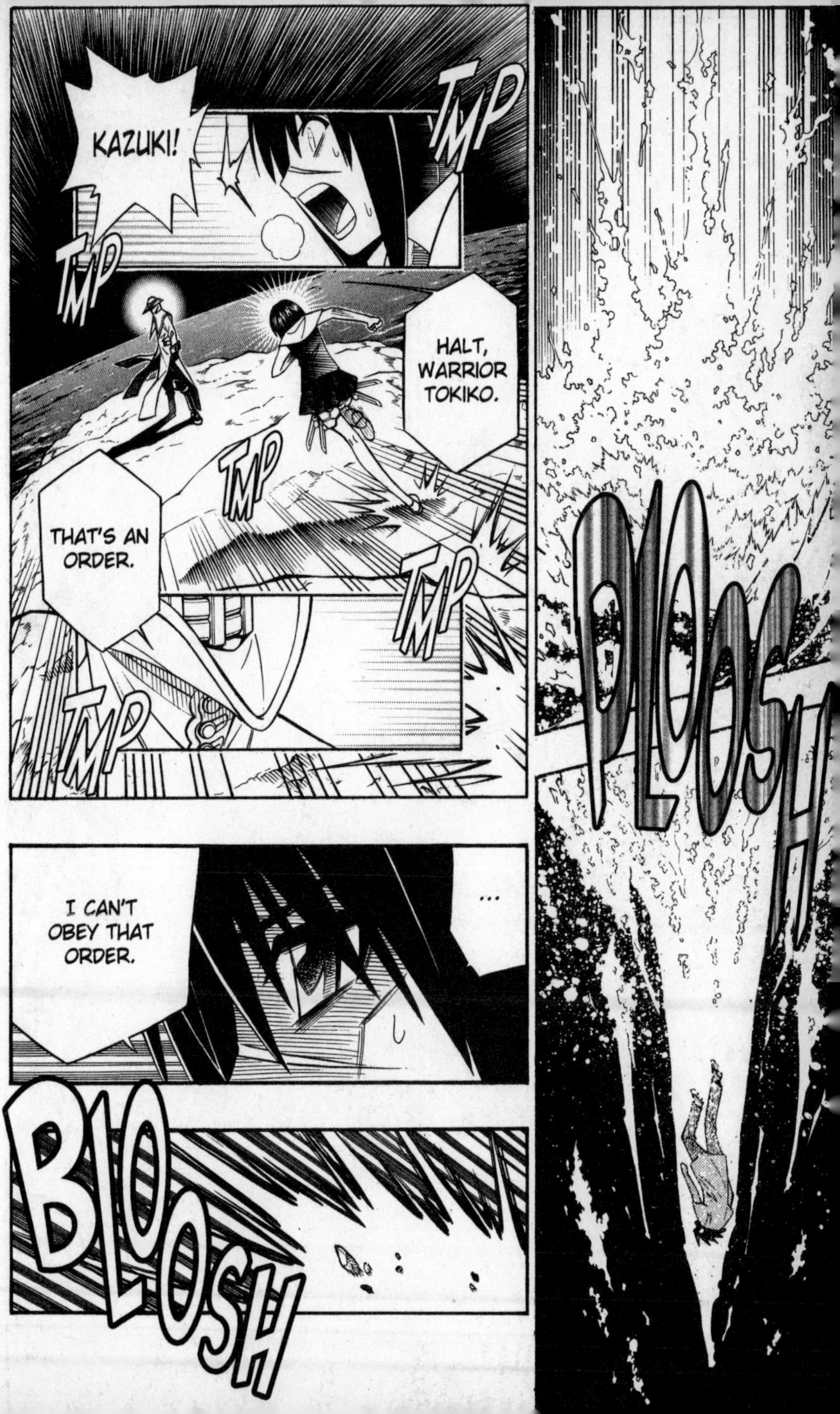
PLOOSH
TMP
KAZUKI!
TMP
HALT, WARRIOR TOKIKO.
TMP
THAT'S AN ORDER.
TMP
TMP
...
I CAN'T OBEY THAT ORDER.
BLOOSH

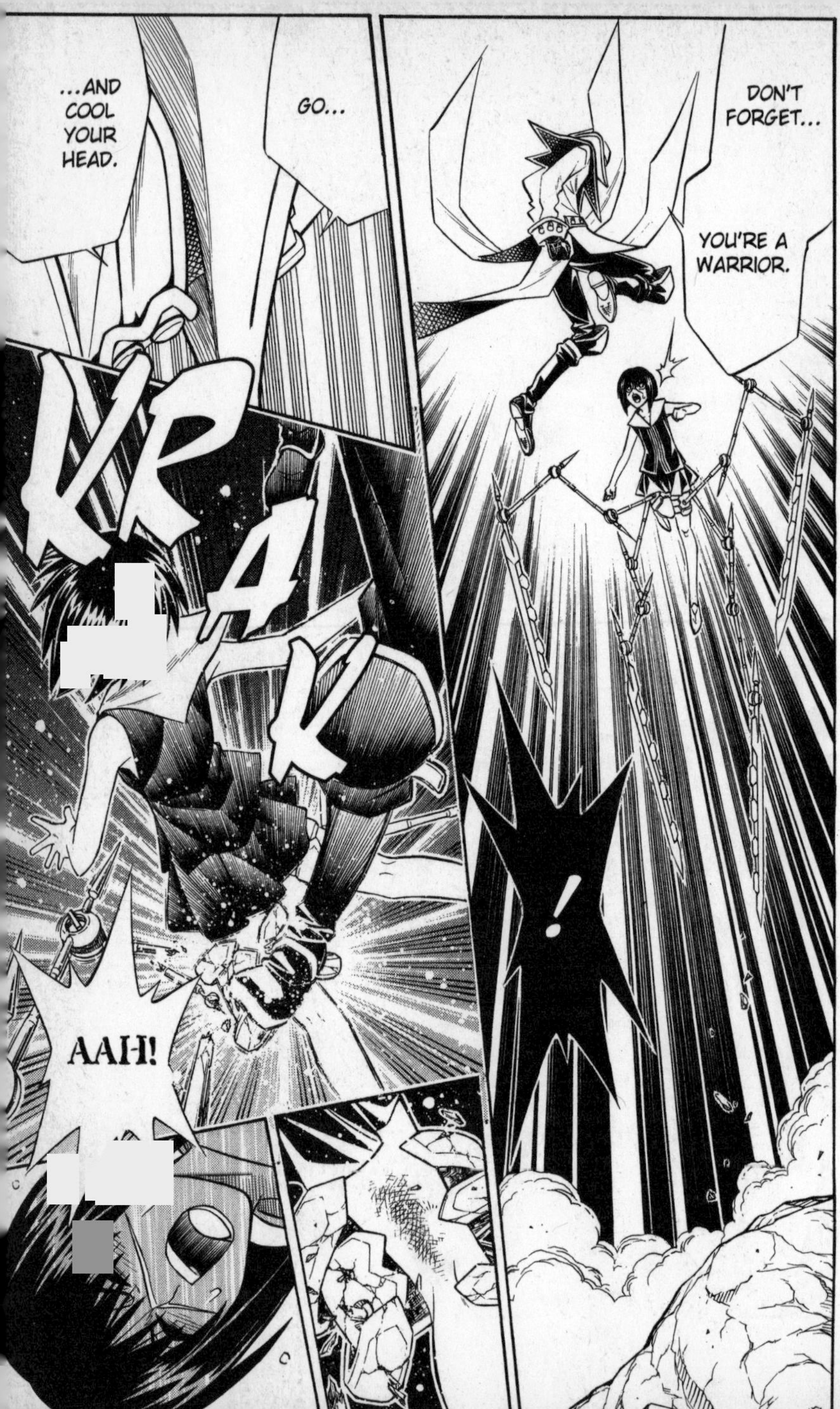

DON'T FORGET...
YOU'RE A WARRIOR.
!
GO...
...AND COOL YOUR HEAD.
KRAK
AAH!

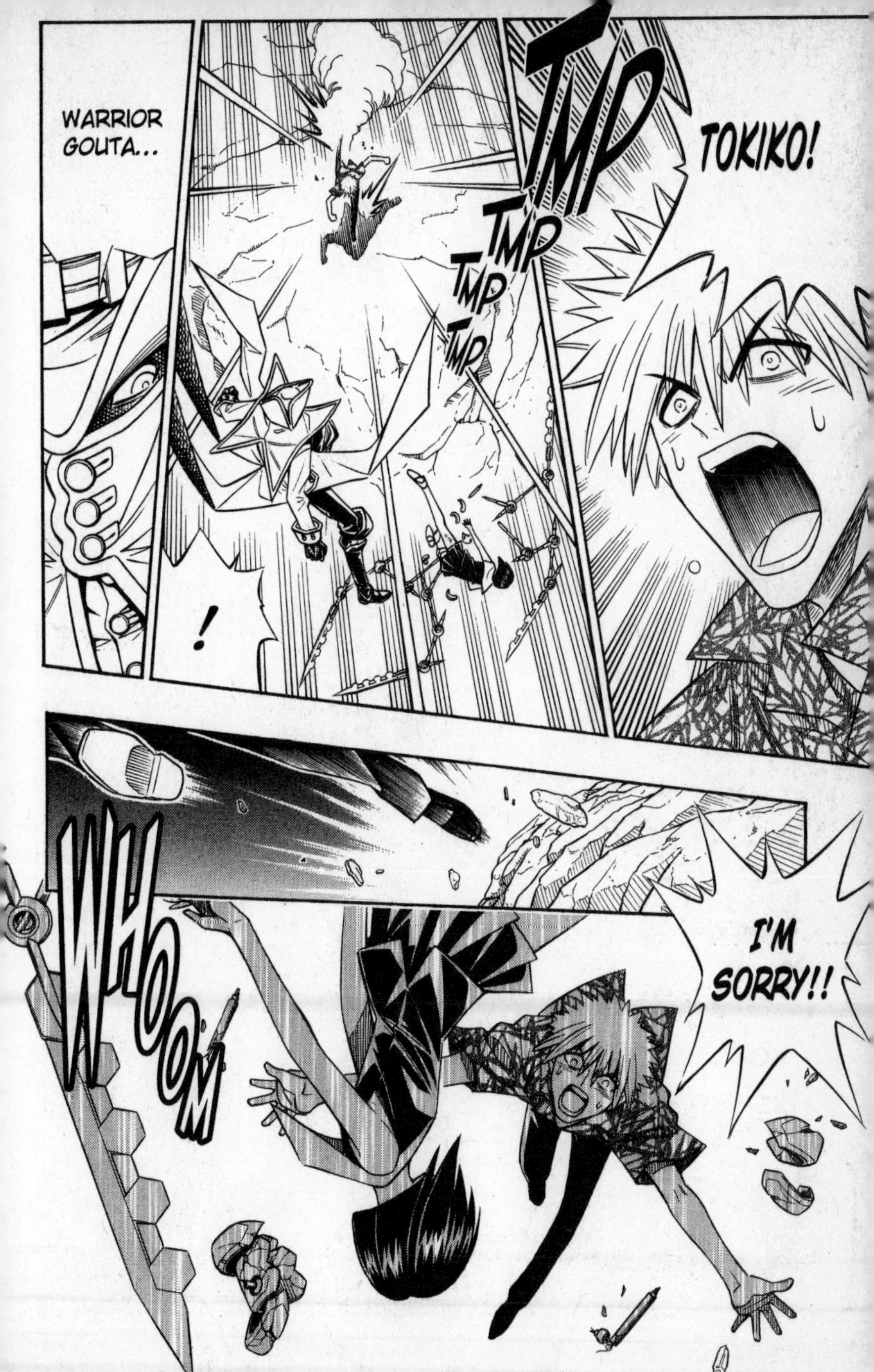
TOKIKO!
TMP
TMP
TMP
TMP
!
WARRIOR GOUTA...
I'M SORRY!!
WHOOM

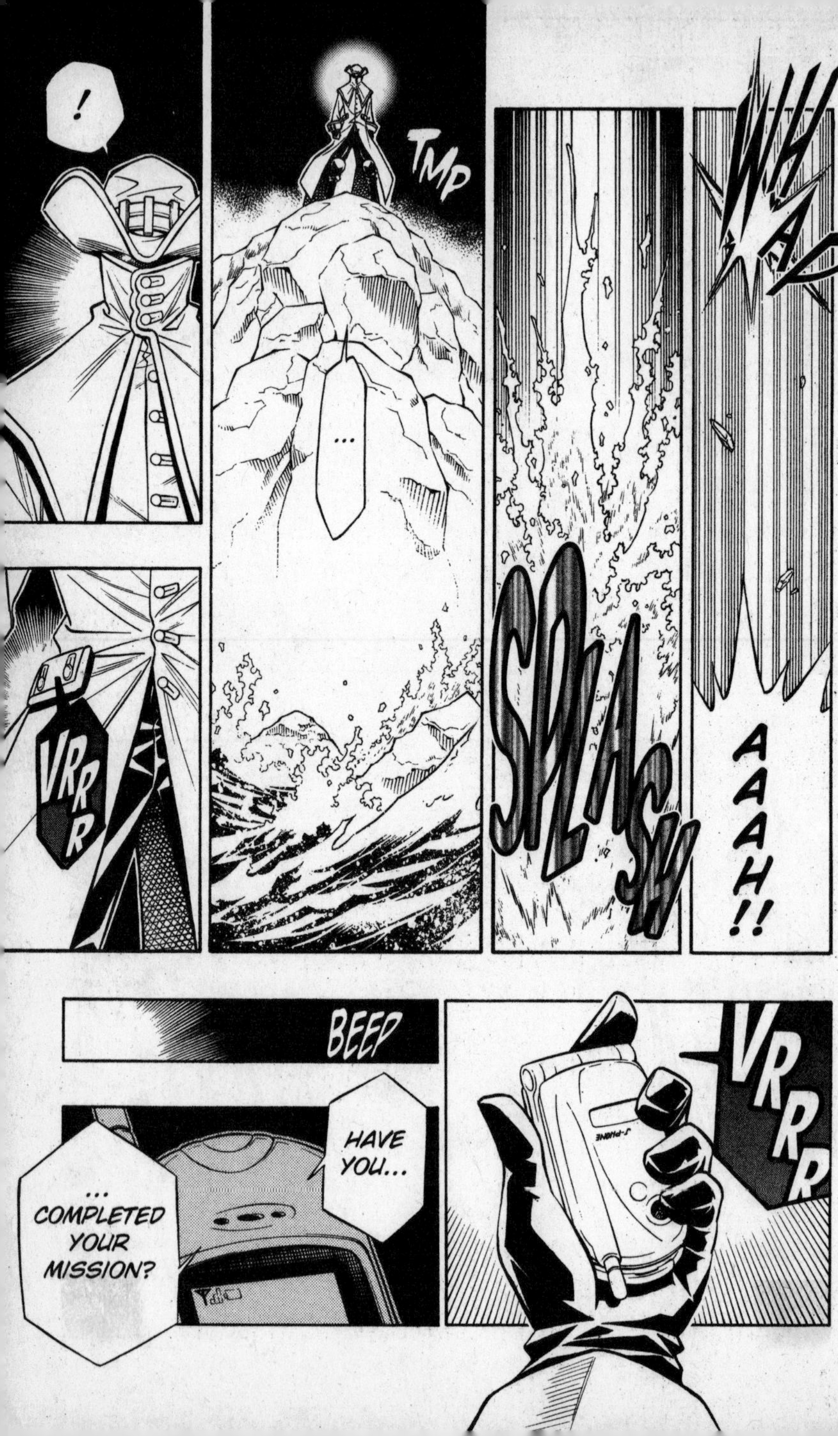
WHAP
AAAAH!!
SPLASH
TMP
...
!
VRRR
VRRR
BEEP
HAVE YOU...
... COMPLETED YOUR MISSION?

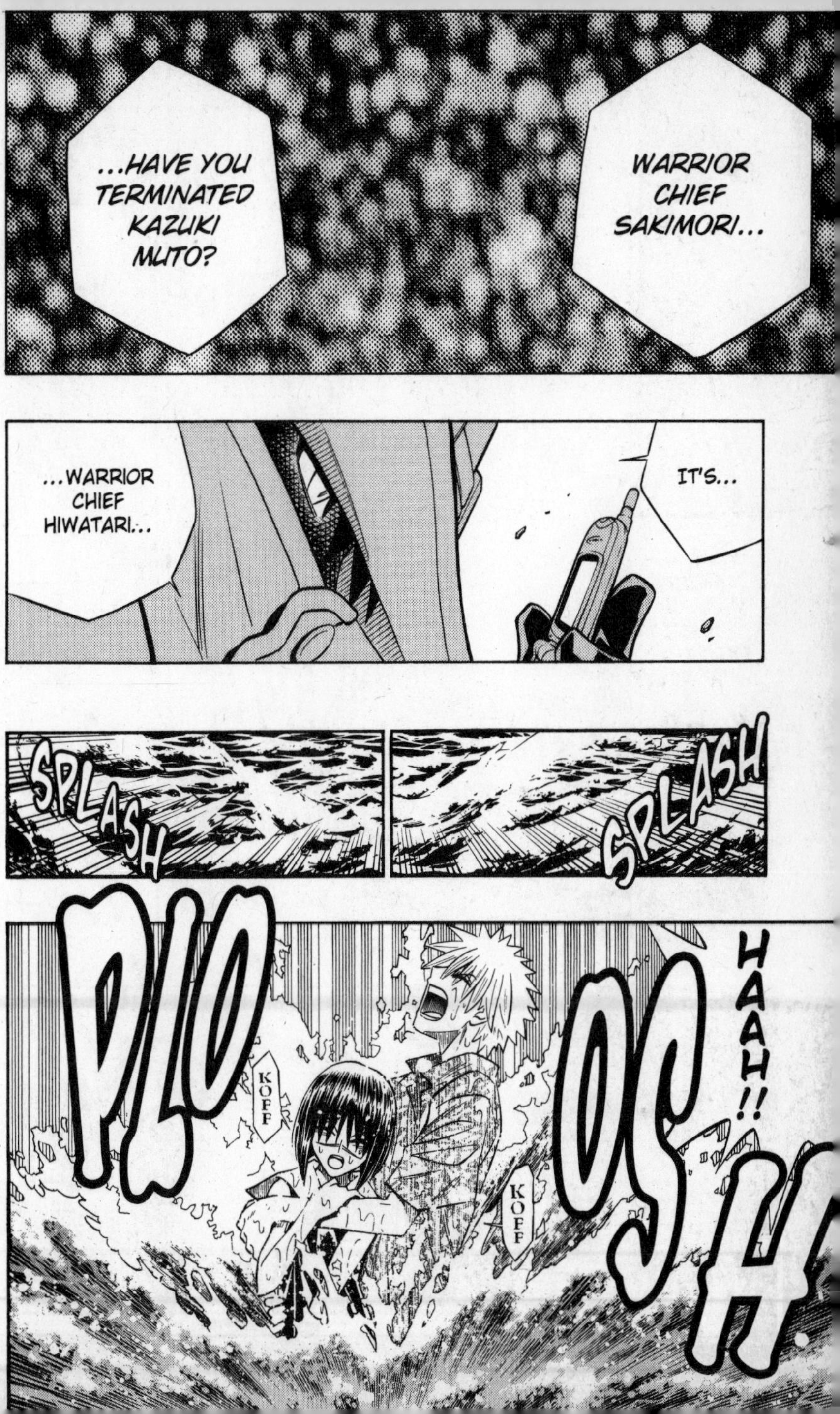
WARRIOR CHIEF SAKIMORI...
...HAVE YOU TERMINATED KAZUKI MUTO?
IT'S...
...WARRIOR CHIEF HIWATARI...
SPLASH
SPLASH
HAAH!!
PLOOSH
KOFF
KOFF

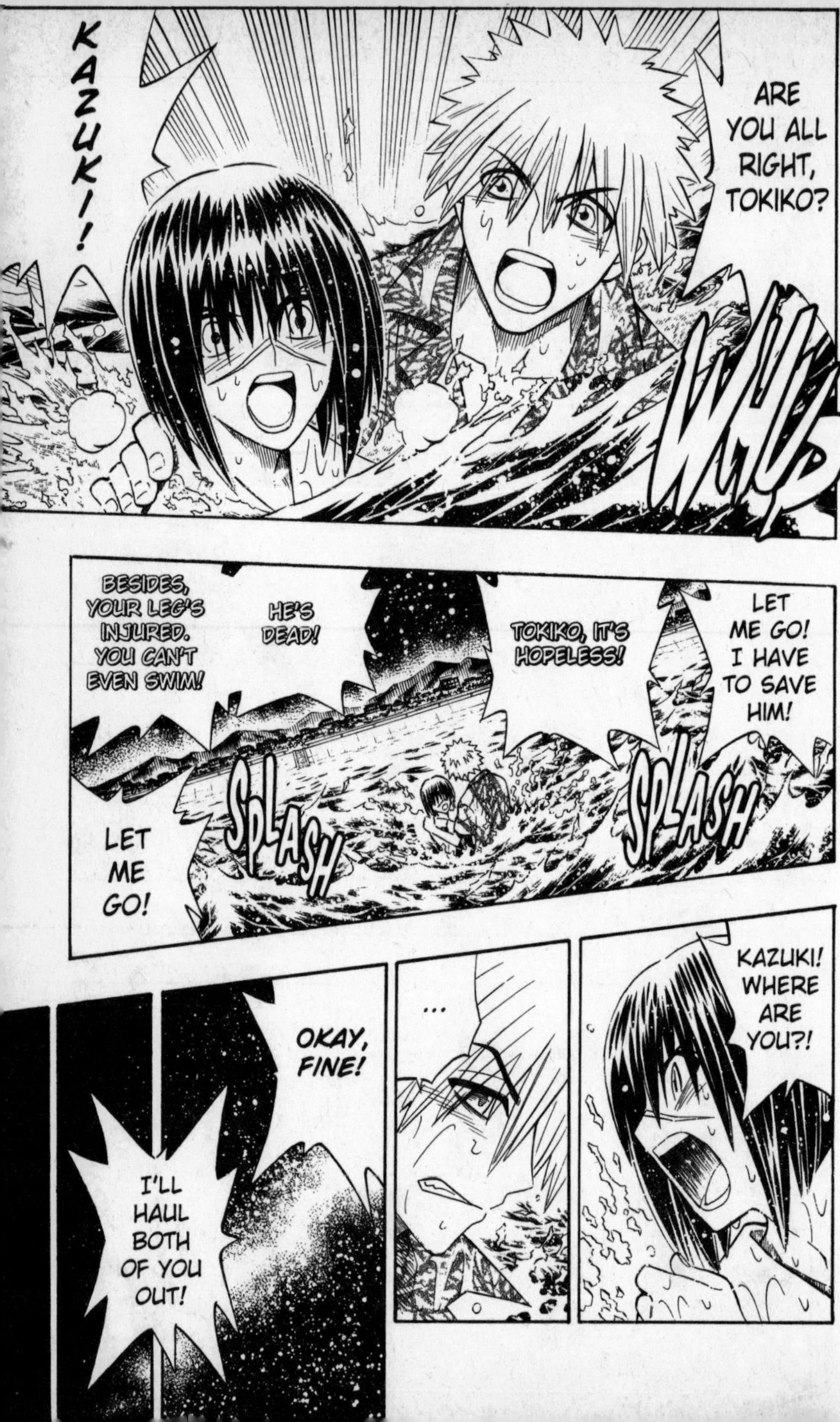
ARE YOU ALL RIGHT, TOKIKO?
KAZUKI!
WHU
LET ME GO! I HAVE TO SAVE HIM!
TOKIKO, IT'S HOPELESS!
HE'S DEAD!
BESIDES, YOUR LEG'S INJURED. YOU CAN'T EVEN SWIM!
SPLASH
SPLASH
LET ME GO!
KAZUKI! WHERE ARE YOU?!
...
OKAY, FINE!
I'LL HAUL BOTH OF YOU OUT!

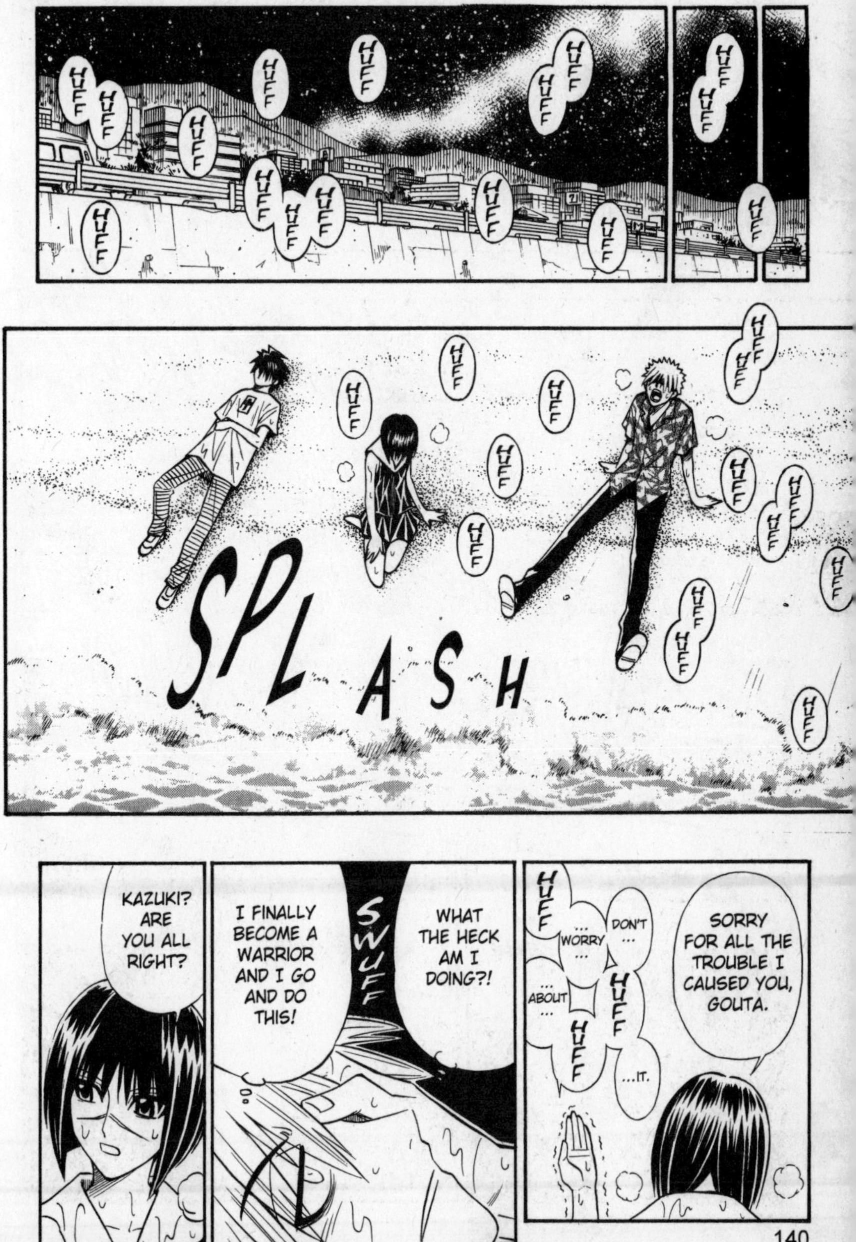
HUFF
HUFF
HUFF
HUFF
HUFF
HUFF
HUFF
HUFF
HUFF
HUFF
HUFF
HUFF
HUFF
HUFF
HUFF
HUFF
HUFF
HUFF
HUFF
HUFF
HUFF
HUFF
HUFF
HUFF
HUFF
HUFF
HUFF
HUFF
HUFF
SPLASH
SORRY FOR ALL THE TROUBLE I CAUSED YOU, GOUTA.
HUFF
...DON'T...
...WORRY...
...ABOUT...
HUFF
HUFF
...IT.
WHAT THE HECK AM I DOING?!
SWUFF
I FINALLY BECOME A WARRIOR AND I GO AND DO THIS!
KAZUKI? ARE YOU ALL RIGHT?

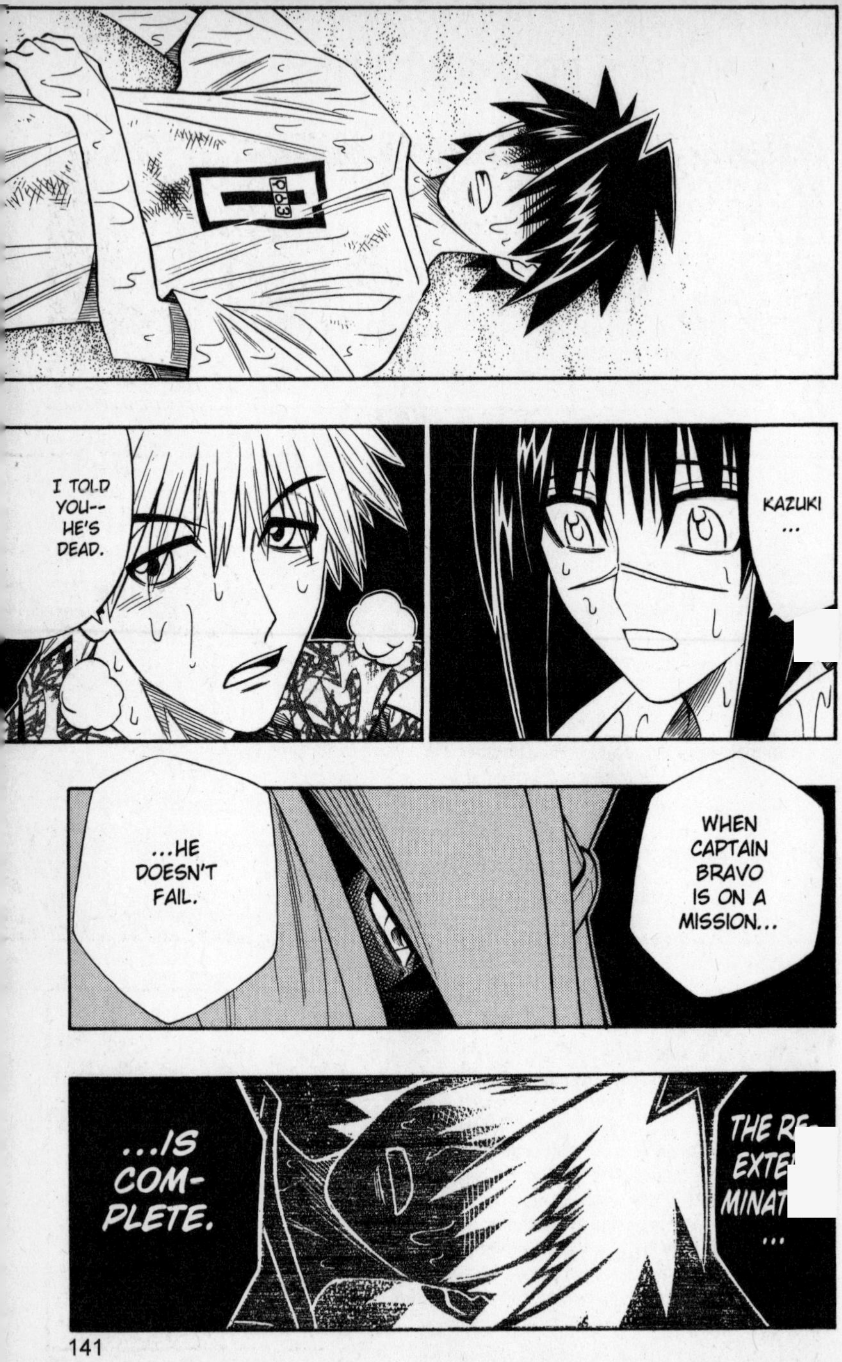
KAZUKI ...
I TOLD YOU-- HE'S DEAD.
WHEN CAPTAIN BRAVO IS ON A MISSION...
...HE DOESN'T FAIL.
THE RE- EXTE MINAT ...
...IS COM- PLETE.

"There are no exits to my Wonderland!"

Buso Renkin File No. 10

アリス・イン ワンダーランド

ALICE IN WONDERLAND

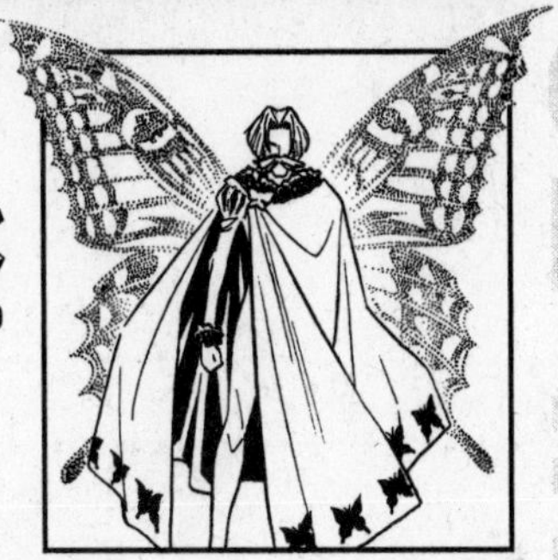

- Kakugane Serial Number: XXII (22)
- Creator: Bakushaku Chouno (Dr. Butterfly)
- Form: Chaff
- Main Color: Platinum White
- Special Abilities:
  - In its scattered form, it confuses the senses of direction and distance. It also disrupts electronics and prevents communication.
  - In its concentrated form, it affects the human brain, causing hallucinations and disrupting the psyche.
- Special Traits:
  - In scattered form, it can cover an area of about one kilometer in diameter.
  - The fog is created by saturating the chaff before deployment and is not a function of the Buso Renkin's power.
  - In its concentrated form, it uses the refractive properties of the chaff to attack the mind via the sense of sight.
  - The visions the victim sees are generated randomly by the brain. A very strong will is required to resist these effects.
- Author's Notes:
  - This special ability came from the idea of making an island on land. In this day of technological wonders like cellular phones and mass transit, it takes extraordinary powers to really cut people off from the rest of the world.
  - I created the concentrated form of the chaff especially for the battle between Dr. Butterfly and Papillon. I'd always wanted to do a psychological battle so that was a lot of fun.
  - The design was meant to be a counterpart for Papillon's Near-Death Happiness, only this one was white instead of black.
  - The weapon is named after the title character of *Alice's Adventures in Wonderland*. In the beginning I wanted all the Buso Renkin of the L.X.E. to be named after fairy tales.

ALICE IN WONDERLAND

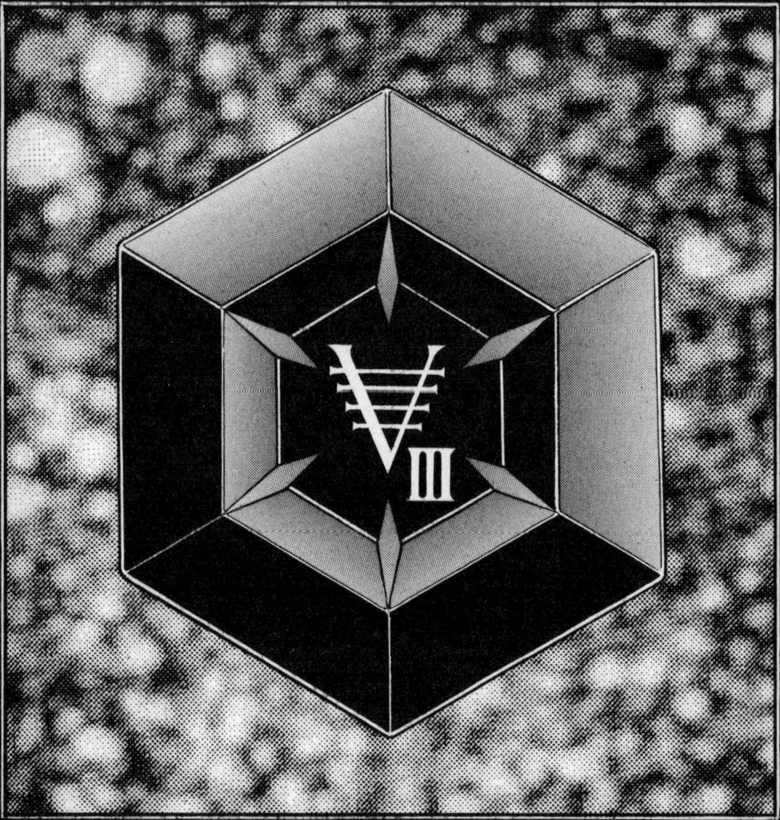

CHAPTER 53:

WHEN THE NIGHT ENDS

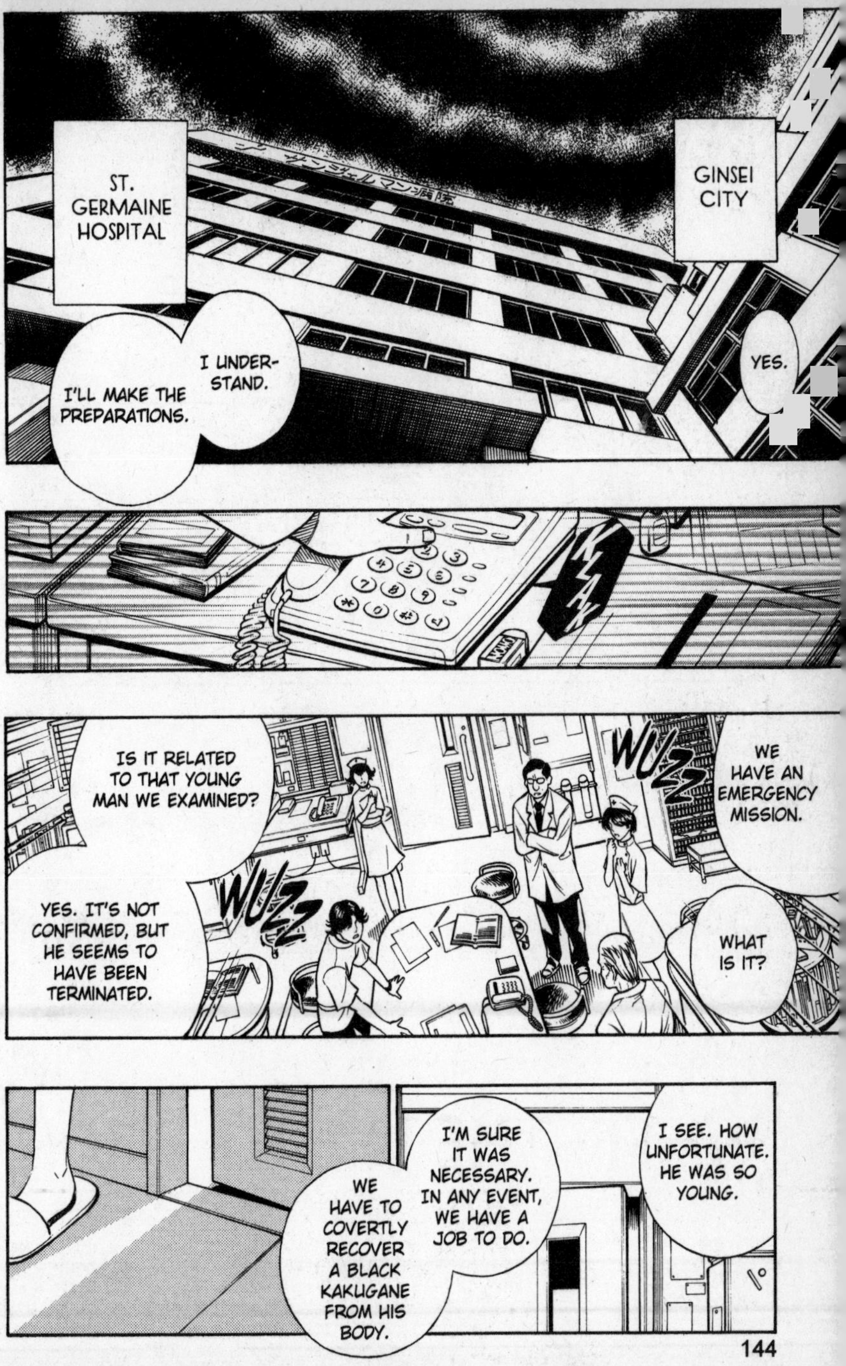
GINSEI CITY
ST. GERMAINE HOSPITAL
YES.
I UNDER-STAND.
I'LL MAKE THE PREPARATIONS.
KLAK
WUZZ
WE HAVE AN EMERGENCY MISSION.
WHAT IS IT?
IS IT RELATED TO THAT YOUNG MAN WE EXAMINED?
WUZZ
YES. IT'S NOT CONFIRMED, BUT HE SEEMS TO HAVE BEEN TERMINATED.
I SEE. HOW UNFORTUNATE. HE WAS SO YOUNG.
I'M SURE IT WAS NECESSARY. IN ANY EVENT, WE HAVE A JOB TO DO.
WE HAVE TO COVERTLY RECOVER A BLACK KAKUGANE FROM HIS BODY.

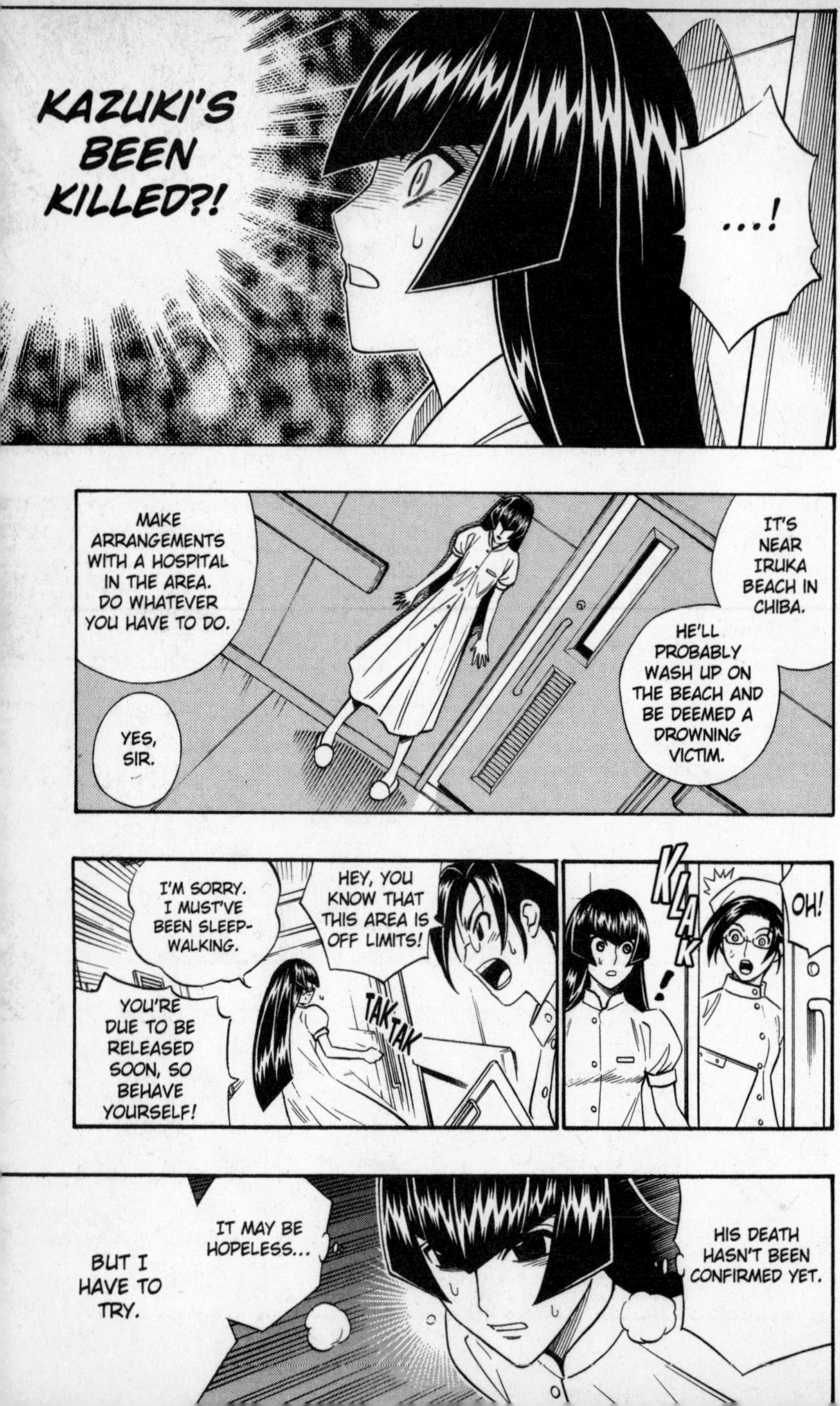
...!
KAZUKI'S BEEN KILLED?!
IT'S NEAR IRUKA BEACH IN CHIBA.
HE'LL PROBABLY WASH UP ON THE BEACH AND BE DEEMED A DROWNING VICTIM.
MAKE ARRANGEMENTS WITH A HOSPITAL IN THE AREA. DO WHATEVER YOU HAVE TO DO.
YES, SIR.
KLAK
OH!
!
HEY, YOU KNOW THAT THIS AREA IS OFF LIMITS!
I'M SORRY. I MUST'VE BEEN SLEEP-WALKING.
TAK TAK
YOU'RE DUE TO BE RELEASED SOON, SO BEHAVE YOURSELF!
HIS DEATH HASN'T BEEN CONFIRMED YET.
IT MAY BE HOPELESS...
BUT I HAVE TO TRY.

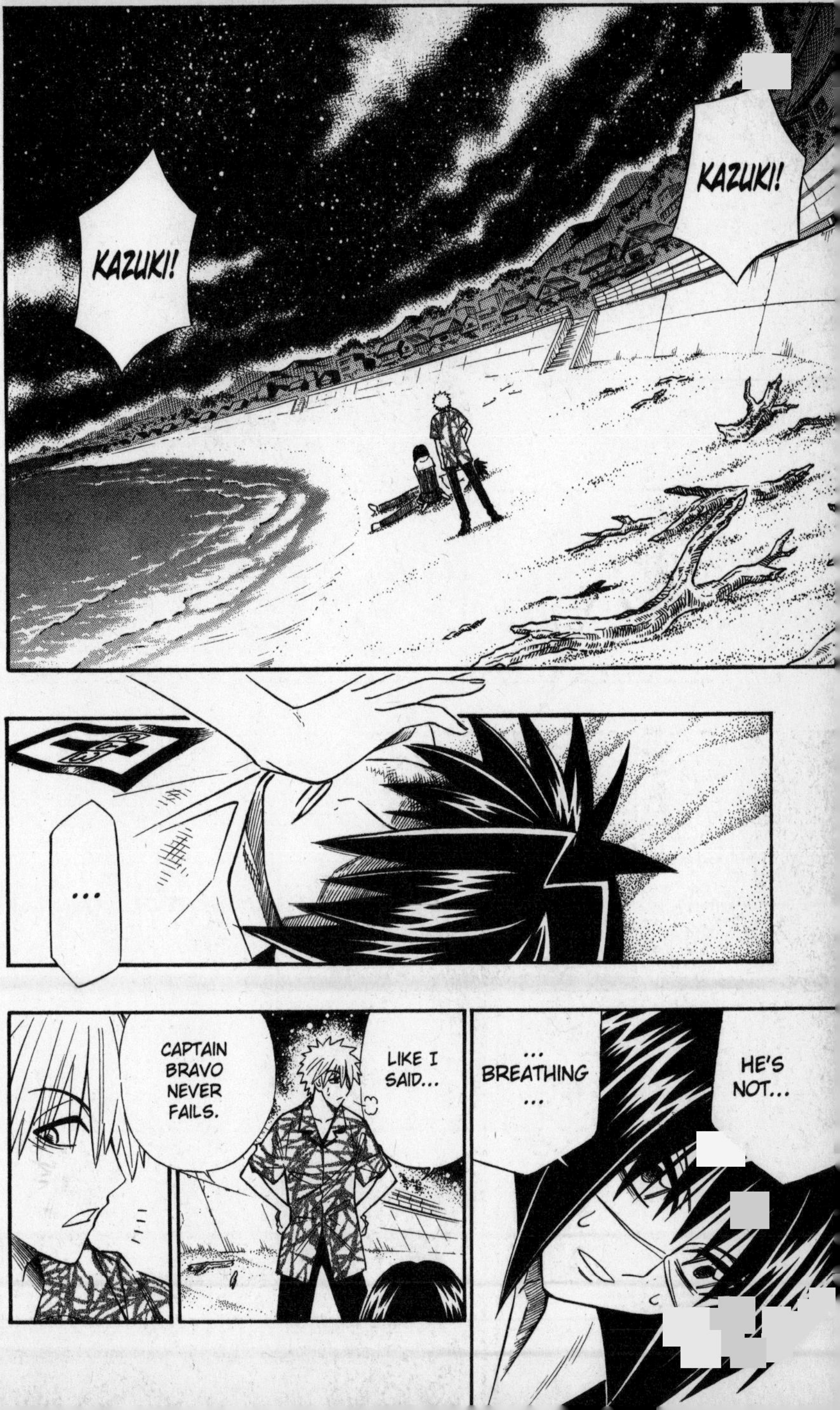
KAZUKI!
KAZUKI!
...
HE'S NOT...
... BREATHING ...
LIKE I SAID...
CAPTAIN BRAVO NEVER FAILS.

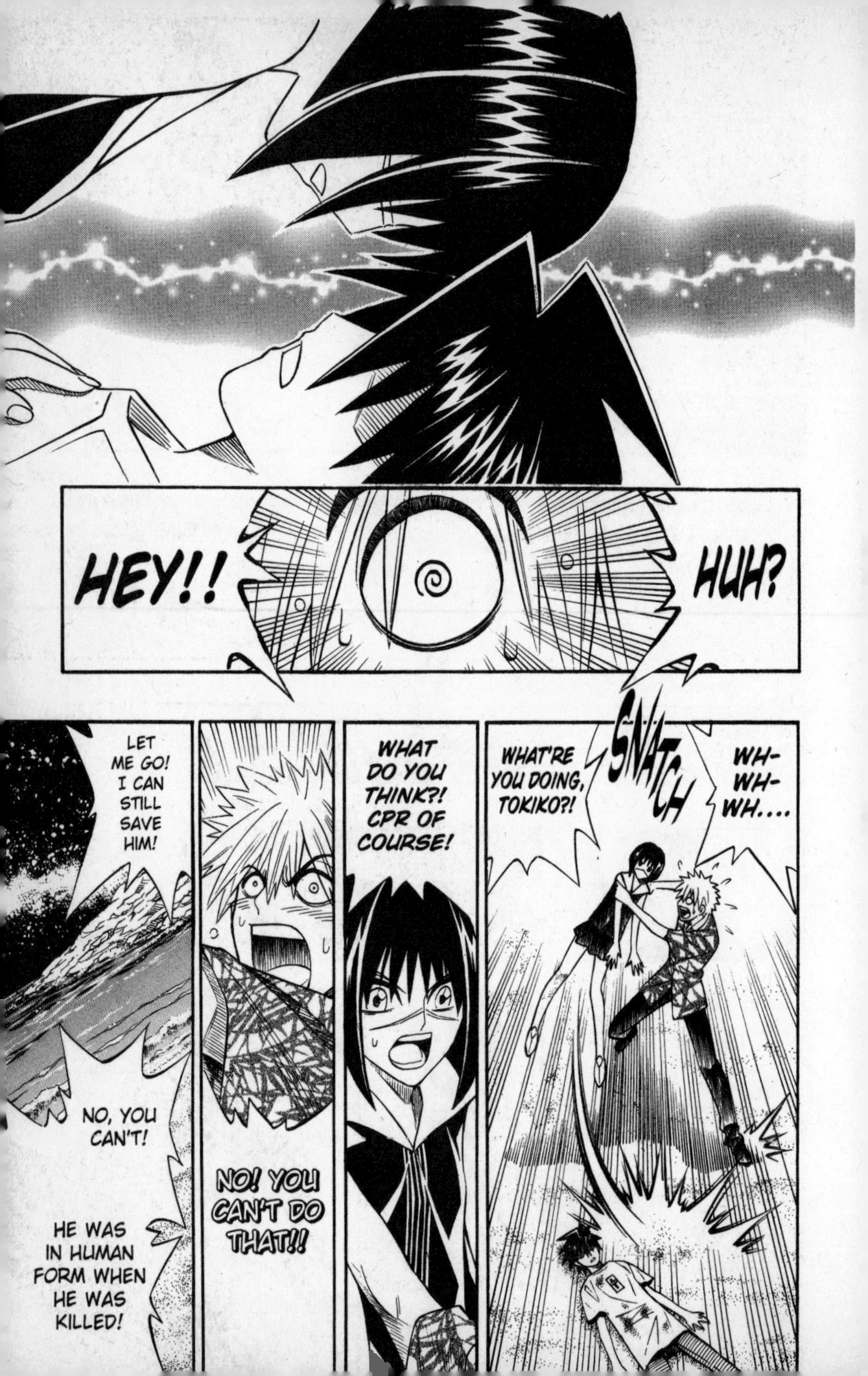
HUH?
HEY!!
WH-WH-WH....
SNATCH
WHAT'RE YOU DOING, TOKIKO?!
WHAT DO YOU THINK?! CPR OF COURSE!
NO! YOU CAN'T DO THAT!!
LET ME GO! I CAN STILL SAVE HIM!
NO, YOU CAN'T!
HE WAS IN HUMAN FORM WHEN HE WAS KILLED!

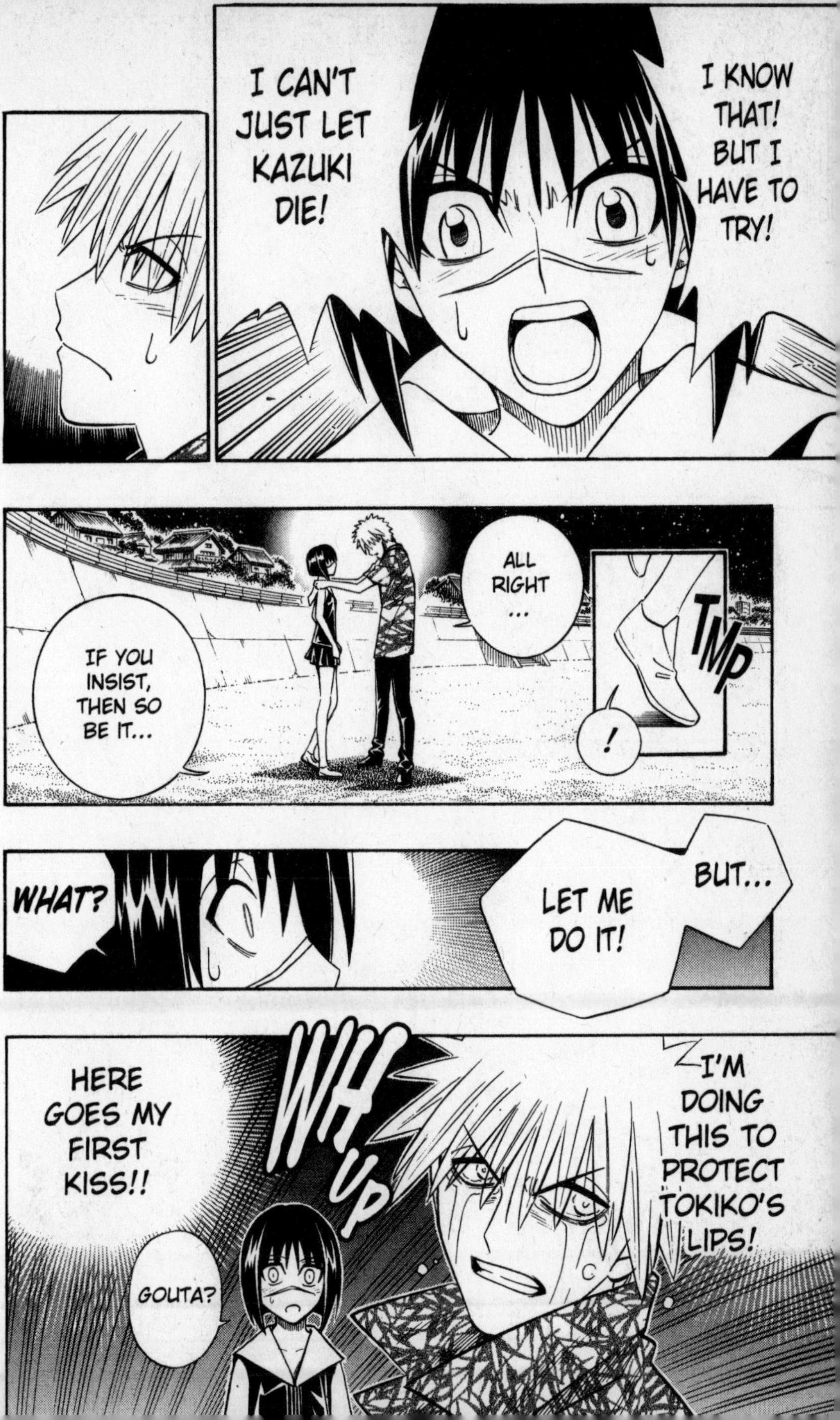
I KNOW THAT! BUT I HAVE TO TRY!
I CAN'T JUST LET KAZUKI DIE!
TMP
!
ALL RIGHT ...
IF YOU INSIST, THEN SO BE IT...
BUT...
LET ME DO IT!
WHAT?
I'M DOING THIS TO PROTECT TOKIKO'S LIPS!
WHUP
HERE GOES MY FIRST KISS!!
GOUTA?

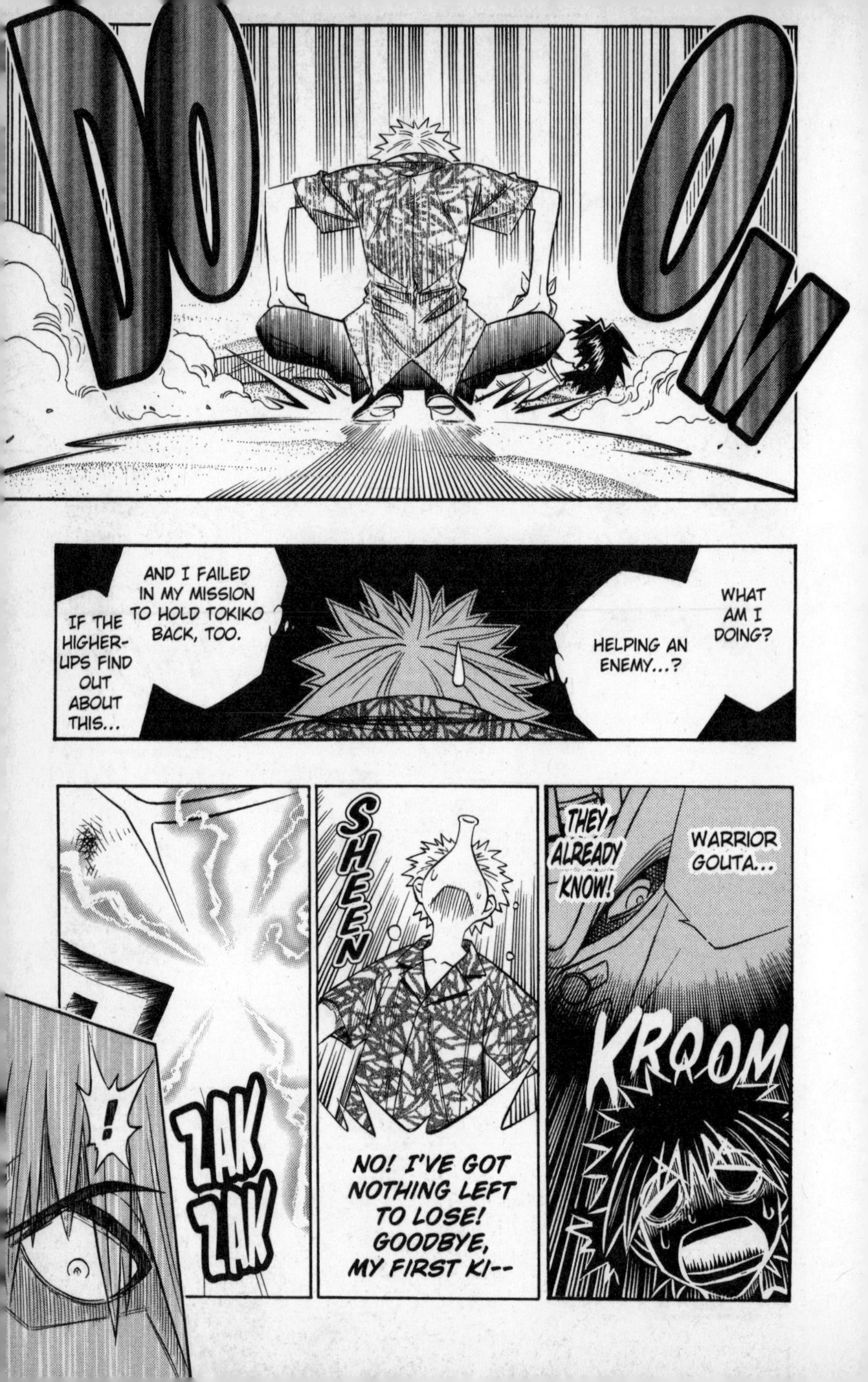
DOON
WHAT AM I DOING?
HELPING AN ENEMY...?
AND I FAILED IN MY MISSION TO HOLD TOKIKO BACK, TOO.
IF THE HIGHER-UPS FIND OUT ABOUT THIS...
WARRIOR GOUTA...
THEY ALREADY KNOW!
KROOM
SHEEN
NO! I'VE GOT NOTHING LEFT TO LOSE! GOODBYE, MY FIRST KI--
!
ZAK ZAK

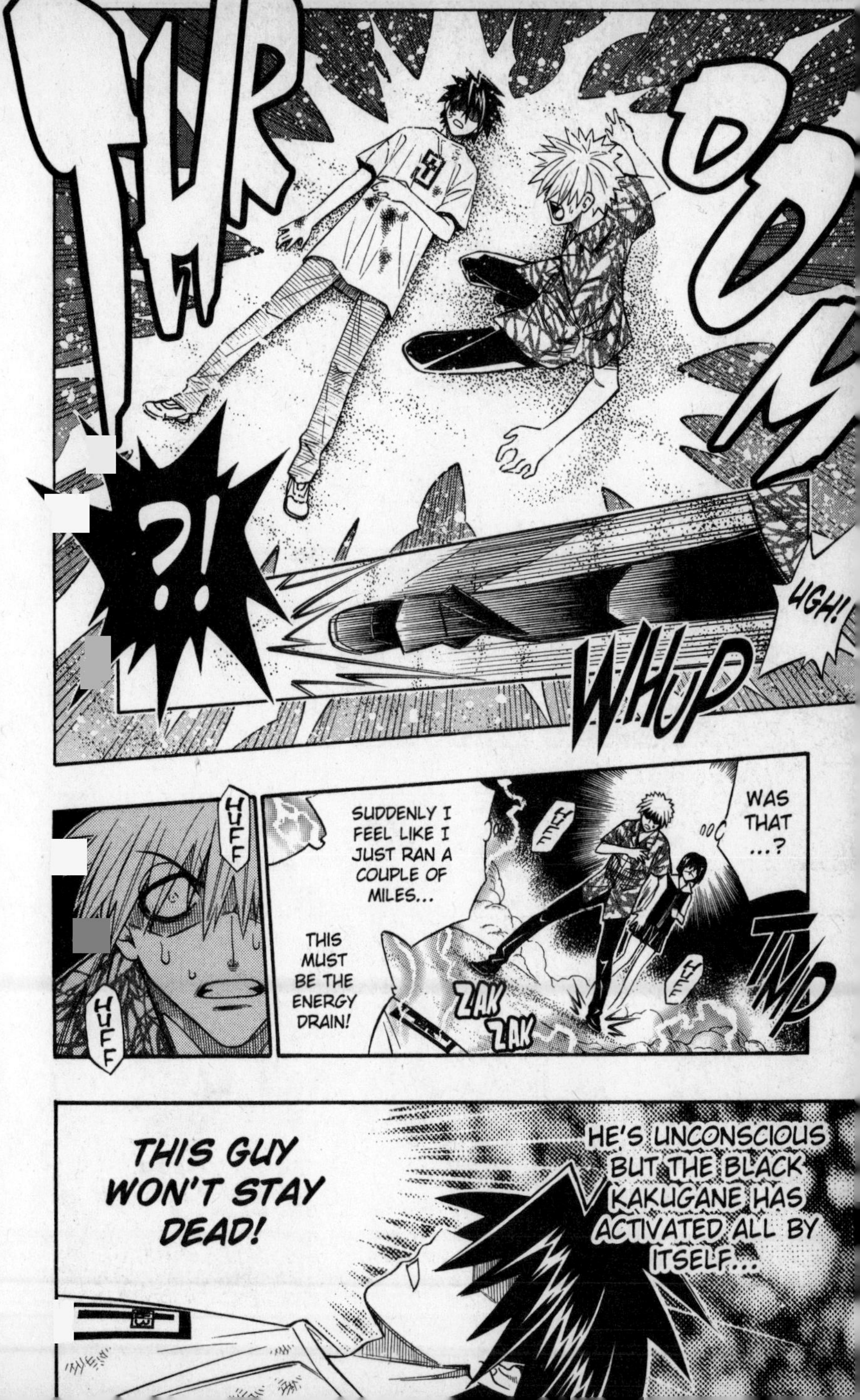
UGH!
WHUP
?!
WAS THAT ...?
HUFF
SUDDENLY I FEEL LIKE I JUST RAN A COUPLE OF MILES...
THIS MUST BE THE ENERGY DRAIN!
ZAK ZAK
HUFF
HUFF
HUFF
HE'S UNCONSCIOUS BUT THE BLACK KAKUGANE HAS ACTIVATED ALL BY ITSELF...
THIS GUY WON'T STAY DEAD!

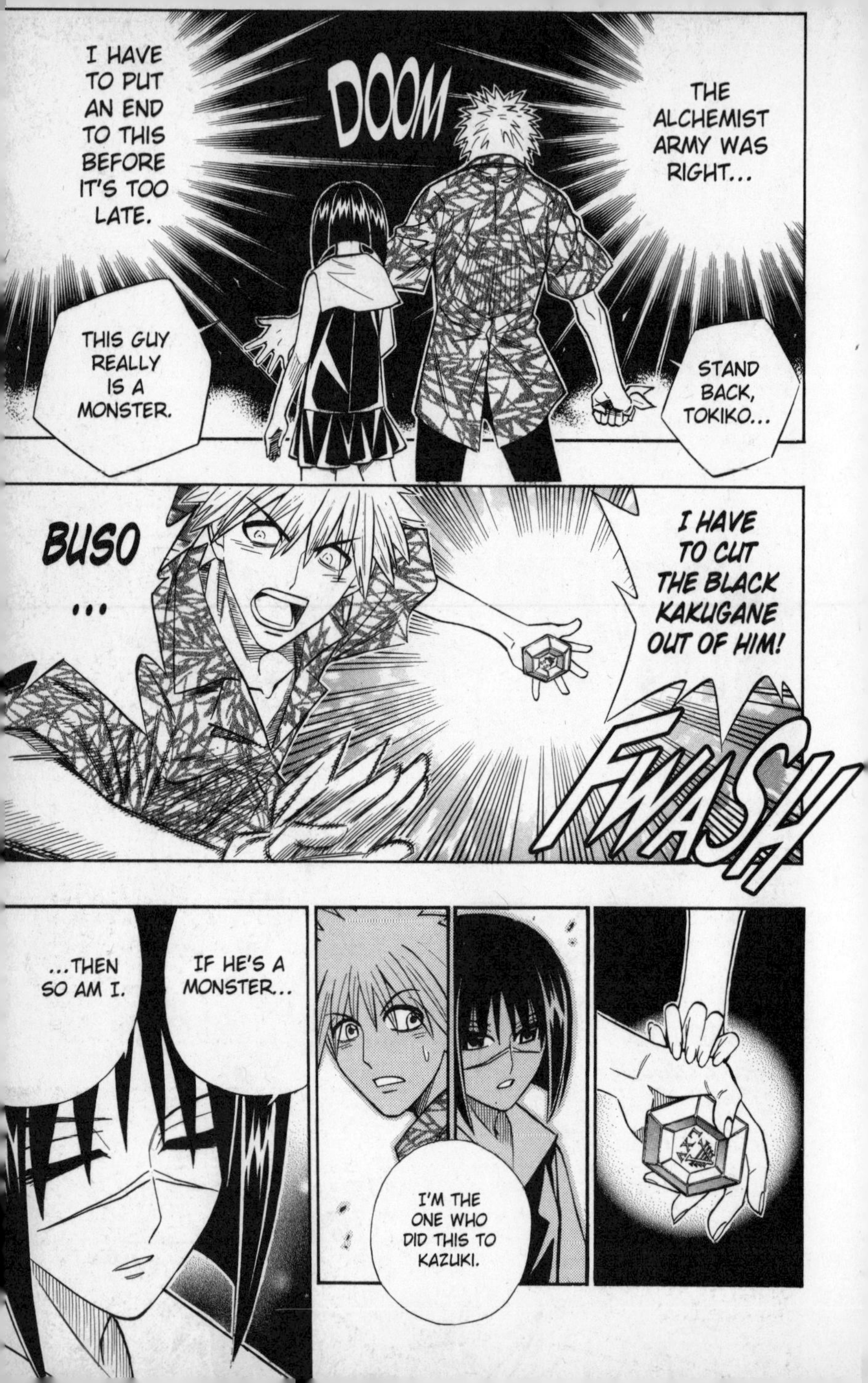
THE ALCHEMIST ARMY WAS RIGHT...
DOOM
I HAVE TO PUT AN END TO THIS BEFORE IT'S TOO LATE.
STAND BACK, TOKIKO...
THIS GUY REALLY IS A MONSTER.
I HAVE TO CUT THE BLACK KAKUGANE OUT OF HIM!
BUSO...
FWASH
I'M THE ONE WHO DID THIS TO KAZUKI.
IF HE'S A MONSTER...
...THEN SO AM I.

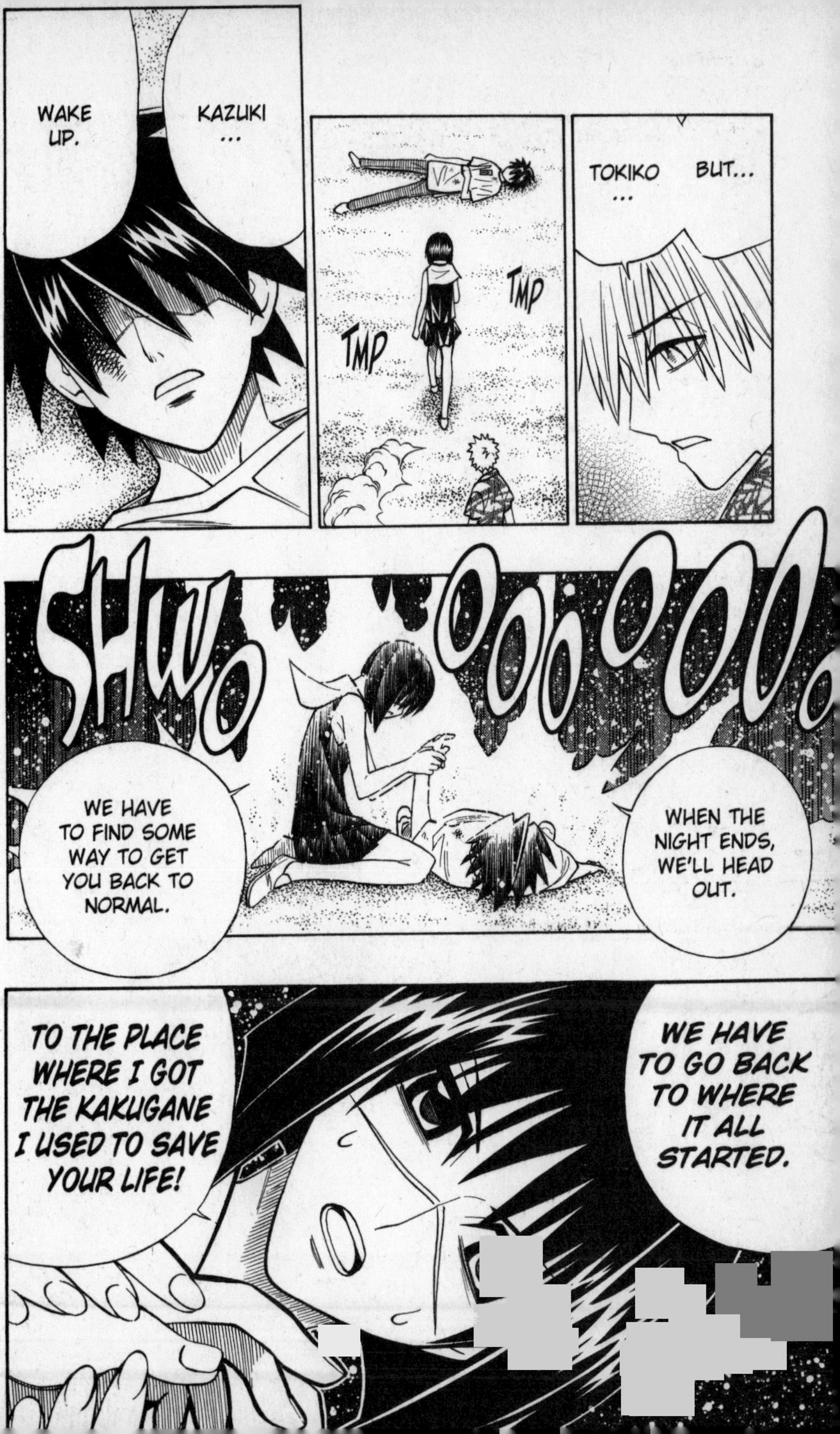

BUT...
TOKIKO ...
TMP
TMP
KAZUKI ...
WAKE UP.
SHUOOOOOOO
WHEN THE NIGHT ENDS, WE'LL HEAD OUT.
WE HAVE TO FIND SOME WAY TO GET YOU BACK TO NORMAL.
WE HAVE TO GO BACK TO WHERE IT ALL STARTED.
TO THE PLACE WHERE I GOT THE KAKUGANE I USED TO SAVE YOUR LIFE!

READ THIS WAY

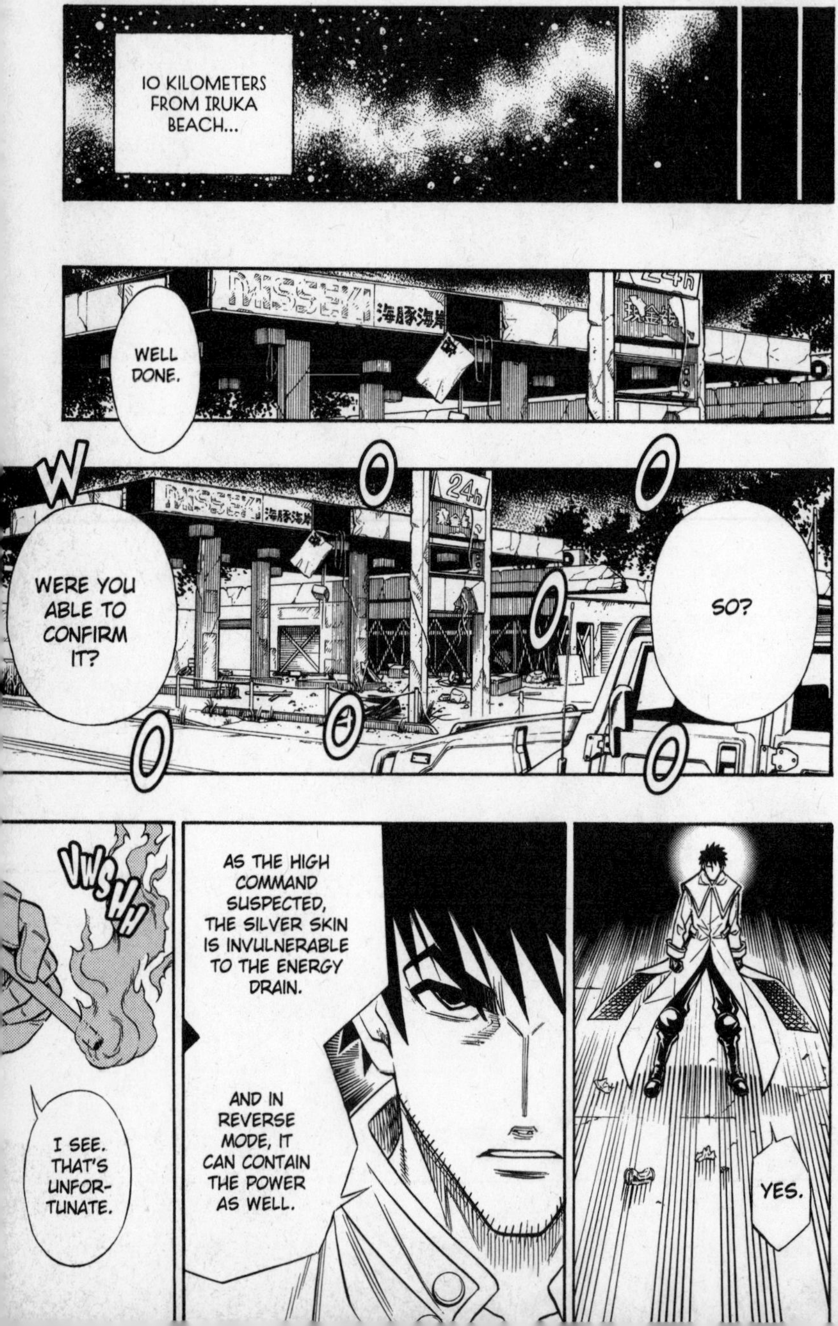
10 KILOMETERS FROM IRUKA BEACH...
海豚海岸
WELL DONE.
SO?
W
WERE YOU ABLE TO CONFIRM IT?
YES.
AS THE HIGH COMMAND SUSPECTED, THE SILVER SKIN IS INVULNERABLE TO THE ENERGY DRAIN.
AND IN REVERSE MODE, IT CAN CONTAIN THE POWER AS WELL.
VWSHH
I SEE. THAT'S UNFORTUNATE.

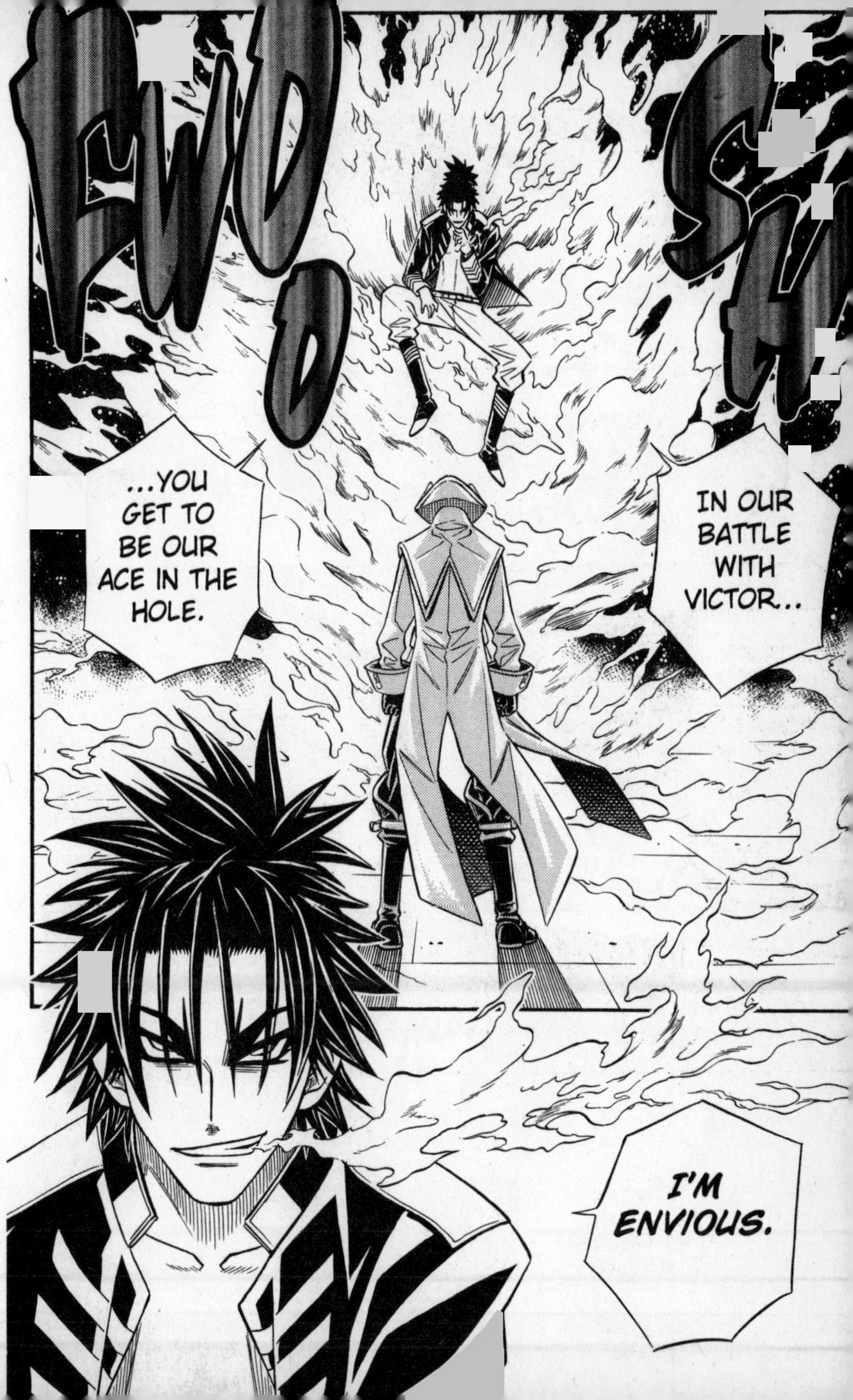
IN OUR BATTLE WITH VICTOR...
...YOU GET TO BE OUR ACE IN THE HOLE.
I'M ENVIOUS.

READ THIS WAY

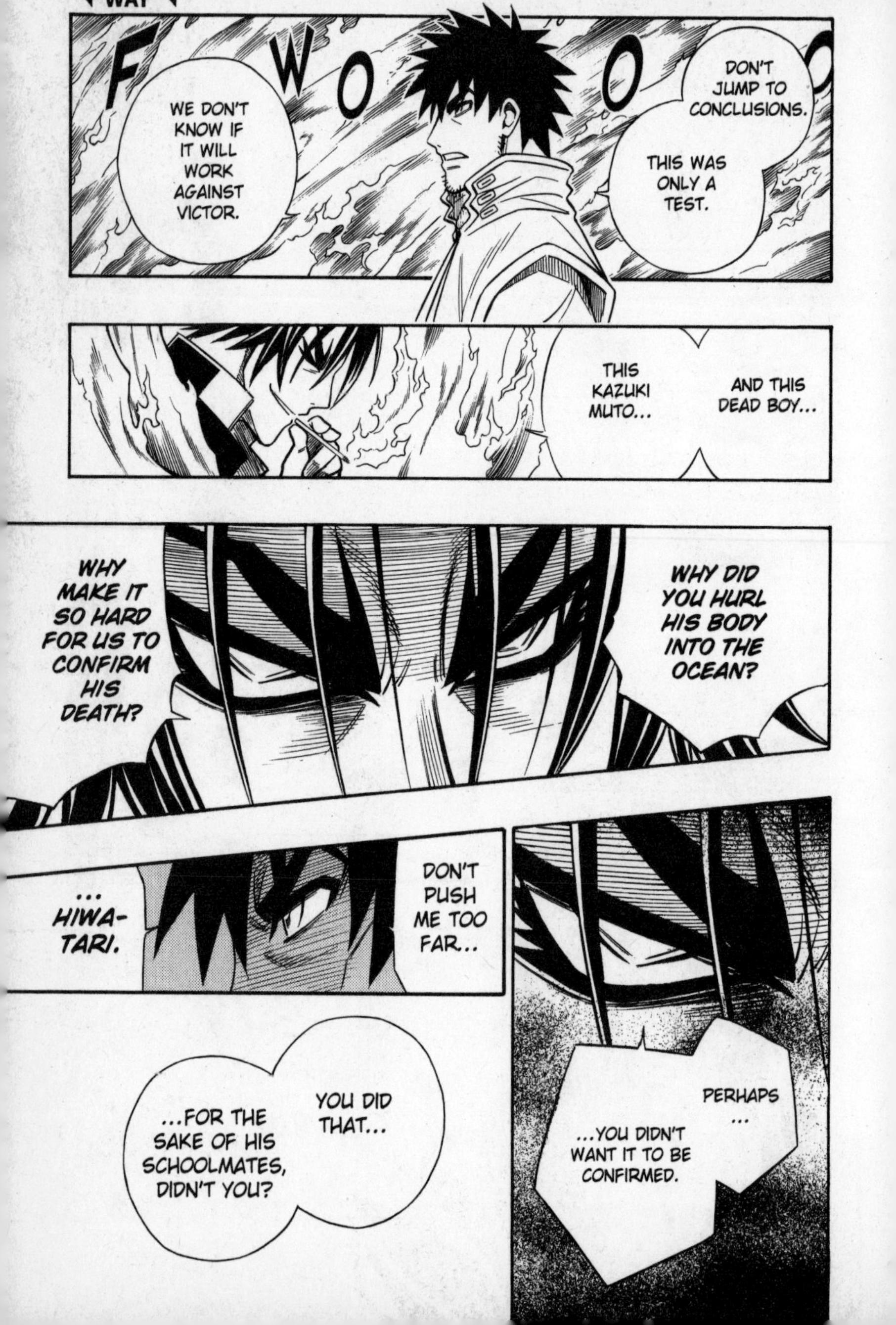
DON'T JUMP TO CONCLUSIONS.
THIS WAS ONLY A TEST.
FWOOO
WE DON'T KNOW IF IT WILL WORK AGAINST VICTOR.
AND THIS DEAD BOY...
THIS KAZUKI MUTO...
WHY DID YOU HURL HIS BODY INTO THE OCEAN?
WHY MAKE IT SO HARD FOR US TO CONFIRM HIS DEATH?
PERHAPS...
...YOU DIDN'T WANT IT TO BE CONFIRMED.
YOU DID THAT...
...FOR THE SAKE OF HIS SCHOOLMATES, DIDN'T YOU?
DON'T PUSH ME TOO FAR...
...HIWATARI.

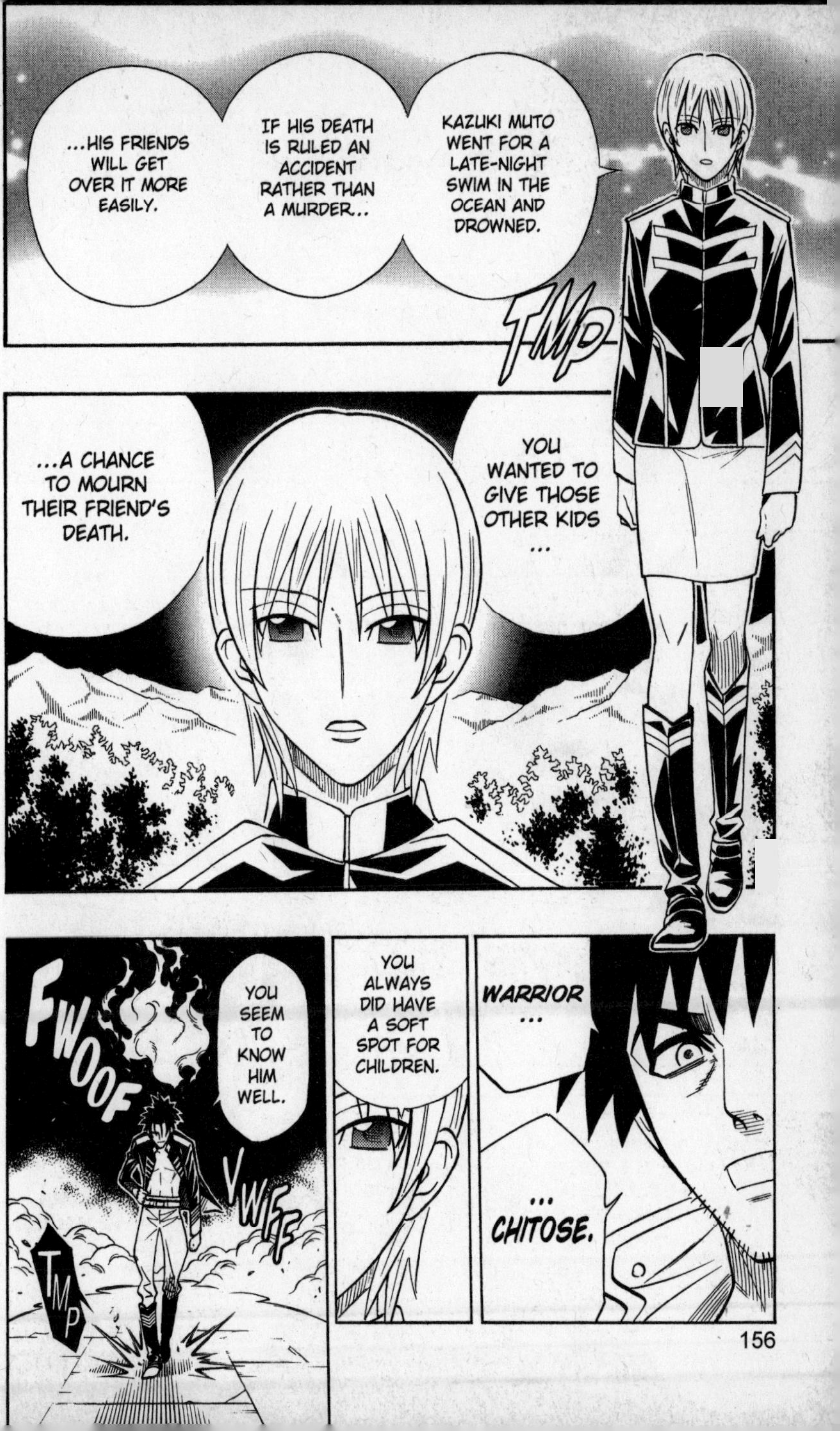
KAZUKI MUTO WENT FOR A LATE-NIGHT SWIM IN THE OCEAN AND DROWNED.
IF HIS DEATH IS RULED AN ACCIDENT RATHER THAN A MURDER...
...HIS FRIENDS WILL GET OVER IT MORE EASILY.
TMP
YOU WANTED TO GIVE THOSE OTHER KIDS ...
...A CHANCE TO MOURN THEIR FRIEND'S DEATH.
WARRIOR ...
... CHITOSE.
YOU ALWAYS DID HAVE A SOFT SPOT FOR CHILDREN.
YOU SEEM TO KNOW HIM WELL.
FWOOF
VWFF
TMP

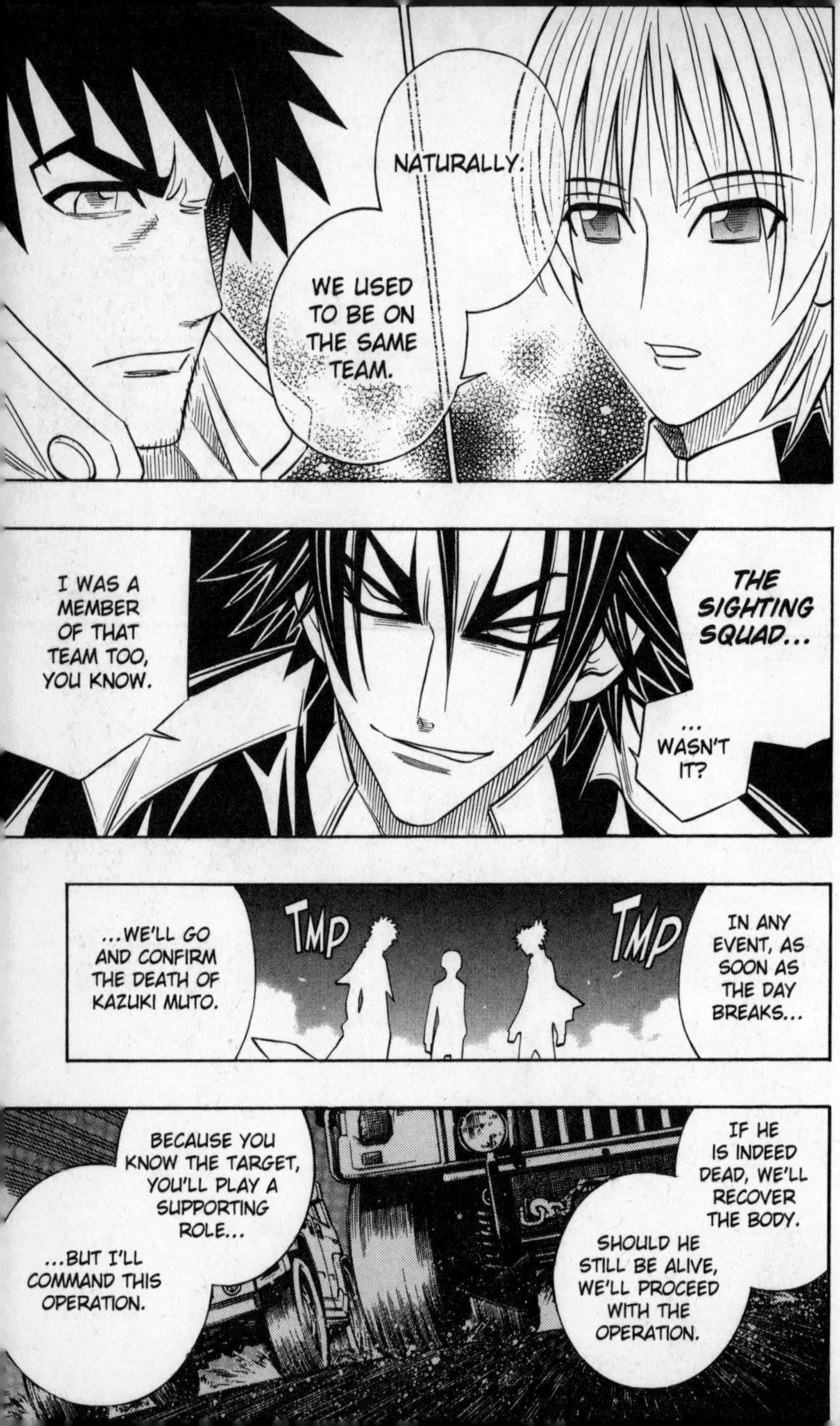
NATURALLY.
WE USED TO BE ON THE SAME TEAM.
THE SIGHTING SQUAD...
...WASN'T IT?
I WAS A MEMBER OF THAT TEAM TOO, YOU KNOW.
IN ANY EVENT, AS SOON AS THE DAY BREAKS...
TMP
TMP
...WE'LL GO AND CONFIRM THE DEATH OF KAZUKI MUTO.
IF HE IS INDEED DEAD, WE'LL RECOVER THE BODY.
SHOULD HE STILL BE ALIVE, WE'LL PROCEED WITH THE OPERATION.
BECAUSE YOU KNOW THE TARGET, YOU'LL PLAY A SUPPORTING ROLE...
...BUT I'LL COMMAND THIS OPERATION.

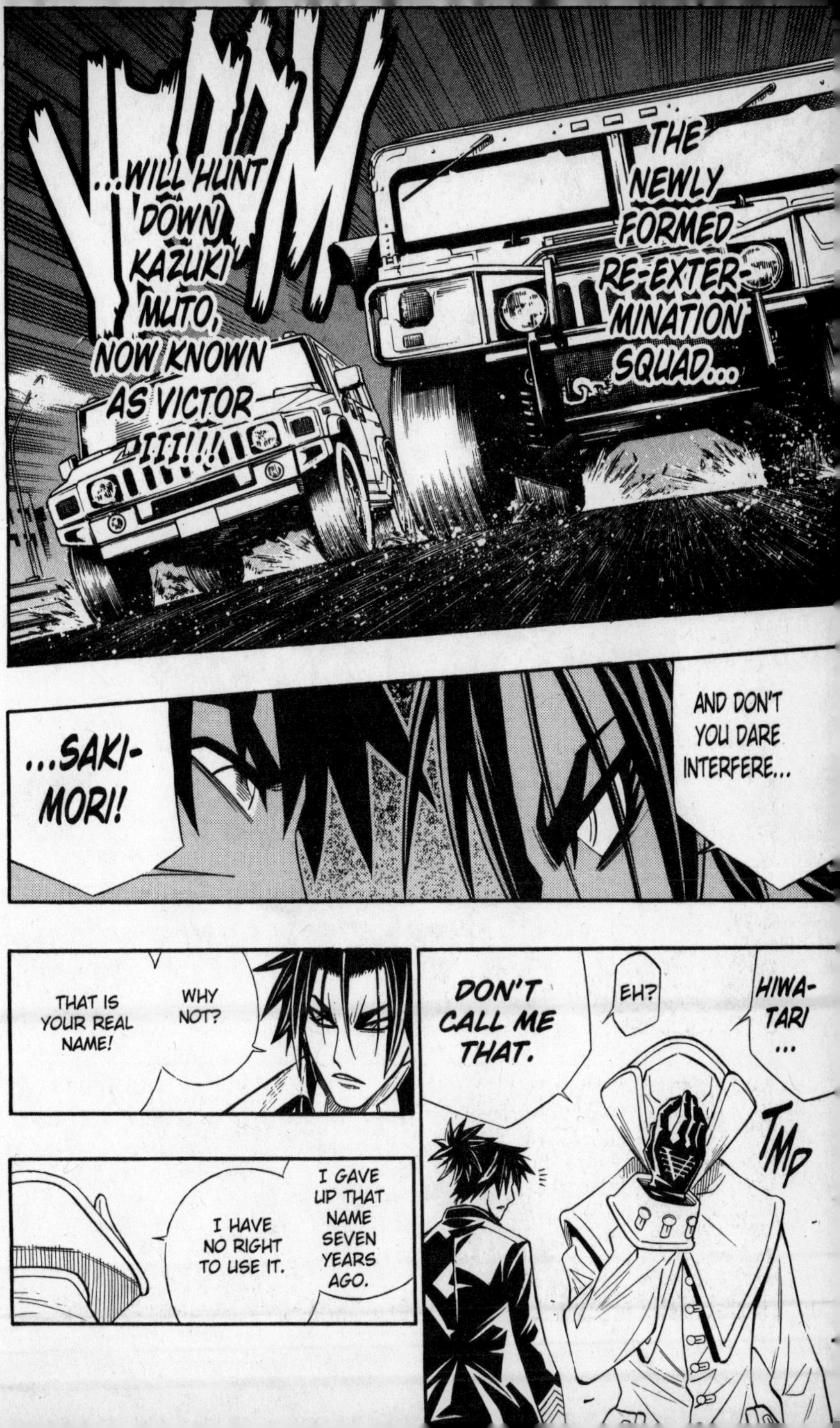
THE NEWLY FORMED RE-EXTER-MINATION SQUAD...
...WILL HUNT DOWN KAZUKI MUTO, NOW KNOWN AS VICTOR III!!!
AND DON'T YOU DARE INTERFERE...
...SAKI-MORI!
HIWA-TARI ...
EH?
DON'T CALL ME THAT.
TMP
WHY NOT?
THAT IS YOUR REAL NAME!
I GAVE UP THAT NAME SEVEN YEARS AGO.
I HAVE NO RIGHT TO USE IT.

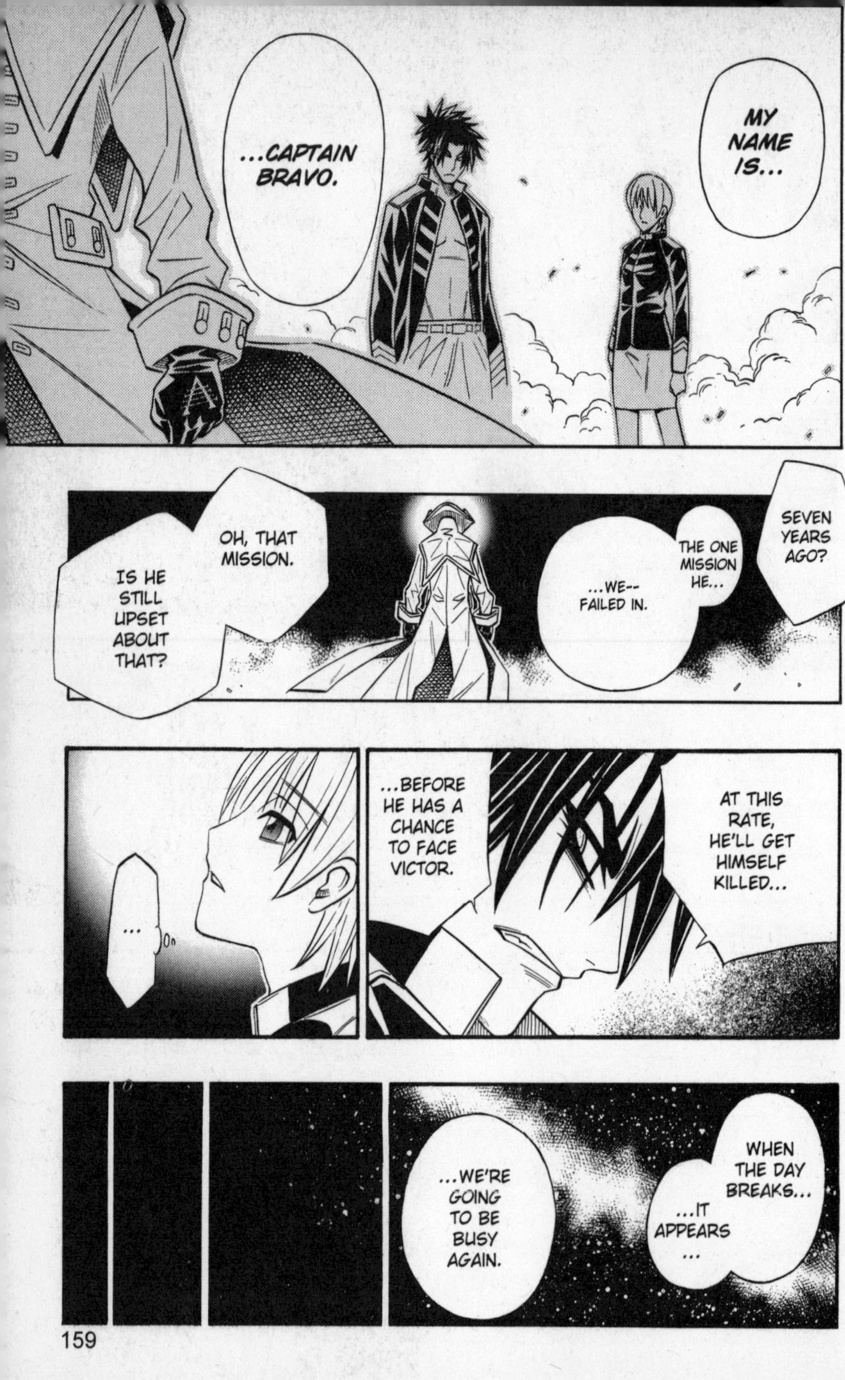
MY NAME IS...
...CAPTAIN BRAVO.
SEVEN YEARS AGO?
THE ONE MISSION HE...
...WE-- FAILED IN.
OH, THAT MISSION.
IS HE STILL UPSET ABOUT THAT?
AT THIS RATE, HE'LL GET HIMSELF KILLED...
...BEFORE HE HAS A CHANCE TO FACE VICTOR.
...
WHEN THE DAY BREAKS...
...IT APPEARS ...
...WE'RE GOING TO BE BUSY AGAIN.

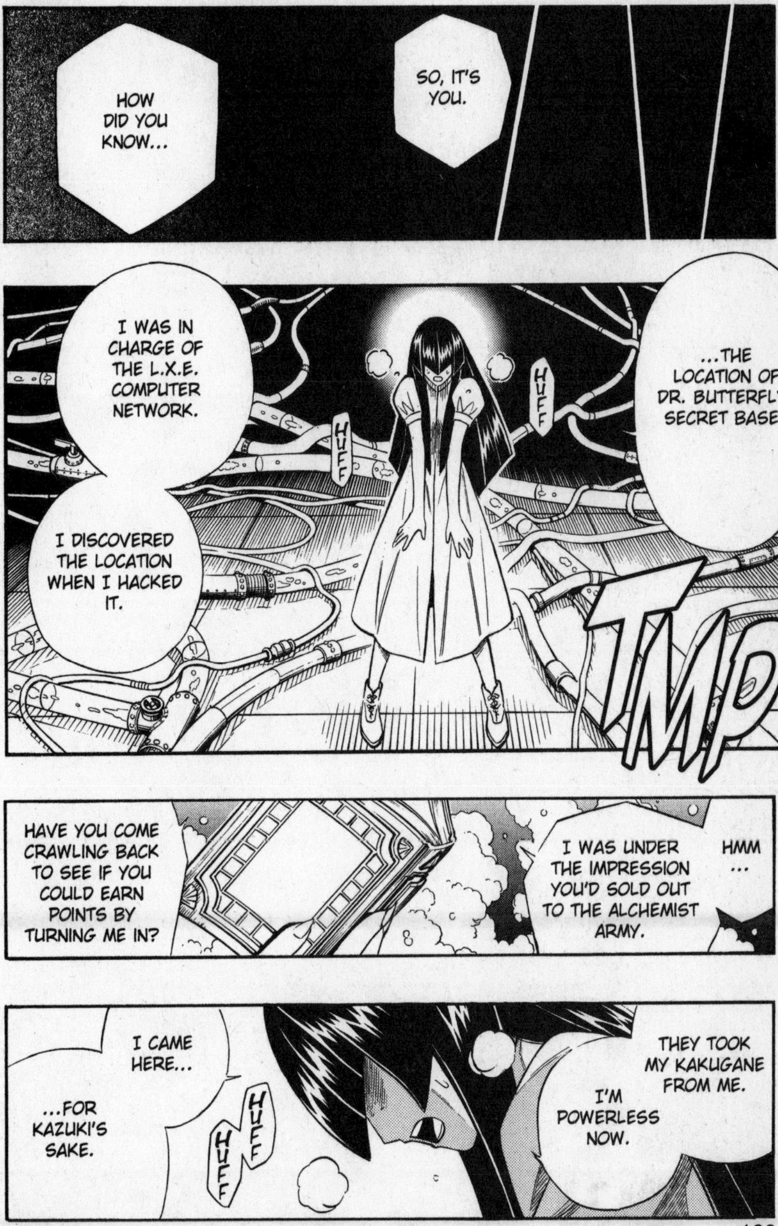
SO, IT'S YOU.
HOW DID YOU KNOW...
...THE LOCATION OF DR. BUTTERFLY'S SECRET BASE?
HUFF
HUFF
I WAS IN CHARGE OF THE L.X.E. COMPUTER NETWORK.
I DISCOVERED THE LOCATION WHEN I HACKED IT.
TMP
HMM...
I WAS UNDER THE IMPRESSION YOU'D SOLD OUT TO THE ALCHEMIST ARMY.
HAVE YOU COME CRAWLING BACK TO SEE IF YOU COULD EARN POINTS BY TURNING ME IN?
THEY TOOK MY KAKUGANE FROM ME.
I'M POWERLESS NOW.
HUFF
HUFF
I CAME HERE...
...FOR KAZUKI'S SAKE.

READ THIS WAY

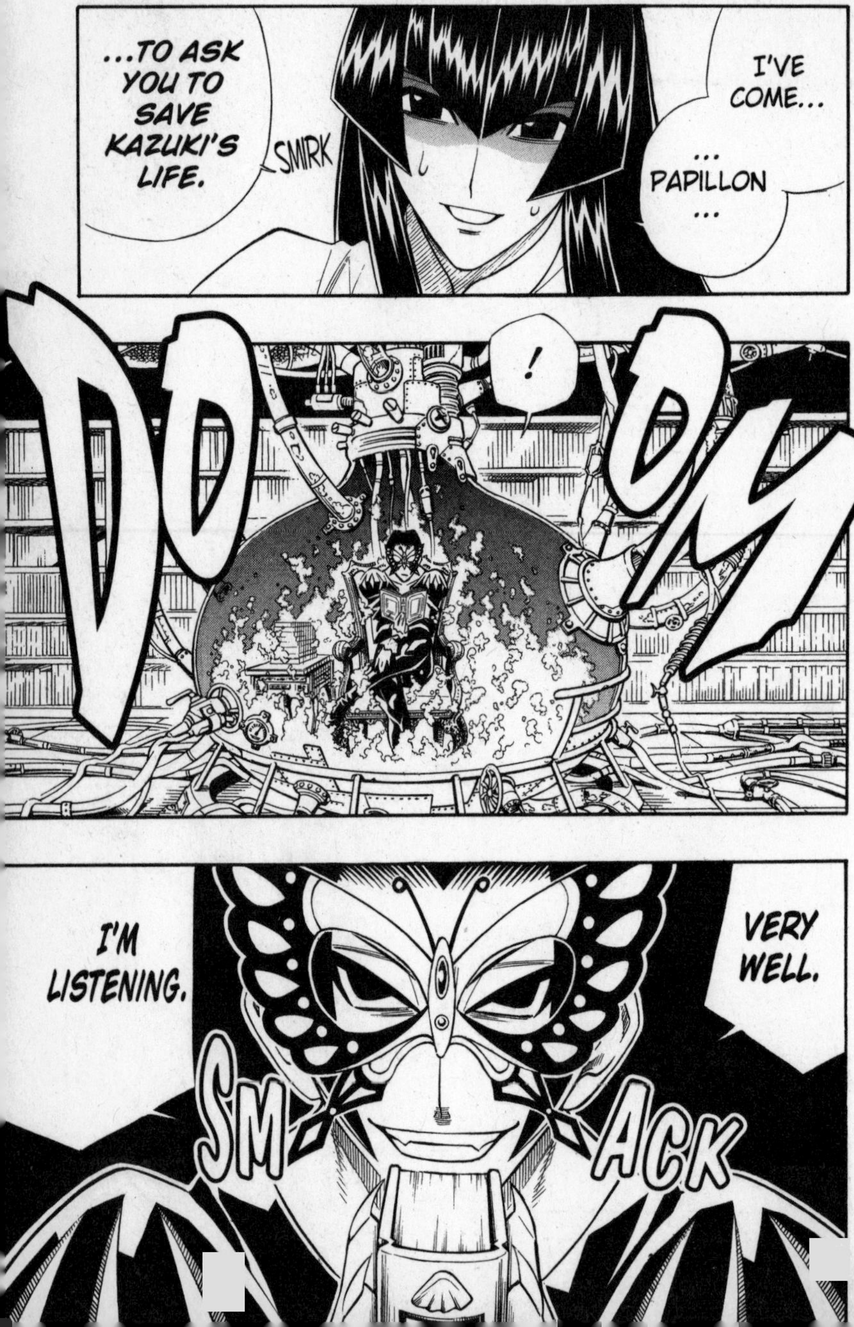
I'VE COME...
... PAPILLON ...
...TO ASK YOU TO SAVE KAZUKI'S LIFE.
SMIRK
DOON
!
VERY WELL.
I'M LISTENING.
SMACK

Buso Renkin
ブソウレンキン

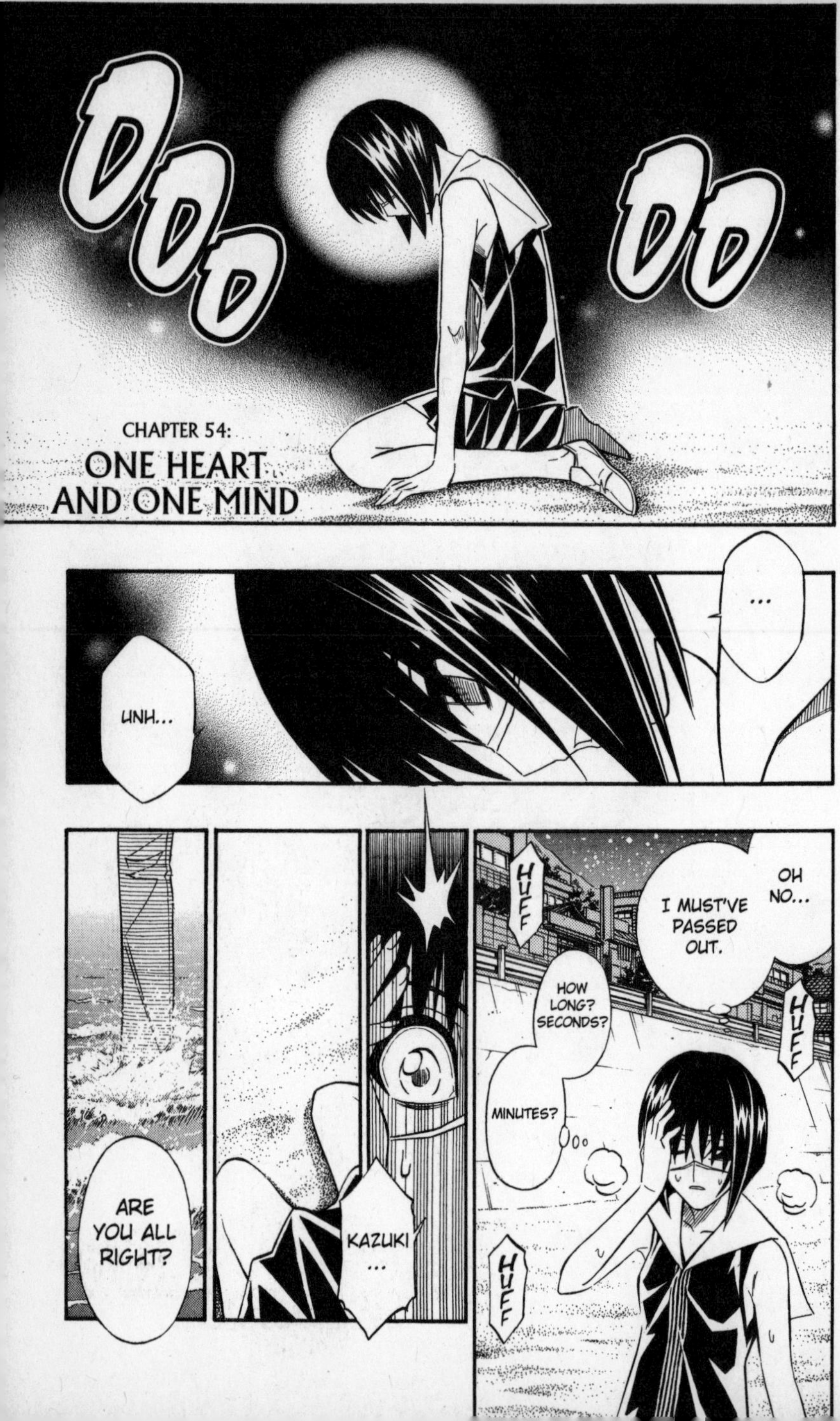
CHAPTER 54:
ONE HEART AND ONE MIND
...
UNH...
OH NO...
I MUST'VE PASSED OUT.
HUFF
HUFF
HOW LONG? SECONDS?
MINUTES?
HUFF
KAZUKI ...
ARE YOU ALL RIGHT?

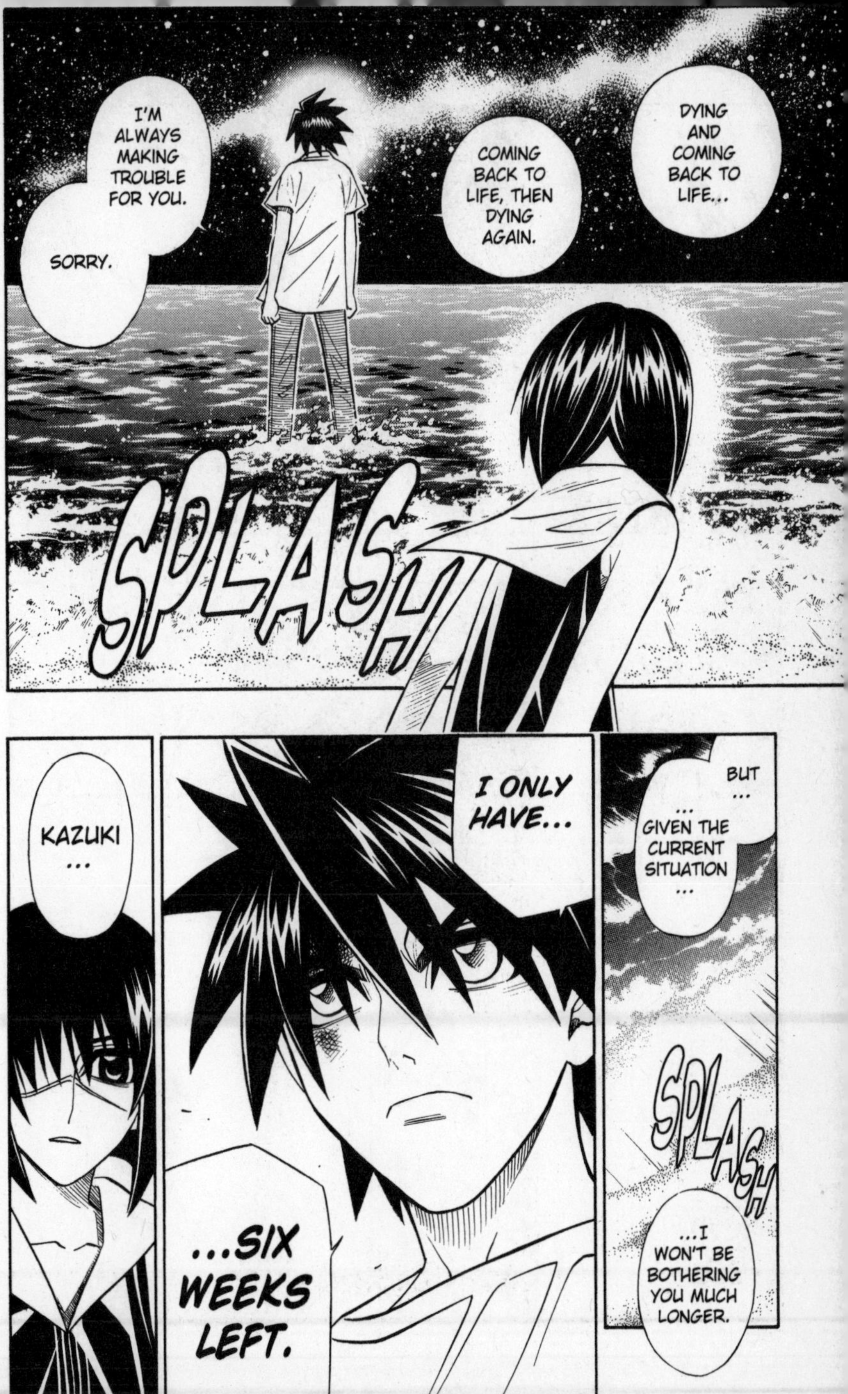
DYING AND COMING BACK TO LIFE...
COMING BACK TO LIFE, THEN DYING AGAIN.
I'M ALWAYS MAKING TROUBLE FOR YOU.
SORRY.
SPLASH
BUT ... ... GIVEN THE CURRENT SITUATION ...
SPLASH
...I WON'T BE BOTHERING YOU MUCH LONGER.
I ONLY HAVE...
...SIX WEEKS LEFT.
KAZUKI ...

CHAPTER 54:
ONE HEART AND ONE MIND

CHAPTER 54: ONE HEART AND ONE MIND

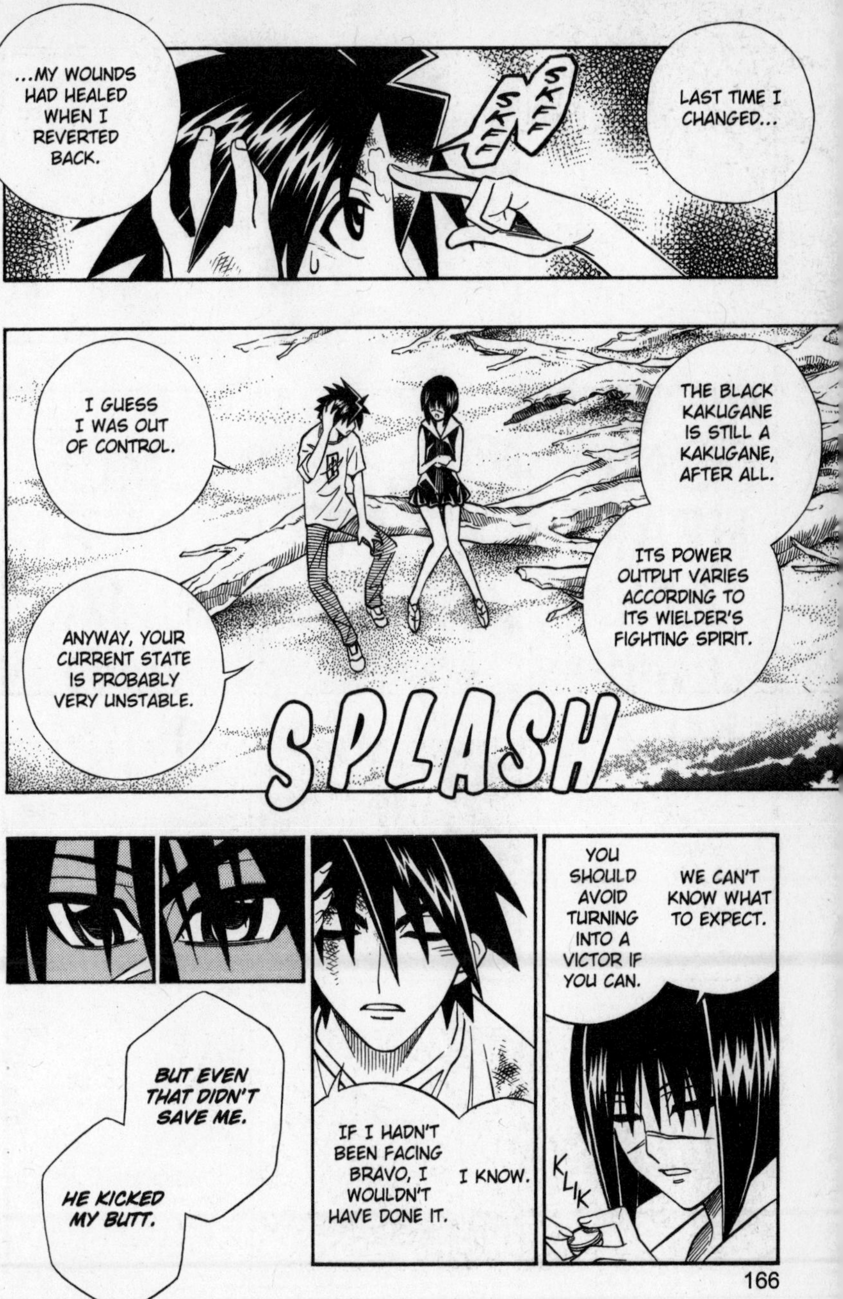
LAST TIME I CHANGED...
SKEFF SKEFF
...MY WOUNDS HAD HEALED WHEN I REVERTED BACK.
THE BLACK KAKUGANE IS STILL A KAKUGANE, AFTER ALL.
I GUESS I WAS OUT OF CONTROL.
ITS POWER OUTPUT VARIES ACCORDING TO ITS WIELDER'S FIGHTING SPIRIT.
ANYWAY, YOUR CURRENT STATE IS PROBABLY VERY UNSTABLE.
SPLASH
WE CAN'T KNOW WHAT TO EXPECT.
YOU SHOULD AVOID TURNING INTO A VICTOR IF YOU CAN.
KLIK
I KNOW.
IF I HADN'T BEEN FACING BRAVO, I WOULDN'T HAVE DONE IT.
BUT EVEN THAT DIDN'T SAVE ME.
HE KICKED MY BUTT.

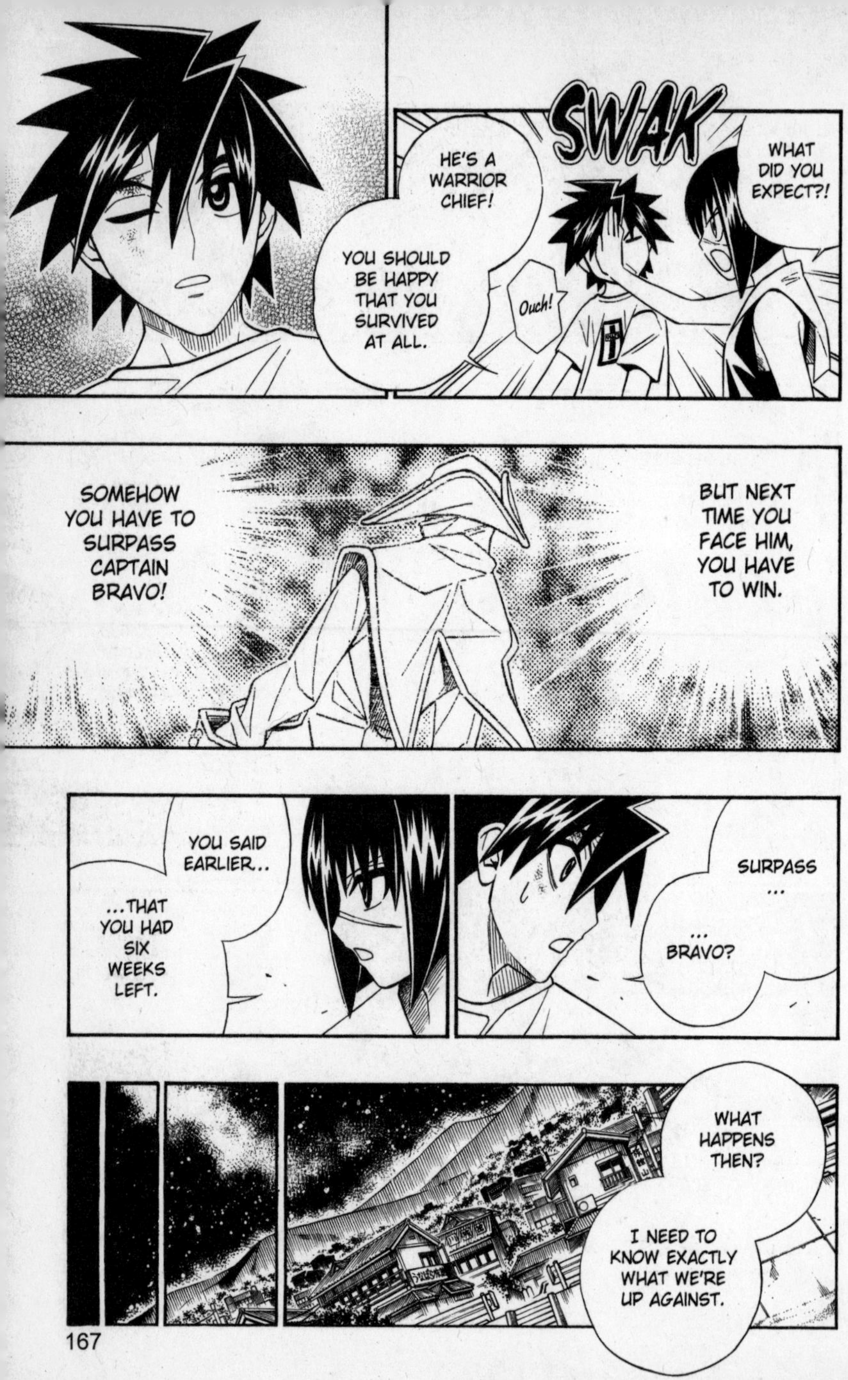
SWAK
WHAT DID YOU EXPECT?!
HE'S A WARRIOR CHIEF!
Ouch!
YOU SHOULD BE HAPPY THAT YOU SURVIVED AT ALL.
BUT NEXT TIME YOU FACE HIM, YOU HAVE TO WIN.
SOMEHOW YOU HAVE TO SURPASS CAPTAIN BRAVO!
SURPASS ...
... BRAVO?
YOU SAID EARLIER...
...THAT YOU HAD SIX WEEKS LEFT.
WHAT HAPPENS THEN?
I NEED TO KNOW EXACTLY WHAT WE'RE UP AGAINST.

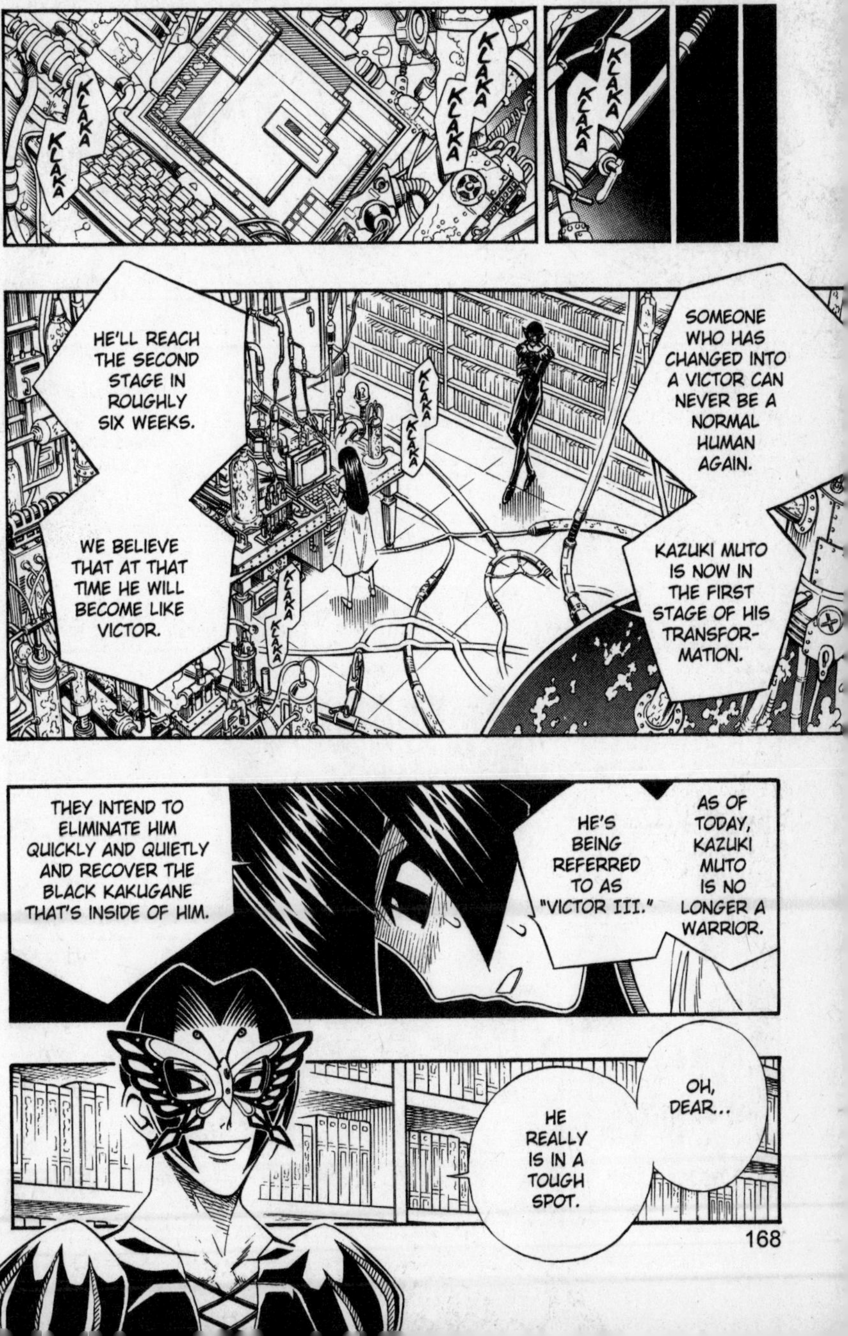
KLAKA KLAKA
KLAKA KLAKA
KLAKA KLAKA
KLAKA KLAKA
SOMEONE WHO HAS CHANGED INTO A VICTOR CAN NEVER BE A NORMAL HUMAN AGAIN.
KLAKA KLAKA
KAZUKI MUTO IS NOW IN THE FIRST STAGE OF HIS TRANSFORMATION.
HE'LL REACH THE SECOND STAGE IN ROUGHLY SIX WEEKS.
KLAKA KLAKA
WE BELIEVE THAT AT THAT TIME HE WILL BECOME LIKE VICTOR.
AS OF TODAY, KAZUKI MUTO IS NO LONGER A WARRIOR.
HE'S BEING REFERRED TO AS "VICTOR III."
THEY INTEND TO ELIMINATE HIM QUICKLY AND QUIETLY AND RECOVER THE BLACK KAKUGANE THAT'S INSIDE OF HIM.
OH, DEAR...
HE REALLY IS IN A TOUGH SPOT.

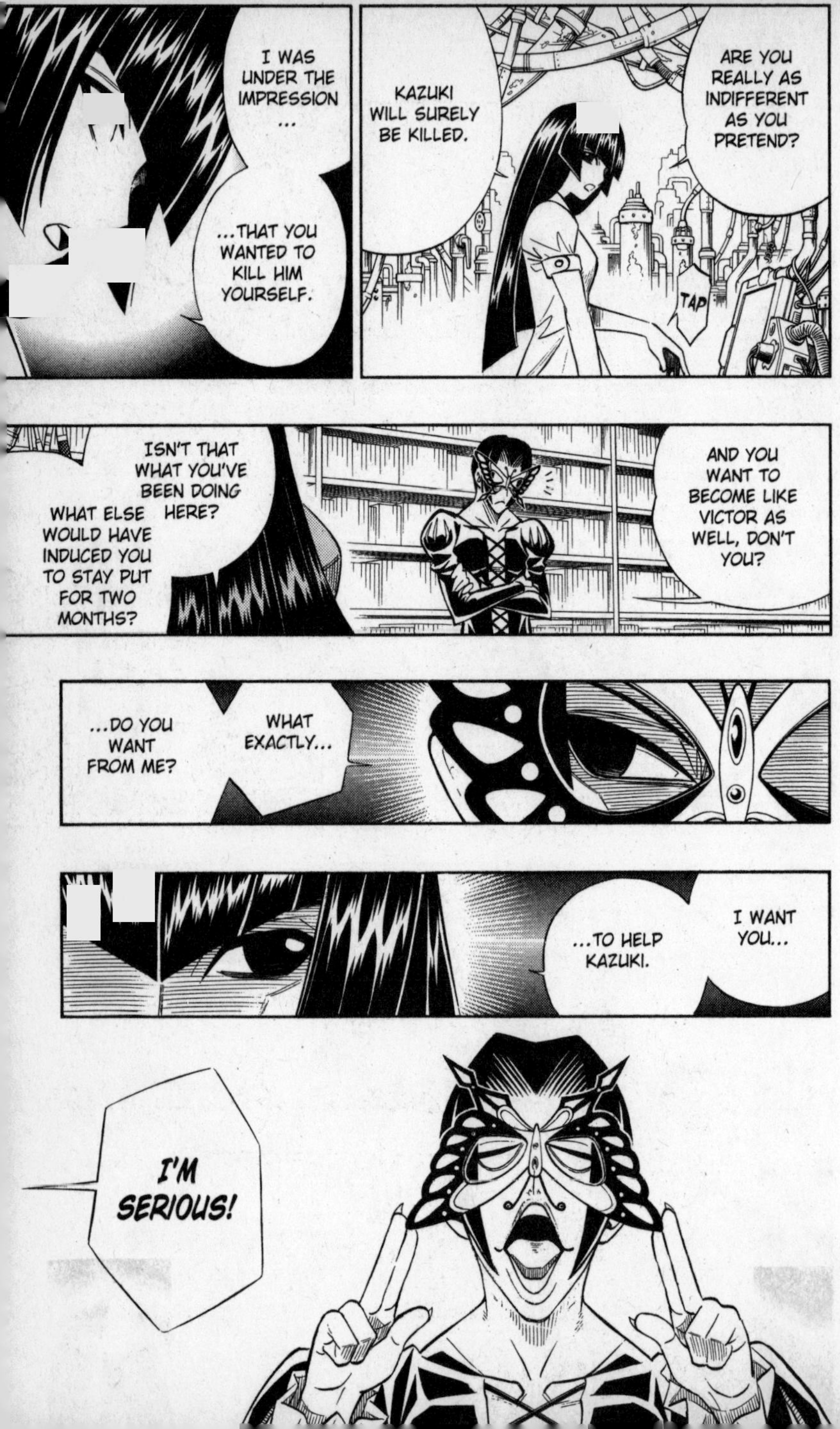
ARE YOU REALLY AS INDIFFERENT AS YOU PRETEND?
KAZUKI WILL SURELY BE KILLED.
TAP
I WAS UNDER THE IMPRESSION ...
...THAT YOU WANTED TO KILL HIM YOURSELF.
AND YOU WANT TO BECOME LIKE VICTOR AS WELL, DON'T YOU?
ISN'T THAT WHAT YOU'VE BEEN DOING HERE?
WHAT ELSE WOULD HAVE INDUCED YOU TO STAY PUT FOR TWO MONTHS?
WHAT EXACTLY...
...DO YOU WANT FROM ME?
I WANT YOU...
...TO HELP KAZUKI.
I'M SERIOUS!

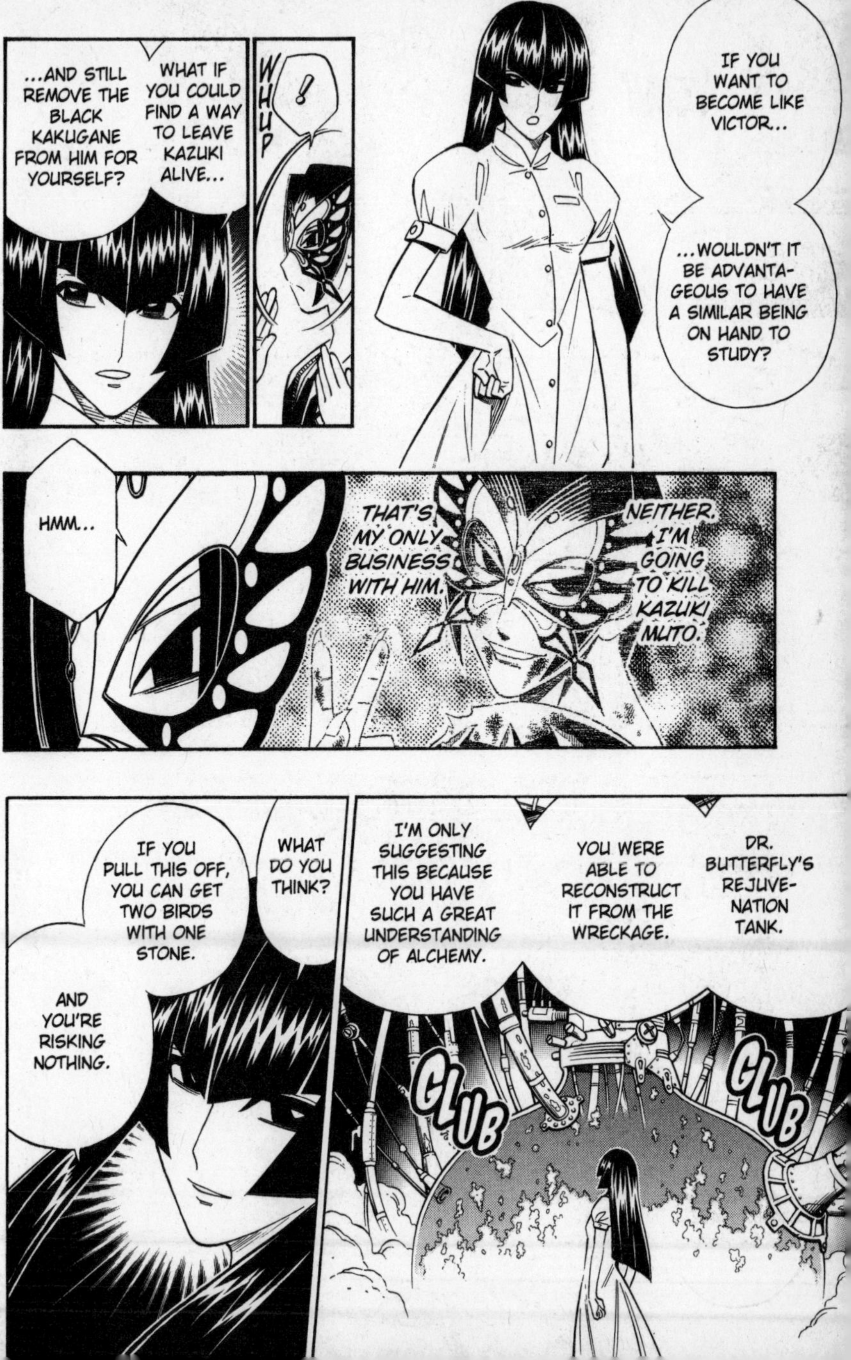
IF YOU WANT TO BECOME LIKE VICTOR...
...WOULDN'T IT BE ADVANTAGEOUS TO HAVE A SIMILAR BEING ON HAND TO STUDY?
WHUP
!
WHAT IF YOU COULD FIND A WAY TO LEAVE KAZUKI ALIVE...
...AND STILL REMOVE THE BLACK KAKUGANE FROM HIM FOR YOURSELF?
NEITHER. I'M GOING TO KILL KAZUKI MUTO.
THAT'S MY ONLY BUSINESS WITH HIM.
HMM...
DR. BUTTERFLY'S REJUVENATION TANK.
YOU WERE ABLE TO RECONSTRUCT IT FROM THE WRECKAGE.
I'M ONLY SUGGESTING THIS BECAUSE YOU HAVE SUCH A GREAT UNDERSTANDING OF ALCHEMY.
CLUB
CLUB
WHAT DO YOU THINK?
IF YOU PULL THIS OFF, YOU CAN GET TWO BIRDS WITH ONE STONE.
AND YOU'RE RISKING NOTHING.

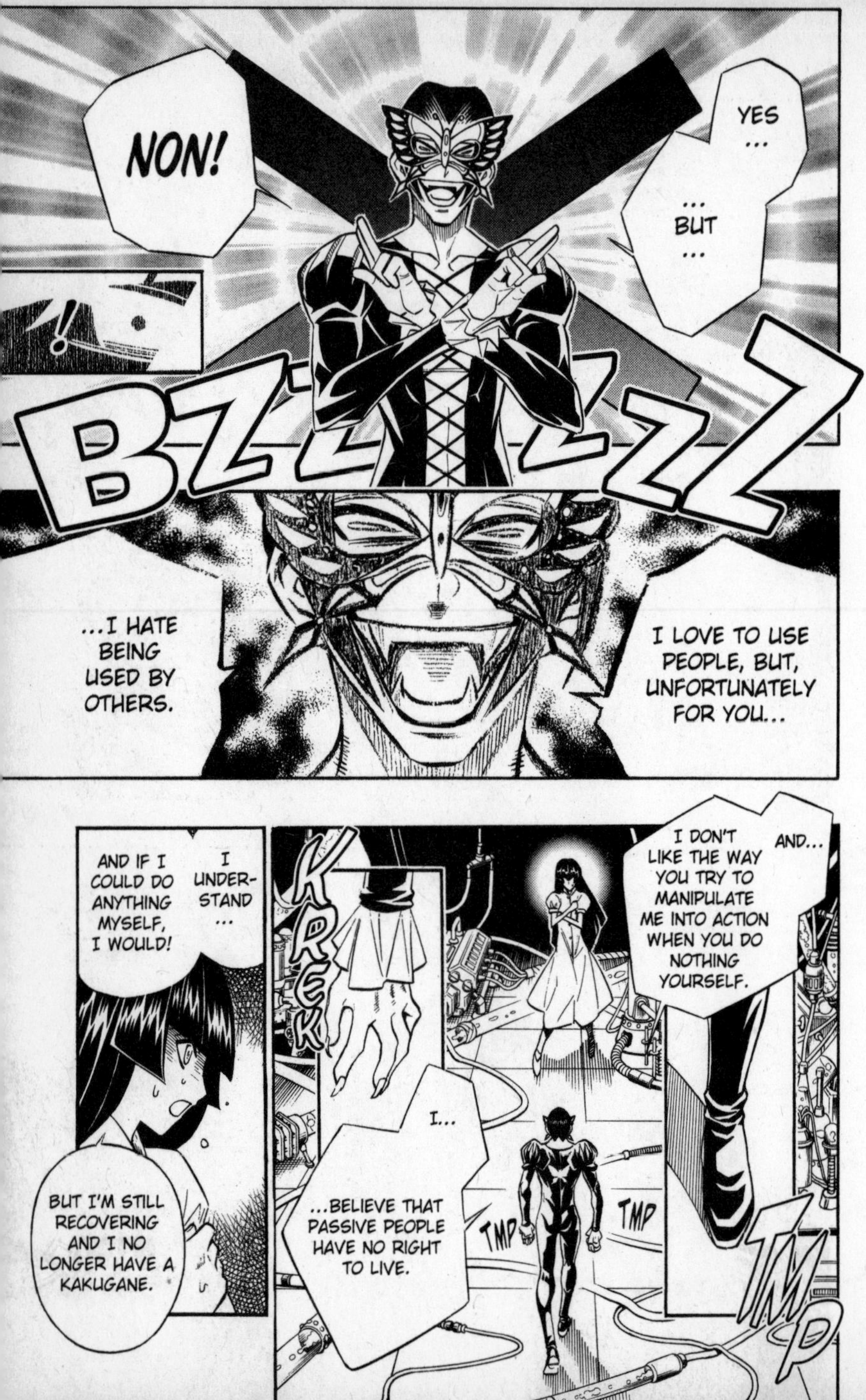
YES ...
... BUT ...
NON!
!
BZZZZZ
I LOVE TO USE PEOPLE, BUT, UNFORTUNATELY FOR YOU...
...I HATE BEING USED BY OTHERS.
AND...
I DON'T LIKE THE WAY YOU TRY TO MANIPULATE ME INTO ACTION WHEN YOU DO NOTHING YOURSELF.
KREK
I...
...BELIEVE THAT PASSIVE PEOPLE HAVE NO RIGHT TO LIVE.
TMP
TMP
TMP
I UNDER-STAND ...
AND IF I COULD DO ANYTHING MYSELF, I WOULD!
BUT I'M STILL RECOVERING AND I NO LONGER HAVE A KAKUGANE.

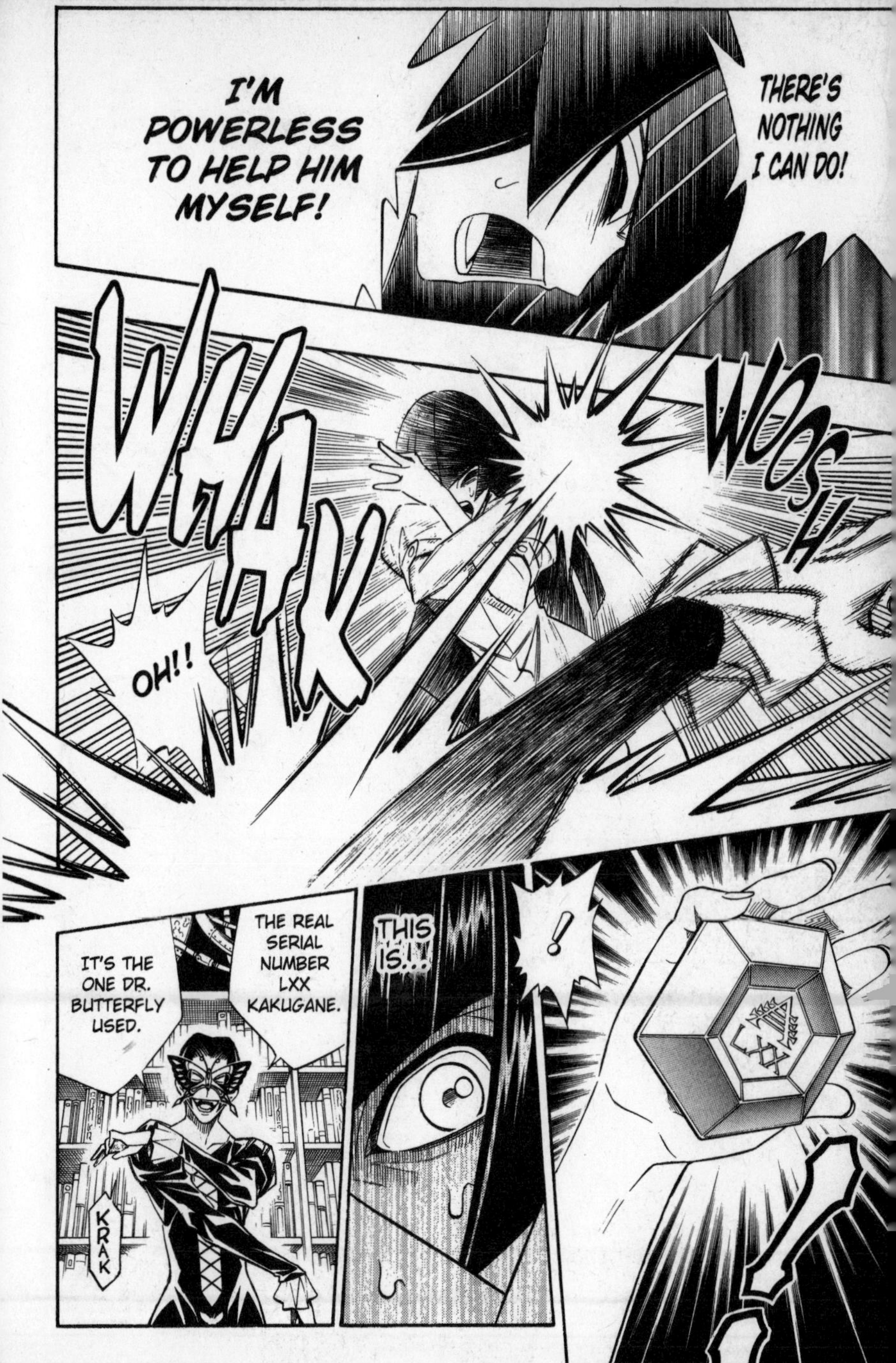
THERE'S NOTHING I CAN DO!
I'M POWERLESS TO HELP HIM MYSELF!
WOOSH
WHAK
OH!!
LXX
!
THIS IS...
THE REAL SERIAL NUMBER LXX KAKUGANE.
IT'S THE ONE DR. BUTTERFLY USED.
KRAK

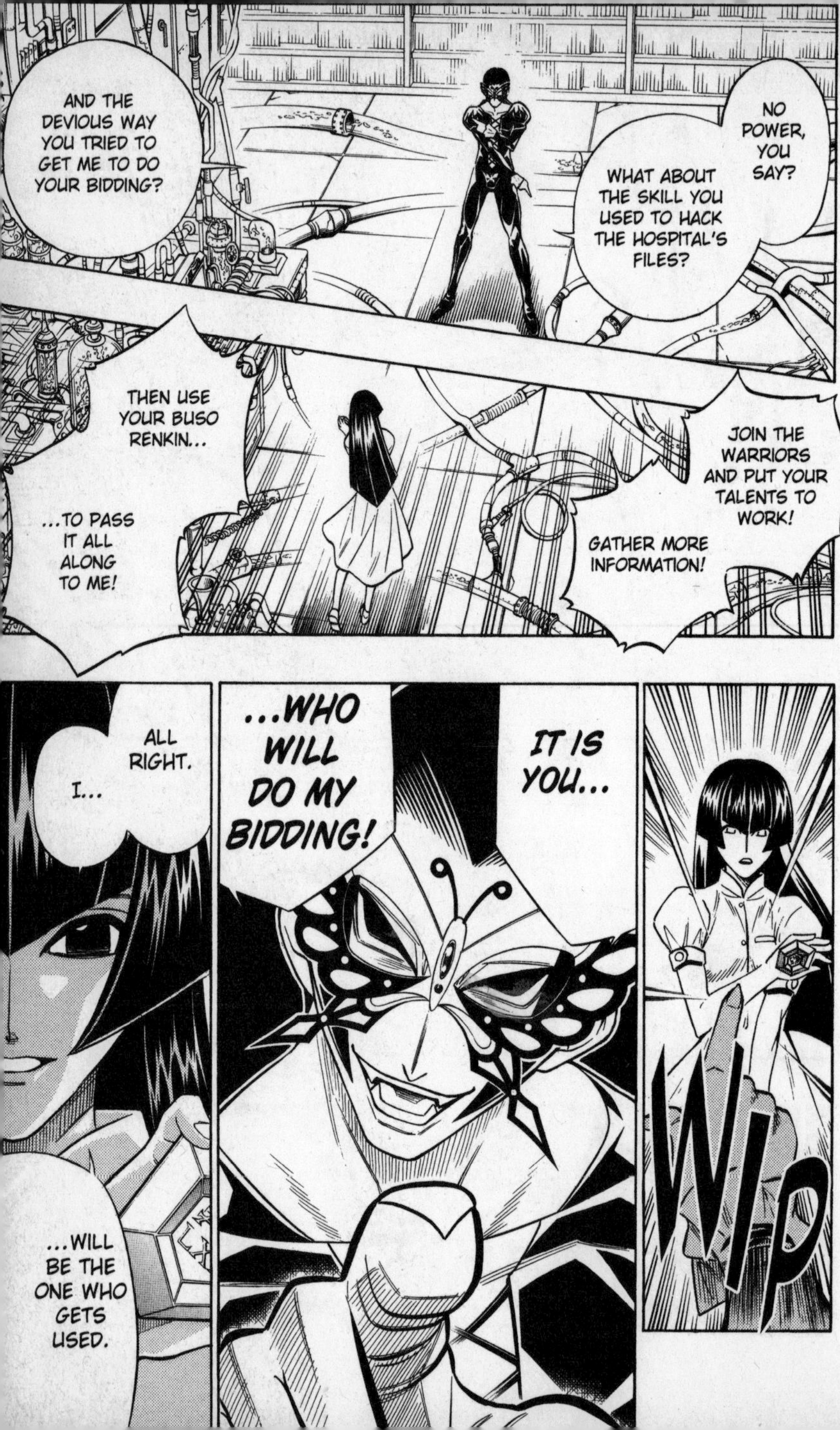
NO POWER, YOU SAY?
WHAT ABOUT THE SKILL YOU USED TO HACK THE HOSPITAL'S FILES?
AND THE DEVIOUS WAY YOU TRIED TO GET ME TO DO YOUR BIDDING?
JOIN THE WARRIORS AND PUT YOUR TALENTS TO WORK!
GATHER MORE INFORMATION!
THEN USE YOUR BUSO RENKIN...
...TO PASS IT ALL ALONG TO ME!
WIP
IT IS YOU...
...WHO WILL DO MY BIDDING!
ALL RIGHT.
I...
...WILL BE THE ONE WHO GETS USED.

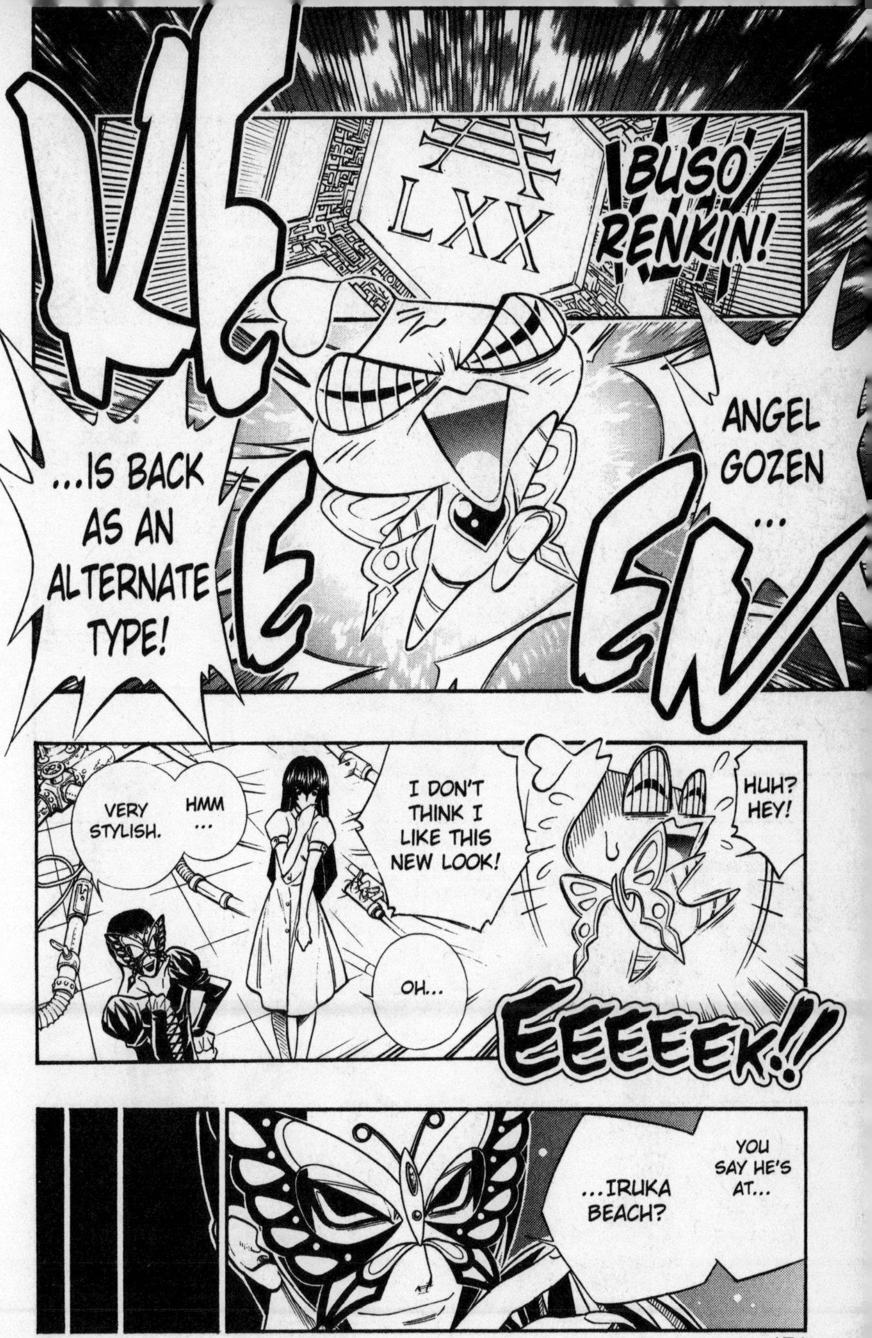

LXX
BUSO RENKIN!
ANGEL GOZEN ...
...IS BACK AS AN ALTERNATE TYPE!
HUH? HEY!
EEEEEEK!!
I DON'T THINK I LIKE THIS NEW LOOK!
OH...
HMM ...
VERY STYLISH.
YOU SAY HE'S AT...
...IRUKA BEACH?

READ THIS WAY

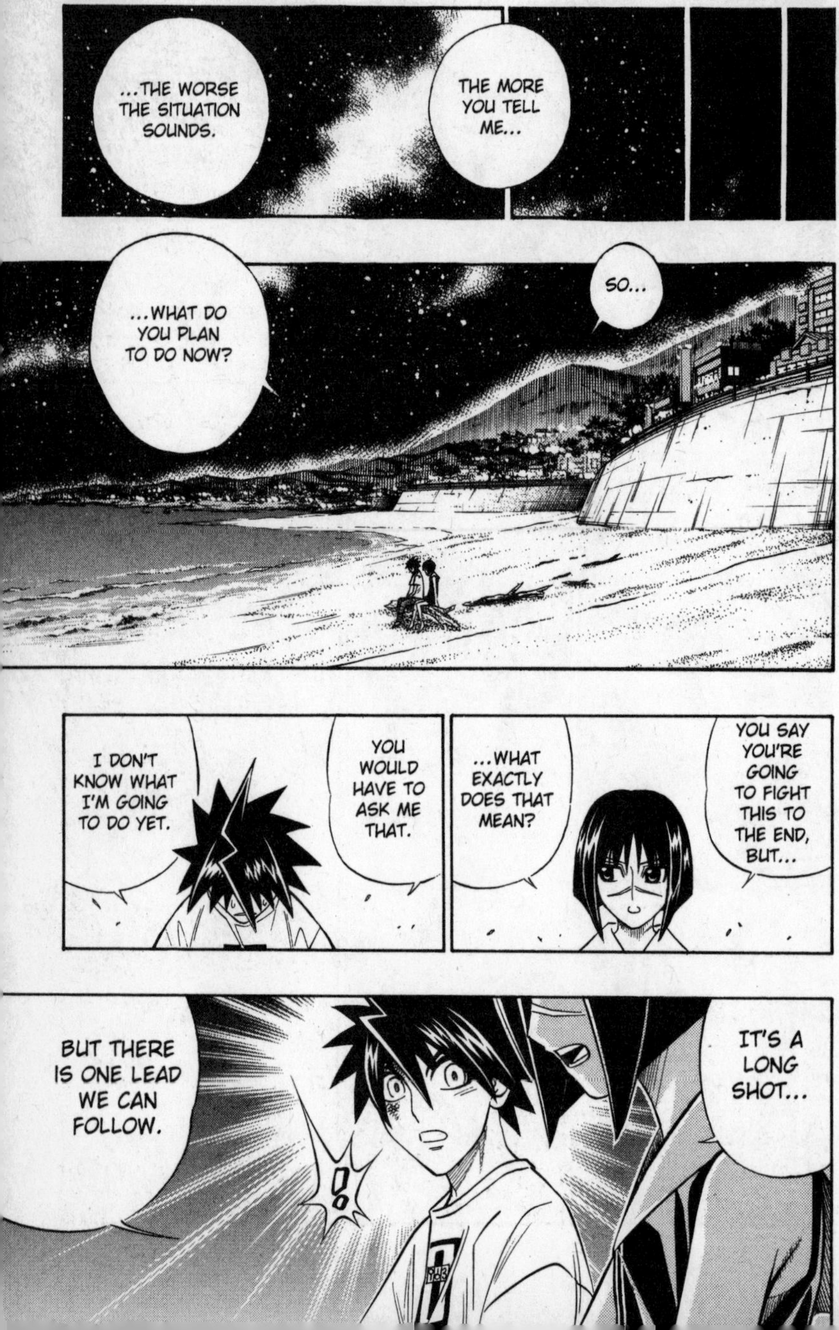
THE MORE YOU TELL ME...
...THE WORSE THE SITUATION SOUNDS.
SO...
...WHAT DO YOU PLAN TO DO NOW?
YOU SAY YOU'RE GOING TO FIGHT THIS TO THE END, BUT...
...WHAT EXACTLY DOES THAT MEAN?
YOU WOULD HAVE TO ASK ME THAT.
I DON'T KNOW WHAT I'M GOING TO DO YET.
IT'S A LONG SHOT...
BUT THERE IS ONE LEAD WE CAN FOLLOW.

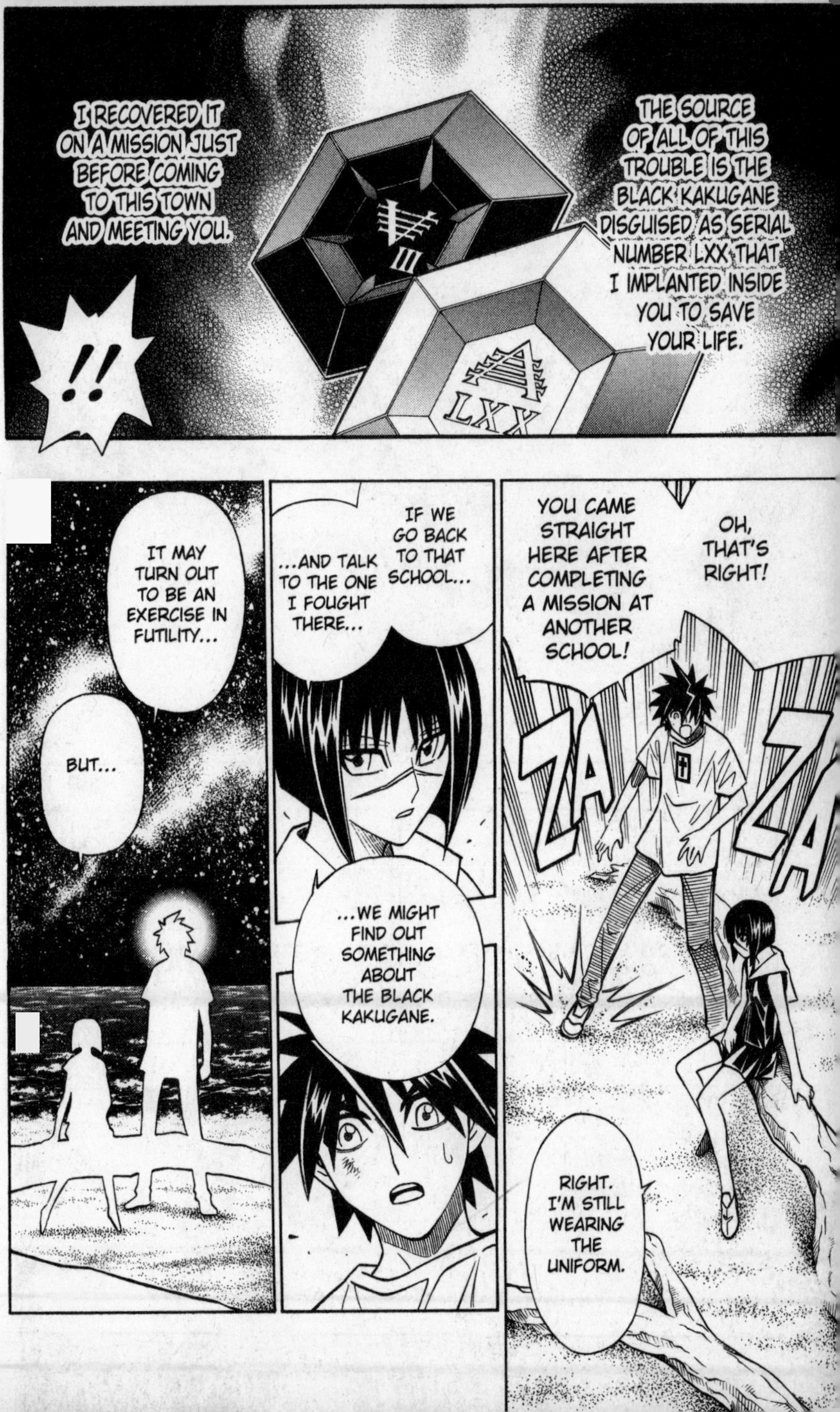
THE SOURCE OF ALL OF THIS TROUBLE IS THE BLACK KAKUGANE DISGUISED AS SERIAL NUMBER LXX THAT I IMPLANTED INSIDE YOU TO SAVE YOUR LIFE.
I RECOVERED IT ON A MISSION JUST BEFORE COMING TO THIS TOWN AND MEETING YOU.
III
LXX
!!
OH, THAT'S RIGHT!
YOU CAME STRAIGHT HERE AFTER COMPLETING A MISSION AT ANOTHER SCHOOL!
ZA
ZA
RIGHT. I'M STILL WEARING THE UNIFORM.
IF WE GO BACK TO THAT SCHOOL...
...AND TALK TO THE ONE I FOUGHT THERE...
...WE MIGHT FIND OUT SOMETHING ABOUT THE BLACK KAKUGANE.
IT MAY TURN OUT TO BE AN EXERCISE IN FUTILITY...
BUT...

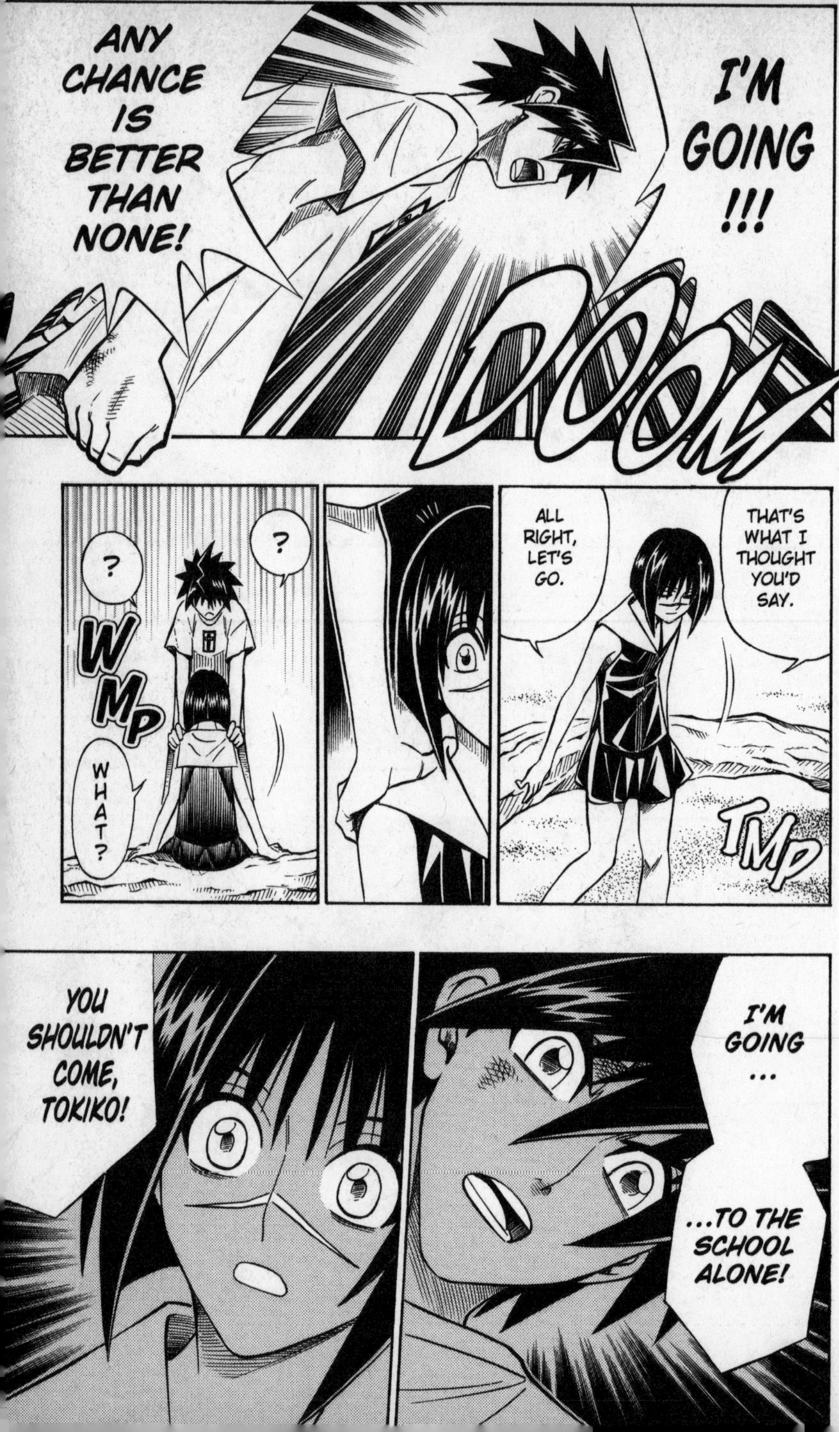
I'M GOING!!!
ANY CHANCE IS BETTER THAN NONE!
DOOM
THAT'S WHAT I THOUGHT YOU'D SAY.
ALL RIGHT, LET'S GO.
TMP
?
?
WMP
WHAT?
I'M GOING...
...TO THE SCHOOL ALONE!
YOU SHOULDN'T COME, TOKIKO!

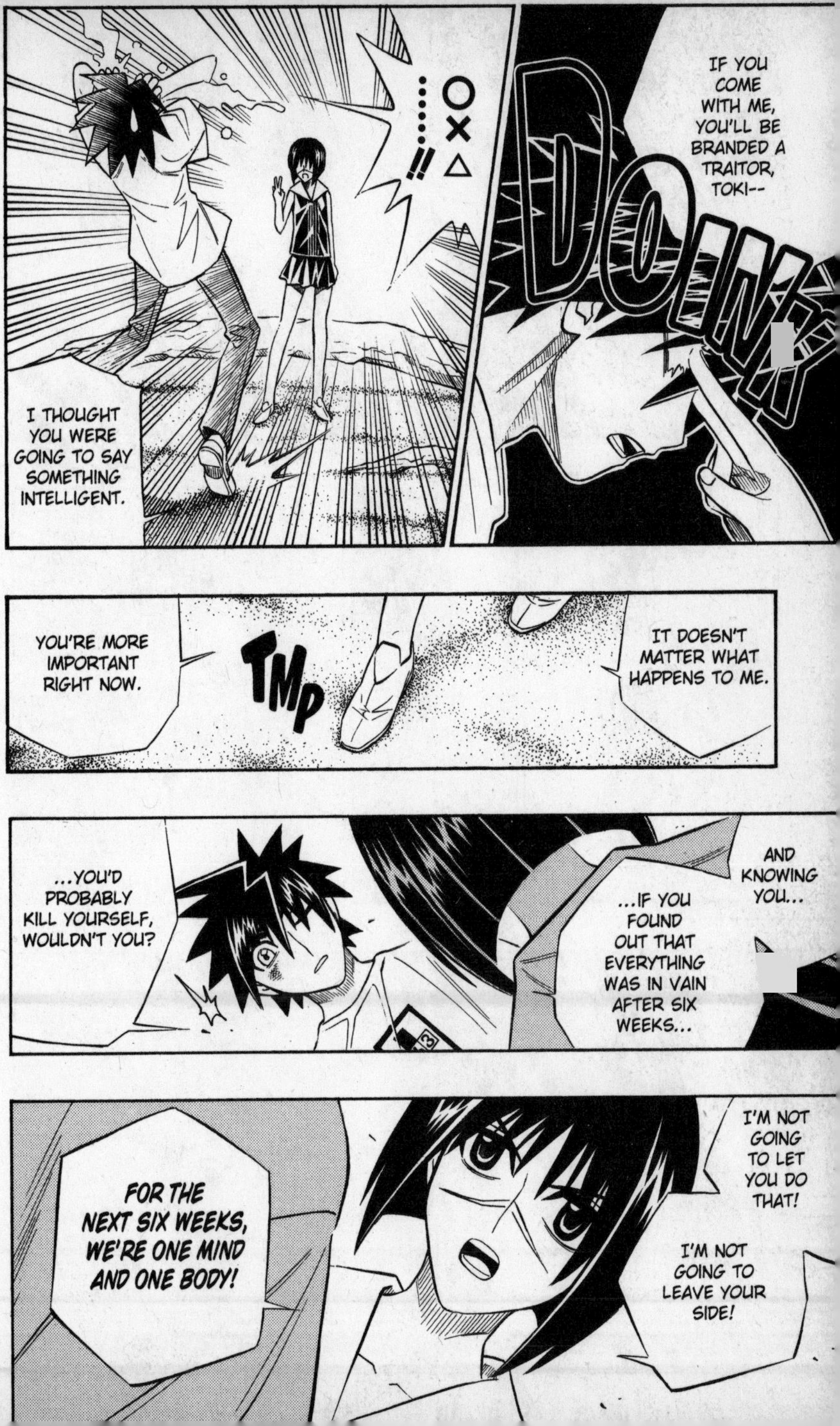
IF YOU COME WITH ME, YOU'LL BE BRANDED A TRAITOR, TOKI--
DOINK
○×△......!!
I THOUGHT YOU WERE GOING TO SAY SOMETHING INTELLIGENT.
IT DOESN'T MATTER WHAT HAPPENS TO ME.
TMP
YOU'RE MORE IMPORTANT RIGHT NOW.
AND KNOWING YOU...
...IF YOU FOUND OUT THAT EVERYTHING WAS IN VAIN AFTER SIX WEEKS...
...YOU'D PROBABLY KILL YOURSELF, WOULDN'T YOU?
I'M NOT GOING TO LET YOU DO THAT!
I'M NOT GOING TO LEAVE YOUR SIDE!
FOR THE NEXT SIX WEEKS, WE'RE ONE MIND AND ONE BODY!

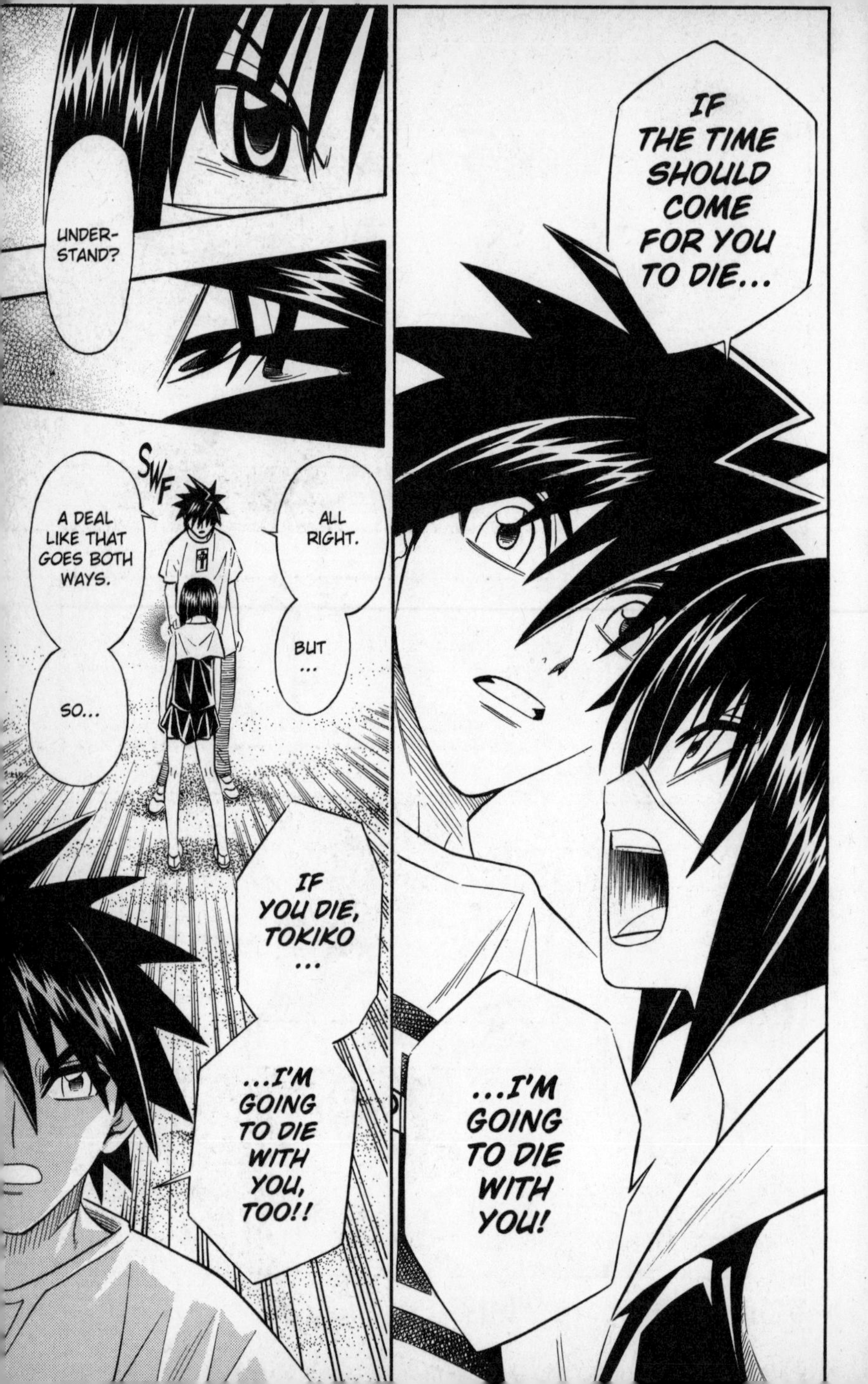
IF THE TIME SHOULD COME FOR YOU TO DIE...
...I'M GOING TO DIE WITH YOU!
UNDER-STAND?
SWF
ALL RIGHT.
BUT...
A DEAL LIKE THAT GOES BOTH WAYS.
SO...
IF YOU DIE, TOKIKO...
...I'M GOING TO DIE WITH YOU, TOO!!

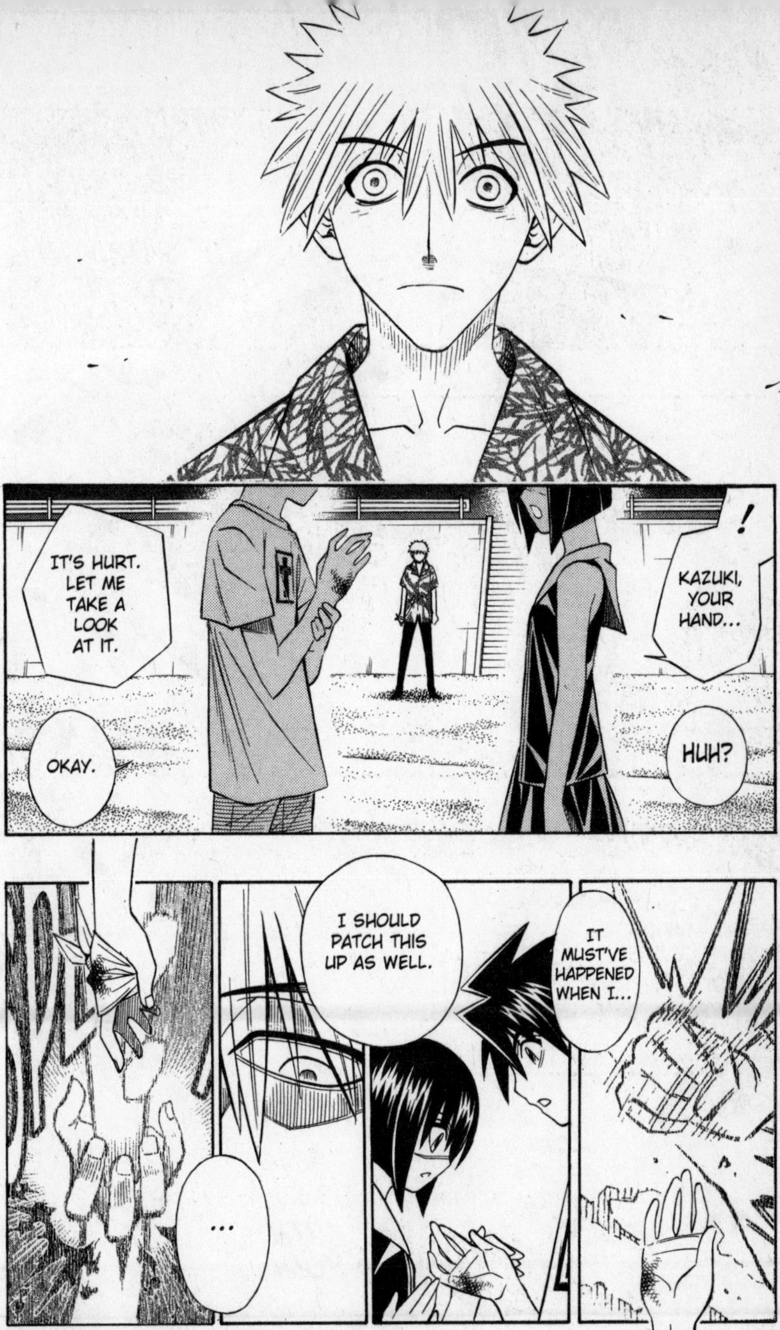
!
KAZUKI, YOUR HAND...
HUH?
IT'S HURT. LET ME TAKE A LOOK AT IT.
OKAY.
IT MUST'VE HAPPENED WHEN I...
I SHOULD PATCH THIS UP AS WELL.
...

VOLUME 6: A NEW MISSION (THE END)

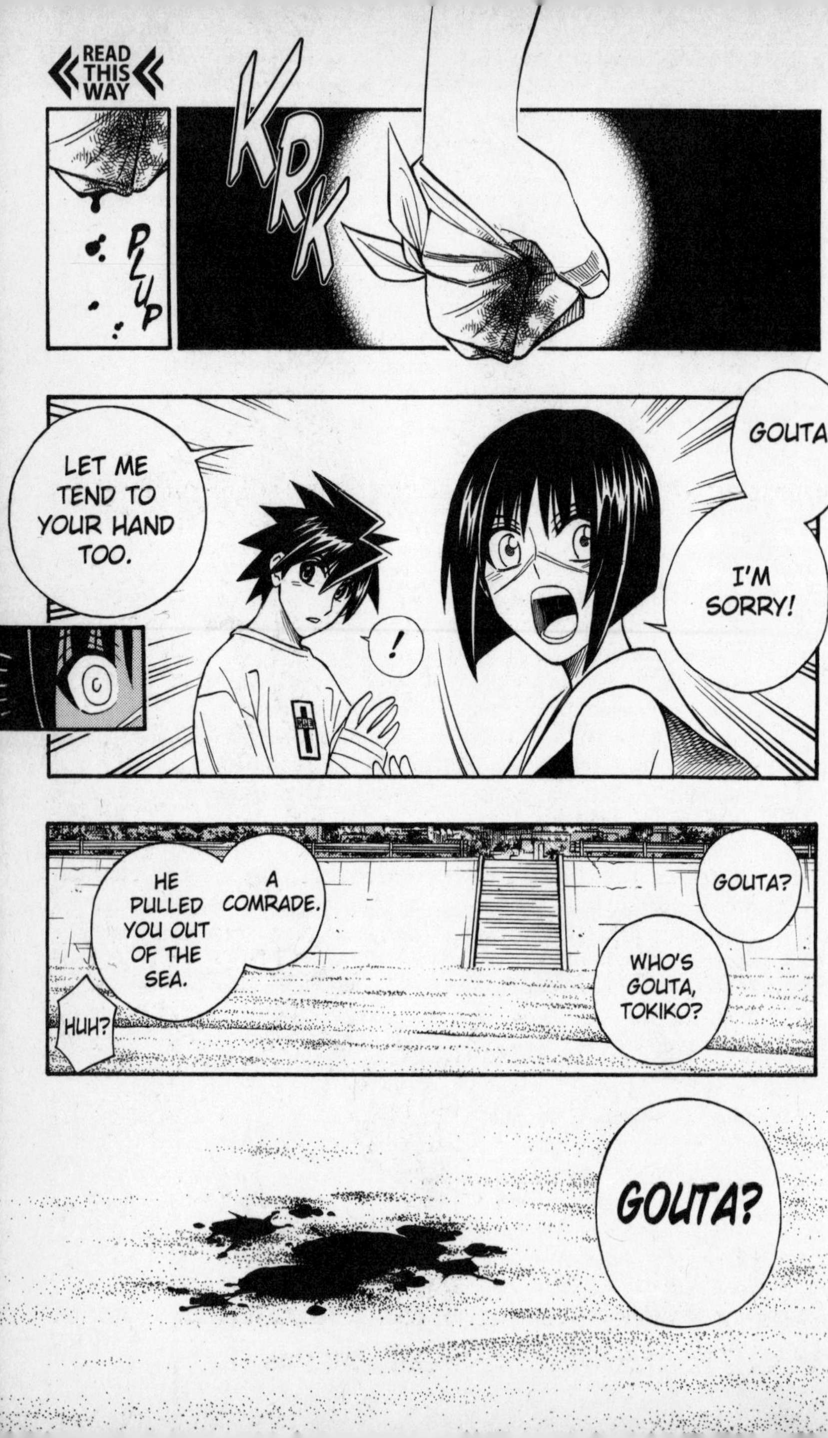
READ THIS WAY
KRK
PLUP
GOUTA!
I'M SORRY!
!
LET ME TEND TO YOUR HAND TOO.
GOUTA?
WHO'S GOUTA, TOKIKO?
A COMRADE.
HE PULLED YOU OUT OF THE SEA.
HUH?
GOUTA?

Chapter 46: Heart Shift

· Kazuki turns into a Victor. The number of tones increased and the number of black fills decreased. I found myself feeling uneasy as I was drawing it. Kazuki's pants and Tokiko's hair seemed to stand out too much.

· Tearing off arms then absorbing them, flying around and causing a lot of mayhem… It's fun to depict super-beings fighting each other, but it's hard to choreograph. I consider this both a low point and a high point in my career. It really made me realize that *Dragon Ball* is something to be admired.

· Tokiko stops Kazuki in his tracks. No matter what form or situation Kazuki is in, he's powerless against Tokiko. Then again, if a girl like her were to hug him from behind like that, what man wouldn't stop? I mean, really.

· One of my friends pointed out that the line, "Please, Kazuki…" being uttered by Tokiko sounded too erotic. If somebody thinks that, it's their problem, if you ask me.

Chapter 47: End of the Battle

· Well, this was the last chapter for the L.X.E. I wondered whether I should shorten the battle between Bravo and Moonface, but in the end I decided to move the story along. My need to put Bravo in a major battle was satisfied when he fought Kazuki later, but I'm not through with Moonface yet. Hmm…

· I was happy with the way the strange relationship between Kazuki and Papillon developed in this chapter. Kazuki accepts Papillon's harsh words without lashing out. If anything, Kazuki is almost kind to Papillon. I really enjoy drawing Kazuki when he's being like that.

· I liked the way Tokiko looked speeding along on that scooter. (Although the scooter was drawn by one my assistants.) I've been a manga artist for over a decade, but I still feel a sense of accomplishment when I draw something I've never drawn before. (But then, when I do, I usually make more work for my assistants…)

· The lines about the Warriors and how they protected the town were almost cut in the planning stage because they seemed too cliché, but I think they worked well. I've decided it's not good to overuse the left side of my brain.

Chapter 48: A Warrior's Respite

· I took the title of this chapter from an episode of *Fang of the Sun Dougram*. Of the real robot anime fans of my generation, most were fans of *Votoms*, but I liked *Dougram* better. The way the first episode began with the main robot in ruins had a big impact on me.

· Who knew that Daihama was a closet swimsuit *otaku*? I think a lot of readers were hoping to see Tokiko in the school swimsuit, but I didn't think she would wear one to the beach. It was fun to do a comedic chapter after that last battle.

- Victor turns out to be a man of his word. He actually went around the world to see it for himself. I included that bit about Antarctica because it's one of the five major continents.
- Originally, I had no intention of depicting the cast at the beach. I was going to have Bravo show up the night before Kazuki left, so I just picked an arbitrary setting. But the reader response was so positive (I never thought my fans would want to see my female characters in swimsuits) that my editor at the time insisted on it. That editor was the second one assigned to me for this series and, to tell you the truth, he was a bigger *otaku* than me. Eventually he was reassigned, but he was very passionate and devoted to manga and I really enjoyed working with him.
- In selecting the swimsuits for the girls, I had the help of Kaoru Kurosaki. For Tokiko we wanted something that she could wear while working out, so we chose a sporty two-piece. For Mahiro we decided on a standard floral print swimsuit and a sarong. For Chisato we picked a standard one-piece with a parka. Saori, being the lively character that she is, we gave a bikini. We put a lot less thought into the guys.
- It would've been strange if teenage boys didn't react to a girl in a swimsuit, but to have their attention drawn to the chest or behind would've been too much. So instead I had Kazuki be fascinated by Tokiko's navel.
- The idea for the surfing Bravo came from the movie *Escape from L.A.* Every time I see that movie, I always think surfing = a good sight gag.
- This was the first appearance of Gouta. I think trying to make him look mysterious made his personality a bit different from what I'd intended.

Chapter 49: A New Mission
- I'm going to make a confession here. While drawing all those panels with swimsuits in them, I really started to enjoy it. Originally swimsuits were only going to be shown during the walk back to the hotel, but I added a few scenes.
- Because of my love of American comic books, I think I've come to enjoy drawing muscles and bodies. While working on the swimsuit designs, I found myself looking at teen fashion magazines and famous Shojo comics. As I looked through them, I noticed that the lines of the swimsuits could be drawn in so many different ways. I don't think it's going to come into play in most of my books, but I've decided to try to make my female characters more attractive.
- After only one chapter, the lines of Tokiko's swimsuit are already pushing the boundary a bit more. As a side note, the emblem on her swimsuit is the one that Getter-2 has on its forehead. I love *Getter Robo*.
- I chose this chapter to reveal the name of the Alchemist Army. There was so much back-story to tell, I really wish I'd had more time to work it all out beforehand. Regarding the Philosopher's Stone, I was staying away from it because of another comic that deals with Alchemy. Now that I've gone through with it, some people are accusing me of stealing ideas. Don't they realize that a lot of what I write is based on general knowledge? Dealing with this kind of stuff has been difficult and a source of many headaches.

Chapter 50: Say It's Not So, Bravo.

· The title of this chapter comes from a phrase that was in my junior high school English book. It refers to the 1919 World Series scandal in which some players were paid to throw the game. The famous phrase, "Say it ain't so, Joe," was shouted at "Shoeless Joe" Jackson by a young fan.

· The battle between Kazuki and Bravo was the biggest problem in this whole volume. I've never made former comrades fight each other, and it was quite a challenge. This was also an opportunity for Kazuki to show off his progress by trying to surpass Bravo.

· Bravo had once encouraged Kazuki with words that now push him away, but Kazuki isn't dissuaded from his resolve. The two clash, each believing in his own truth. I thought it went well, but the fan response wasn't so good. Maybe it was my lack of skill or maybe readers just didn't want Kazuki and Bravo to fight, or both. It's hard to tell. Combined with the unexpected popularity of the beach episode recently, this caused some turmoil in my life. I've still got a lot to learn.

Chapter 51: Crimson Ocean

· This chapter marked the series' one-year anniversary. This year seems both long and short to me. It was hard, but it was fun, too. In all, I think it was more fun.

· Thank you for your continued support.

· I rushed a bit because I wanted the newly reformed Sunlight Heart to be in the color pages at the beginning of this chapter. But in the end, it didn't make it, and my efforts were in vain.

· Bravo uses his chop to part the ocean. One might think that Bravo was a bigger monster than Kazuki for being able to perform such a feat. It was a lot of work, but reader response was very positive so it was worth it. Viva Super-being battles!

· Kazuki becomes a "Victor" again. I still think these panels are kind of off somehow. I have to do something about this.

Chapter 52: Re-Extermination Complete

· The Silver Skin Reverse. It's Bravo's secret attack, but I had to think twice about having such an invincible character become even more powerful. Once again, I'm experiencing first-hand the "power-inflation" that occurs in fighting manga.

· I got the idea for the hexagon panels from an old video game I was hooked on called *Cyber Trooper Virtual-On*. But it turned out to be a lot of work for my assistants. It made me think that computer graphics might be worth using. Then again, I'm not very good with electronics so I think I'm better off drawing things by hand for the time being. But in the near future, I may start incorporating some CG into my work.

· The line "We've said our goodbyes" and "We've already parted ways" come from the opening theme song of *Armored Trooper Votoms*.

The number of people who recognized them confirm that there are more fans of *Votoms* than of *Dougram* out there.

Chapter 53: When the Night Ends

· Gouta is an idiot. He's manly, but he's still an idiot.

· When Hiwatari first appears, there's no reason for him to be sitting on a blazing fire, but I had to decide whether to do something realistic or fantastic. I usually go with something realistic. After making the choice, it occurred to me that the old me would've made it without a moment's hesitation. In the old days I really didn't care if something worked well or not.

· The term "Re-Extermination Squad" is also from Kenji Otsuki's novel *Stacy*. Sorry, I'm just a huge fan of Kenji Otsuki.

· Bravo's real name is Mamoru Sakimori. In this chapter Chitose also makes her debut, but by coincidence, these two names are also found in another series in the magazine in which *Buso Renkin* was originally published. It made me believe the old myth that writers and artists get ideas from outer space and that people in a given field sometimes pick up the same signals at the same time.

· Ouka and Papillon. I really like the interplay between these two manipulative and devious people. I hope I get to do more of this.

Chapter 54: One Heart and One Mind

· The line about dying and coming back to life was really a jab at myself. I really need to plan my stories out better.

· Papillon wins the battle of manipulation. Again I have to say that I really enjoyed drawing that scene. Hyahoo!

· The lines about "I'll die when you die" would seem like declarations of love if not for the situation. And of course to Gouta all of this looks like Romeo and Juliet stuff. I put Gouta in the scene only at the very end for maximum impact. Readers found this chapter both funny and moving. But I do feel bad for Gouta. Maybe I went too far. Sorry, Gouta.

· Where will Gouta go next with his broken heart?

· And so →

To be continued.

Coming Next Volume

Kazuki meets a new Alchemist Warrior named Gouta Nakamura who trained under Tokiko. They head toward Apple Newton Academy, the very same place Kazuki's mysterious black kakugane came from. Unfortunately, on their way they discover that they're being hunted!

Available in August 2007!

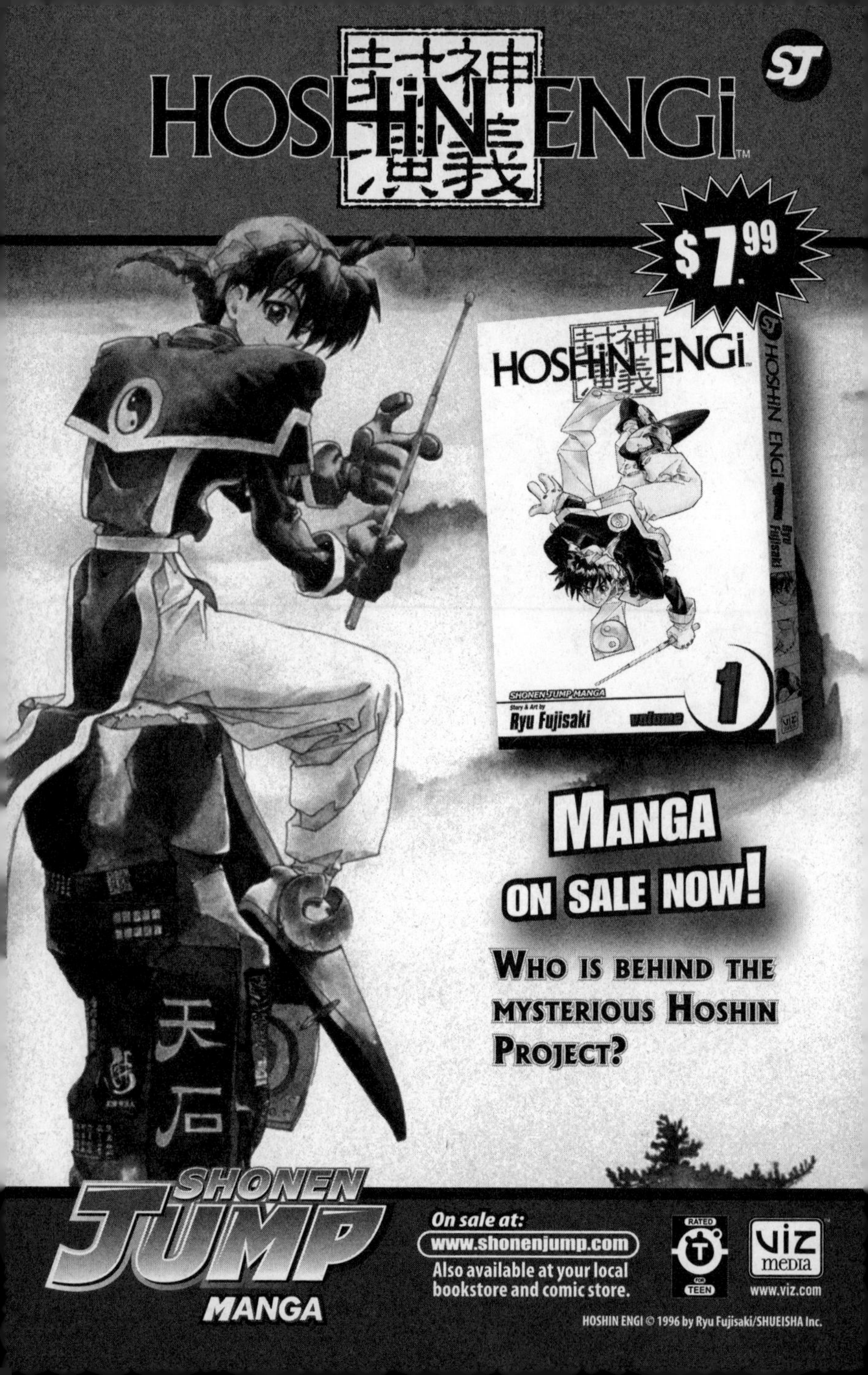
HOSHIN ENGI™
封神演義
SJ
$7.99
HOSHIN ENGI
SHONEN JUMP MANGA
Story & Art by
Ryu Fujisaki
volume 1
MANGA
ON SALE NOW!
WHO IS BEHIND THE
MYSTERIOUS HOSHIN
PROJECT?
SHONEN JUMP MANGA
On sale at:
www.shonenjump.com
Also available at your local
bookstore and comic store.
RATED T FOR TEEN
viz media
www.viz.com
HOSHIN ENGI © 1996 by Ryu Fujisaki/SHUEISHA Inc.

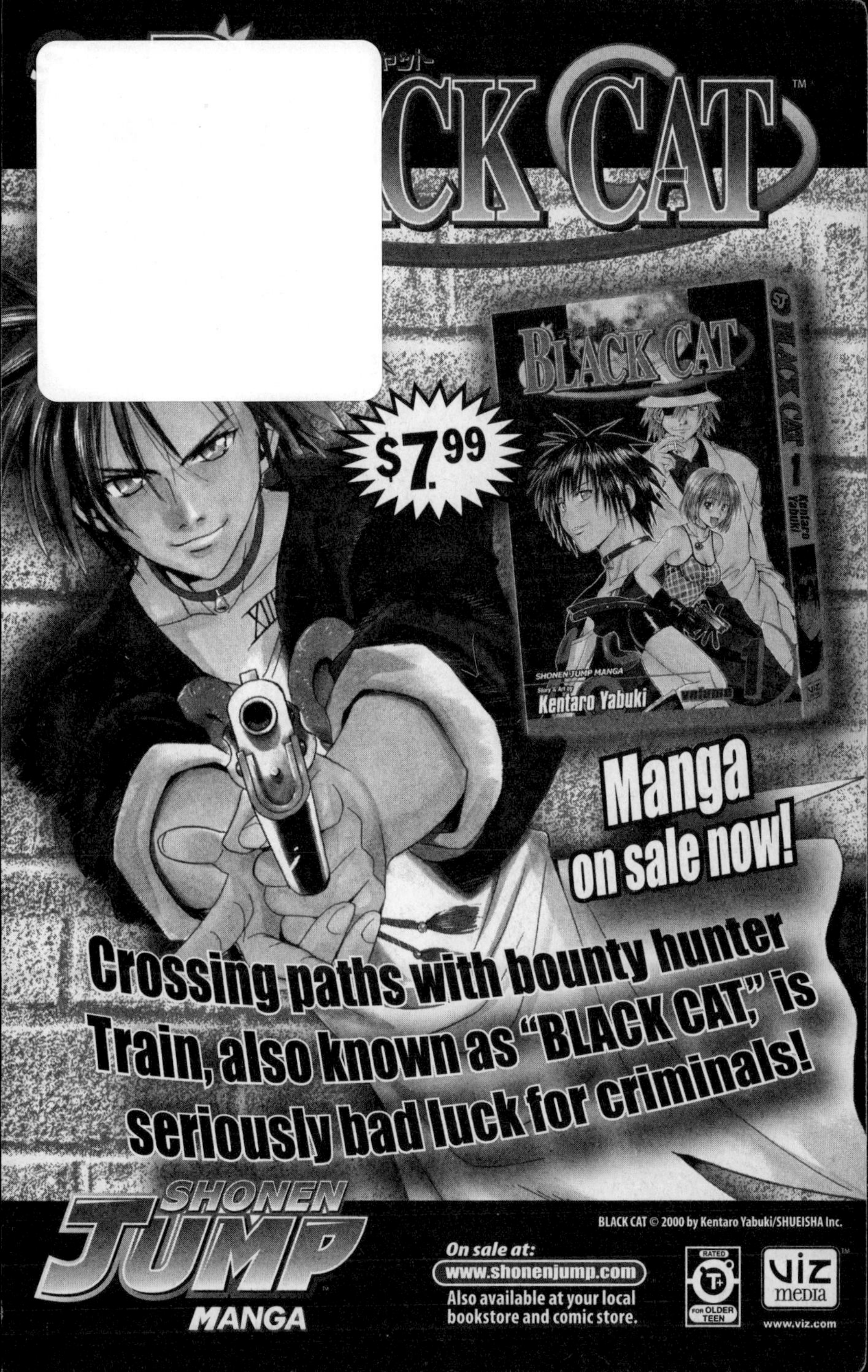

BLACK CAT™
$7.99
BLACK CAT
SHONEN JUMP MANGA
Story & Art by Kentaro Yabuki
Manga on sale now!
Crossing paths with bounty hunter Train, also known as "BLACK CAT," is seriously bad luck for criminals!
SHONEN JUMP MANGA
BLACK CAT © 2000 by Kentaro Yabuki/SHUEISHA Inc.
On sale at:
www.shonenjump.com
Also available at your local bookstore and comic store.
RATED T+ FOR OLDER TEEN
viz media
www.viz.com

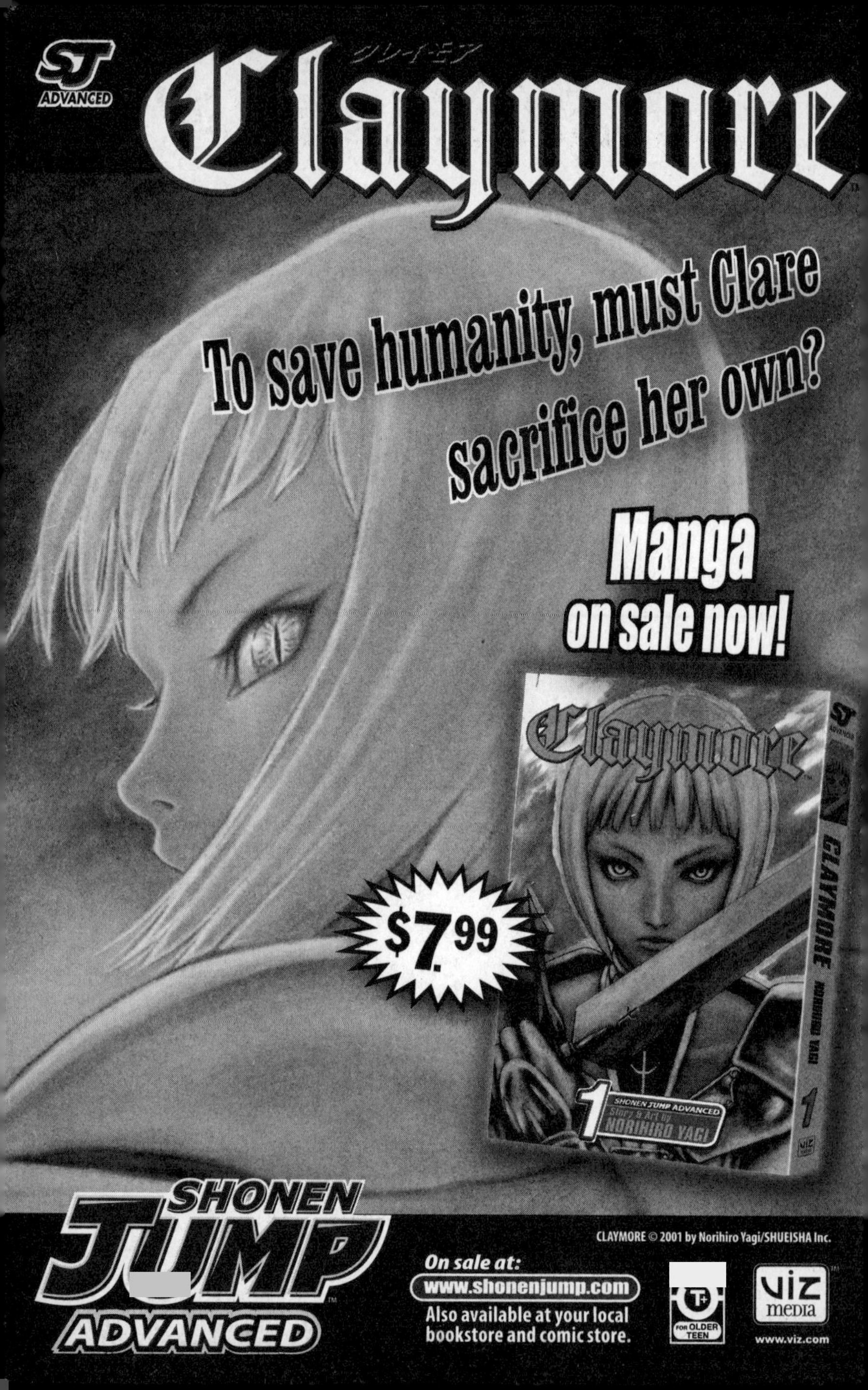
SJ ADVANCED
Claymore
To save humanity, must Clare sacrifice her own?
Manga on sale now!
$7.99
Claymore
SJ ADVANCED
CLAYMORE
NORIHIRO YAGI
1
SHONEN JUMP ADVANCED
Story & Art by NORIHIRO YAGI
SHONEN JUMP ADVANCED
CLAYMORE © 2001 by Norihiro Yagi/SHUEISHA Inc.
On sale at:
www.shonenjump.com
Also available at your local bookstore and comic store.
T+ FOR OLDER TEEN
VIZ media
www.viz.com

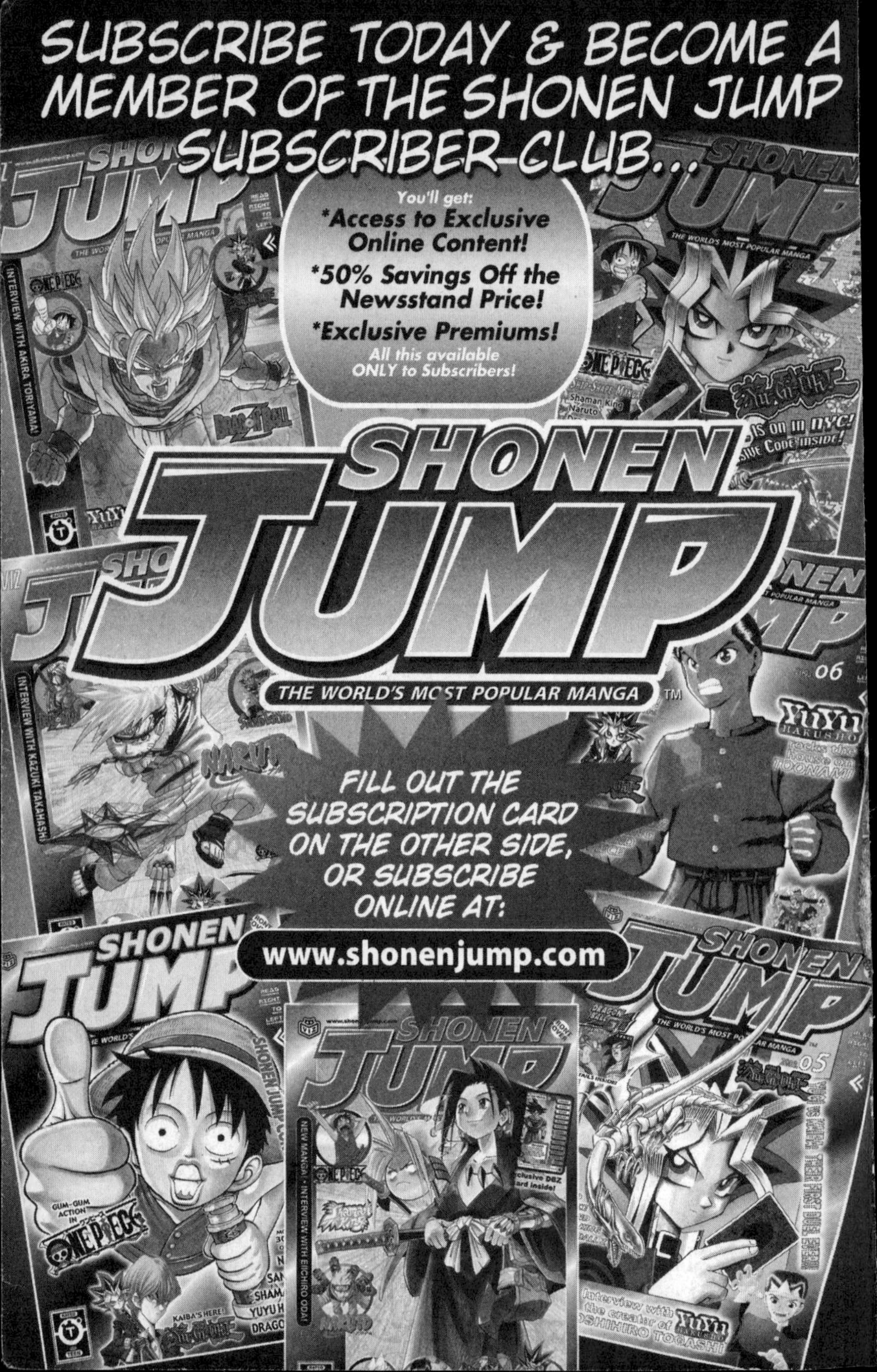
SUBSCRIBE TODAY & BECOME A MEMBER OF THE SHONEN JUMP SUBSCRIBER CLUB...
You'll get:
*Access to Exclusive Online Content!
*50% Savings Off the Newsstand Price!
*Exclusive Premiums!
All this available ONLY to Subscribers!
SHONEN JUMP
THE WORLD'S MOST POPULAR MANGA
TM
FILL OUT THE SUBSCRIPTION CARD ON THE OTHER SIDE, OR SUBSCRIBE ONLINE AT:
www.shonenjump.com